Robert Penner's
Programming
Macromedia Flash™ MX

Robert Penner

McGraw-Hill/Osborne

New York / Chicago / San Francisco
Lisbon / London / Madrid / Mexico City / Milan
New Delhi / San Juan / Seoul / Singapore / Sydney / Toronto

McGraw-Hill/Osborne
2600 Tenth Street
Berkeley, California 94710
U.S.A.

To arrange bulk purchase discounts for sales promotions, premiums, or fund-raisers, please contact
McGraw-Hill/Osborne at the above address. For information on translations or book distributors outside the
U.S.A., please see the International Contact Information page immediately following the index of this book.

Robert Penner's Programming Macromedia Flash™ MX

1234567890 CUS CUS 0198765432

ISBN 0-07-222356-1

Publisher
Brandon A. Nordin

Vice President & Associate Publisher
Scott Rogers

Acquisitions Editor
Jim Schachterle

Project Editor
Monika Faltiss

Acquisitions Coordinator
Timothy Madrid

Technical Editor
Dave Yang

Copy Editor
Mike McGee

Proofreaders
Cheryl Abel
Susie Elkind

Indexer
Jack Lewis

Computer Designers
Tabi Cagan, Lucie Ericksen, Kelly Stanton-Scott

Illustrators
Lyssa Wald, Jackie Sieben, Michael Mueller

Series Design
Kelly Stanton-Scott

Cover Design
Greg Scott

This book was composed with Corel VENTURA™ Publisher.

*To William Ronald and Wilma June Penner, who
made me "go outside and get some fresh air."*

About the Author

Based in Vancouver, Canada, Robert is a freelance Flash developer, consultant, and speaker, whose focus is on math and object-oriented design. A moderator and featured artist at Ultrashock.com, Robert is known worldwide for his technical innovation and organic style. He has developed such innovations as Flash back-button integration and mathematical easing equations. Having not only moderated several forums on Ultrashock and wrangled OOP with the Chattyfig Flashcoders, Robert's work with Axis-media.com has also earned him two Flash Film Festival finalist nominations. His portfolio and experiments can be viewed online at http://www.robertpenner.com.

Contents at a Glance

Table of Contents

Part II   Foundational Concepts   65

3   Math 1: Trigonometry and Coordinate Systems   67

6   Event-Based Programming   163

Part III   Dynamic Visuals   189

7   Motion, Tweening, and Easing   191

Introduction

Well over a year ago, Jim Schachterle approached me about writing a book on Flash for Osborne/McGraw-Hill. He had a very specific concept in mind for the project—it was to represent "the intersection of programming and design." In other words, it was about creating visual elements with code. I had been exploring this area for a while, and had a number of experimental animations on my site (www.robertpenner.com) that I had done for fun.

Jim was also adamant that this was *not* to be a tutorial book. Rather, the material would be conceptually based, teaching principles that could be applied in many different ways. I was more than happy to oblige. I had many ideas bouncing around my head that I wanted to write about, and it would take this kind of approach to be able to discuss the material with sufficient depth.

This book, then, is about my approach to creating dynamic visuals in ActionScript, broken down conceptually. The fundamental elements are object-oriented programming, trigonometry, coordinate systems, vectors, and event-based programming. Once these are understood sufficiently well, motion, physics, color, and shapes can be explored. I endeavor to explain the over-arching principles of these areas, as well as ways to realize them in ActionScript. Flash and the ActionScript language will continue to evolve in coming years, and the code we use to realize scripted animation will doubtless change as well. But the skills you learn in this book, an understanding of the timeless principles of math and movement, will transfer reasonably well to new contexts.

What this Books Covers (Part and Chapter Descriptions)

Part I, "Entering the Process," relates a personal context which precedes and shapes programming and a conceptual context for programming.

Chapter 1, "The Flash Disciple: Process and Disciplines," is autobiographical. I share my story of discovering Flash and the life experiences that have influenced my work. I also relate some personal disciplines that shape the day-to-day routine of my vocation.

Chapter 2, "Object-oriented Programming," is an introduction to object-oriented analysis, design, and programming. It shows a process of moving from project requirements to object-oriented code, and how to implement OOP concepts like classes, methods, and inheritance in ActionScript.

Part II, "Foundational Concepts," outlines fundamental math and programming theory; covered in Chapters 2 through 6.

Chapter 3, "Math 1: Trigonometry and Coordinate Systems," establishes a mathematical foundation useful for ActionScript animation, and for the vector chapters that follow. Key concepts include angles, triangles, the Pythagorean theorem, and polar coordinates.

Chapter 4, "Math 2: Vectors in Two Dimensions," teaches the concept of vectors and how they can be implemented in ActionScript. Vector addition, multiplication, dot product, and other concepts are taught alongside their code implementations.

Chapter 5, "Math 3: Vectors in Three Dimensions," extends the previously learned vector concepts to three dimensions. Also, 3-D coordinates and their projection and rotation are explained alongside ActionScript implementation.

Chapter 6, "Event-Based Programming," covers the new event model in Flash MX, and how it differs from Flash 5. Event handlers and listeners are explained, and I show how to define custom event sources that can broadcast messages.

Part III, "Dynamic Visuals," builds on the previous chapters and extends them to the areas of motion, physics, color, and shape, presented in Chapters 7 through 10.

Chapter 7, "Motion, Tweening, and Easing," discusses the conceptual and mathematical basis of motion. Various equations for easing are explored, and an object-oriented approach to scripted tweening is developed.

Chapter 8, "Physics," explains key concepts of physics such as acceleration, friction, and force, as well as the features of waves.

Chapter 9, "Coloring with ActionScript," develops a multitude of approaches for dynamically coloring graphics with code, using Flash's *Color* class.

Chapter 10, "Drawing with ActionScript," goes over the Flash MX Shape Drawing API for drawing lines, curves, and fills, and shows how to extend it to draw more complex shapes.

Part IV, "Case Studies," takes an in-depth look at four of my experimental animations in Chapters 11 through 14.

Chapter 11, "Aurora Borealis," outlines an interactive two-dimensional particle system that emulates the northern lights.

Chapter 12, "Snowstorm," highlights a three-dimensional particle system modeled upon falling snowflakes.

Chapter 13, "Fractal Dancer," introduces a self-similar (fractal) tree that responds to mouse interaction, recording, and can play back movement.

Chapter 14, "Cyclone," describes a particle system that produces an interactive tornado.

How to Read this Book

This book is probably best read in a non-linear and iterative fashion. Naturally, the chapters are laid out in a logical order, and there is a progression of ideas that build upon each other. At the same time, some concepts may only be understood fully when revisited with more context in mind. Thus, I suggest making several passes to absorb the information, feeling free to skip around a bit to cross-pollinate ideas.

About the Online Files

The source files discussed in the book will be available online at the publisher's web site at http://www.osborne.com, and at my personal site at http://www.robertpenner.com/profmx/.

Acknowledgments

Osborne/McGraw-Hill—for taking a chance on me.

Jim Schachterle—for developing a brilliant vision for the book and for constant encouragement and professionalism.

Bill Spencer—for believing in me and whispering in Jim's ear.

Brandon ("Ahab") Williams—for your passion for math.
Macromedia—for Flash.

The Flash Community—for never a dull moment, with special thanks to Flashcoders and Ultrashock.

Andy Park, Karen Cook, Alan and Nechama Wiseman, and Mark Anderson—for your wisdom and support in the writing process.

Dave, Kevin, Darren, and Willy—for post-modern experiences and dirty bathrooms.

The Creator—for fractals.

Part I

Entering the Process

Chapter 1

The Flash Disciple: Process and Disciplines

We are what we repeatedly do. Excellence, then, is not an act, but a habit.

— Aristotle

I am a Flash disciple. For this period of my life, I am devoted to discovering what Flash can do, and using it in creative ways. Flash is incredibly fun, and it pays the bills. It has captured my heart and head—how can I resist?

I am also fascinated by how people learn and grow. It thrills me to see a few key concepts and skills open up a whole new world for people. I don't claim to be an expert communicator—just a passionate one. Because I want to see people grow, I try to convey concepts in a clear and simple manner. Have you ever heard someone speak who made a complex concept suddenly become crystal-clear? If I can find the right language to do that for my fellow Flashers for a few key ideas, I'll be happy.

In this book, I want to share with you the best ideas and code I've developed. We will explore the dynamic creation of visuals with code. We will design with ActionScript, using object-oriented principles. First and foremost, though, this is a book about *process*. I don't want to convey mere facts about Flash or ActionScript. I approach Flash in a particular way because of my past experiences and habits, and so will endeavor to expose the thought process behind my work.

Personal Background

My first passion in life was music. I started taking piano lessons at age four, from my mother. She tells me that for the first few years, I would practice piano two hours a day. I have no idea why I was intense about it, but my mother says I would do everything in two hour blocks, whether reading, playing with Lego blocks, or practicing music. Over the next 14 years, I studied piano and competed annually in local and provincial festivals. For quite a while growing up, my long-term goal was to become a concert pianist. At school, I played trombone and bassoon in band, and sung in choir. After high school, I picked up the acoustic guitar, the Celtic whistle, and the djembe (an African drum).

Reading was my next love. Any decent fiction book I owned would be read at least twice. I would pick a letter from our 1969 World Book encyclopedia set (*today I feel like... "K"*), and read it for the afternoon. I would read the instructions on the shampoo bottles and the manuals for every electronic device in the house. At one point, my parents actually grounded me from reading for a day.

My next big discovery was computers. When I was ten, my parents bought an XT. If you can remember the 486, well, the XT was basically a 086. Green monochrome screen, 640 kilobytes of RAM, 20 megabyte hard drive. (A wise man once said, "No one should need more than 640K." He now owns Microsoft.) I learned MS-DOS and, to my delight, eventually discovered the program Basica on my computer—a run-time interpreter for the BASIC language. I bought a book of BASIC programs that purported to contain a multitude of Olympic games. After dutifully typing in what seemed like reams of code, I was a little disappointed to be rewarded with dancing ASCII characters that were vaguely reminiscent of swimming and the 100-meter dash. Nevertheless, a door had been opened. I kept on with BASIC, eventually discovering how to switch into different graphics modes and plot pixels and shapes.

In high school, I was overjoyed when my parents bought CorelDRAW! 2.0. We had upgraded to a 286, which ran at 12MHz with one megabyte of RAM. I could run Windows 3.1 on it—slowly. Using CorelDRAW! on this machine required extreme patience; I probably saw that spinning hourglass more often than the cursor. But I learned vector graphics and Bezier curves, along with a plethora of hideous gradients and graphics that seemed brilliant at the time. My parents started a new business during this period: "Rainbow Copy Center," which had the first full-color copies in town. I worked there weekends and summers, and regularly used CorelDRAW! to design brochures and t-shirts.

Math was the next thing that ignited me, although it almost misfired at first. In the ninth grade, I was bored with math and annoyed with my teacher. I gradually stopped doing my homework, and started goofing around with the back-of-the-class crowd. One day, on a whim, I decided to print creepy, cryptic messages in tiny letters all over the math test I was writing. Shortly after the tests were marked, I was called to the school counselor's office. She asked if everything was ok. I said I was fine. Then why, she asked, did I write "WOE IS ME" on my math test? I laughed and explained I was just goofing around because I was bored. Out of the blue, I asked, "Is there any way I could skip a grade of math?" The counselor said she would look into it. Soon after, I was given the Math 9 outline, and finished learning it by Christmas. A year-and-a-half later, I had completed most of Math 12 by correspondence. (It's scary to think what would have happened had I stayed in Math 9.) In grade 11, I was introduced to physics and calculus, and we've been good friends ever since. It wasn't long before I could *see* physics happening all around me: force, acceleration, gravity, and friction, everywhere I looked.

My University Years

At the end of high school, I planned to become either a programmer or a math professor. I entered university confident of my direction, and studied math and computer science for two years. I took five math courses (Calculus I & II, Multivariable Calculus, Linear Algebra, and Complex Analysis), physics, and three computer science courses. Once again, however, my course was altered because of a teacher I didn't like. I was so frustrated with my computer science classes that I thought, "I don't want to spend the rest of my life programming," and looked for another major. I switched to philosophy, and worked towards becoming a philosophy professor.

I was already analytical by nature, but philosophical training increased that ten-fold. Two of the required courses were devoted to logic. We learned how to symbolize logical (and illogical) arguments. With semi-mathematical rules, we proved the validity (or lack thereof) of their conclusions. We learned exactly how constructs like *and*, *but*, *or*, and *if-then* worked logically. Besides the logic courses, the philosophy curriculum was filled with abstract concepts in the extreme. It was an alternate universe of multisyllabic "isms" (like *epiphenomenalism*) that challenged every assumption we had about the universe.

I learned to organize ideas into mental categories and find interesting relationships between them. Like a well-structured XML document, the different nodes and hierarchy of information became clear to me. I grew skilled at distilling the essence of an idea and communicating it in different ways to different people. Because philosophers are ruthless in their scrutiny of language, my writing was forced to become tighter, more precise. These habits have followed me into the language of ActionScript. As future chapters show, I have a passion for clean, organized, and optimized code. I love object-oriented programming (OOP); it's quite gratifying philosophically (and practically). My training in philosophy may seem like an expensive rabbit trail, but it has served me well in other areas.

However, at the end of my Bachelors degree, my brain was basically fried. To graduate on time, I had to take 12 philosophy courses in two years, which really did a number on me. It was hard to be sure of anything anymore, physical or metaphysical. Hungering for something practical, I was drawn to computers once again. Only this time, I wanted to do something with the Internet. I wanted to create web pages and connect them with links. And if I could one day make a menu bar with *rollovers*—well, that would be the ultimate (or so I thought at the time).

Technical School

And so it happened that, a week after graduating from university, I began an intensive nine-month program at a technical school. The institution purported to "turn university graduates into IT professionals," and sure enough, it did. We studied object-oriented programming and design, and learned the process of rapid application development. School ran five hours a day, five days a week—two hours in class, and three hours in "team time."

This collaborative approach was a unique aspect of the program. In teams of five or six, we developed four substantial applications in the core areas of HTML, Visual Basic, Java, and Oracle. For example, we created Windows software and a web site that allowed a fictitious career agency to manage its database of applicants, companies, and jobs. As each project evolved over two to three months, we were led through the entire application development process. We were given an RFP (Request For Proposal) from the fictitious client, and had to collaboratively develop a response document and make a bid for the project. Following that, we were given the client's requirements for the project. We carefully planned the architecture for the application and drafted design documents using UML (Unified Modeling Language, which I'll touch upon in Chapter 2).

I haven't done any development in Java, Visual Basic, or Oracle since technical school, but it was there that I gained an understanding of object-oriented methodology that applies across many platforms. Most importantly, I internalized a *process*—the disciplines related in this chapter that have shaped my life and career.

Finding Flash

My first awareness of something called "Flash" was probably the site for The Matrix (www.whatisthematrix.com). I had previously seen a few sites with the Shockwave plug-in. They had generally annoyed me because of the hassle getting the plug-in, and then waiting (and waiting) for the Shockwave site to download. When the Matrix site said it needed the "Shockwave Flash" plug-in, I remember thinking, "What's this 'Flash' thing? Oh great, *another* plug-in!" The Matrix site took forever to load, but what an interface! There was so much animation going on, all these screens everywhere with complex rollovers that almost looked like video. And the sound... the effects made such an impact, in a web that was quite silent at the time.

A few months later, in tech school, I started to see Flash sites more frequently. Turtleshell.com was one of the first immersive web experiences I remember. I felt like I had fallen into the site, and was gliding through it from section to section. I loved the calm, clean aesthetic, which has influenced my work ever since. In late 1999, the Balthaser site knocked me off my chair. I couldn't believe this was happening in my browser: it was like full-screen video, but… better.

Some classmates in my tech school were learning Flash at that time, and I once looked over a friend's shoulder as he worked on a Flash 4 movie. I could make out some sort of timeline: a mysterious tangle of layers, dots, and horizontal lines with little arrows. Flash just seemed intimidating, so I left it alone. That is, until a fateful day two months from the end of tech school. The Java final exam was fast approaching, but I was tired of studying. For something to do, I installed the trial version of Flash 4 and started playing around. Within a day or so, I had completed the eight lessons in the Help menu as well as the tutorial in the documentation, and found some more tutorials on Webmonkey. Three days later, I completed my first Flash project: slides for my Java team's final presentation. All the other teams used PowerPoint, and I loved how smooth the Flash tweens and anti-aliasing looked in comparison.

Thus began my obsession with Flash. During the last two months of tech school, most of my waking moments were spent learning Flash or dreaming up new things to try. During class, all us students used laptops, and I would be tinting and tweening symbols while the instructor explained PL/SQL. I took on several small Flash projects in my spare time. Thankfully, these occurred at that perfect point in my learning—just barely within reach using my present skills, forcing me to stretch myself and go deeper into Flash.

Nearing the end of tech school, I was conflicted. Programming in Visual Basic and Java was enjoyable, but Flash was heavenly. I wished I could immediately launch into a Flash career. Unfortunately, Flash jobs were few and far between, and I had little in the way of experience or a portfolio. I resigned myself to finding a programming position for the time being, and working towards a future career in Flash in my spare time.

However, a lucky break came in the last week of school. A friend of a friend with a small web development company called me in for an interview. He liked my potential, and the day after graduation, I started working for monkeymedia.net. It was almost too good to be true—getting paid to be creative in Flash, two months after picking it up. Over the next year, I worked with monkeymedia.net and then Axis Interactive (axis-media.com) on contract. During that time, I grew by leaps and bounds in my Flash abilities. It seemed that, almost every month, something revolutionary came along—a new concept that forever changed the way I approached Flash.

This was the Flash 4 era, and animation was my primary work during this period. The company designers would develop layout, graphics, and storyboards for projects. I would take these into Flash and make them dance and sing. I painted the timeline with motion and shape tweens, and cooked up music and sound effects to match. ActionScript was limited, and so was my use of it, consisting mostly of button actions telling movie clips to play or stop.

During this time, I began to develop my own portfolio site and make connections in the Flash community. I eventually started finding clients on my own, mostly in the United States. In February 2001, I attended the FlashForward conference in San Francisco. This impacted me significantly, as I'll describe later in the chapter.

Flash was a phenomenon that took me by surprise. But it was such a perfect fit, that it's almost as if my prior experiences were all preparation for a career in multimedia development. Music, BASIC, CorelDRAW, math, philosophy—they all converged to a focal point. The disciplines of my past became the underpinnings of my new passion—Flash.

The Centrality of Discipline

I've heard it said that "success is when preparation meets opportunity." One angle on this is that you will only be successful if opportunity comes your way. And if you have more natural ability, then in a sense, you have more opportunity. However, opportunity and ability do not *guarantee* success. The other necessary ingredient is preparation. When a pivotal moment comes along, success will be grabbed by those who have built the necessary foundation in their lives. This preparation is called discipline.

What Are Disciplines?

The word "discipline" can have negative connotations for some people, along the lines of "control" or "punishment." This is unfortunate, since discipline, at the core, is about being a disciple—a learner working towards maturity, strength, and success. I am particularly interested in *disciplines*, in the sense that there are many different activities, each a discipline.

Dallas Willard gives a brilliant description of disciplines in one of my favorite books, *Spirit of the Disciplines*. He defines a discipline as an activity you practice in order to accomplish something you cannot achieve by direct effort. We are all familiar with this concept. For example, I know I would not be able to run a marathon by simply showing up on race day and trying to run a marathon. However, if I start small, and take practical steps, I could eventually reach the point where a marathon is within my reach.

These practical steps involve many areas besides the actual running. Preparing for a marathon requires a certain kind of lifestyle, encompassing patterns of work, sleep, diet, and mental tenacity. The foundation for success is built with many interlocking disciplines, many stepping stones, many habits.

Habits

Our lives are ruled by habits, both good and bad. Much of the success and failure we encounter can be traced to habits formed long ago, often as children. Are we stuck, then, enslaved to the bad habits of our upbringing? Thankfully, no. As humans, we have a unique ability to think about the state of our own minds, and make changes to some degree. In a sense, our brain is a special type of hardware and software that has the ability to rewrite itself. This is where disciplines come in.

Disciplines are conscious attempts to unravel bad habits in our lifestyle, and weave in good habits in their place. It can be very hard to quit a bad habit merely by trying not to do it. Strong habits are automatic and involuntary; that's what makes them habits. The word that keeps slipping off the tongue, the important occasions that keep being forgotten—these happen despite our best intentions. Habits take on a life of their own. Some of them become so strong that you might have better luck trying to change your style of handwriting than killing them off. Sometimes it takes some unusual measures.

University for me was a time of little structure or consistency. Classes were a slalom course of changing timeslots, around which studying, socializing, and sleep were scattered randomly. Most of my essays were written at the last minute, and ended up being late despite the inevitable all-nighters. After years of this madness, I started a career—self-employed no less! It has been an incredibly challenging process to learn the ropes of business and keep money coming in. More than anything, though, I battled the bad habits that had taken root in my lifestyle.

At one point, I was engaged in a long-term project which demanded I make steady progress and keep consistent working hours. It was difficult to make this happen, though. Living on my own, I had too much freedom, and too little self-control. Work and free time intermingled and disrupted each other. I was falling behind on the project and becoming desperate.

One day, while I was describing the situation to a few close friends, one of them came up with an idea. He suggested I buy a cheap laptop, and then set in place some hours of the day when I would have to leave the house to "go to work." I liked the idea, and suggested we also come up with a tangible consequence for missing the work hours, to help motivate me. We tossed a few interesting ideas around, and settled on this: I would have to clean one of their bathrooms every time I failed to keep my hours. A funny idea, but it worked. I was suddenly motivated to kick myself out of bed and out the door in the morning. My hatred of soap scum became a source of positive energy; my aversion to toilet bowls, a spring of renewal. I eventually did have to endure the consequences of missed work hours, but no more than a few times. After a while, my working schedule became more habitual, forming a core of consistency that now helps me structure the rest of my day.

Without a strong foundation, built over time through discipline, we will not be able to achieve our goals, despite our good intentions. Natural ability plays a notable part in achievements, but discipline is always necessary for holistic success in the long-term.

My Disciplines

I want to relate a number of disciplines I have found especially helpful on my path as a Flash devotee. Success in any vocation takes a multitude of good principles and habits. Some are obvious, for example, people skills, honesty, perseverance, and punctuality. Though easy to understand, these can be hard to master. I am working on these areas personally, with no small effort. There are other personal disciplines, though, which are deeply embedded in my life. I would like to share how these have aided me in becoming a Flash disciple.

Self-learning

I'm an independent person by nature. When it comes to learning, I have always assumed, deep down, that I am responsible for my own education. When I want to know something, I hunt it down in reference material. When reading a book or writing an essay, if I run into an unfamiliar word, I'll often drop what I'm doing and look it up in the dictionary right away. Similarly, in Flash, when I encounter some uncertainty, I try to find the answer myself. When I was learning Flash (version 4.0 at the time), I would consult the built-in Help *every time* I ran into a problem. After six months, I must have visited 95 percent of the pages in the documentation.

This is such a strong habit that it hardly feels like a discipline. I don't really have to work at it; it's just a part of my life. I grew up believing that, most of the time, with a little effort, I *can* figure out what I need. When I've honestly tried my best, then I ask for help. Of course, it's true that people have different learning styles and personalities. Some learn better socially, verbally, or kinesthetically. My life is not a standard to impose upon others.

I can't pretend that reading the encyclopedia and dictionary for fun is "normal," not by any stretch, but I do want to say that consulting reference materials has benefited me a great deal. It has enabled me to learn quickly and empowered me to use many tools more effectively.

I have a friend from my university who ventured into self-employed print and web design right after graduating in biology. He told me about how he read the Macromedia Dreamweaver 2 manual in two days. A while later, he read through the Flash 4 manual in one sitting. Today, he runs his own successful design company.

I have to admit that his approach is pretty intense, and wouldn't work for everyone. Personally, I haven't read through an entire manual so quickly. The point is that the manual is there to be read. This takes determination, but it is very rewarding. In January 2001, I decided that I was finally going to switch over to Flash 5 and learn the new ActionScript. I chose to sit down on the couch with the ActionScript reference and read it like a novel, an hour here, an hour there. This discipline, along with some customized practice (see what follows), helped me to become familiar with Flash 5 fairly quickly.

If you're not naturally someone who reads manuals, I encourage you to try it as a discipline. Choice information on myriad devices and programs is sitting on the shelf in uncracked manuals. R.T.F.M. (Read The "Friendly" Manual) is not a condemnation, but an invitation to independence and growth.

Customized Practice

For most of my piano-learning years, I generally practiced less than I should have. In high school, I aimed for an hour a day, but never quite reached that goal consistently. I did, however, learn to practice *efficiently*. Over time, I developed various approaches and strategies to conquer my piano pieces. I focused on key areas of the music and tried all sorts of tricks to bring them under my control, eventually turning a stubborn mule of a melody into a racehorse.

The goal of practicing is to be able to play the music normally, but achieving that end requires a tremendous amount of *abnormal* playing. I purposefully played fast parts slow, soft notes loud, smooth lines staccato, and straight rhythms in swing. And above all, I repeated things over and over. (I pity my poor family, who had to endure this mind-numbing cacophony. They eventually changed the ceiling and installed a sliding glass door to lessen the sound from the basement where I practiced.) Often, I would work on a piece from a higher grade level; rising to its technical challenges made it easier to learn my regular music. With these and other techniques, I made the most of my limited practice time. My skills advanced quickly enough for me to complete all of the piano grades by the end of high school. At one point, I placed second in my province's piano competition, and today I am left with a large repertoire of challenging and beautiful pieces under my belt.

When it came to learning Flash, I quickly saw the need for customized practice. For every skill I gained, I saw two more that needed to be learned. I started writing down the techniques I wanted to learn as I came across them, forming a to-do list. In my Flash 4 days, my list looked something like this:

Flash things to learn:

- Pop-up menu

- Drag and drop movie clip

- Load movie

- Load variables from a text file

- Set movie clip properties

And so on…

Bit by bit, I worked my way through the list. I researched the concepts (in the manual, of course), and practiced them either in projects or in small test movies.

It's important to know what it is that you don't know. I remember seeing a Flash 4 article headlined: "Are You a Load Movie Virgin?" I immediately thought, "Load Movie? Say what? I guess I am a virgin, then." The article went on to say that loading external SWFs was a pivotal skill that affected one's approach to Flash development entirely. I took the author's word for it and decided to learn the Load Movie command. Before I read the article, I was ignorant of my ignorance. I had no idea how important this technique would become for my Flash career. The author was right—as I practiced using Load Movie, the structure of my projects was revolutionized.

At whatever stage you find yourself in the journey, take stock of the holes in your knowledge that need to be filled. Examine your own learning style, find the tricks that help you advance more quickly, and develop a customized curriculum of practice for yourself.

Example: Learning Keyboard Shortcuts

Most commands in Flash can be accessed through the menus. However, many of these have keyboard shortcuts associated with them. Early on, I decided to learn and use as many of these shortcuts as possible. This process is one example of how I applied the disciplines of self-learning and customized practice. I felt that the keyboard commands were a necessary part of "mastering the fundamentals," and I developed some customized practice to make this happen.

Table 1-1 lists my core keyboard shortcuts. I use these constantly now, without even thinking about it.

NOTE: I haven't included the many other shortcuts not specific to Flash, such as cut, copy, paste, undo, switching, closing windows, and so on. Also, I listed only Windows key combinations; I'm sure Mac users are savvy enough to translate these for their own use.

It took some effort to memorize these keyboard commands. I forced myself to use the shortcuts by creating a new discipline: when I needed to use a command, I would find it in the menu and note its keyboard equivalent. Then I would actually back out of the menu and call the command with the keyboard instead. I figured that if I waited until the next time I needed that command, I would probably forget the key combination, and end up using the menu again. This practice of backing out of the menus slowed me down a bit at first, but caused me to learn the shortcuts quickly. Now I hardly use the main or right-click menus at all.

Key Combination	Description
F8	Convert to Symbol
CTRL-F8	New Symbol
F5	Insert Frame
SHIFT-F5	Remove Frames
F6	Insert Keyframe
SHIFT-F6	Clear Keyframes
F7	Insert Blank Keyframe
CTRL-ALT-X	Cut Frames
CTRL-ALT-C	Copy Frames
CTRL-ALT-V	Paste Frames
CTRL-SHIFT-V	Paste in Place (one of my personal favorites)
CTRL-ENTER	Test Movie
CTRL-F12	Publish Preview (F12 in Flash 5)
SHIFT-F12	Publish

TABLE 1-1

My Core Keyboard Shortcuts for Flash

Why am I making such a big deal about keyboard commands? Are they essential to a successful Flash career? Well, no—I'm sure one can manage well enough without SHIFT-F5 and CTRL-F8. What's important about this example is the process surrounding it. I wanted to be able to work quickly in Flash. I had the foresight to see how learning keyboard shortcuts would help me reach that goal, and I acted upon it. By intentionally disrupting my normal routine, I was able to engrain good habits early on, and I am still enjoying the benefits of these today. The shortcuts have saved me many hours of development time, and they make my workflow smoother in general. This is one small but tangible example of the power of discipline.

Community

Wherever there is a discipline, art, or craft, there is usually a community that has evolved along with it. The craft first gives rise to a community, then the community perpetuates the craft. It is difficult to work in complete isolation. Working alongside peers produces a combination of camaraderie and competition, which is a large part of motivation.

When I was learning piano, my year revolved around the music festival that occurred every spring. Each year, I would learn new pieces of music, my focus being those brief moments when I presented the result of my efforts publicly, receiving the audience's applause and the adjudicator's critique. I probably focused too much on the competitive aspect of the music festival. Certainly, uncovering the beauty of a Chopin nocturne should always have been more important than "beating Bev and Genevieve this year." Nevertheless, it was genuine friendship with local musicians, teachers, and parents that supported and spurred me onwards.

The online Flash community is an interesting phenomenon. It's amazing the intensity with which people around the world have congregated around a single piece of software. Yet it's more than that. Flash has a way of turning into a lifestyle, of flooding your brain with ideas while you're trying to get to sleep, of interrupting everyday activities with the thought, "I bet I could do that in Flash."

When I've been stuck in a rut, the community has exposed me to new ideas. When I've been tempted to think I've mastered it all, individuals in the Flash community have astounded me with fantastic feats of innovation. Two specific disciplines relating to community that have developed in my life are *learning by teaching* and *open source*.

Learning by Teaching

It's well known that teaching is one of the best ways to gain a deeper understanding of a topic. In high school, I tutored in math and computer skills occasionally, and had several piano students for two years. In university, I was a computer science teacher's assistant, marking programming assignments and helping students in the computer lab.

I once had a conversation where I was describing to a friend some new concepts I'd learned in my philosophy courses. I vividly remember her saying to me, "Robert, you're a good student."

"What do you mean?" I protested. "I'm constantly sleeping in and missing class, procrastinating, and handing in assignments late."

"That's not what I mean," she replied. "You take what you've learned to heart." I'd have to say she was right. I was genuinely interested in what was being taught in class, and I was constantly telling people about it. For instance, I was quite impacted by existentialism, and I talked my friends' ears off about it. I couldn't use all the technical jargon from the material, though, so I found ways to communicate the concepts in different terms. I enjoyed seeing people grasp the ideas, and I learned them more thoroughly by teaching.

In the learning phase of my Flash journey, I started by digging into the manual and supplied lessons. But I gained an in-depth knowledge of Flash largely by answering questions on the Flash discussion forums. I knew there were a lot of details that I hadn't looked into yet. What helped motivate me to discover different areas was looking at what information other people were seeking out.

For instance, someone might ask, "How do you remove an item from an array?" I would see this and think, "Good question: how *do* you remove an item from an array?" So I would search for the answer, first in the Flash manual, and if I couldn't find it there, the Internet. Then I would write up some code to try it out, test it in Flash, and post the answer on the forum. This is really a great system. You get to kill two birds with one stone— helping someone else and yourself at the same time.

Open Source

The biggest turning point in my Flash career came in February 2001, and it had to do with the concept of "open source." The site I had developed on contract with Axis Interactive (www.axis-media.com) was nominated twice in the Flash Film Festival. Consequently, Axis brought me with them to San Francisco to attend the festival and the FlashForward conference. I was tremendously inspired by the sessions as well as the people I met.

At that time, I was decidedly "closed source" personally. I felt it was necessary to keep my FLAs offline to protect my original ideas and maintain a competitive edge. As well, I had recently been burned when someone ripped off my favorite experiment. They stole the code right out of the SWF with ActionScript Viewer, and then passed it off as their own, offering an FLA for download. I was able to resolve the situation, but remained wary and protective.

In San Francisco, however, I attended Joshua Davis' session and heard his thoughts on open source. I was inspired by his generosity, passion, and personal journey. I saw a beautiful paradox: sometimes you receive more by giving things away. I realized that I had more to gain by opening up my work than I had to lose. In fact, I had already seen that it's nearly impossible to protect a SWF, anyway. I resolved to post my FLAs online once I returned from the conference.

Heeding Samuel Wan's FlashForward exhortation to write clean code, I immediately rewrote my ActionScript and added numerous comments. After announcing my FLAs on the Flash boards, I saw the traffic to my site skyrocket (from 5 unique visitors a day to 100). I found that releasing my code actually helped protect me from being ripped-off. Now that more people knew my work, it was more difficult for others to pretend it was theirs.

Open source is a great way to refine your work by gathering suggestions and improvements from others. Going public can also motivate you to polish your ideas a bit more and develop a personal style. It's a way to give back to the Flash community, and in return, receive recognition for your unique ideas that may interest designers more than clients.

There is a saying that "a rising tide lifts all boats." I believe a significant part of Flash's success is the generous sharing of ideas in an active online community. That said there is also a place for *commercial* Flash resources, and these will become increasingly important as Flash matures as a development platform. Various people are investing huge amounts of time developing quality Flash tools, components in particular—and I'm glad if they can be supported financially by their work.

Iterative Process

One phrase I heard over and over at technical school was this: "It's an iterative process." This became almost a running joke. When the application we were developing would crash spectacularly, we'd just look at each other and quip, "well, it's an iterative process." An iteration is simply a repetition or a cycle. The idea of an iterative process is that a project is developed in stages, needing several laps around the track. Sometimes the easiest way to get from point A to point B isn't a straight line—it's a series of circles, like a spiral staircase.

Think of how a tree grows. It doesn't first grow a full trunk, then one complete branch, then another branch, and so on. The tree starts as a simple sapling, a "prototype," if you will. A young tree has much of the "functionality" of an older tree, but the scale is smaller and the structure is less detailed. The tree goes through cycles in rhythm with the seasons, building on itself and branching out. The tree's rings are a record of its iterative process.

Most things in our world naturally grow in cycles. They start out basic, but gradually expand in functionality and complexity. Organisms are obvious examples, but so are organizations. For example, a community/ resource web site starts small, but as people join, it adds more features, which attracts more people, and so on.

Growing in Circles

I've found that the path of learning is not very linear. Knowledge isn't a long procession of individual "facts" on an assembly line which one absorbs one-by-one. Knowledge is more like a tangled web of ideas. It's like an Internet in your head, steadily growing over the years. Knowledge expands in cycles and multiple directions. Our initial understanding of a new concept is sketchy—loosely linked to other concepts more familiar to us. Our knowledge grows as we revisit the idea again and again, forming new connections and enhancing the context.

I often come across code or ideas that are over my head, especially on the Flashcoders mailing list. When the length or density of the material becomes overwhelming, I don't try to fully understand it. Instead, I just skim the text and try to pick out the main points. If it seems important, I put it aside for a later time. Sometimes I'm just not ready to take in a new idea; I may not have the mental framework to support it. However, I can still expose myself to ideas, forming a fuzzy node in my brain that can eventually grow into something useful.

In the spring of 2001, I remember a Flashcoders discussion on listeners and event handlers that went sailing right over my head. I saved the lengthy posts, though, and read them repeatedly over the next few weeks. Eventually, it clicked for me, and listeners are now one of my favorite coding concepts.

ActionScript learners can take a similar iterative approach to learning the language. They can delve into the ActionScript Dictionary with several passes, starting shallow and going deeper. The first pass could be core language structures: operators, if-then-else statements, for and while loops, function declarations, and so on. The second pass could be an overview of ActionScript's built-in classes: *Array, Button, Color, MovieClip, TextField*, and so forth. It is a tremendous help just to be aware of all the different supplied tools at one's disposal. The next phase could be a skim of all the *methods* available for the objects. The principle is that it's good to paint first with broad strokes, then gradually fill in the details.

Prioritizing

In technical school, one concept that was particularly impressed upon us was the relative importance of "required features" vs. "extended features." For each project, we were given a detailed specification listing core functionalities that needed to be developed—required features. For instance, one project was a career placement application, which managed participating companies, available positions at those companies, and job applicants. The client "must-haves" included adding and editing companies, positions, and applicants, as well as automatic matching of applicants to jobs. If our application was lacking any of these required features, we would be severely penalized.

We were also given a list of "extended features," which the client would enjoy having if time was available to implement them. These would be rewarded by bonus dollars, or grade points in our case. However, if any *required* features were absent, we would not receive credit for any of the extended features. As a result of this setup, we students learned to prioritize. Most projects ended up having some extended features, but we worked doggedly to finish those required features first.

The principle here is that extra *wants* are worthless unless the core *needs* are met first. The client would like "icing on the cake," but would prefer plain cake over "icing on the plate." This was an important lesson for me to learn. I am naturally drawn to the icing, so much so that I sometimes forget about the cake. I find myself obsessing over details, seeking elusive perfection in one area while neglecting the others. Over time, I've learned to stop periodically and check that my priorities and progress are in line with reality.

Prioritizing is especially important in the hurried world of Internet development. When time and resources are limited, you have to pick and choose which features can be reasonably included in the current release of a project. This comes back to iterative process: it helps to think of an endeavor as Project 1.0. A first version doesn't need to have every conceivable feature. It's a starting point, a foundation to build on.

Building for the Future

Another key principle of iterative process is to *build with the future in mind*. Many projects will evolve through several stages. Even when they seem to be finished, often they will need to be modified or expanded in the future.

For example, I just heard that my university is in the process of planning a new university center, which includes a larger gymnasium. The building will be one of the largest on campus, and the project will cost many millions of dollars. To make it more financially manageable, the center will be built in stages. The university will first construct a core facility, which it can use while building additions in the following years. It takes extra time and money in the design stage, to create a development plan that allows this multi-stage expansion. However, this upfront investment will bring many long-term benefits to the university.

Building with the future in mind is common sense. We all understand the peril of "painting yourself into a corner." Nevertheless, we may fail to apply this principle as often as we need to, especially when developing in Flash. With movie clips, timelines, and a few commands, it's all too easy to build something that merely "works." A poorly planned movie can look good on the surface, but the insides are a tangle of confusing structure and hardwired, non-modular code. Try to use it in another project, or make some customizations, and the whole thing tumbles like a house of cards.

I have come across dozens of Flash pieces online that look practical; but when I open the FLA, the code makes me cringe. For example, these often have dozens of lines of code tossed into `onClipEvent` handlers with no encapsulating functions, and plenty of absolute, non-dynamic references to `_root` and other variables. The principles of object-oriented programming (OOP) are absent, to the detriment of the project's readability and reusability. I pity the person who tries to make sense of the mess and make it work in another project. Flashers, I beg you: learn OOP and build with the future in mind!

I hate mundane and repetitive tasks with a passion. Paradoxically, I often work hardest when I'm trying to save myself work in the future. I remember when, on one summer job, I was given the task of folding and stuffing several thousand pieces of promotional material. The job was going to take several hours, and I just wanted to finish as quickly as possible. I took a few minutes before starting the job to think about the most efficient way to proceed. I experimented with different techniques of folding and stacking, and came up with a good system. It saved me perhaps a half hour or more; but when you're a teenager, 30 minutes less of stacking and folding is no small victory. And more importantly, I was developing a discipline, a habit of planning before starting projects.

When ideas come along, we programmers are often tempted to jump in and just start coding. I do this myself sometimes, when I want to sketch out an idea quickly, or with small projects. However, this approach does not work effectively when things are more complex. A quick start often means time is wasted fixing a flimsy structure later. Sometimes the project will even have to be scrapped and redone with proper planning. Overall, a slow and careful start will result in a shorter development time throughout the life cycle of a project.

An example of this is when Bill Spencer ("Pope de Flash") invited me to develop an animation for him to showcase at his 3-D session at FlashForward 2001 in New York. He wanted something that combined prerendered 3-D with ActionScript. The time prior to the conference was quite busy, and thus, two days before I was to fly to New York, I found myself with my 3-D object (an asteroid) rendered, but no ActionScript written. The urge came to rush into the code, but I knew that I had to slow down *because* I was so pressed for time. I would never finish in time if I didn't organize my thoughts.

I sat down with a pen and paper and began to plan. I covered page-after-page with paragraphs, lists, diagrams, and pseudocode. It took several hours, but at the end of it, I had improved on my initial ideas considerably and drawn a clear path to my goal. I had used the principles of object-oriented analysis and design, which enabled me to code in an organized manner. I was confident that my approach would work because I had charted out most of the logic on paper. And I did manage to finish it on time, though just barely—I stayed up all night and had an hour to spare before leaving for the airport. If I had not taken the time to plan, though, the development would have taken longer, and the project would never have been finished in time.

Take a few moments at the beginning of a project to work out a good system. Imagine yourself a month down the road, having just received a request from the client to change the highlight color on all the interfaces. Is your current system making the future-you happy, or angry? It helps to look at the requirements of the project and abstract them—work from specific tasks to generalizations that can be customized. As we shall see in Chapter 2, the object-oriented paradigm helps a great deal in this area.

The Direction of this Book

I have laid out this book in a particular way. Sections build on those that came before them. The next chapter, object–oriented programming, establishes a foundation of ActionScript proficiency. This places the reader in a good position to tackle the math concepts in the following three chapters. All of these concepts have to do with space—both two-dimensional and three-dimensional. Within the math chapters, there is also a carefully chosen order. Trigonometry and coordinate systems form a foundational language for locating points in space, and describing spatial relationships. The vector chapters, on the other hand, assume knowledge of trigonometry, and introduce higher-level math concepts. Vectors are convenient and powerful objects for working with graphics and motion. The vector code libraries are used in later chapters of the book. Chapter 6, meanwhile, returns to code concepts to round out the section on fundamentals. It explains the event-based programming paradigm that has emerged in Flash MX.

The Dynamic Visuals section covers four pillars of ActionScripted visuals. Chapter 7 covers motion, tweening, and easing—animation that was once restricted to the timeline, but can now be controlled dynamically. Chapter 8 covers animation that is generated entirely differently— using combinations of force, acceleration, and velocity. The color and drawing chapters showcase the graphic capabilities made possible by MX and a little ingenuity.

In the final section, I explore four of my visual experiments. I deconstruct my thought process and the application of various concepts used earlier in the book.

Overall, this book presents my vision—a coherent, multi-disciplinary system for approaching dynamic visuals in ActionScript, executed with passion and discipline. In the next chapter, we move forward with object-oriented programming—a paradigm for organizing your ideas and code.

Chapter 2

Object-oriented Programming

At the beginning of my Flash career, I created simple, linear animations. But as Flash became more familiar, I started adding interactivity—a button here, a script there. Gradually, I shifted to the coding side of things, to the point where, today, I spend most of my time in ActionScript, hardly using the timeline at all. Flash itself has had a similar journey over the years, progressing from a simple animation tool to a powerful code-centric environment.

What's more, ActionScript is really coming into its own as a language for object-oriented programming (OOP). Years ago in technical school, I studied and used OOP in ASP, Visual Basic, and Java, but it took some time for me to realize how I could apply this background to ActionScript development.

OOP makes it easier to represent real-life situations. It improves organization in both your planning and coding, making your programs easier to debug, update, and reuse. OOP allows you to be more creative and have more fun coding. In what follows, we'll explore the philosophy, principles, and practice of the object-oriented paradigm. Since OOP is such a huge territory, this chapter is not meant to be comprehensive, like an aerial map. Rather, I want to take you on a narrated hike through the terrain, giving you the lay of the land from my particular perspective.

The Essence of Programming

I like to think about things and boil them down to their philosophical essence. Thinking about programming, it seemed to me that there are two fundamental components: *knowing* and *doing*. I found that these were a yin and yang of sorts, mirrored in a host of related dualities, listed in the following table.

Knowing	Doing
Information	Power
Thinking	Action
Brains	Brawn
Head	Hands
Memory	Ability
Characteristics	Behavior
Data	Procedures
Variables	Functions
Properties	Methods

Reading each column from top to bottom, notice how the words morph into each other: *Information*, *Brains*, *Head*, *Memory*, and so on. The two columns are concept clusters that can be found in a multitude of contexts, both inside the computer and out.

Memory and Variables

Imagine how difficult life would be if you couldn't remember anything. One of my favorite movies, *Memento*, depicts the existential agony of Leonard Shelby, a man with no short-term memory. It's as if his brain would reboot every ten minutes, wiping out all the information that had accumulated in RAM (reminds me of trying to work in Windows 98).

Leonard's life illustrates how power without knowledge is usually misdirected. Leonard *does* many things, but his lack of data renders his actions meaningless. He is also incapable of knowing himself, because memory is foundational for self-understanding.

Variables are named bits of memory. You stick information in a variable so you can use it in the future. In ActionScript, the data can be of various types, but the variable name is always a string. With many variables, you can accumulate a respectable knowledge base within the run-time programming environment. But what are you going to *do* with all that information?

Abilities and Functions

Power without knowledge is dangerous, but knowledge without power is useless. Imagine another existential nightmare, which would also make a great movie: you're lying in a coma, in full possession of your memory, mental faculties, and sense of hearing. However, you cannot move a muscle.

You have no ability to communicate to the outside world. You have no control over your bodily "functions," so to speak.

We all need some measure of personal power, a way to bridge the gap between our thoughts and the molecules around us. Physicist Stephen Hawking's physical abilities are fairly limited. Nonetheless, he has enough power to manipulate a special computer and communicate his knowledge. He "functions" rather well, writing books and lecturing on advanced theoretical physics.

Now, imagine a programming language where you could only use variables—no functions. You could store information in memory, perhaps multiply some numbers together, but you couldn't even print the contents of a variable to the screen. Without functions, the language is comatose. If, on the other hand, a programming language *has* functions, but you don't know about them, you're no better off. Read the manual, or code in a coma.

Functions are the primary way of exercising power in ActionScript. The built-in functions expose abilities of the Flash Player to the ActionScript programmer. You can also create your own abilities and package them as functions. At the most basic level, a function wraps a series of tasks into a bundle and slaps a name on it. When I was young, my mother showed me how to make mashed potatoes. Once I was familiar enough with the process, the many steps merged into one task—a function, if you will. To this day, I carry with me the power to make mashed potatoes. When I get that special craving, I simply call my *makeMashedPotatoes( )* function, and before I know it, I've rinsed, peeled, sliced, boiled, drained, mashed, spooned, and buttered those potatoes to fluffy perfection.

Objects: Memory and Abilities

Objects combine information and power into one convenient package. They're like little life-forms you create, each possessing knowledge and abilities, which are implemented in *properties* and *methods*.

Properties and Methods

An object's *properties* are variables, which store the object's knowledge, while an object's *methods* are functions, which enable the object to perform tasks. Flash gives you many predefined objects to use—strings, arrays, and so on—each of which has its own set of properties and methods. Let's look at the most familiar object for Flash programmers: the movie clip.

Movie clips have built-in properties, which give us information about their status. The following table lists a sampling of the *MovieClip* properties, and the information that each represents.

Property	Information
mc._x	Represents the movie clip's horizontal position
mc._y	Represents the movie clip's vertical position
mc._width	Shows the width of the movie clip
mc._height	Shows the height of the movie clip
mc._alpha	Shows the movie clip's level of transparency

These properties act as a movie clip's "memory." They are pieces of information that allow the movie clip to have a "self-understanding"—in other words, knowledge of its current status.

Furthermore, only that particular movie clip, and nothing else, possesses this up-to-date knowledge. Practically speaking, if another object wants to know where the mc movie clip is, the object has to ask mc for that information. In other words, the outside object has to look up, or *reference*, the movie clip (using mc), then ask for a specific property (_x).

In addition to properties, movie clips also have built-in methods, which give them various behaviors. The following table lists three *MovieClip* methods, and their corresponding behaviors.

Method	Behavior
mc.gotoAndPlay( )	Plays from a specified frame in the movie clip
mc.startDrag( )	Makes the movie clip follow the cursor
mc.getBytesTotal( )	Returns the movie clip's size in bytes

Take a real-life situation where you want to meet up with a friend, but don't know where she is. Think about the steps involved, and how they relate to object-oriented properties and methods:

1. Find her cell phone number. This is the *object reference*. It so happens that you have her number stored on your cell phone under "Alice."

2. Dial the number. This is *evaluating the object reference*, which puts you in contact with the object.

3. Ask her where she is. This is *evaluating a property of the object*. In this case, you find her location at `alice.address`.

4. Memorize her address. This is *assigning the result to a variable*. A piece of information comes from Alice's memory and is added to yours. You store it in your "destination" slot as:
   `this.destination = alice.address;`

5. You drive to meet her. This involves invoking your own "driveTo" behavior, or *method,* represented as:

    ```
    this.driveTo (this.destination);
    ```

Classes

In OOP, a *class* is a blueprint for an object, and an object derived from a specific class is called an *instance* of that class. A class is much like a species, defining what a category of things has in common. For instance, individual cats and dogs vary greatly in their appearance, but it's still easy to tell whether a particular "instance" is a cat or a dog.

I live in a recently developed suburban neighborhood whose landscape is dominated by gated communities of cookie-cutter townhouses. This was done because development costs are reduced by designing one template— a *Townhouse* class—and constructing many instances of it. The parts of the townhouses are also members of various classes, allowing the developers to save quite a bit of money by bulk-ordering 100 or more doors from the same class.

Flash's Built-in Classes and Objects

From Flash 5 onward, ActionScript has come with a smorgasbord of powerful classes and objects built into the language. Table 2-1 lists the 17 built-in classes and objects in Flash 5.

Flash MX more than doubled the number of built-in classes and objects, shown in Table 2-2.

It's interesting to note that half of these were not included in the original documentation for Flash MX. Macromedia packed many new features into the Flash MX Player, but decided to reveal them in stages.

How did I separate these entities into classes and objects, you might ask? Simply put, if you can make instances of it, it's a class; otherwise, it's an object. Can you create multiple *Sound* objects? Yes. Can you make *Math* instances? No. Thus, *Sound* is a class, and *Math* is an object. The built-in objects are sometimes called *static objects*, because they don't "dynamically" spawn new instances.

You may have noticed that Flash's documentation generally does not divide the built-in entities into classes and objects. The ActionScript Dictionary calls them all objects—the *Array* object, the *Color* object, the *Math* object, and so on—stubbornly refusing to refer to the classes as "classes."

This really irritated me, until I read the ECMA-262 (ECMAScript) specification, upon which ActionScript and JavaScript are based. The ECMA

Flash 5 Classes	Flash 5 Objects
Array	Cookie*
Boolean	Key
Color	Math
Date	Mouse
MovieClip	Selection
Number	
Object	
Sound	
String	
XML	
XMLNode*	
XMLSocket	

* undocumented in original release

TABLE 2-1

Flash 5 Built-in Classes and Objects

document also calls them "objects," and explains that ECMAScript is technically not a class-based language. It doesn't have "true classes," the way C++ and Java do. Rather, ECMAScript is a "prototype-based language."

Nevertheless, my position is that *Array* and *Color* simply *are* classes, in all the ways that matter. All the essentials of a class are there: constructor, methods, properties, and inheritance. I could care less about the specifics of the *implementation* (prototypes and so on)—*philosophically*, they are classes. Interestingly, portions of Flash's *Using Flash* documentation refer to "built-in classes." For instance, there are these quotes:

"In the Actions panel, the built-in ActionScript classes are called objects."

"All movie clips are instances of the built-in class MovieClip, and all buttons are instances of the built-in class Button."

NOTE: Colin Moock's *ActionScript: The Definitive Guide* (O'Reilly & Associates, 2001) shares my perspective, distinguishing between classes and objects. For example, *Array* and *Color* are consistently referred to as "classes."

To me, the built-in classes and objects are like X-Men: beings that have fallen out of the sky, offering to help us with their special powers. We don't really understand how they obtained these abilities, but they sure are fun to work with. Are you close friends with the built-in classes and objects? *Stage*, *TextField*, *String*—these mutants want to assist you with their special

New Flash MX Classes	New Flash MX Objects
Button	Accessibility
Camera*	ASBroadcaster*
Function	CustomActions
LoadVars	Stage
LocalConnection*	System
Microphone*	System.capabilities
NetConnection*	System.security*
NetStream*	
SharedObject*	
System.Product*	
TextField	
TextFormat	
Video*	

* undocumented in original release

TABLE 2-2

New Flash MX Built-in Classes and Objects

powers. But first, you have to know what those powers are. As G.I. Joe says, "Knowing is half the battle." So crack open that ActionScript Dictionary and do some reference surfing.

Class Constructors

A class constructor is a special function that creates new instances of the class. For example, we can create an array using the *Array( )* constructor like this:

```
list = new Array();
```

In the above example, "Array" is the name of a constructor function, but is also the class to which list belongs. This is common practice in object-oriented programming: the constructor is given the same name as the class. In ActionScript, a class constructor is invoked with new, as in the previous example. The new keyword tells the function to manufacture a new object and deliver it to the outside world.

A constructor will often take arguments, which are used to customize the new object at the moment of creation. To take an example from ordinary life, imagine you've been coding into the wee hours of the morning. Taking a bathroom break, you are suddenly reminded of your physicality, and the fact that you haven't eaten anything in six hours. Quite famished, you pull into an all-night burger joint and blurt out, "Give me a new Hamburger object." This makes perfect sense to you, since you're still thinking in code:

```
mySnack = new Hamburger();
```

You called the constructor without arguments, so you get a plain burger.

On the other hand, if you're feeling a bit more particular, you might say, "I'd like a new Hamburger object with cheese equals true and patties equals two." The cashier gives you a blank stare, so you scribble the order on a napkin and slide it over. The cashier picks it up and reads:

```
mySnack = new Hamburger (true, 2);
```

This time around, you have called the constructor with parameters, to get a customized burger. Fortunately, the cashier is a laid-off JavaScript programmer, and chuckling to himself, he calls to the kitchen for a double cheeseburger.

The *Array* class has quite a versatile constructor, and can be used three ways. We saw the first approach in a previous example:

```
list = new Array();
```

This is the constructor without parameters, which yields an empty array.

The second approach is to use one parameter:

```
greatLakes = new Array (5);
```

Here, the parameter— 5 in this case—determines the length of the array. The greatLakes array now has five empty elements. If we then trace greatLakes to the Output window, we see it represented by four commas, separating five nothings:

```
trace (greatLakes); // output: ,,,,
```

The last option is to pass two or more parameters to the constructor. This results in each argument being added as an element of the array. For example, we can create a `weekdays` array which stores the names of the weekdays as strings:

```
weekdays = new Array ("Monday", "Tuesday",
    "Wednesday", "Thursday", "Friday");
```

As a side note, you can do the same thing using a shortcut square bracket syntax:

```
weekdays = ["Monday", "Tuesday",
    "Wednesday", "Thursday", "Friday"];
```

Some constructors must always be passed one or more parameters. A Color object, for instance, always targets a movie clip. Thus, the *Color( )* constructor always requires one argument, a movie clip reference:

```
col = new Color (mc);
```

We'll take an in-depth look at the Color class in Chapter 9.

In general, be sure to read the documentation for class constructors specifically. Some may have parameters you may not be aware of, that you can use to customize new objects. Or you may simply discover why a piece of code isn't working. Perhaps a constructor is being passed the wrong data or data type.

Instantiating the Visual Classes

Three of the built-in classes are what I call *visual classes*: *Button*, *MovieClip*, and *TextField*. They are unique in that they can be created "by hand" in the Flash authoring environment. Text fields, movie clips, and buttons can be placed on the stage at author-time and edited visually. At run time, they become instances of their respective classes.

By contrast, an array cannot be dragged onto the stage. You have to create it with ActionScript. The built-in classes are instantiated with the `new` keyword:

```
instance = new Class();
```

However, this approach won't work for the three visual classes:

```
// these don't work
mc = new MovieClip();
```

```
btn = new Button();
tf = new TextField();
```

The new keyword can't be used to create instances of the visual classes.

There's no way to directly create *Button* instances with ActionScript. However, a movie clip can be dynamically created by using the *MovieClip* methods *attachMovie( )*, *duplicateMovieClip( )*, or *createEmptyMovieClip( )*. Similarly, a text field can be created dynamically with the *MovieClip.createTextField( )* method. In design patterns terminology, these would be called *factory methods*—they create and return an instance of a class.

In summary, the three visual classes do not have normal constructors. However, MovieClip and TextField instances can be created using MovieClip methods.

NOTE: The undocumented *Camera* and *Microphone* classes also use factory methods instead of constructors to create instances. For example, the *Camera.get( )* method returns a new *Camera* instance, and *Microphone.get( )* produces a *Microphone* instance.

The Prototype Property

In ActionScript, each constructor function has a property called prototype, which is an object. You can verify this yourself with the following code:

```
trace (typeof Array.prototype); // output: object
trace (typeof Color.prototype); // output: object
trace (typeof String.prototype); // output: object
```

As previously discussed, the constructor functions of the visual classes do not create instances. However, they are not entirely useless. *Button*, *MovieClip*, and *TextField* each have a prototype object, as demonstrated in the following code:

```
trace (typeof Button.prototype); // output: object
trace (typeof MovieClip.prototype); // output: object
trace (typeof TextField.prototype); // output: object
```

However, the static built-in objects, such as *Math*, *Stage*, and *Mouse*, do not have prototypes:

```
trace (typeof Math.prototype); // output: undefined
trace (typeof Stage.prototype); // output: undefined
trace (typeof Mouse.prototype); // output: undefined
```

Without prototype properties, *Math*, *Stage*, and *Mouse* can neither be constructor functions nor classes. The prototype object is the glue that holds a class together.

A class starts with a constructor function, say *Widget( )*:

```
function Widget();
```

Widget( ) is then automatically assigned a prototype property, `Widget.prototype`:

```
trace (typeof Widget.prototype); // output: object
```

We can now stick new properties in `Widget.prototype`, for instance, a `size` property:

```
// add a property to Widget.prototype
Widget.prototype.size = 10;
```

If we then create new *Widget* instances, the size property is automatically inherited:

```
// create an instance
w = new Widget();
// test the size property
trace (w.size); // output: 10
```

This holds true for all ActionScript classes. Every instance inherits properties from the prototype of its class constructor. For example:

➧ All movie clips inherit from `MovieClip.prototype`

➧ All arrays inherit from `Array.prototype`

➧ All text fields inherit from `TextField.prototype`

And so on down the list of classes.

How does the class-to-instance inheritance actually happen? Well, the __proto__ property is the key. Every instance of a class is given a __proto__ property that points to the prototype of its class. When you call a property of an object, the run-time interpreter looks for the property first in the object itself. If it cannot be found there, the interpreter looks for the property in the object that __proto__ points to. The interpreter repeats this process, searching along the prototype chain from __proto__ to __proto__, until the property is found or the chain ends.

To illustrate, let's look at an array:

```
arr = new Array();
trace (typeof arr.__proto__); // output: object
trace (arr.__proto__ == Array.prototype); // output: true
```

In the preceding code, we create an instance of the *Array* class, arr. We check the type of arr.__proto__ and see that it is an object. Comparing arr.__proto__ to Array.prototype, we see they are equal. The former points to the latter. Suppose we call *Array* method *push( )* on arr:

```
arr.push ("data");
```

The arr object itself does not have a *push( )* method. However, as we saw, arr.__proto__ is equal to Array.prototype, which does have a *push( )* method. Thus, arr gets to use *Array.prototype.push( )* as its own method, borrowing it, if you will, like a teenager using his parents' credit card.

Later in the chapter, we'll explore the process of creating custom classes using the prototype property. For now, let's continue looking at Flash's built-in classes.

Adding Methods to Classes

Have you ever wanted to play Dr. Frankenstein with the built-in ActionScript classes? To take a simple example, suppose you'd like every movie clip to have a method to flip itself horizontally, something like *mc.flipX( )*. In other words, each movie clip in your movie would automatically inherit your *flipX( )* method.

This actually isn't very difficult. If you know the right syntax, you can add your method to the prototype of the built-in object. For example, this is how you would add the *flipX( )* method to the *MovieClip* class:

```
MovieClip.prototype.flipX = function () {
    this._xscale = -this._xscale;
};
```

Now you can flip any movie clip by calling your method like so:

```
mc.flipX();
```

Here is a *flipY( )* method to match:

```
MovieClip.prototype.flipY = function () {
    this._yscale = -this._yscale;
};
```

In general, you can add a method to any class object using this syntax:

```
Class.prototype.method = function () {
// code
};
```

This works both with the built-in classes and custom classes.

NOTE: I have heard many creative uses of the word *prototype*, so here is a clarification on the terminology. The custom *MovieClip.flipX( )* method is *not a prototype*. It is simply a *method*, which happens to be attached to a prototype object. The *MovieClip* class only has one prototype, so you can't *add* a prototype to it.

Overwriting Built-in Methods

Not only can you *add* new methods to the built-in classes, you can actually *overwrite* their built-in methods. A well-known example of overwriting is Branden Hall's collection of *String* methods, which were substantially faster than the default ones in the Flash 5 Player. All I had to do was include his code in my movie, and my string operations would execute faster. Since his methods overwrote the built-in methods, I didn't have to change my syntax, and suddenly the horribly slow *String.split( )* became a not-so-pokey *String.split( )*.

NOTE: The *String* class in Flash 5 was actually written in ActionScript. In Flash MX, the String class is now a "native object," which means that its methods are written in C++, and exist as compiled code in the Flash Player. As a result, string operations such as *split()* are faster than they were in Flash 5. The *XML* and *Array* classes have been upgraded in the same manner.

To overwrite a built-in method, just use the same syntax you do for adding a method. For example, the *Array.push( )* method is fairly slow in Flash 5. You can overwrite it with this code:

```
Array.prototype.push = function (data) {
    this[this.length] = data;
};
```

The preceding code inserts data into the end of the current array. Notice that the this keyword is used to refer to the current instance object from inside the method.

Extending Static Objects

Math, *Selection*, *Key*, and *Mouse* are "static objects," as opposed to *classes* like *Array* and *Date*. They are called "static" because there's just one object that sits there; you can't instantiate any more of them. For instance, you can't create more *Math* objects.

Extending the static objects needs to be done a little differently than classes. Static objects don't have a prototype property. Consequently, you attach new properties and methods to the static object itself. For example, this is how you could write a *Math.cube( )* function that cubes a given number:

```
Math.cube = function (x) {
    return x*x*x;
};
// test Math.cube()
trace ( Math.cube (20) ); // output: 8000
```

In general, you can use this syntax to extend static objects:

```
StaticObject.method = function () {
// code
};
```

However, *don't* try to extend static objects with this syntax:

```
StaticObject.__proto__.method = function () {
// code
};
```

Using __proto__ in this manner will actually add the method to Object.prototype, which we definitely don't want. All objects inherit from Object.prototype, so it's best not to stick anything there unless you really need to.

NOTE: If you add properties to Object.prototype, you should use the undocumented feature ASSetPropFlags( ) to "hide" them from for..in loops, with this syntax: ASSetPropFlags (Object.prototype, null, 1); Otherwise, the properties will show up in all objects, causing trouble for XML nodes in particular. For more information on *ASSetPropFlags( )*, see the Flashcoders Wiki: http://chattyfig.figleaf.com/flashcoders-wiki/ index.php?ASSetPropFlags

Classic OOP Concepts

When we think in the object-oriented paradigm, we see a program not as a series of sequential steps, but as a system composed of several components, each of which is designed for a specific purpose. These objects communicate with each other, working together to form a larger collaborative system. Using the classic concepts of *abstraction*, *encapsulation*, and *polymorphism* will help us to see the system in object-oriented terms.

Abstraction

I remember getting the living daylights scared out of me, around age twelve, watching the movie *Predator*. (It didn't help that my brother and I were alone in the house that night, having illicitly rented the video while our parents were out of town.) One of the creepiest parts was seeing the alien's point of view. The doomed earthlings showed up as blotches of red, yellow, and green, caricatured and dehumanized by some sort of heat map, while strange symbols buzzed around them in the viewfinder. The alien viewed an *abstraction* of the other life forms, which removed certain characteristics (skin color), and highlighted others (body temperature).

In a similar way, you are abstracted when you interact with various computer systems. When you use a bank machine, for example, you can almost imagine the machine scanning you, like an alien. It doesn't care how tall you are or whether you're having a good day. It simply pulls up your number, processes more numbers associated with your number, and decides whether to throw some paper at you.

Abstraction is a technique that is central to both "real life" and object-oriented programming. (It's scary sometimes how the two can merge.) It is the process by which we focus on what's important and ignore what is irrelevant for our current needs. We live in a complex world that threatens to overwhelm us unless we simplify, distill, *abstract*. If our minds need to manage complexity in this way, how much more does a computer have to?

For example, imagine you had to build a system for an online job agency. It would allow jobseekers to search for open positions, and companies to search for applicants based on their skills. Sounds simple, but the process becomes quite involved. In the technical school I attended, we spent a total of five months analyzing, planning, and developing this system—first in Visual Basic, then in Java. In the early stages, we described how such a system would operate from the user's perspective. Then we had to abstract out the fundamental entities of the system in order to move towards an object-oriented design.

In practical terms, we identified a few key objects in the system: Applicant, Position, Company, and Skill. Most of the system's operations could be described in terms of interactions among these. With each object, we asked, "What characteristics of this object are important to us, in terms of this system?" An applicant, for example, is a person. An *Applicant*, however, is an *abstract representation* of that person from the system's point of view. We singled out the person's essential characteristics, such as name, password, e-mail address, phone number, and job skills. Naturally, we had to ignore most of the applicant's other qualities, like shoe size and political persuasion.

In case you haven't already guessed, Applicant, Position, Company, and Skill became custom classes as we progressed through the project life cycle. Abstraction, then, occurs at an early stage, and has a significant formative influence on the custom objects that evolve.

Encapsulation

An encapsulated object is like the proverbial "black box." You don't need to know the inner workings of the black box in order to use it; you simply feed it an input, and it gives you an output. A well-designed object is like a vending machine. Chances are, you won't be able to understand how it works internally. Nevertheless, if you follow the directions, stick in the right coins, and press the right button, you can get what you want.

Imagine for a second how an *unencapsulated* vending machine might operate. You feed it some quarters, press a button and wait. Nothing happens. You kick and rock the stupid thing, but nothing comes out. Finally, you give up and leave, frustrated. When you arrive home, though, you notice something small outside the front door. It's a chocolate bar. In fact, it's *the* chocolate bar—the one you were trying to buy from the machine. Mystified, you check for razor blades, and then proceed to eat this Hershey from heaven. The next day, however, you check your online banking, and discover that the vending machine has charged five dollars to your credit card! Stupid machines.

The example is a bit silly, but this is often what happens in sloppy ActionScript. In open-source FLAs, I often see people use functions that are not encapsulated. Like the wacky vending machine, a poorly coded function will: 1) change things in distant places, and 2) fail to return its output where you would normally expect it.

Let's look at a function guilty of crimes against encapsulation. The following is a *spin( )* function I cooked up:

```
function spin () {
    _level5.box._rotation += 10;
```

```
    _root.result = _level5.box._rotation;
}
```

The general purpose of *spin( )* is to rotate a movie clip and store the new value of _rotation. As it stands, though, the function's natural beauty is hidden beneath unsightly hard-coding and lack of encapsulation. Let's give it a makeover.

We can start by generalizing *spin( )* to make it more dynamic. Instead of having it rotate one particular movie clip, _level5.box, let's have it affect any clip we specify. We add an mc argument, and use it in place of _level5.box:

```
function spin (mc) {
    mc._rotation += 10;
    _root.result = mc._rotation;
}
```

That looks better already. We would now call *spin( )* like this:

```
result = spin (_level5.box);
```

Next, let's get rid of the _root.result assignment. Putting the result on _root is like finding the chocolate bar on your doorstep in the earlier vending machine example. Better to have the function directly return the result instead:

```
function spin (mc) {
    mc._rotation += 10;
    return mc._rotation;
}
```

If we wanted to take it further, we could make this a *MovieClip* method. We simply attach the function to MovieClip.prototype and refer to the movie clip a little differently:

```
MovieClip.prototype.spin = function () {
    this._rotation += 10;
    return this._rotation;
};
```

Now that *spin( )* is being invoked as a method of the movie clip, we use this to refer to the clip, and we don't need the mc parameter. We also call *spin( )* differently, like so:

```
result = _level5.box.spin();
```

Our function is now a method of an object, and is completely self-contained. It doesn't change anything outside the object, and returns its result where we expect it.

We can take it yet another step further, and replace our value of 10 with a dynamic parameter:

```
MovieClip.prototype.spin = function (angle) {
    this._rotation += angle;
    return this._rotation;
};
```

Then our code would look like this:

```
result = _level5.box.spin (10);
```

It's good practice to eliminate hard-coded numbers, so-called "magic numbers," with parameters. This generalizes a function so it can be used in a greater variety of ways.

NOTE: If we want to get really fancy, we can change the rotation and return the result in one line instead of two:
```
return (this._rotation += angle);
```

Encapsulated code is cleaner and easier to debug. Here are some rules of thumb on how to keep code self-contained:

> **Use relative references instead of absolute references.**   This will allow your code to be more portable. To use an analogy, if you build a web site with all absolute links, good luck trying to move it later.

> **Ban _root from your classes.**   Class encapsulation is shattered by _root. If you need to use a movie clip reference, pass it in as a parameter.

> **Fall in love with the word "this."**   Focus objects and their methods primarily on themselves. Take a page from pop psychology—navel-gaze and change yourself instead of others. If a method needs to affect an outside object, pass the object in as a parameter or use a local property (this.targetObj, for example).

> **Keep your variables local to the method.**   Declare new variables with var to keep them inside the function, otherwise they will become timeline variables (properties of the enclosing movie clip) and will not be cleaned up when the function finishes executing.

Polymorphism

One of the best things about being an object-oriented programmer is that you get to throw around words like *polymorphism,* which sounds like a possible synonym for "colorful shapeshifter." The concept of polymorphism, though, can be summed up in the phrase: *same interface, different implementation.*

For example, remote controls for both VCRs and DVD players have play, stop, fast forward, and rewind buttons. The *interface* for the basic controls is the same. However, VCRs and DVD players have vastly different *implementations* of play, stop, fast forward, and rewind. If these machines were two different classes, their buttons would be methods. You would have *VCR.play( )* and *DVD.play( ), VCR.stop( )* and *DVD.stop( ).*

This is an example of polymorphism—different classes are purposefully given methods with the same names. The advantage of polymorphism is that it can make it easier to interact with objects of different classes, using the same interface.

If you were developing an adventure game, you might create several Player and Enemy classes to represent different characters. It could be advantageous to look at the similar behaviors between these objects, and give them methods with the same names. For instance, the objects would probably all need *move( )*, *attack( )*, and *die( )* methods.

Developing a Custom Class

We have looked at Flash's built-in classes, and discussed some key object-oriented concepts. Now we'll explore the process of building a custom class, using a hands-on example.

We're going to apply some object-oriented techniques to a task that isn't too complex, yet requires a bit of thought. It is also practical. I developed a *PhotoAlbum* class for a small Flash site recently, and realized it would make a good example for this chapter.

The site needed a simple gallery of photos. No thumbnails, just one image changed by Back and Forward buttons. The gallery would consist of JPEGs (loaded dynamically), and would wrap from the end to the beginning, and vice versa.

These requirements aren't too difficult. One could throw down some code and movie clips and get the job done fairly quickly. However, I'm at the point now where I can't *not* create a class for something like this. I love OOP so much that I'll use any excuse to design a custom class, even for simple jobs.

An object-oriented approach is slower in the beginning, but saves you time later during development, debugging, and modification. Let's enter the first stage of this approach: *analysis*.

Analysis

Analysis is the process of taking things apart, breaking complex entities into simpler pieces. By contrast, *synthesis* moves in the opposite direction, creating a larger whole out of the parts. This we will do later in the design phase, but a good synthesis is usually preceded by a thorough analysis.

The analysis stage is where you clarify your goals by spelling them out in detail. It's important to thoroughly understand the problem *before* trying to solve it. This is especially poignant in developer-client relations. If you skip the analysis stage, you may find that you've developed something completely different from what the client had in mind. Gather as many specifics about the client's expectations as possible, and write them out in detail.

There are numerous tools and methodologies to assist in this process. Entire books have been written on object-oriented analysis, so I'm giving it merely cursory treatment here. One particularly helpful analysis tool I learned in technical school was the *use case*.

Use Cases

One of the first rules of public speaking is "know your audience." In particular, what do they expect to gain from the experience you bring to them? The same holds true in application development. The analysis and design of the system should center around the *user experience*. Use cases are a tool from UML (Unified Modeling Language) that help us focus on the user.

The first question, then, is "Who is the user?" In our case, we are building some ActionScript to encapsulate a photo album—a collection of code. Since the actual "end user" of the application won't see the code, our user is the actually ActionScript developer.

The next step is to break the user experience down into task-based components, or *use cases*. With the photo album, there are four main activities from the ActionScript developer's perspective:

❭ Create a Photo Album

❭ Display the Next Photo

❭ Display the Previous Photo

❭ Display the Photo at a Specific Index

These are our use cases for this project, and were fairly easy to extract from the initial description of the system. In a more complex project, you may need further dialogue with the client to develop the use cases.

Use Case Scenarios

The next step is to fill out the use cases into *use case scenarios*. A use case scenario describes, step by step, how a use case unfolds *from the user's perspective*. It is important to break out of your own perspective as the system developer. At this stage, you should ignore the behind-the-scenes mechanisms, and simply describe changes in the system that are *visible to the user*.

Here are the four use case scenarios for the photo album:

Create a Photo Album

1. The user defines a location to hold the photos.

2. The user defines a list of photo URLs.

3. The user issues the *create photo album* command, supplying the location and photo list.

4. The photo album is created.

5. The first photo in the album is displayed.

Display the Next Photo

1. The user issues the *next photo* command.

2. The next photo in the album is displayed.

3. If the album reaches the end, it wraps to the first photo.

Display the Previous Photo

1. The user issues the *previous photo* command.

2. The previous photo in the album is displayed.

3. If the album reaches the beginning, it wraps to the last photo.

Display the Photo at a Specific Index

1. The user issues the *show photo at index* command, supplying a number.

2. The photo at the specified index is displayed.

3. If the new number is too small for the album, the last photo is displayed instead.

4. If the new number is too large for the album, the first photo is displayed instead.

Hopefully, this gives you a general sense of what use case scenarios look like. The preceding listings were simple, but even then, I wrote them in several passes. It takes time to think through the steps involved, tighten the ideas, and refine the language. In several of these scenarios, I found that "implementation language" had slipped in, making it sound too much like pseudocode. In those spots, I had to simplify the wording and bring it back to the user's perspective. At this stage, the descriptions should be fairly high-level, and float above the implementation.

Design

Now that we've clarified our goals through analysis, we're ready to move on to the design stage. Because we're using an object-oriented approach, it's safe to assume we'll end up with a system containing one or more objects. In the design stage, we identify the main objects of the system and sketch out their features. Choosing the objects is an intuitive and inexact process, since it involves an interpretation of everyday language. In general, though, look for the *nouns* that occur frequently in the use case scenarios. Objects are *things*, so look for the main things that figure in the descriptions.

In our project, the use case scenarios are dominated by two nouns: *photo* and *photo album*—good candidates to become custom objects. Now we can engage in some object-oriented design (OOD).

NOTE: Sometimes I use the terms "custom object" and "custom class" interchangeably, especially in relation to object-oriented design. Though the concepts are different, they are quite closely related. A custom class is a template for a custom object. Hence, if you're designing a custom class, you're designing a custom object.

Remember that objects are a combination of knowledge and abilities. Thus, when we're fleshing out our own objects, we ask these questions:

1. What does this object know?

2. What does this object do?

The first question gives us the object *properties*, while the second gives us the object *methods*.

Choosing Properties

Let's start with the photo album, and give it a class name of *PhotoAlbum*. What does a *PhotoAlbum* object know? Re-reading our use case scenarios and thinking it through, I arrived at this list of property names and descriptions, shown in the following table.

Property Name	Description
holder	The object used to hold the photos — a movie clip
photos	A list of the photos in the album — an array
index	The index of the currently displayed photo — a number

When we look at the other object, *Photo*, we notice it doesn't know very much. In our use case scenarios, a photo really has only one property: the URL of its JPEG file. Given this, here's the sole property, shown in the following table.

Property Name	Description
url	The location of the JPEG photo — a string

Choosing Methods

Having specified the knowledge of the objects, we turn to their abilities. The behaviors we see in the use case descriptions are good candidates for class methods.

In our example, I looked at the use cases and saw that the last three are behaviors of a *PhotoAlbum* object. I then defined methods corresponding to each of these, as shown in the following table.

Method Name	Description
next( )	Display next photo in the album
prev( )	Display previous photo in the album
showPhotoAt( )	Display the photo at a specific index

As for the *Photo* class, what behaviors does it have? Does the photo "display itself," or is it "displayed by" the album? I decided that the photo should be passive—it will be *displayed by* the album. The *Photo* class has no behaviors, and thus, it has no methods.

There are often ambiguities in the interpretation process. With questions like our previous one, the answer can go either way, and may be decided by considerations of implementation or style. In a similar vein, choosing good method names is often an exercise in aesthetics, as one attempts to balance descriptiveness with brevity. Thankfully, object-oriented design is an iterative process, so you can do rough sketches and refine them in subsequent passes.

Object Relationships

After identifying the main objects and their properties and methods, we examine the relationships between the objects. The primary relationships are called *aggregation, composition, collaboration,* and *inheritance.*

Aggregation

Aggregation is a "has a" relationship, where one object is part of another. For example, a computer *has a* hard drive, *has a* CPU, and so on. The relationship between the computer and its parts is one of aggregation. With our project, we see that a photo album *has a* photo, therefore they are related by aggregation.

Composition

Like aggregation, composition is a "has a" relationship. The difference between the two is slight, and subtle: objects collected through composition are not independent of the containing object. The parts of your body are related to you by composition—you are composed of arms, legs, and so forth. By contrast, aggregated photos have more independence from the photo album that contains them.

Collaboration

Collaboration is the "uses a" relationship, where one object controls or calls upon another object to accomplish a task. However, though the objects are connected, neither object is part of the other. Likewise, your relationship with your computer is one of collaboration.

Inheritance

Inheritance is the "is a" relationship, where one object is the child of another. The child object inherits the abilities and characteristics of the parent, but possesses additional abilities. The child, or subclass, is usually more specialized than the parent, or superclass. You yourself have an inheritance relationship with the vertebrate, mammal, and human classes, therefore you *are* all of these.

Class Diagrams

The class diagram is a UML tool for depicting object relationships. The notation and rules for class diagrams are somewhat involved, so I'll give just a brief introduction to them here. Figure 2-1 shows the class diagram for our project.

Each class is represented by a box, which is separated into three sections. At the top of the box is the class name. Underneath are listed the class properties and then the methods. The *Photo* class has no methods, so it has a blank section at the bottom. The data type for each property and method is also listed. For instance, the `photos` property of *PhotoAlbum* is an array, so it is followed by a colon and "Array." A value of "void" indicates that a function either does not return a value or doesn't take any parameters, depending on its placement.

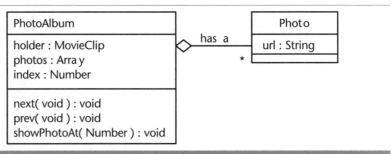

FIGURE 2-1

The class diagram for PhotoAlbum and Photo

NOTE: Class diagrams often include access signs in front of the properties and methods. Public properties are preceded by a plus sign (+), private properties by a minus (−), and protected properties have a number sign (#). ActionScript does not give us the option of hiding or protecting properties (apart from the undocumented function *ASSetPropFlags( )*). In other words, all properties are public in ActionScript. However, some classes, like those in the FUI components, have comments specifying that certain properties or methods are public or private. This approach is useful, but depends on "the honor system." Developers are "not supposed to" access private properties, but there is no (documented) way to enforce this.

In a class diagram, relationships between classes are depicted by lines between the boxes, with various accompanying symbols. As we discussed previously, *PhotoAlbum* and *Photo* are related by aggregation. The symbol for aggregation is a hollow diamond. Thus, the diamond is placed on the line of relationship, adjacent to the possessing class—*PhotoAlbum* in this case. The phrase "has a" is an optional addition to the line of relationship.

NOTE: In contrast to the hollow diamond for aggregation, the symbol for *composition* is a solid diamond, usually black.

An aggregation relationship has the characteristic of *multiplicity*, which can be *one-to-one* or *one-to-many*. In our case, one photo album can have many photos, so it is a one-to-many relationship. The asterisk (*) in Figure 2-1 indicates the one-to-many multiplicity. A one-to-one multiplicity would be represented by the numeral 1.

NOTE: One-to-many multiplicity can also be specified with a minimum and a maximum. For example, if you specify that a stool can have between three and five legs, the multiplicity between Stool and Leg would be 3 . . 5 . When there is no upper limit, an asterisk is used in place of the second number, for instance, 1 . . *.

Our project is extremely simple, having only two classes, and the class diagram may seem trivial as a result. However, many projects require a multitude of interdependent classes, with complex relationships. For these, class diagrams are crucial for understanding and designing the structure of the system. If you have found this brief introduction interesting, I recommend you do further reading on UML and class diagrams. In particular, I recommend Ivar Jacobsen's book *Object-Oriented Software Engineering* (Addison-Wesley, 1992).

Class Development in ActionScript

After the analysis and design stages, we are now in a position to start coding the class. In general, we create a class constructor, which initializes properties of the class, and then a function for each method.

In our example, the *PhotoAlbum* class has three properties and three methods. The *Photo* class, on the other hand, has just one property—the url string—and no methods. For our purposes, a photo can be represented by just a single string. We don't really need to create a custom *Photo* object, and thus, we won't define a *Photo* class.

The PhotoAlbum Constructor

The constructor function of the class is used to create the custom object and initialize its properties. In this project, we have a use case called *Create a Photo Album*, to which we will return for inspiration:

Create a Photo Album

1. The user defines a location to hold the photos.

2. The user defines a list of photo URLs.

3. The user issues the *create photo album* command, supplying the location and photo list.

4. The photo album is created.

5. The first photo in the album is displayed.

Step 1 in the preceding list mentions "a location to hold the photos." In the Flash implementation, external JPEGs must be loaded into a movie clip. Thus, the procedure will involve creating a movie clip (whether at author-time or run time), and passing the movie clip reference to the class constructor. Also, the "list of photo URLs" translates practically into an array of strings. So it appears that our constructor will take two parameters: a movie clip reference and an array.

Here is the *PhotoAlbum* constructor I came up with:

```
_global.PhotoAlbum = function (holder_mc, photos_arr) {
    this.holder = holder_mc;
    this.photos = photos_arr;
    this.showPhotoAt (0);
};
```

Each of the two arguments is assigned to an object property: `holder_mc` to `this.holder`, and `photos_arr` to `this.photos`. The constructor function is attached to the `_global` object to make it globally accessible. As a result, in any scope, we can access *PhotoAlbum* without the need for a prefix.

As you may recall, a *PhotoAlbum* instance has three properties: `holder`, `photos`, and `index`. The first two have been set directly, but what about `index`? We know from the use case scenario that the first picture should be displayed when the object is created. Since the photos are stored in an array, the first index is zero. Could we just set index to zero, then?

```
this.index = 0;
```

This code initializes the `index` property, but does nothing to display the photo at that index. Remember, though, that we gave *PhotoAlbum* three methods in the design stage: *next( )*, *prev( )*, and *showPhotoAt( )*. We also said that *showPhotoAt( )* would display a photo at a specified index. It would make perfect sense, then, to use the *showPhotoAt( )* method here in the constructor to display the photo at index zero:

```
this.showPhotoAt (0);
```

At this point, we haven't coded the *showPhotoAt( )* method. However, because we have already defined its purpose, we trust that *showPhotoAt( )* will take an index argument, "make it happen," and display the photo for us. Imagine if, for some reason, you were assigned to code the constructor, but another programmer was responsible for *showPhotoAt( )*. If the other coder properly encapsulates the method, you can call the method in your own code without knowing anything about its internal implementation.

The showPhotoAt( ) Method

With our constructor function complete, we can now add methods to the class by defining more functions and attaching them to the prototype of the class. The behavior of the *showPhotoAt( )* method needs to follow one of our use case scenarios:

Display the Photo at a Specific Index

1. The user issues the *show photo at index* command, supplying a number.

2. The photo at the specified index is displayed.

3. If the new number is too small for the album, the last photo is displayed instead.

4. If the new number is too large for the album, the first photo is displayed instead.

We need to do some interpretation of these descriptions to move towards the eventual code. First off, we must decide how "too small" and "too large" will be determined. Our photos are stored in the photos array, which is indexed from zero. If there are five photos, the last index will be 4. Thus, if we try to set the index to 5, that would be too large, and so the first photo (index 0) would be displayed.

That makes the process clearer, but we still need to generalize the "too large" condition. How about this: when the new index is greater than the last index, set the index to zero. We can now write some preliminary pseudocode as follows:

```
if newIndex > lastIndex
then index = 0
```

But how do we find the last index of the photos list? Being an array, it has a *length* property. In general, the last index is one less than the length of the array. So we can rewrite our pseudocode:

```
lastIndex = photos.length - 1
if newIndex > lastIndex
then index = 0
```

We also need to check if the new index is too small. This is easier because the lowest index is always zero. So, if the new index is less than zero, we set the index to the last available index:

```
if newIndex < 0
then index = lastIndex
```

Of course, if the new index isn't too large or too small, we just set the index to that value:

```
index = newIndex
```

We can then combine these three conditions into one if..else block of pseudocode:

```
lastIndex = photos.length - 1
if newIndex > lastIndex
then index = 0
else if newIndex < 0
then index = lastIndex
else index = newIndex
```

With the new index sorted out, the last step is to display the photo at that index in the array. The pseudocode can be simply stated as this:

```
display photos[index]
```

This pseudocode can now be translated into ActionScript fairly easily. Here, at last, is the *showPhotoAt( )* method:

```
PhotoAlbum.prototype.showPhotoAt = function (n) {
    var lastIndex = this.photos.length - 1;
    if (n > lastIndex) n = 0;
    else if (n < 0) n = lastIndex;
    this.index = n;
    this.holder.loadMovie (this.photos[this.index]);
};
```

The function is attached to `PhotoAlbum.prototype`, ensuring that all instances inherit the method. The one argument, n, is the new index. The internal code follows the pseudocode closely. To display the photo, the *loadMovie( )* command is invoked as a method of the container movie clip. The JPEG URL is then located with `this.photos[this.index]` and passed to *loadMovie( )*.

The next( ) Method

Now, let's explore the *next( )* method. We look again to the corresponding use case scenario:

Display the Next Photo

1. The user issues the *next photo* command.

2. The next photo in the album is displayed.

3. If the album reaches the end, it wraps to the first photo.

How is the "next photo" determined, we ask? It is the index that is one greater than the current index. We already have a command to change the index, so we can reuse it here. The pseudocode is naturally quite simple:

```
showPhotoAt (index + 1)
```

Here's the ActionScript for the *next( )* method:

```
PhotoAlbum.prototype.next = function () {
    this.showPhotoAt (this.index + 1);
};
```

This setup is simple and elegant. All the validation and wrapping logic is in one place—*showPhotoAt( )*.

NOTE: When I was first developing this class, I had some validation logic in *next( )* and *prev( )*. It was only after starting to code *showPhotoAt( )* that I realized I could consolidate all the validation code into that method, and just call *showPhotoAt( )* from *next( )* and *prev( )*.

The prev( ) Method

Although we have a hunch the *prev( )* method will look much like *next( )*, we dutifully consult the original use case scenario:

Display the Previous Photo

1. The user issues the *previous photo* command.

2. The previous photo in the album is displayed.

3. If the album reaches the beginning, it wraps to the last photo.

The "previous photo" is found by taking the current index and subtracting one.

Here's the ActionScript for *prev( )*:

```
PhotoAlbum.prototype.prev = function () {
    this.showPhotoAt (this.index - 1);
};
```

It's basically the same as the *next( )* code, except we're subtracting rather than adding one. Our *PhotoAlbum* class is now finished, and ready to be tested.

PhotoAlbum in Action

If we developed our project correctly, we should be able to create a photo album by following our original use case scenario:

Create a Photo Album

1. The user defines a location to hold the photos.

2. The user defines a list of photo URLs.

3. The user issues the *create photo album* command, supplying the location and photo list.

4. The photo album is created.

5. The first photo in the album is displayed.

For step one, let's create a movie clip dynamically with the *MovieClip.createEmptyMovieclip( )* method:

```
this.createEmptyMovieClip ("holder_mc", 1);
```

In step two, we'll create an array of strings to hold the URLs for the photos:

```
photos_arr = ["pic1.jpg", "pic2.jpg", "pic3.jpg"];
```

For step three, we call the class constructor to create a new photo album, passing our movie clip and array:

```
album = new PhotoAlbum (holder_mc, photos_arr);
```

Steps 4 and 5 in the scenario are now carried out automatically. The photo album is created, and referenced by `album`. And the first photo in the list, `pic1.jpg`, is loaded into the movie clip `holder_mc`.

The last thing we need to do is set up a basic interface for scrolling through the album. This couldn't be simpler. We just create two buttons, and have them call the *PhotoAlbum.next( )* and *PhotoAlbum.prev( )* methods. We place this code on the left button instance:

```
on (release) {
    album.prev();
}
```

And this code goes on the right button instance:

```
on (release) {
    album.next();
}
```

We now have a simple photo album system that fulfills both the client requirements and the principles of object-oriented programming. If need be, we can build on this base, adding more features and methods to the class, or perhaps convert it into a component.

In my original situation, my client requested another photo album that functioned much the same but cross-faded between pictures. I was able to extend my *PhotoAlbum* class, keeping its structure but rewriting the *next( )* and *prev( )* methods. I used polymorphism there—having the same method names for two similar classes, *PhotoAlbum* and *FadePhotoAlbum*. In the final section of the chapter, we'll look at how to extend classes with inheritance.

Class Inheritance

We've looked at the concept of the class—a specification for a group of objects with common characteristics and abilities. Sometimes classes are arranged in a hierarchy, something like the biological classifications *vertebrate—bird—sparrow*. The hierarchy moves from general to specific— for instance, a bird is a specialized vertebrate, and a sparrow is a specialized bird. If we modeled these categories with classes, the characteristics of each would be passed down in a process of *class inheritance*. Let's look at how to implement this in ActionScript.

Method vs. Property Inheritance

Remember that objects have both information and abilities, which correspond to properties and methods, respectively. As a result, there are two different components to inheritance: *method inheritance* and *property inheritance*. Method inheritance passes *abilities* from a superclass to a subclass, whereas property inheritance passes on the *knowledge*.

In ActionScript, class methods are attached to the prototype property. Thus, methods are also *inherited* through the prototype. Properties of the class, on the other hand, generally belong to the instance object itself, not the prototype. These are called *instance properties*, and are created in the constructor.

 NOTE: There are exceptions to this general rule. Not only can you put methods in the prototype of the superclass, but properties as well, which are then inherited by the subclass through the prototype chain. These could be called "class properties" instead of "instance properties." Conversely, you can create methods for an object in the constructor instead of in the prototype. These could be called "instance methods." However, this last approach is not recommended for methods because it wastes memory and complicates the inheritance process.

Property Inheritance with super( )

We'll look at property inheritance first since it has less attendant issues than method inheritance. In a nutshell, property inheritance passes the knowledge of a superclass on to a subclass.

Let's take a simplified example of a *Parent* class:

```
Parent = function (a, b) {
    this.sum = a + b;
};
```

A *Parent* object has one property, sum, which is found by adding the two parameters a and b.

Suppose we want to define a *Child* object that knows everything a *Parent* knows, plus a little more. Specifically, a *Child* instance will store the *product* of the two supplied numbers, not just the sum. We can code this in the constructor easily enough:

```
Child = function (a, b) {
    this.product = a * b;
};
```

But how do we make the *Child* instance inherit instance properties from the *Parent* class? What we do is call the superclass constructor, *Parent( )*, but run it in the scope of the subclass. This creates the superclass properties inside the subclass instance. In Flash 5, we would do it like this:

```
// Flash 5 property inheritance
Child = function (a, b) {
    this.base = Parent;
    this.base (a, b);
    delete this.base;
    this.product = a * b;
};
```

Flash MX, though, gives us the *super( )* function, which calls the superclass constructor directly. As a result, we have this much simpler code:

```
// Flash MX property inheritance
Child = function (a, b) {
    super (a, b);
    this.product = a * b;
};
```

We pass the two parameters up through *super( )*, which calls the *Parent( )* constructor, creating the sum property. Then the additional product property is created.

NOTE: As a general rule, the superclass constructor should be called first before any other code in the subclass constructor. This principle is strictly enforced in the Java language, but ActionScript is not so strict.

The property inheritance procedure is performed instance by instance. Method inheritance, on the other hand, is performed only once per class, as we'll soon see.

Method Inheritance

Method inheritance allows a subclass to inherit the abilities of its superclass. In our example, let's give our *Parent* class a simple method:

```
Parent.prototype.printSum = function () {
    trace (this.sum);
};
```

When method inheritance is correctly established, we will be able to call *printSum( )* as a method of both a *Parent* object and a *Child* object.

Method inheritance is implemented in ActionScript via a prototype chain. The `__proto__` property of a subclass' prototype will point to the `prototype` of its superclass. In other words, if the *Child* class is a subclass of the *Parent* class, `Child.prototype.__proto__` should point to `Parent.prototype`. When this chain is in place, all methods and properties in `Parent.prototype` are passed on to `Child.prototype`. How do we test if the prototype chain is established correctly? We can simply run this code:

```
trace (Child.prototype.__proto__ == Parent.prototype);
```

The result of this Boolean condition will be `true` if the *Parent* class is the superclass of the *Child* class.

NOTE: With multilevel inheritance, one class can actually be the *grandparent* of another. In our example, if the *Parent* class is a subclass of a *Grandparent* class, `Parent.prototype.__proto__` points to `Grandparent.prototype`, and `Child.prototype.__proto__.__proto__` points to `Grandparent.prototype` as well. The `instanceof` operator can detect multi-level inheritance.

The super Object

When method inheritance is implemented, we can both override individual methods in the subclass, but still call the original superclass methods. For this, we use the `super` *object*, which behaves differently from the *super ( )* function (discussed later in the chapter).

Remember that the *Parent* class has a *printSum( )* method:

```
Parent.prototype.printSum = function () {
    trace (this.sum);
};
```

We can *override* this method in the *Child* subclass by defining a method with the same name in Child:

```
Child.prototype.printSum = function () {
    trace ("Child printSum()");
};
```

Additionally, what we can do is use *Parent.printSum( )* in *Child.printSum( )*, allowing us to call the superclass method with `super.printSum( )`:

```
Child.prototype.printSum = function () {
    super.printSum();
    trace ("Child printSum()");
};
```

Thus, the `super` object allows subclass methods to "add on" to superclass methods.

Method Inheritance with new

We've seen how method inheritance looks when it has been established. The question now is, *how* do we set up the correct prototype chain, on which method inheritance depends?

The "official" approach, recommended by Macromedia, uses the *new* keyword:

```
Child.prototype = new Parent();
```

This syntax is used in Flash MX's documentation and the supplied FUI components, such as *FUIScrollbar* and *FUIListbox*.

Unfortunately, *new* syntax has many problems. To sum it up, *new* syntax forces the superclass constructor to execute needlessly. This results in the following undesirable effects:

> The execution of the constructor code wastes CPU cycles.

> Instance properties are erroneously created in the prototype. These are junk properties, which serve no purpose but to waste memory.

> If the constructor creates new movie clips, extra clips will appear when the prototype chain is established with *new* syntax.

> The existing class prototype is replaced with a new object. As a result, any methods that were in the prototype are wiped out.

> ❱ The `constructor` property of the subclass prototype is incorrectly set to the superclass. It should be set to the subclass.

> ❱ In relation to OOP methodology, one should not have to run the superclass constructor in order to establish method inheritance.

These issues have been discussed at length in the Flashcoders archives (see http://chattyfig.figleaf.com) and documented on Dave Yang's Flash inheritance page: www.quantumwave.com/html/flash_setInheritance.html.

Method Inheritance with __proto__

The more direct and efficient way to establish method inheritance is to use the __proto__ property. Remember that in a proper prototype chain, `Child.prototype.__proto__` points to `Parent.prototype`. In that case, it makes perfect sense to just set the former to the latter:

```
Child.prototype.__proto__ = Parent.prototype;
```

This sets up the prototype chain in the simplest way possible.

We can encapsulate this procedure into a function by using the new Flash MX class *Function*. All user-defined functions are actually objects, instances of *Function*. Thus, we can create *methods for function objects*. Our inheritance method looks like this:

```
Function.prototype.extend = function (superclass) {
    this.prototype.__proto__ = superclass.prototype;
};
```

We call *extend( )* like this:

```
Child.extend (Parent);
```

In the above example, `Child` and `Parent` are existing constructor functions.

NOTE: I used the name "extend" because "extends" is a future reserved word for ECMAScript languages. In other words, languages like JavaScript and ActionScript might conceivably implement *extends* functionality in the future, and so use of that word is strongly discouraged.

Unfortunately, due to a bug in the Flash MX Player, the *super( )* function does not work when inheritance is established with __proto__ syntax. There are two workarounds, however.

The __constructor__ Solution

The first solution to the conflict between __proto__ and *super( )* involves an undocumented feature. The __constructor__ property is a hidden property of most objects that is apparently used in the Flash Player's internal inheritance procedures. It was discovered that by manipulating __constructor__, we can "re-enable" *super( )* so that it works with __proto__ inheritance.

Specifically, we set the __constructor__ property of the subclass prototype to the superclass:

```
Child.prototype.__constructor__ = Parent;
```

For ease of use, we can include this code in our *extend( )* function:

```
Function.prototype.extend = function (superclass) {
    this.prototype.__proto__ = superclass.prototype;
    this.prototype.__constructor__ = superclass;
};
```

With our example, then, we have this code when we pull it all together:

```
Function.prototype.extend = function (superclass) {
    this.prototype.__proto__ = superclass.prototype;
    this.prototype.__constructor__ = superclass;
};

Parent = function (a, b) {
    this.sum = a + b;
};
Parent.prototype.printSum = function () {
    trace (this.sum);
};

Child = function (a, b) {
    super (a, b);
    this.product = a * b;
};
Child.extend (Parent);
Child.prototype.printSum = function () {
    super.printSum();
```

```
    trace ("Child printSum()");
};
```

We can now run a small test of the *Child* class and its *printSum( )* method:

```
// test Child class
c = new Child (6, 3);
c.printSum();
// output: 9
// output: Child printSum()
```

The *Child* instance works as we would expect. Without the setting of the __constructor__ property in the *extend( )* function, though, "undefined" would be traced instead of "9." The reason is that *super( )* would not successfully pass the a and b arguments to the superclass constructor.

There is a drawback to the __constructor__ approach, though. As mentioned, __constructor__ is undocumented, and is actually one of the lesser-known of Flash's many undocumented features. It was added in Flash MX, and there is no guarantee that Macromedia will keep it around in the next release of Flash. (In my opinion, the undocumented features *ASSetPropFlags( )* and *ASBroadcaster* have a much better chance of being kept in future versions of Flash than __constructor__.) I deleveoped a different workaround, however—a custom method called *superCon( )*.

The superCon( ) Solution

When Flash MX was released, I was quite disappointed that __proto__ inheritance and *super( )* would not peacefully co-exist. My solution to the problem was to find an alternative to the *super( )* function itself.

I thought about what *super( )* actually does. It locates the superclass constructor function, relative to the current constructor function. If I could somehow find a reference to that superclass constructor with my own code, I could replace *super( )* with a custom function. I eventually discovered that the following code would give me the reference to the constructor I was looking for:

```
arguments.caller.prototype.__proto__.constructor
```

I worked this into a method I called "superCon," for "superclass constructor." The method can be attached to any class you want, including our *Child* class:

```
Child.prototype.superCon = function () {
    arguments.caller.prototype.__proto__.
constructor.apply (this, arguments);
};
```

The method can now be called in place of *super( )*. The *Child* constructor would then be rewritten like this:

```
Child = function (a, b) {
    this.superCon (a, b);
    this.product = a * b;
};
```

More adventurous ActionScripters may consider adding *superCon( )* to *Object.prototype* to make all objects inherit the method:

```
Object.prototype.superCon = function () {
    arguments.caller.prototype.__proto__.
constructor.apply (this, arguments);
};
ASSetPropFlags (Object.prototype, "superCon", 1);
```

The use of *ASSetPropFlags( )* is necessary to avoid pollution of for..in loops. *ASSetPropFlags( )* is an undocumented feature, but people are using it so often now that Macromedia will likely be forced to keep it around in future versions of Flash. If you prefer to stay away from undocumented features altogether, you can stick with adding *superCon( )* to just custom classes instead of the *Object* class.

In summary, the *superCon( )* method allows us to use __proto__ inheritance and still have the functionality of *super( )*. What's more, *superCon( )* uses no undocumented commands. Consequently, you can be sure it will work in the next release of Flash. All things considered, I think *superCon( )* (together with __proto__ inheritance) is the best all-around solution for class inheritance, and it's what I use in my own projects.

Conclusion

This concludes our initial discussion of object-oriented programming. We've lightly touched upon topics that are vast areas of study in themselves, such as object-oriented analysis and design, use cases, and class diagrams. If any of these have piqued your interest, I hope you'll practice the time-honored discipline of self-learning, mentioned in Chapter 1, and research these subjects further.

In the chapters that follow, you'll see OOP in action, and watch its principles applied to all aspects of dynamic animation with ActionScript, including motion, physics, color, and shape. In the next chapter, we explore the dimension of space, using the mathematics of trigonometry and coordinate systems.

Part II

Foundational Concepts

Chapter 3

Math 1: Trigonometry and Coordinate Systems

Math is essentially relationships. We all know that relationships make the world go round. An equation may look complex, but it's simply a way of describing a relationship. The precise relationships of science have math as their native language.

It is also the framework of beauty. As I write this, I can see a water fountain shooting 30 feet into the air, cascading down around itself and sending hundreds of thin rings on a slow journey across a still pond. The scene is gorgeous in its own right, but appears all the more beautiful because I can see the equations behind the movement. The parabola in the curve of the falling water. The sine waves in the ripples on the pond. The angles of incidence and reflection in the wavering mirror of the birch trees.

Math is power. Power to re-create the water fountain in a computer animation. Power to understand and control behavior. Power to solve a riddle, given a few clues. Power to interpret the past, create the present, and predict the future. We all use math on a regular basis to fill gaps in our knowledge—probably more than we realize. Our minds are constantly crunching numbers to get us to appointments on time, or leave a tip that's big (or small) enough. Math is an essential part of the problem-solving process. If you can convert a piece of information into a number, it is easier to work with in a programming context.

For the ActionScript animator, the subjects of trigonometry and coordinate systems are fundamental. They allow you to work with *space* with confidence and precision. This chapter will introduce these topics, laying out the concepts and providing encapsulated ActionScript code you can plug into your projects.

Trigonometry

Though it may seem intimidating, trigonometry is simply the measuring of triangles ("tri-gon" is Greek for triangle). The triangle is one of the simplest two-dimensional shapes possible. Take any three points on a plane, connect them with lines, and you have a triangle. You may remember a few special triangles—the *equilateral* and *isosceles* triangles, for instance—but in animation one is particularly useful: the *right triangle*.

The Right Triangle

A right triangle has one 90-degree angle, or "right angle." Figure 3-1 shows a generic right triangle, with the right angle marked by a small square in the corner. The horizontal and vertical sides of the triangle are labeled *a* and *b*, respectively. The longest side, *c*, is called the *hypotenuse*.

Modern civilization was built on the right triangle. Our space is filled with rectangles and cubes, each composed of right angles. Our squared-off boxes, buildings and streets reveal our obsession with the perpendicular. The 90-degree angle symbolizes order and precision. The mathematical relationships within the right triangle, between its three sides and three angles, are foundational for the architect, the engineer, and the ActionScript animator.

The Pythagorean Theorem

Most students learn this famous equation in junior high school. The Greek mathematician Pythagorus discovered a relationship between the three sides of a right triangle. By taking the squares of the short sides, *a* and *b*, and adding them together, you can find the square of the hypotenuse *c*.

Pythagorus' Theorem:

$$c^2 = a^2 + b^2$$

If we want to solve for *c*, we take the square root of both sides of the equation:

$$c = \sqrt{(a^2 + b^2)}$$

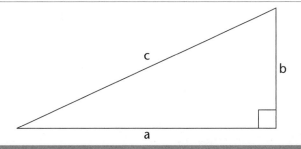

A right triangle with sides *a*, *b*, and *c*

Let's explore this equation with an example from ordinary life. We know intuitively that "cutting a corner" gives us shorter trips and saves time. If you wanted to walk from one corner of a football field to the other, cutting straight across would obviously be faster than walking along the sides. But how much time do you actually save?

If the field is 40 meters wide and 100 meters long (see Figure 3-2), your trip would be 140 meters if you walked along the sides a and b. On the other hand, you could cut through the middle, along line c.

The lines a, b, and c form a right triangle. To find the value of c, we use the Pythagorean Theorem:

$$c^2 = a^2 + b^2$$
$$c = \sqrt{(a^2 + b^2)}$$
$$c = \sqrt{(100^2 + 40^2)}$$
$$c = \sqrt{(10000 + 1600)}$$
$$c = \sqrt{(11600)}$$
$$c = 107.7$$

If you cut across the field, along line c, your trip is about 108 meters. Compared to walking along sides a and b, you saved yourself 32.3 meters of walking, or 23 percent. You would see the biggest percentage difference with a square field (of any size). In this scenario, cutting across diagonally saves about 41 percent. If you're interested, you can derive this number yourself as an exercise, using the Pythagorean theorem.

Distance Between Two Points

A common task in ActionScripted animation is to find the distance between two points. Figure 3-3 shows two arbitrary points, with the coordinates (x_1, y_1) and (x_2, y_2). The Pythagorean Theorem can be used to find this distance if a right triangle is constructed. First, draw a line d between the two points,

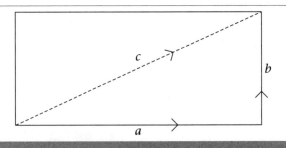

FIGURE 3-2

Cutting across a field

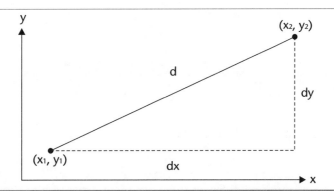

FIGURE 3-3

Finding the distance between two points

followed by the appropriate horizontal line *dx*, and vertical line *dy*. Side *d* is now the hypotenuse of a right triangle, and its length is the distance between the two points.

Our distance equation will have this form:

$$d = \sqrt{dx^2 + dy^2}$$

Translated into ActionScript, the code reads like this:

```
d = Math.sqrt (dx * dx + dy * dy);
```

We can easily write a function to return the distance based on *dx* and *dy*:

```
function distance (dx, dy) {
    return Math.sqrt (dx * dx + dy * dy);
}
```

However, this setup is not as convenient as we might like. The parameters *dx* and *dy* must be calculated before calling the function. What we really want is to take the coordinates for any two points (x_1, y_1) and (x_2, y_2), pass them to a function, and receive back the distance between the points. Here is such a function, *Math.distance( )*:

```
Math.distance = function (x1, y1, x2, y2) {
    var dx = x2 - x1;
    var dy = y2 - y1;
```

```
        return Math.sqrt (dx * dx + dy * dy);
};
```

The calculation of *dx* and *dy* has been moved inside the function, which saves steps. The function has also been placed in the *Math* object, where it can be easily accessed from any timeline.

Angles in Right Triangles

So far, we've explored the Pythagorean relationship between the three sides of a right triangle. We will soon look at more interesting connections between triangle sides. But first, we must turn our attention to the *angles* of the right triangle. A triangle has three angles, which always add up to 180 degrees. In a right triangle, one of the angles is 90 degrees. Thus, the other two angles must add up to 90 degrees.

Radian Measurement of Angles

Degrees are the most common unit of measurement for angles in everyday life. There are 360 degrees in a circle, but this number is completely arbitrary. The radian unit was developed by mathematicians as a standard, metric way to measure angles. Radians are based on π (pi), a property inherent to circles. Computer programming languages typically work with angles in radians. JavaScript and ActionScript have an identical built-in *Math* object, which calculates sines and cosines in radians, not degrees.

NOTE: The following is a mathematical definition of a radian: When two lines extend from the center of a circle to its edge, an angle and an arc are subtended between them. The angle between the two lines is *one radian* when the length of the subtended arc exactly equals the radius.

Converting from Degrees to Radians

How does one convert from degrees to radians? The basic relationship is that π radians equals 180 degrees—a ratio of π : 180. Thus, there are 2π radians in 360 degrees, a full circle. The conversion equation is:

$$\text{radians} = \frac{\text{degrees} \times \pi}{180°}$$

In ActionScript, we can create a function to perform this conversion:

```
Math.degreesToRadians = function (angle) {
    return angle * (Math.PI / 180);
};
```

The *Math.degreesToRadians( )* function accepts an angle in degrees as a parameter. It converts the angle to radians and returns the result. The following code demonstrates how to use this function:

```
// test Math.degreesToRadians()
angleDegrees = 180;
angleRadians = Math.degreesToRadians (angleDegrees);
trace (angleRadians) // output: 3.14159265358979
```

NOTE: In the *Math.degreesToRadians( )* function, I put parentheses around (Math.PI / 180) for a reason. When Flash publishes a SWF, it compiles the ActionScript into bytecode. During that process, it evaluates whatever constant values it can to optimize the file for performance. For instance, Math.PI is always replaced with the numerical value 3.14159265358979; it is not looked up dynamically at run time. The parentheses around (Math.PI / 180) cause the compiler to evaluate the expression to 0.0174532925199433. This eliminates the need for the division to occur at run time, and thus improves performance.

Converting from Radians to Degrees

Converting angles in the opposite direction, from radians to degrees, requires a simple inversion of the ratio. The angle is multiplied by 180 / π:

```
Math.radiansToDegrees = function (angle) {
    return angle × (180 / Math.PI);
}
// test the Math.radiansToDegrees() function
trace ( Math.radiansToDegrees (Math.PI) ); // output: 180
```

Sine

At their essence, sine and cosine are simply *ratios*. A ratio is a mathematical relationship where one number is directly proportional to another. Sine and cosine describe relationships between the sides of a right triangle. In many scenarios, the sine ratio deals with the *height* of a right triangle, and cosine governs the *width*. There are more formal definitions of sine and cosine you may have heard, but here's a little thought experiment to help develop an intuitive understanding.

Imagine you have your arm flat on a table, holding a piece of string in the tip of your hand. Raising your hand changes your arm's angle with the table, and swings your hand in an arc. Meanwhile, the string hangs straight down from your hand. A triangle is formed between the table, your arm, and the string (see Figure 3-4).

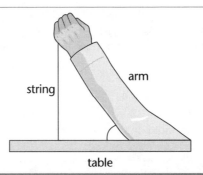

FIGURE 3-4

Exploring the sine ratio with your arm and a length of string

The length of the string changes as you change the angle of your arm relative to the table. The string gives a measurement of your hand's height above the table. The question is: how high will your hand be (that is, how long is the string) for a particular angle? Zero degrees is easy: the height is zero because your hand is flat on the table. It's also simple to find the angle at 90 degrees. The string is as long as your arm, so if your arm is three feet long, the tip of your hand is three feet above the desk.

What about 45 degrees, though? When the angle is half of 90 degrees, is the string half the length of your arm—1.5 feet long? Looking at the string, you should be able to see that this is not the case. In fact, the angle that would give you a height of half your arm is 30 degrees.

Here's where sine comes in: the sine of 30 degrees is 0.5. And for our other angles, the sine of 0 degrees is 0, and the sine of 90 degrees is 1. Are you beginning to see how sine might be related to the angle and the string? Think back to when your arm is straight up and down. Your arm is three feet long, and so is the string. The angle is 90 degrees, and the sine of the angle is 1. Remember how I said that sine is a ratio? Well, the ratio of the string to your arm length is 1, at 90 degrees.

To find the length of the string at a certain angle, you take the length of your arm and multiply by the height ratio for that angle:

string length = arm length × height ratio for angle

A sine is basically a height ratio for a given angle:

height ratio for angle = sine of angle

Thus, we can change the first equation by replacing the height ratio with the sine:

string length = arm length × sine of angle

We can test this last equation with our example. We start with an arm length of 3, and an angle of 0 degrees:

string length = 3 × sine of 0°

Since we know that the sine of 0 degrees is 0, we can see that the equation will be this:

string length = 3 × 0
string length = 0

With an angle of 90 degrees, the sine is 1, so the equation is:

string length = 3 × sin 90°
string length = 3 × 1
string length = 3

Those are fairly simple cases. Now let's try a 30-degree angle. If you have a scientific calculator (hint: there's one on your computer), you can punch in **30** and hit **sin** to find the sine of 30 degrees, which is 0.5. As a result, our equation is

string length = 3 × sin 30°
               = 3 × 0.5
               = 1.5

Now, with this equation, we will be able to see how long the string is at 45 degrees. If you take the sine of 45 degrees on your scientific calculator, you'll find that it is approximately 0.707. Plugging that value into our equation:

string length = 3 × sin 45°
               = 3 × 0.707
               = 2.121

Formal Definition of Sine

So far, I have presented sine in an informal fashion. It is important to develop an intuitive understanding of the sine ratio, so you can apply it in real-world situations. We will now round out our discussion of sine with a look at its more formal definition:

$$\sin \theta = \frac{opposite}{hypotenuse}$$

In our right triangle, side b is opposite from the angle θ, and the hypotenuse is c, (see Figure 3-5).

Thus, we can rewrite the equation as:

$$\sin \theta = \frac{b}{c}$$

ActionScript – Math.sin( )

The syntax to find the sine of an angle in ActionScript is simply this:

```
Math.sin (theta);
```

The variable `theta` is an angle in radians. Here is a simple example of how to use *Math.sin( )*:

```
// test Math.sin()
trace ( Math.sin (0) ); // output: 0
trace ( Math.sin (Math.PI) ); // output:
1.22460635382238e-16 (approx. 0)
```

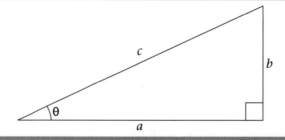

FIGURE 3-5

A right triangle with angle θ

NOTE: Because of the way floating-point numbers are stored in binary format, small rounding errors appear in calculations. As a result, you will sometimes get values like 1.22460635382238e-16 when you were expecting zero. This decimal number is approximately 1.22 divided by 10^{16}, or 0.000000000000000122. Thus, it is extremely close to zero.

I prefer to work in degrees wherever possible, so I wrote a new function for the *Math* object to help me out. The following *Math.sinD( )* function takes an angle in degrees and returns its sine:

```
Math.sinD = function (angle) {
    return Math.sin (angle × (Math.PI / 180));
};
```

Math.sinD( ) is a *wrapper function*. It wraps around *Math.sin( )*, providing a different interface that better suits our purposes. The following code demonstrates how to take the sine of various angles in degrees:

```
// test Math.sinD()
trace ( Math.sinD (0) ); // output: 0
trace ( Math.sinD (90) ); // output: 1
trace ( Math.sinD (180) ); // output: 0
```

Cosine

Similar to sine, cosine is a ratio between two sides of a right triangle. However, whereas sine is generally a height ratio, cosine is a width ratio. Returning to our example with the arm and string, imagine there is a light directly above your arm, casting a shadow onto the desk beneath it. To find the length of this shadow for different angles, we call upon cosine. Figure 3-6 shows how we can explore cosine in this scenario.

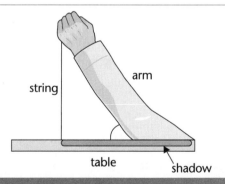

FIGURE 3-6

Exploring the cosine ratio with your arm and the width of shadow

Let's start with an easy case again. Think about how long your arm's shadow would be when your arm is straight up and down. At 90 degrees, there isn't really a shadow, so the length is zero. Without knowing anything more about cosine, could you hazard a guess as to what the cosine of 90 degrees is? If you came up with zero, give yourself a gold star—the cosine of 90 degrees is, in fact, zero. How about when your arm is flat on the desk—what would the shadow's ratio be then? Since the shadow is as long as your arm, the ratio between the two is simply 1:1. The angle of elevation is 0 degrees, and the cosine of 0 degrees is 1, as you might have guessed.

As a final exercise, let's look at 45 degrees. Remember that earlier, we found the sine of 45 degrees to be 0.707 (approximately). If you take the cosine of 45 degrees with a scientific calculator, you'll find that it is also 0.707. Plugging this value into our equation, we get:

shadow length = 3 $\times$ cos 45°

shadow length = 3 $\times$ 0.707

shadow length = 2.121

We can see that at 45 degrees the string and the shadow are the same length—2.121 feet—because the sine of 45 degrees is equal to the cosine of 45 degrees. This makes a lot of sense when you consider that the triangle between your arm, the string, and the shadow is actually half of a square. The sides of a square are equal, and the diagonal line is always at 45 degrees.

The Formal Definition of Cosine

Cosine is formally defined as "adjacent over hypotenuse," where "adjacent" refers to the side of the right triangle *closest* to the angle:

$$\cos \theta = \frac{adjacent}{hypotenuse}$$

In our right triangle (see Figure 3-5), side a is adjacent to the angle θ, and the hypotenuse is c.

Thus, we can rewrite the equation like this:

$$\cos \theta = \frac{a}{c}$$

ActionScript – Math.cos( )

The syntax to find the cosine of an angle in ActionScript is similar to finding the sine:

```
Math.cos (theta);
```

The variable `theta` is an angle in radians, naturally. Here is a simple example of using *Math.cos( )* to take the cosine of various angles in radians:

```
// test Math.cos()
trace ( Math.cos (0) ); // output: 1
trace ( Math.cos (Math.PI / 2) ); // output:
6.12303176911189e-17 (approx. 0)
```

Here, as before, I would prefer to specify the angle in degrees rather than radians. I wrote a *Math.cosD( )* function for this purpose:

```
Math.cosD = function (angle) {
    return Math.cos (angle × (Math.PI / 180));
};
```

The following code demonstrates how to take the cosine of various angles in degrees:

```
// test Math.cosD()
trace ( Math.cosD (0) ); // output: 1
trace ( Math.cosD (90) ); // output:
6.12303176911189e-17 (approx. 0)
```

Tangent

We have explored two trigonometric ratios: sine, which often governs height, and cosine, which often governs width. *Tangent*, the third fundamental ratio in trigonometry, governs slope.

Slope

As the angle of a line changes, so does its steepness. We can express steepness mathematically, in a ratio called *slope*. You may remember the expression "slope equals rise over run" from high-school math. *Rise* means the vertical change in position; *run* means the horizontal change. Thus, slope is calculated by dividing *vertical change* by *horizontal change*:

$$\text{slope} = \frac{rise}{run} = \frac{vertical\ change}{horizontal\ change}$$

We can transfer this concept to our familiar right triangle (see Figure 3-1). The slope of the hypotenuse *c* is the ratio of *b* to *a*:

$$\text{slope of } c = \frac{b}{a}$$

The Slope of a Line at a Given Angle

There is a particular relationship between the slope of the hypotenuse c and the adjacent angle θ. This relationship is captured in the tangent ratio. The tangent of an angle is the slope of a line at that angle:

$$\text{slope of } \theta = \text{tangent of } \theta$$

Given the angle of a line, you can find the line's slope by using the *tan* function on a scientific calculator. The slopes of some common angles are listed in Table 3-1.

The Formal Definition of Tangent

Tangent is formally defined as "opposite over adjacent." *Adjacent* is the side of the right triangle closest to the angle, and *opposite* is the side farthest away.

$$\tan \theta = \frac{opposite}{adjacent}$$

In our right triangle (Figure 3-5), side b is opposite to the angle θ, and side a is adjacent.

Thus, we can rewrite the equation like this:

$$\tan \theta = \frac{b}{a}$$

θ	$\tan \theta$	Explanation
0°	0	A line at 0 degrees is horizontal, so its slope is 0.
30°	0.577...	The exact value is $1/\sqrt{3}$.
45°	1	A 45-degree line balances the horizontal and vertical, so its slope is 1.
60°	1.732...	The exact value is $\sqrt{3}$.
90°	∞	A line at 90 degrees is straight up and down, so its slope is not a finite number.
180°	0	A 180-degree line is horizontal, so its slope is also 0.

TABLE 3-1

Values of Tangent for Common Angles

ActionScript – Math.tan( )

You can calculate the tangent of an angle in Flash using the ActionScript function *Math.tan( )*. The syntax is simple:

```
Math.tan (angle);
```

Again, the angle must be given in radians. I wrote my own function *Math.tanD( )* that lets me specify the angle in degrees:

```
Math.tanD = function (angle) {
    return Math.tan (angle × (Math.PI / 180));
};
```

The following code demonstrates how to take the tangent of various angles in degrees:

```
// test Math.tanD()
trace ( Math.tanD (0) ); // output: 0
trace ( Math.tanD (45) ); // output: 1
trace ( Math.tanD (90) ); // output:
1.63317787283838e+16 (approx. infinity)
```

Inverse Tangent

We've seen that the tangent operator turns an angle into a slope ratio. How do we perform the reverse operation? We can take the *inverse tangent* of a slope to turn it into the corresponding angle. Inverse tangent is usually written as $tan^{-1} \theta$, but it makes occasional appearances as arctan θ or atan θ.

ActionScript – Math.atan( )

There are two functions which calculate the inverse tangent in ActionScript. The first, *Math.atan( )*, takes a single number as a parameter:

```
angle = Math.atan (slope);
```

The returned angle is in radians. Before calling *Math.atan( )*, you would usually calculate *slope* by dividing *y* by *x*:

```
slope = y / x;
angle = Math.atan (slope);
```

Finding the correct angle with *Math.atan( )* is a complicated process. The inverse tangent of any number can be one of two angles. For instance, *tan⁻¹* (1) can be 45 degrees or 225 degrees. In general, two angles 180 degrees apart will have the same slope and tangent:

tan θ = tan(θ + 180°)

However, *Math.atan( )* will only return one of these angles. Consequently, determining the correct angle requires a cumbersome "quadrant-checking" procedure. On top of that, the tangent of 90 degrees and 270 degrees is infinity because of a division by zero; this can be difficult to manage in code. For these reasons, I avoid *Math.atan( )* altogether and employ the more user-friendly *Math.atan2( )*.

ActionScript – Math.atan2( )

The *Math.atan2( )* function takes two parameters, y and x:

```
angle = Math.atan2 (y, x);
```

What's truly beautiful about *Math.atan2( )* is that it returns the correct angle every time, no fuss, no muss. Quadrant checking is done internally, using the x and y parameters.

Since *Math.atan2( )* returns an angle in radians, I wrote my own function *Math.atan2D( )* to calculate degrees instead:

```
Math.atan2D = function (y, x) {
    return Math.atan2 (y, x) × (180 / Math.PI);
};
```

The following code demonstrates how to take the inverse tangent of various angles in degrees:

```
// test Math.atan2D()
trace ( Math.atan2D (7, 7) ); // output: 45
trace ( Math.atan2D (0, -4) ); // output: 180
trace ( Math.atan2D (-6, 0) ); // output: -90
```

NOTE: Be careful to put *y* first, then *x*. Ordered pairs are usually written (*x, y*), but this is an exception.

Finding the Angle Between Two Points

The *Math.atan2( )* function returns the angle of a line between a point (x, y) and the origin $(0, 0)$. But how do we calculate the angle of a line between *any* two points (x_1, y_1) and (x_2, y_2)? We simply subtract the x and y coordinates of the two points to form a new point $(x_2 - x_1, y_2 - y_1)$. This new point can now be passed to *Math.atan2( )* to find the angle.

I wrote a function called *Math.angleOfLine( )* that takes x and y coordinates for two points, and returns the angle between them:

```
Math.angleOfLine = function (x1, y1, x2, y2) {
    return Math.atan2D (y2 - y1, x2 - x1);
};
```

For convenience, the returned angle is in degrees.

In the following code example, *Math.angleOfLine( )* is used to find the angle of a line between the points $(3, 3)$ and $(5, 5)$:

```
// test Math.angleOfLine()
theta = Math.angleOfLine (3, 3, 5, 5);
trace (theta); // output: 45
```

N O T E :   *Math.angleOfLine( )* depends on the custom function *Math.atan2D( )*, so be sure to include it in your movie.

Inverse Cosine

Taking the cosine of an angle produces a ratio between –1 and 1. To work backwards, from the ratio to the angle, we take the *inverse cosine* of the ratio. In ActionScript, the process looks like this:

```
// first take the cosine
cosRatio = Math.cos (angle);
// reverse the process to find the original angle
angle = Math.acos (cosRatio);
```

The *Math.acos( )* function takes a ratio between –1 and 1 and returns an angle in radians. I wrote a *Math.acosD( )* function to produce degrees instead:

```
Math.acosD = function (ratio) {
    return Math.acos (ratio) × (180 / Math.PI);
};
```

The inverse cosine is commonly used to find the angle between two vectors, as we will see in Chapter 4.

Inverse Sine

Similar to inverse cosine, the inverse sine is used to find an angle. The difference is that the inverse sine operates on a sine ratio instead:

```
sinRatio = Math.sin (angle);
// in reverse
angle = Math.asin (sinRatio);
```

The *Math.asin( )* function takes a ratio between –1 and 1 and returns an angle in radians. I wrote a *Math.asinD( )* function to produce degrees instead:

```
Math.asinD = function (ratio) {
    return Math.asin (ratio) × (180 / Math.PI);
};
```

Compared to the trigonometric functions, inverse sine isn't used very often. I have included it for the sake of completeness.

We have now established a base knowledge of trigonometry, the study of triangles. We have learned the fundamental relationships between angles and sides in a right triangle. These include the Pythagorean Theorem, as well as the sine, cosine, and tangent ratios, and their inverses. Several practical applications of trigonometry have been explored, such as finding the distance between two points, and finding the angle of a line. Finally, we accumulated a library of functions that encapsulate different operations of trigonometry. These include wrapper functions for several built-in *Math* methods, that allow us the convenience of using degrees instead of radians— for example, *Math.sinD( )* instead of *Math.sin( )*. This knowledge is a good foundation for moving ahead into custom coordinate systems, and in later chapters, vectors.

Coordinate Systems

We have all encountered graphs and grids, whether in school or graphics programs. Each graph has a coordinate system, which defines how things are measured on its grid. As ActionScript animators, we need to understand different coordinate systems in order to properly render graphics. Additionally, we can define more advantageous coordinate systems and convert from one system to another.

Cartesian Coordinates

The Cartesian coordinate system is a widely used grid. Most line graphs we see, whether for the stock market or mathematical functions, use the Cartesian system.

The X and Y Axes

The grid has two axes, x and y. The x values increase to the right of the grid, and the y values increase towards the top. The location of a point on the grid is given as an ordered pair (x, y). The two axes intersect at (0, 0); this point is called the *origin* (see Figure 3-7).

Grid Quadrants

The x and y axes split the Cartesian grid into four quadrants, numbered from 1 to 4, which start at the upper right and work counterclockwise. Figure 3-8 indicates the numbering of the quadrants.

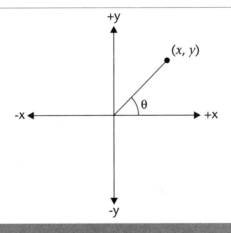

FIGURE 3-7

The Cartesian coordinate system

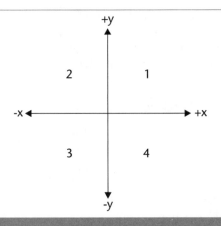

FIGURE 3-8

The four quadrants of the Cartesian grid

The Cartesian quadrants have several properties, which are summarized in Table 3-2.

Angle Measurement

When angles are measured in Cartesian coordinates, the starting point is the x-axis. From there, angles are measured in a counterclockwise direction (see Figure 3-8).

Flash Coordinates

Similar to the Cartesian system, Flash has coordinates along the x and y axis. Each movie clip has an $\_x$ property which stores its horizontal position relative to the origin (0, 0), and a $\_y$ property which stores its vertical position. The origin of a movie clip is called its *registration point*, and is denoted by a small cross. The origin of the _root movie clip is at the upper-left corner of the main stage (see Figure 3-9).

Quadrant	Corner	*x* Values	*y* Values	Angle Range
Quadrant 1	Upper right	+	+	0° to 90°
Quadrant 2	Upper left	-	+	90° to 180°
Quadrant 3	Lower left	-	-	180° to 270°
Quadrant 4	Lower right	+	-	270° to 360°

TABLE 3-2

Properties of the Cartesian Quadrants

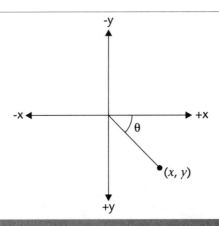

FIGURE 3-9

The Flash coordinate system

The _x property increases to the right of the screen, the same direction as the Cartesian x. Thus, no conversion is necessary for the _x property:

Flash _x = Cartesian *x*

The _y property, on the other hand, increases in value towards the bottom of the screen. This is directly opposite to the Cartesian *y* coordinate, which increases towards the top (Figure 3-9). The Cartesian *y* needs to be inverted (multiplied by –1) before being assigned to _y:

Flash _y = -(Cartesian *y*)

Angle Measurement: the _rotation Property

All movie clips have a _rotation property which stores their angle of rotation. These angles are measured differently in Flash than on the Cartesian grid. They are measured in a clockwise direction, the opposite of the Cartesian system (see Figure 3-8 again). Thus, 10 degrees in Cartesian is –10 degrees in Flash.

Flash _rotation = -(Cartesian angle in degrees)

Also, Flash stores the _rotation property in degrees, so radian angles will have to be converted before being assigned to movie clips.

Flash _rotation = -(Cartesian angle in radians) $\times$ 180 / π

On a final note, the `_rotation` property always returns a number between 180 and –180. In mathematical terms:

$-180 \leq \_rotation \leq 180$

However, you can set `_rotation` to any number you want. For example, you can give a movie clip a rotation of 370 degrees:

```
mc._rotation = 370;
```

The movie clip will be rendered at the correct angle. However, the `_rotation` property will internally store 10 degrees, which is equivalent to 370 degrees. If we check the `_rotation` value immediately after setting it to 370, we find it has been changed to 10, which lies between –180 and 180:

```
trace ( mc._rotation ); // output: 10
```

Standardizing an Angle

When doing certain calculations in ActionScript, I may need to ensure that an angle falls in the "standard" range between 0 and 360 degrees. For instance, 380, 740, and –340 degrees are all equivalent to 20 degrees (380 – 360 = 20, -340 + 360 = 20, etc.). I wrote a *Math.fixAngle( )* function that will take an angle in degrees and return the equivalent standardized angle between 0 and 360 degrees:

```
Math.fixAngle = function (angle) {
    angle %= 360;
    return (angle < 0) ? angle + 360 : angle;
};
```

In the first line of code inside *Math.fixAngle( )*, the *modulo* operator is used to set angle to the remainder of a division with 360. This step forces angle to fall between –360 and 360. Our goal is an angle between 0 and 360 (that is, a positive number). Thus, we need to check if angle is negative at this stage. If it is less than zero, we add 360 to convert it to the equivalent positive angle.

NOTE: The internal code may be difficult to follow, simply because the function is highly optimized for speed, and uses abbreviated syntax. However, the beauty of a good function is that you don't have to understand the internal workings of the "black box." As long as you know what to put in, and what comes out, you'll be fine.

The following example demonstrates how to standardize angles using *Math.fixAngle( )*:

```
// test Math.fixAngle()
trace ( Math.fixAngle (740) ); // output: 20
trace ( Math.fixAngle (-340) ); // output: 20
trace ( Math.fixAngle (20) ); // output: 20
```

The normalized angle for all three input angles (740, -340, and 20) is 20.

Converting from Cartesian to Flash Coordinates

I prefer to think in Cartesian coordinates as much as possible. When I want to code complex dynamic movement in Flash, as in my *Black Star* or *Sphere Burst* experiments, I start by developing the concept on a Cartesian grid—either mentally or on paper. Animations such as these usually require conversions into polar coordinates (discussed later in this chapter) and back again. At some point, movie clips will be moved around by changing _x, _y, or _rotation. These conversions are easiest if I stay in Cartesian coordinates as long as possible. However, I will eventually need to render the graphics in Flash coordinates.

When it comes to the ActionScript implementation, I find it best to store the positions of objects in x, y, and rotation *variables*, which are separated from the _x, _y, and _rotation *properties*. This gives me the flexibility to perform my calculations in the Cartesian coordinate system. When it comes time to render these coordinates to the screen, I convert to Flash coordinates, with the following code:

```
// convert Cartesian coordinates to Flash coordinates
// x, y, and rotation are existing number variables
// and mc is a movie clip instance
mc._x = x;
mc._y = -y;
mc._rotation = -rotation;
```

The x variable doesn't need to be changed during the conversion. However, y and rotation run in opposite directions to their Flash counterparts _y and _rotation. Consequently, they must be inverted.

Converting from Flash to Cartesian Coordinates

Converting coordinates in the reverse direction, from Flash to Cartesian, is easy: the equations are simply reversed. Once again, _x is assigned straight across, while _y and _rotation are multiplied by –1. This is how the procedure looks in ActionScript:

```
// convert Flash coordinates to Cartesian coordinates
// x, y, and rotation are existing number variables
// and mc is a movie clip instance
x = mc._x;
y = -mc._y;
rotation = -mc._rotation;
```

Polar Coordinates

In a two-dimensional world, there are two fundamentally different approaches to defining a location. The first, as we've seen, is to give the horizontal and vertical distances *x* and *y* from the origin (0, 0). For instance, we would say, "Point A is at (3, 4)," which means "Point A is three units to the right and four units up from (0, 0)." Thus, Cartesian coordinates are defined on a rectangular grid.

However, the same point in space can be defined in a different way, using a circular grid (see Figure 3-10). The circles on the grid correspond to the distance from the origin. Under this system, Point A in our example could be described as "5 units away from the origin, at 53.13 degrees."

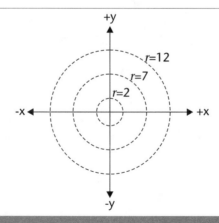

FIGURE 3-10

A circular grid of distances from the origin

When a distance and angle are used together to define a location, they are called *polar coordinates*. The notation for polar coordinates is (r, θ). The r coordinate is the point's distance or "radius" from the origin. The θ coordinate specifies the direction of the point from the origin, "as the crow flies."

Though less familiar than the Cartesian system, polar coordinates are extremely useful. For certain situations, x and y coordinates do not work as well as distance and angle. An airplane pilot, for example, needs to know the heading and distance of his destination. It's true that his start and end positions are defined on a semi-rectangular grid, in terms of longitude and latitude, which are similar to x and y values. Nevertheless, longitude and latitude do not *automatically* tell the pilot which direction to fly the plane, or how far away the destination is. Longitude and latitude must be converted into angle and distance; someone has to convert between coordinate systems.

NOTE: The pilot's situation is actually more mathematically complex than my simplified example. The surface of a globe such as the earth is measured with *spherical coordinates*. In this system, a point in 3D space is defined by (ρ, θ, ϕ) — *rho, theta, phi*. In a standard mathematical model, ρ would be the radius of the earth, θ the angle of longitude, and ϕ would be the angle from the North Pole. Another three-dimensional system is *cylindrical coordinates*, which define a location using (r, θ, z). I have used both of these systems in two of my experimental Flash pieces — cylindrical coordinates in "Photon Ring," and spherical coordinates in "Sphere Burst" (displayed at www.robertpenner.com).

Converting from Cartesian to Polar Coordinates

How does one take a point in Cartesian coordinates—an (x, y) pair—and convert it to the equivalent polar coordinates (r, θ)?

Finding r and θ Manually   You can do this conversion manually by plotting the point, for example, (3, 4), on graph paper. Then you can draw a line r from the origin to the point (3, 4). (See Figure 3-11.) You can now find the value of r by measuring its length with a ruler. You would find the distance to (3, 4) is about 5 units. To find θ, you can use a protractor to measure the angle between the line to (3, 4) and the x-axis. You would find the angle to be about 53 degrees.

This manual approach helps form an intuitive understanding of polar coordinates. However, it doesn't help us very much in a programming setting. We want to be able to convert between these coordinate systems dynamically, finding precise values with ActionScript.

Finding r Mathematically   Thankfully, mathematicians figured out a way to find r long ago. The line r is the hypotenuse of a right triangle with sides x, y, and r. Thus, we can calculate r using the Pythagorean Theorem:

$$r = \sqrt{x^2 + y^2}$$

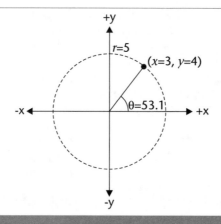

Polar coordinates *r* and θ for the point (3, 4)

If we pick the point (3, 4), this is how we use the equation to find the point's *r* value:

$$r = \sqrt{3^2 + 4^2}$$
$$r = \sqrt{9 + 16}$$
$$r = \sqrt{25}$$
$$r = 5$$

The value of *r* shows that the point (3, 4) is 5 units from the origin.

Finding θ Mathematically   If we have a point (*x*, *y*), we can find the point's angle θ by dividing *y* by *x* and taking the inverse tangent:

$$\theta = \tan^{-1}(y / x)$$

We can take our familiar point (3, 4), and plug the *x* and *y* values into our equation to find θ:

$$\theta = \tan^{-1}(4 / 3)$$
$$\theta = 53.1301...$$

With the core mathematical equations for *r* and θ under our belts, we are now just a step away from performing these calculations in Flash.

Finding r and θ with ActionScript   In ActionScript, we can use the following syntax to perform the conversion from the Cartesian coordinates (*x*, *y*) to the polar coordinates (*r*, θ):

```
// convert Cartesian coordinates to polar coordinates
radius = Math.sqrt (x * x + y * y);
theta = Math.atan2 (y, x);
```

Note that θ will be calculated in radians in this code. If degrees are preferred, we can use my custom function *Math.atan2D( )*, discussed earlier in this chapter:

```
theta = Math.atan2D (y, x); // theta in degrees
```

Converting Cartesian to polar coordinates is a task we will need to perform repeatedly. It would be smart to encapsulate this process in a function. The most important features of a function are its input and output values. In this case, our input values are (*x*, *y*) and our output values are (*r*, θ). The tricky part here is that a function can only return one value. How can we use one function to give us two values, *r* and θ?

Using a Point Object   The solution is to use a *point object* to store the coordinates for one point. So far, we have stored *x* and *y* in separate variables. What we can do instead is create a generic ActionScript object and give it *x* and *y* properties. Here is the basic procedure:

```
var p = new Object(); // create an object to represent a point
p.x = 3;  // assign a property for x
p.y = 4;  // assign a property for y
```

We can also use a shorthand notation to create the point object:

```
var p = { x:3, y:4 };
```

NOTE: The curly brace {} syntax is called the *anonymous object constructor*.

We can access the x and y values of the point object like this:

```
trace (p.x); // output: 3
trace (p.y); // output: 4
```

This point object is a convenient little package. It binds x and y together, and can be easily passed to and from functions. A point is really a single entity, so it makes sense to create a single object to represent it. Manipulations of points in code can be cleaner and easier with this approach. Chapters 4 and 5 will extend this concept. There, we will create custom *vector* objects which represent points in a similar way, but with additional functionality.

A cartesianToPolar( ) Function   We have covered the basic code that will convert Cartesian coordinates to polar coordinates. We have also prepared a special point object. Now we're ready to create a custom function that encapsulates the conversion process. Here's how the function looks:

```
Math.cartesianToPolar = function (p) {
    var radius = Math.sqrt (p.x * p.x + p.y * p.y);
    var theta = Math.atan2D (p.y, p.x);
    return {r:radius, t:theta};
};
```

The *Math.cartesianToPolar( )* function accepts one parameter: a point object p, which contains x and y properties. Using p.x. and p.y., the point's radius and theta are calculated. These values are assigned to the temporary variables radius and theta, respectively. In the last line of the function, a new object is created with two properties. The object's r property is assigned the value of radius, and the t property is assigned the value of theta. The function concludes by returning this new object to the outside world. Thus, when you call *Math.cartesianToPolar( )*, you need to assign the result to a variable.

Here is an example of how to create a point in Cartesian coordinates and convert it to polar coordinates:

```
// test Math.cartesianToPolar()
var cartesianPt = { x:3, y:4 };
var polarPt = Math.cartesianToPolar (cartesianPt);
trace (polarPt.r); // output: 5
trace (polarPt.t); // output: 53.1...
```

In the example, a point is created at the coordinates (3, 4). After converting the point to polar coordinates, we find that the point is 5 units from the origin, at approximately a 1-degree angle.

Notice that *Math.cartesianToPolar( )* calculates the angle in degrees. I used my custom function *Math.atan2D( )*, discussed earlier in this chapter, because I prefer to think in degrees. If you want to find theta in radians instead, you can easily modify *Math.cartesianToPolar( )* by replacing `Math.atan2D` with `Math.atan2`.

Converting from Polar to Cartesian Coordinates

To convert from polar to Cartesian coordinates, we start with *r* and θ, and convert them to *x* and *y*. The basic equations for this conversion are as follows:

$$x = r \cos\theta$$

$$y = r \sin\theta$$

This process is sometimes called "splitting/resolving into *x* and *y* components," especially when done with vectors (discussed in Chapter 4).

In ActionScript, these equations translate to the following code:

```
// convert from Polar coordinates to Cartesian coordinates
// theta is in degrees
x = radius × Math.cosD (theta);
y = radius × Math.sinD (theta);
```

Here is the *Math.polarToCartesian( )* function, which converts polar coordinates to Cartesian:

```
Math.polarToCartesian = function (p) {
    var x = p.r × Math.cosD (p.t);
    var y = p.r × Math.sinD (p.t);
    return { x:x, y:y };
};
```

Similar to *Math.cartesianToPolar( )*, the *Math.polarToCartesian( )* function takes a single parameter: a point object. In this case, the object contains *r* and *t* properties, representing the point's radius and theta. These values are fed into the trigonometric equations to calculate *x* and *y* values. The function concludes by wrapping *x* and *y* into a new object, and returning it. Once again, I use the custom functions *Math.cosD( )* and *Math.sinD( )* so that we can specify angles in degrees.

Here is an example of how to create a point in polar coordinates and convert it to Cartesian coordinates:

```
// test Math.polarToCartesian()
var p = { r:5, t:90 };
var c = Math.polarToCartesian (p);
trace (c.x); // output: 3.06151588455594e-16 (approx. 0)
trace (c.y); // output: 5
```

In this example, a point is created that is 5 units from the origin, at a 90-degree angle. After converting the point to Cartesian coordinates, we find that the point is at $(x, y) = (0, 5)$—five units straight up the y-axis, as we would expect.

Conclusion

This chapter has been an introduction to trigonometry and coordinate systems. The concepts discussed in these two areas are crucial to understanding how objects relate within space. Our exploration has been both conceptual and practical, placing mathematical definitions and ActionScript side by side. Already, we have amassed a library of encapsulated and optimized functions, along with code examples. As it stands, this code can be put to many different uses, especially in projects that involve ActionScripted animation. In the next chapter, we will build on this foundation and take these concepts to another level. We will explore vectors: their qualities, relationships, and practical benefits for animation, physics, and dynamic design.

Chapter 4

Math 2: Vectors in Two Dimensions

Animation with ActionScript is a prominent feature of my work, and hence, of this book. I create dynamic movement in the two-dimensional world of Flash, and often I create my own three-dimensional worlds in ActionScript. Higher dimensions demand higher concepts—in particular, vectors. This chapter will show you how to break out of the world of one-dimensional variables and harness the power of two-dimensional data structures.

In addition to explaining math concepts, this chapter serves as a reference for the *Vector* library I use throughout this book, particularly in physics-based animation. My *Vector* class is designed to be reusable across many projects. The code also demonstrates many OOP principles of Chapter 2. Indeed, it may be helpful to consult Chapter 2 when reading this chapter for the first time. In the same way, you may want to refer back to this chapter while reading later chapters that use vectors. Don't worry if the vector concepts are a bit fuzzy after an initial read. The *iterative process* described in Chapter 1 applies here: understanding will develop as you read the concepts, see vectors in action, and then revisit these ideas in context.

Vectors

Suppose you asked someone how to find the nearest phone booth and they responded, "It's five blocks from here." Would you thank them and be on your way? Hopefully not, because you're missing crucial information. On the other hand, suppose you were given only the direction to the phone booth: "It's south of here." This is not very helpful, either. You could head in that direction and hope to recognize your destination, but will you be traveling two blocks or two miles?

This is an example of *displacement*—the distance and direction from one point to another. Some quantities, like weight, temperature, and age, are defined by just one number. These are called *scalar* quantities in math, and they are one-dimensional. However, in a two-dimensional grid (such as city streets), properties like displacement are only meaningful when they are represented by two numbers. These types of quantities are known as *vectors*, and have at least two dimensions, perhaps even more. Displacement, velocity, and acceleration are all vector quantities, and they are key components of both physics and dynamic animation.

The definition of a two-dimensional vector is quite simple: it has an x value, and it has a y value. In mathematical notation, it is represented as:

$$\boldsymbol{V} = [x, y]$$

The boldface $\boldsymbol{V}$ indicates a vector. If we graph a vector, we depict it as an arrow coming from the origin (0, 0) and leading to the point (x, y) (see Figure 4-1).

Suppose we want to define a vector 5 units long that points to the right. If we know our Cartesian coordinates (discussed in Chapter 3), we can see intuitively that x should be 5, and y should be 0. Thus, we define the vector like this:

$$\boldsymbol{V} = [5, 0]$$

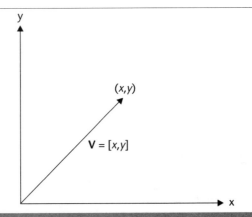

FIGURE 4-1

Representing a vector graphically

A Vector Class

There are many different ways to code vector functionality. The object-oriented approach is to create a custom template—a vector class. Classes and associated concepts are explained in Chapter 2. I remember first seeing an ActionScript *Vector* class implemented by Brandon Williams (known as *ahab* on the discussion forums). It was, in fact, one of the first useful ActionScript classes I found in the early days of Flash 5.

I have spent many hours developing my own implementation of a vector class, taking it through several iterations. We will work through this *Vector* class, defining and coding custom functionality that all vectors will inherit. I will work through the vector concepts, explaining the math and the code simultaneously. For some people, the code illuminates the math; for others, vice versa.

The Vector Constructor

The constructor function is used to name our *Vector* class and to create new instances. All we need to instantiate a *Vector* are two numbers: x and y. Thus, the constructor function is quite simple:

```
// constructor for Vector class
function Vector (x, y) {
    this.x = x;
    this.y = y;
};
```

The two arguments are copied into x and y properties for the *Vector* instance. Here is an example of how to use the constructor:

```
// test Vector constructor
v = new Vector (-9, 4);
trace (v.x); // output: -9
trace (v.y); // output: 4
```

Vector.toString( )

It would be nice to have a shorter way of checking both properties of a *Vector* object. We can give the *Vector* class a *toString( )* method, which returns a string representation of the object. This is especially useful when we use *trace( )* for debugging. Here is the method:

```
Vector.prototype.toString = function () {
    var rx = Math.round (this.x * 1000) / 1000;
    var ry = Math.round (this.y * 1000) / 1000;
    return "[" + rx + ", " + ry + "]";
};
```

When a *Vector* object is evaluated as a string, *toString( )* will be called
automatically. The method returns the values of *x* and *y*, formatted with
a comma and brackets—for example, [5, 8]. I'm choosing to round the
coordinates to three decimal places. This is purely for formatting purposes;
the actual values are unaffected.

Here is a code example:

```
// test Vector.toString()
position = new Vector (5, 8);
trace (position.toString()); // output: [5, 8]
trace (position); // output: [5, 8]
```

As you can see, *toString( )* allows the *Vector* object to be easily traced.

Vector.reset( )

The x and y values of a *Vector* are set when we create the object. However,
we may want to change these values later. I often give my custom classes a
reset( ) method that reinitializes the object:

```
Vector.prototype.reset = function (x, y) {
    this.constructor (x, y);
};
```

The *reset( )* method is a wrapper for the constructor function of the *Vector*
object. It takes *x* and *y* values and passes them to *this.constructor( )*. The
built-in constructor property is discussed in more detail in Chapter 6.

Normally, an object's constructor function is invoked using the new
keyword. However, it can also be called as a method from within the object.
In this case, I call the constructor to reinitialize the *Vector* without creating a
new object. The advantage of this approach is that I keep the initialization
code in one place—the constructor. Because *reset( )* points to *this.constructor( )*,
I can update the initialization code without having to change the *reset( )*
method as well.

Here is a code example:

```
// test Vector.reset()
velocity = new Vector (0, 0);
velocity.reset (-9, 7);
trace (velocity); // output: [-9, 7]
```

Vector.getClone( )

Suppose we need to make a copy of a *Vector* object. At first, one might think that you can just assign the *Vector* to another variable to make a copy, as in this code:

```
forceA = new Vector (5, 1);
forceB = forceA;
trace (forceB); // output: [5, 1]
```

This doesn't work, however. There is still only one *Vector* object, but now both forceA and forceB point to it. Consequently, if forceB is changed, so is forceA. We can see this if we extend our example by resetting forceB, as the following code shows:

```
forceB.reset (2, 2);
trace (forceB); // output: [2, 2]
trace (forceA); // output: [2, 2]
trace (forceA == forceB); // output: true
```

The two objects are equal because they point to the same spot in memory that contains that particular *Vector*. We need an alternative, a way to copy a *Vector's* values into a new object. The *Vector.getClone( )* method does just that:

```
Vector.prototype.getClone = function () {
    return new this.constructor (this.x, this.y);
};
```

The *getClone( )* method returns a new *Vector* object containing the x and y values of the current object. It uses the *this.constructor( )* property to find the*Vector* class constructor. Here is a code example:

```
// test Vector.getClone()
forceA = new Vector (2, 4);
forceB = forceA.getClone();
trace (forceB); // output: [2, 4]
trace (forceA == forceB); // output: false
```

The vectors forceA and forceB are now two distinct objects. Changes to one will not affect the other.

Vector.equals( )

Now that we're starting to spawn *Vectors* left and right, we may need to run some comparisons between objects. Suppose two *Vectors* look suspiciously like clones; how do we determine if they're identical? One might be tempted to try a simple equality comparison:

```
// v and w are separate Vector objects
trace (v == w);
```

However, because v and w are objects, not numbers, the equality operator (==) doesn't help us. The values being compared in the preceding code example are object references, not the internal properties of the objects. Unless v and w happen to be pointing to the same object, the output will always be `false`.

Two vectors are equal when each of their components is equal. Thus, we need to test the equality of the two x components and the two y components. The *Vector.equals( )* method performs this comparison, returning `true` if the numbers line up, and false otherwise:

```
Vector.prototype.equals = function (v) {
    return (this.x == v.x && this.y == v.y)
};
```

In the following code example, a force *Vector* is cloned, and the two *Vectors* are compared:

```
// test Vector.equals()
forceA = new Vector (2, 4);
forceB = forceA.getClone();
trace (forceB.equals (forceA)); // output: true
forceA.reset (0, 0);
trace (forceB.equals (forceA)); // output: false
```

When the clone is compared to the original *Vector*, the values are identical, so the *equals( )* method returns `true`. After the `forceA` *Vector* is changed, a comparison with `forceB` yields `false`.

Adding Vectors

Two vectors can be added together to produce a new vector. It is easiest to add vectors when they are in *x* and *y* components—in other words, the

Cartesian mode. The sum of the two vectors is found by adding the *x* components together and the *y* components together:

If $A = [x_A, y_A]$ and $B = [x_B, y_B]$

$A + B = [x_A + x_B, y_A + y_B]$

To try an example, suppose that $A = [1, 3]$ and $B = [3, 0]$. You can add A and B together to produce a new vector C with this procedure:

$A = [1, 3]$

$B = [3, 0]$

$C = A + B$

$C = [1 + 3, 3 + 0]$

$C = [4, 3]$

You can also see how the addition works spatially by graphing it (see Figure 4-2). The first vector A starts at the origin and extends to [1, 3]. Vector B is added to A by placing "tail-to-tip": the tail of B starts at the tip of A. From there, B extends 3 units to the right because it is [3, 0]. You can see that it ends up at the point [4, 3]—the same result as our previous approach.

Vector.plus( )

The *plus( )* method performs vector addition quite easily. The function takes a *Vector* object as a parameter and adds it to the current *Vector*:

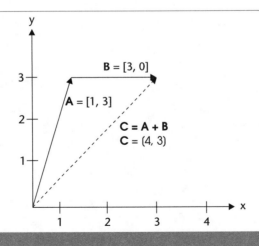

FIGURE 4-2

Adding vectors *A* and *B* graphically

```
Vector.prototype.plus = function (v) {
    this.x += v.x;
    this.y += v.y;
};
```

The following code is a classic example of how *Vectors* can be used in dynamic animation:

```
// test Vector.plus()
position = new Vector (1, 3);
velocity = new Vector (3, 0);
position.plus (velocity);
trace (position);  // output: [4, 3]
```

First, a `position` *Vector* is created to represent a point in two-dimensional space. Then a `velocity` *Vector* is created: it represents the point's two-dimensional speed. The point is moved or *translated* in space by adding `velocity` to `position`. This process is explained further in Chapter 8.

NOTE: The object passed to the *plus( )* method doesn't have to be a *Vector* object. It can be any object with *x* and *y* properties. For instance, you could pass an object literal like {x:3, y:2} to the *plus( )* method.

Vector.plusNew( )

The *plusNew( )* method is similar to *plus( )*. However, it returns the result of the addition as a new *Vector*, instead of changing the current object:

```
Vector.prototype.plusNew = function (v) {
    return new this.constructor (this.x + v.x, this.y + v.y);
};
```

This method allows you to easily store the sum of two *Vectors* in a new object.

The following code example is similar to the preceding one for *Vector.plus( )*. However, with *plusNew( )*, an additional *Vector* `newPosition` is created, which stores the sum of `position` and `velocity`:

```
// test Vector.plusNew()
position = new Vector (4, 1);
velocity = new Vector (-2, 0);
newPosition = position.plusNew (velocity);
trace (newPosition);  // output: [2, 1]
```

Subtracting Vectors

Similar to addition, vector subtraction is straightforward. Simply subtract the *x* components of each vector, and then subtract the *y* components:

if $A = [x_A, y_A]$ and $B = [x_B, y_B]$

$A - B = [x_A - x_B, y_A - y_B]$

Vector.minus( )

Vector subtraction is performed by the *minus( )* method. The function takes a *Vector* as an argument and subtracts it from the current *Vector*:

```
Vector.prototype.minus = function (v) {
    this.x -= v.x;
    this.y -= v.y;
};
```

The following code example shows how a force could be subtracted from another force:

```
// test Vector.minus()
forceA = new Vector (1, 1);
forceB = new Vector (-2, -1);
forceA.minus (forceB);
trace (forceA);   // output: [3, 2]
```

NOTE: Finding the net force by canceling vectors is another topic of Chapter 8.

Vector.minusNew( )

Like *minus( )*, the *minusNew( )* method subtracts two *Vectors*. However, it returns the result as a new *Vector*:

```
Vector.prototype.minusNew = function (v) {
    return new this.constructor (this.x - v.x, this.y - v.y);
};
```

The following code example demonstrates how the *displacement* between two points can be found, using *Vectors* and *minusNew( )*:

```
// test Vector.minusNew()
pointA = new Vector (0, 1);
pointB = new Vector (-2, 0);
displacement = pointB.minusNew (pointA);
trace (displacement);  // output: [-2, -1]
```

NOTE: Displacement differs slightly from distance. Distance is one-dimensional, but displacement can have two or more dimensions. In the preceding example, the 2D `displacement` *Vector* contains x and y distances.

Reversing a Vector

To reverse the direction of a vector, we *negate* it—multiply each component by -1:

if $A = [x_A, y_A]$

$-A = [-x_A, -y_A]$

Figure 4-3 shows how vector negation looks graphically:

Notice that negating a vector has the same result as rotating it by 180 degrees. The length of the vector is not changed by negation.

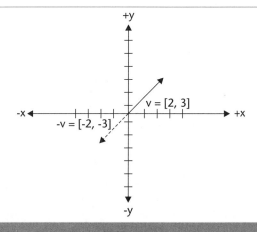

FIGURE 4-3

Negating the vector *v*

Vector.negate( )

The *negate( )* method points a *Vector* in the opposite direction:

```
Vector.prototype.negate = function () {
    this.x = -this.x;
    this.y = -this.y;
};
```

The following code example shows a `direction` *Vector* being reversed:

```
// test Vector.negate()
direction = new Vector (2, 3);
direction.negate();
trace (direction);  // output: [-2, -3]
```

Vector.negateNew( )

The *negateNew( )* method creates and returns a reversed *Vector*:

```
Vector.prototype.negateNew = function (v) {
    return new this.constructor (-this.x, -this.y);
};
```

Here is a code example to demonstrate:

```
// test Vector.negateNew()
forward = new Vector (99, 0);
backward = forward.negateNew();
trace (backward);  // output: [-99, 0]
```

Scaling Vectors

At times, you may like the direction of a vector, but need to scale it up or down a bit. To enlarge a vector by a certain factor, we multiply each of its components by that factor. In mathematical terms:

$$\text{if } \mathbf{A} = [x_A, y_A]$$
$$s\mathbf{A} = [sx_A, sy_A]$$

The variable *s* is a scalar (one-dimensional) number. Scaling a vector does not change its angle, unless *s* is negative. Negative scaling causes a vector to reverse direction. Figure 4-4 shows how vector scaling looks graphically.

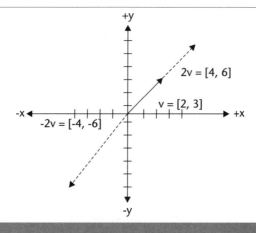

Scaling the vector *v*

NOTE: You may have noticed that vector negation and scaling are related. Negating a vector is the same as scaling it by a factor of -1.

Vector.scale( )

The *scale( )* method changes the length of a *Vector* by a scale factor. Its code is quite simple:

```
Vector.prototype.scale = function (s) {
    this.x *= s;
    this.y *= s;
};
```

The *x* and *y* properties of the *Vector* are multiplied by the scale factor. Here is a code example that shows how a wind's force could be doubled:

```
// test Vector.scale()
windForce = new Vector (2, 3);
windForce.scale (2);
trace (windForce);  // output: [4, 6]
```

Vector.scaleNew( )

The *scaleNew( )* method is similar to *scale( )*. However, it returns a new, scaled *Vector* instead of changing the current object:

```
Vector.prototype.scaleNew = function (s) {
    return new this.constructor (this.x * s, this.y * s);
};
```

This allows you to grab a scaled copy of a *Vector* in one step. Here is a code example which creates a new force vector twice as large as the original:

```
// test Vector.scaleNew()
windForce = new Vector (-2, 1);
galeForce = windForce.scaleNew (2);
trace (galeForce);  // output: [-4, 2]
```

Vector Length

The length of a vector represents its magnitude. It is also called the *absolute value* or *norm* of the vector. The mathematical notation for the length of a vector **A** is |**A**|. We can find the length by applying the versatile Pythagorean theorem to the *x* and *y* components of the vector. In mathematical terms, it looks like this:

If $A = [x, y]$,
$$|A| = \sqrt{(x^2 + y^2)}$$

NOTE: The *norm* should not be confused with the *normal* of a vector. The *norm* is the absolute value of the vector, while the *normal* is a vector perpendicular to the current vector. The latter is discussed later in this chapter.

Vector.getLength( )

The *Vector.getLength( )* method tells you the size of a *Vector*. Here is its code:

```
Vector.prototype.getLength = function () {
    return Math.sqrt (this.x*this.x + this.y*this.y);
};
```

This is classic Pythagorus. To find the length, the *x* and *y* components are both squared, and *Math.sqrt( )* takes the square root of their sum.

In the following example, the speed of a velocity *Vector* is calculated by finding the length of the *Vector*:

```
// test Vector.getLength()
velocity = new Vector (3, 4);
speed = velocity.getLength();
trace (speed); // output: 5
```

NOTE: The terms "speed" and "velocity" are often used interchangeably. In physics, however, there is a difference. Speed is one number, a scalar quantity, while velocity is a vector quantity. Thus, it has a direction, and is composed of two or more numbers. As the preceding example illustrates, the length of a velocity vector is its speed. In other words, speed is the magnitude of velocity.

Vector.setLength( )

We can change the magnitude of a *Vector*—give it a new length—with the *setLength( )* method:

```
Vector.prototype.setLength = function (len) {
    var r = this.getLength();
    if (r) this.scale (len / r);
    else this.x = len;
};
```

The *setLength( )* method works by calculating the ratio between the desired length and the current length, and then scaling the *Vector* by that amount. For example, if the current length is 5, and the desired length is 10, the ratio is 10 / 5 = 2. Thus, the *Vector* needs to be scaled by a factor of 2.

Notice that *setLength( )* calls two other *Vector* methods, *scale( )* and *getLength( )*. Our object-oriented approach allows us to build up levels of functionality easily and intuitively. The *Vector* object is gaining many different abilities through its methods, and these abilities can interact with one another.

Here is a code example, showing how *setLength( )* can be used to set a velocity vector to a new speed.

```
// test Vector.setLength()
velocity = new Vector (3, 4);
newSpeed = 10;
// set a new speed, in the same direction
velocity.setLength (newSpeed);
trace (velocity); // output: [6, 8];
```

```
// check the new speed of the velocity vector
trace (velocity.getLength()); // output: 10
```

Vector Angle

It is often useful to know the angle that a vector makes with the x-axis. In Figure 4-5, we see a simple example: vector *v* is [5, 5]. We know intuitively that its angle is 45 degrees, but other vectors are not so easy. Remember how, in Chapter 3, we converted Cartesian coordinates to polar coordinates. The same mathematical principles apply with vectors. When a vector is defined in *x* and *y* Cartesian coordinates, we can calculate its polar angle by taking the inverse tangent of *y* / *x*.

Vector.getAngle( )

The *getAngle( )* method calculates the *Vector's* angle in degrees and returns it:

```
Vector.prototype.getAngle = function () {
    return Math.atan2D (this.y, this.x);
};
```

In my *Vector* implementation, the angle isn't stored as a property of the *Vector* object. Rather, it is calculated on demand using the *getAngle( )* method.

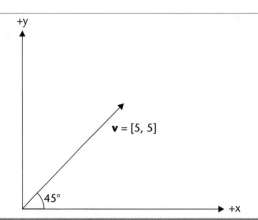

The angle of vector *v*

NOTE: *Math.atan2D( )* returns the angle in degrees rather than radians. Since *Math.atan2D( )* is a custom function, its code must be included in the movie as well.

In the following example, the angle to a destination point is found using the *getAngle( )* method:

```
// test Vector.getAngle()
destination = new Vector (5, 5);
compassBearing = destination.getAngle();
trace (compassBearing); // output: 45
```

Vector.setAngle( )

Suppose we want to keep a *Vector* at the same length, but give it a different angle from the origin. We can change its angle with the *setAngle( )* method:

```
Vector.prototype.setAngle = function (angle) {
    var r = this.getLength();
    this.x = r * Math.cosD (angle);
    this.y = r * Math.sinD (angle);
};
```

The *Vector.setAngle( )* method doesn't set an angle property. Rather, it calculates new x and y coordinates that match the new angle and the current length of the *Vector*. These equations come from the polar to Cartesian coordinates conversion procedure discussed in Chapter 3.

The following code example demonstrates how to turn a velocity vector by 180 degrees:

```
// test Vector.setAngle()
velocity = new Vector (7, 0);
newBearing = 180;
// head in a new direction
velocity.setAngle (newBearing);
trace (velocity); // output: [-7, 0]
```

The vector pulls a u-turn, but keeps the same speed (a magnitude of 7).

Rotating a Vector

Rotating a vector is similar to setting its angle. The difference is that a *relative* angle is used for rotation, rather than an *absolute* angle. In other words, you specify the *change* in the angle, rather than the final angle itself.

Vector.rotate( )

The *rotate( )* method takes an angle in degrees and rotates the *Vector* by that amount:

```
Vector.prototype.rotate = function (angle) {
        var ca = Math.cosD (angle);
        var sa = Math.sinD (angle);
    with (this) {
        var rx = x * ca - y * sa;
        var ry = x * sa + y * ca;
        x = rx;
        y = ry;
    }
};
```

NOTE: I have used the `with` statement in this function for purposes of optimization. The *rotate( )* method has a lot of mathematical operations. Using `with` squeezes a little more speed out of the code by avoiding repeated lookups of "this."

In the following example, a direction *Vector* starts at a 45 degree angle, then is rotated to the right by 90 degrees:

```
// test Vector.rotate()
direction = new Vector (5, 5);
trace (direction.getAngle()); // output: 45
direction.rotate (-90);
trace (direction); // output: [-5, -5]
trace (direction.getAngle()); // output: -45
```

Vector.rotateNew( )

The *rotateNew( )* method returns a new *Vector* that has been rotated by a specified angle:

```
Vector.prototype.rotateNew = function (angle) {
    var v = new this.constructor (this.x, this.y);
    v.rotate (angle);
    return v;
};
```

In the following example, a new direction *Vector* is created that is 10 degrees off from the original direction:

```
// test Vector.rotateNew()
direction = new Vector (5, 5);
newDirection = direction.rotateNew (10);
trace (newDirection.getAngle()); // output: 55
```

Dot Product

Two vectors can be multiplied together in a certain way to produce a number, called the *dot product*. The mathematical notation is **A·B**, read "A-dot-B." The dot product of two vectors is found by adding the product of the *x* components to the product of the *y* components. In mathematical terms, it looks like this:

if $A = [x_A, y_A]$ and $B = [x_B, y_B]$

$A·B = x_A x_B + y_A y_B$

The dot product can be found another way as well—by multiplying the lengths of both vectors by the cosine of the angle between them:

$A·B = |A| \, |B| \cos\theta$

Meaning of the Dot Product

The dot product is a common vector operation that produces information about the relationship between two vectors. For instance, if the dot product is 0, the vectors are perpendicular to each other. The dot product is sometimes called the *scalar product* because it produces a scalar number.

Vector.dot( )

The *dot( )* method returns the dot product of the current *Vector* with another *Vector*:

```
Vector.prototype.dot = function (v) {
    return (this.x * v.x + this.y * v.y);
};
```

In the following example, two *Vectors* are created and their dot product is taken:

```
// test Vector.dot()
v = new Vector (2, 3);
w = new Vector (4, 5);
trace ( v.dot (w) ); // output: 23
trace ( w.dot (v) ); // output: 23
```

As you can see, **v·w** produces the same result as **w·v**. Thus, it doesn't matter what order you multiply the vectors; the dot product is the same either way.

Perpendicular Vectors

Sometimes you have a vector and need to find a vector at a 90-degree angle to it. This perpendicular vector is called the *normal* to the original vector. Figure 4-6 shows the vector **v** and its normal **v**$_\perp$.

Finding a Normal Vector

The normal of a vector is found by swapping the *x* and *y* components, and taking the negative of one of them:

if **A** = [*x*, *y*],

A$_\perp$ = [-*y*, *x*]

Figure 4-6 illustrates this numerical relationship: the vector [3, 5] has a normal of [-5, 3].

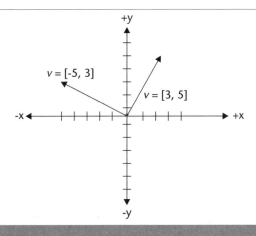

FIGURE 4-6

Vector *v* and its normal *v*⊥

Vector.getNormal( )

The *getNormal( )* method finds a normal for the current *Vector*, and returns it as a new *Vector*:

```
Vector.prototype.getNormal = function () {
    return new this.constructor (-this.y, this.x);
};
```

Normal vectors are often useful in situations where a surface exerts force. For instance, when a ball hits a wall, the wall exerts a force on the ball and changes its direction. The direction of the force is outwards, perpendicular to the wall's surface.

In the following example, the direction of a straight wall is represented by the *Vector* [3, 5]. From an overhead view, the wall appears as a straight line between (0, 0) and (3, 5) (see Figure 4-6). The direction of the wall's force is found by getting the normal *Vector* to the wall:

```
wallDirection = new Vector (3, 5);
forceDirection = wallDirection.getNormal();
trace (forceDirection); // output: [-5, 3]
```

NOTE: There are actually two possible angles for any normal vector. These two angles differ by 180 degrees. Thus, the two normal vectors are in opposite directions to one another, but are both perpendicular to the original vector.

Checking for Perpendicularity

Suppose you have two vectors, and you suspect that they are at right angles to each other. How can you check to be sure? If two vectors are perpendicular, their dot product will be zero:

if $\boldsymbol{A} \perp \boldsymbol{B}$,

$\boldsymbol{A} \cdot \boldsymbol{B} = 0$

Let's try this test on the vectors in Figure 4-6: $\boldsymbol{v}$ and $\boldsymbol{v}_\perp$. They are perpendicular to each other, but what is their dot product?

$\boldsymbol{v} = [3, 5]$

$\boldsymbol{v}_\perp = [-5, 3]$

$\boldsymbol{v} \cdot \boldsymbol{v}_\perp = 3 * -5 + 5 * 3$

$\boldsymbol{v} \cdot \boldsymbol{v}_\perp = -15 + 15$

$\boldsymbol{v} \cdot \boldsymbol{v}_\perp = 0$

The dot product of $\boldsymbol{v}$ and $\boldsymbol{v}_\perp$ is, in fact, zero. So, our test holds true.

Vector.isPerpTo( )

The *isPerpTo( )* method tests if the current *Vector* is perpendicular to another *Vector*:

```
Vector.prototype.isPerpTo = function (v) {
    return (this.dot (v) == 0);
};
```

The *isPerpTo( )* method takes the dot product of the input vector v with the current *Vector*. The function returns `true` if the dot product is zero (indicating perpendicularity), and `false` otherwise.

In the following example, several direction *Vectors* are created, and tested to see if they are at right angles to each other. First, two "left" *Vectors* are created. Since they are parallel, they are not perpendicular. An "up" *Vector* is then created, which is at right angles to the left *Vectors*:

```
// test Vector.isPerpTo()
goingLeft = new Vector (-3, 0);
goingLeft2 = new Vector (-5, 0); // parallel vector
trace (goingLeft.isPerpTo (goingLeft2) ); // output: false
goingUp = new Vector (0, 8);
trace (goingUp.isPerpTo (goingLeft) ); // output: true
trace (goingUp.isPerpTo (goingLeft2) ); // output: true
```

Finding the Angle Between Two Vectors

Between two vectors, there lies an angle θ, as shown in Figure 4-7. In this situation, we know the x and y components for the two vectors. However, this does not automatically tell us what angle separates them. How do we find the angle θ?

Equation to Find the Angle

If we look again at the dot product of two vectors, we can see that one of its definitions contains θ:

$$A \cdot B = |A|\ |B|\ \cos θ$$

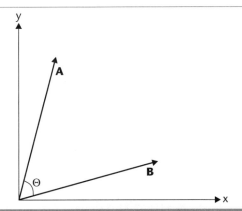

FIGURE 4-7

The angle θ between vectors *A* and *B*

We can rearrange this equation to solve for θ, using algebra. First, we divide both sides by |A||B| to isolate *cos* θ:

$$\cos\theta = \frac{A \cdot B}{|A|\ |B|}$$

To solve for θ, we take the inverse cosine of both sides. The inverse cosine of cos θ yields θ on the left side:

$$\theta = \cos^{-1}\left(\frac{A \cdot B}{|A|\ |B|} \right)$$

We now have a mathematical expression that defines θ in terms of the vectors A and B. In plain English, this equation means that finding the angle between vectors A and B involves the following steps:

1. Find the dot product of A and B.
2. Divide by the length of A.
3. Divide by the length of B.
4. Take the inverse cosine of the result.

Vector.angleBetween( )

The preceding steps may seem involved, but the *Vector* class has a method to find the angle easily. If you understand vectors, all you need to know is how to use the *angleBetween( )* method:

```
Vector.prototype.angleBetween = function (v) {
    var dp = this.dot (v);
    var cosAngle = dp / (this.getLength() *
    v.getLength());
    return Math.acosD (cosAngle); // take the inverse
cosine
};
```

The *angleBetween( )* method is one of the most complex *Vector* methods we've seen thus far. However, this is where the power of object-oriented programming really shines. *Vector.angleBetween( )* manipulates two *Vector* objects, and calls upon the other *Vector* methods *dot( )* and *getLength( )*.

Simple abilities of the object are combined to build up complex functionality.

The following example finds the angle between two forces acting on an object. One *Vector* represents a force pulling the object to the right. Another *Vector* represents the force of friction in the opposite direction.

```
// test Vector.angleBetween()
pullForce = new Vector (4, 0);
frictionForce = new Vector (-1, 0);
theta = pullForce.angleBetween (frictionForce);
trace (theta); // output: 180
```

Treating Points as Vectors

You may have noticed by now that there are many similarities between points and vectors. Both are multidimensional, represented by two or more numbers. Both vectors and points can be represented with Cartesian coordinates (x, y) or polar coordinates (r, θ). So what's stopping us from using *Vector* objects as points? Nothing at all.

The *Vector* class lends itself easily to being used for points. It has such a convenient structure, and its methods are powerful for manipulating positions in space. Vector objects will be used abundantly in the chapters to come. Here is a classic example of how vectors can be used in animation:

```
position = new Vector (0, 0);
velocity = new Vector (2, 3);
position.plus (velocity);
trace (position); // [2, 3]
```

The position variable stores (0, 0), the starting point. Then the velocity is set to 2 in the x-direction and 3 in the y-direction. To produce movement, we add the velocity vector to the position. We can produce continuous, fairly automatic movement by putting this simple code in a frame loop:

```
position.plus (velocity);
```

With this setup, we are free to change `velocity` whenever we like, and it will automatically be reflected in the changing `position`. This will be explained further in Chapter 7.

Perhaps you're still wondering why you should bother using custom vector objects instead of normal variables. For instance, the preceding example could be written without vectors:

```
positionX = 0;
positionY = 0;
velocityX = 2;
velocityY = 3;
positionX += velocityY;
positionY += velocityY;
trace (positionX); // 2
trace (positionY); // 3
```

Notice, however, that this takes twice as many lines of code. There are also twice as many variable names to deal with. This is just a simple example: a mere moving of a point. But what if we want to manipulate the position and velocity in more complex ways, such as setting rotation or magnitude, or finding the angle between them? This is much more complicated when the *x* and *y* components are not joined into a single object.

As an analogy, think about *Array* objects. Like a *Vector*, an *Array* contains multiple properties. The difference is that the *Array* indexes them with 0, 1, 2... instead of x and y. You could store a list of information in multiple variables instead of using an *Array*. In fact, this is what we were forced to do in Flash 4 ActionScript, which didn't have *Arrays*. We used variables like list_0, list_1, list_2, and so on to make lists of related information. The resulting code was a bit convoluted, using statements like eval ("list_" + i) to look up values by index. Manipulating these pseudo-arrays was difficult because the *Array* methods, such as *push( )*, *splice( )*, and *sort( )*, were unavailable. I doubt that any ActionScripter who has delved into Flash 5 *Arrays* would want to go back to the Flash 4 method.

I am proposing a similar shift with *Vectors*. A point in two-dimensional space is a single entity. We can represent this entity with two variables, or with a *Vector* object containing two properties. It certainly isn't *wrong* to use the former approach. In fact, separate variables are usually the best option for small scripts and simple situations.

However, when you start coding complex two-dimensional animations and interactions, *Vectors* are more convenient. For example, when you're passing a list of names from function to function, it's much easier to pass a single *Array*, rather than multiple string variables. In fact, since a function can only return one value, it is practically necessary to use an *Array*. Similarly, a *Vector* is a nice way to package coordinates and ship them from here to there. The *Vector* class is also powerful, like the *Array* class, because of its methods. Given any *Array* object, you know that it can easily be sorted, reversed, or otherwise changed, using the built-in *Array* methods. Likewise, a *Vector* object can be rotated, translated, and lengthened with straightforward commands.

Conclusion

This chapter has explained what vectors are and how they work, both in math and in ActionScript. These concepts will prove to be the foundation for motion, physics, and drawing, as well as other topics in following chapters. The *Vector* library and code examples in this chapter should prove useful for a multitude of ActionScript projects. Also, through my *Vector* class, I have endeavored to set an example of clean and reusable object-oriented code. Now that we have conquered the second dimension, it's time to take on the third, in our next chapter.

Chapter 5

Math 3: Vectors in Three Dimensions

Flash has a two-dimensional stage, which lends itself naturally to 2-D points and vectors. If we're feeling more adventurous, we can also define a three-dimensional world in ActionScript. Since we can represent points with vectors in two dimensions, then the same holds true for the third.

Much has been written about 3-D in Flash, in books, tutorials, and open-source FLAs. Relatively little of it, however, is object-oriented. The code you often see, though instructive in terms of algorithms, is not easily reusable. In a sense, the code has melted onto the graphics, like a plastic bag on a stove, making it difficult to scrape the math and logic off of the movie clips and apply them to a different project. I prefer to encapsulate 3-D operations in a custom ActionScript class. Following the principles of object-oriented design, I have developed a clean, developer-friendly framework for 3-D graphics in ActionScript. Let's explore this approach, starting with the cornerstone: the three-dimensional vector.

X, Y, and Z Axes

The three axes for three-dimensional space can be set up in various ways. I use the axis configuration that is most common in 3-D graphics, shown in Figure 5-1.

The x and y axes are laid out the same way as the two-dimensional Cartesian system: x increases to the right, and y increases upwards. The z values, meanwhile, correspond to the distance from the screen, meaning distant objects have higher z values.

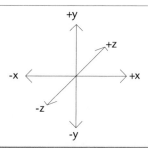

FIGURE 5-1

The axis configuration for *x*, *y*, and *z*

The Vector3d Class

I have created a *Vector3d* class to manipulate three-dimensional entities—objects defined by numbers along *x*, *y*, and *z* dimensions. In many respects, the *Vector3d* class is similar to the 2-D *Vector* class we explored in Chapter 4. Many of the 3-D methods are identical to their 2-D counterparts, except for the addition of the z component.

The Vector3d Constructor

The constructor is straightforward, defining x, y, and z properties for a new *Vector3d* instance:

```
function Vector3d (x, y, z) {
    this.x = x;
    this.y = y;
    this.z = z;
};
```

This is how you would create a new *Vector3d* object to represent a position in 3-D space:

```
position = new Vector3d (4, 0, 1);
```

Vector3d.toString( )

As with 2-D *Vector* objects, it is useful to have a custom *toString( )* method that gives a snapshot of the *Vector3d*'s status:

```
Vector3d.prototype.toString = function () {
    var rx = Math.round (this.x * 1000) / 1000;
    var ry = Math.round (this.y * 1000) / 1000;
    var rz = Math.round (this.z * 1000) / 1000;
    return "[" + rx + ", " + ry + ", " + rz + "]";
};
```

The *x*, *y*, and *z* coordinates are rounded to three decimal places, for formatting purposes.

Here is a code example which creates a position vector and traces it to the output window:

```
// test Vector3d.toString()
position = new Vector3d (2, 4, 6.952013);
trace (position); // output: [2, 4, 6.952]
```

Vector3d.reset( )

As with *Vector*, *Vector3d*'s *reset( )* method is used to re-initialize the coordinates:

```
Vector3d.prototype.reset = function (x, y, z) {
    this.constructor (x, y, z);
};
```

The x, y, and z arguments are passed to the constructor. The constructor is then called as a method of the object (this.constructor( )), assigning the new values to this.x, this.y, and this.z, respectively.

In the following code example, an acceleration vector is created and then reset to different values:

```
// test Vector3d.reset()
acceleration = new Vector3d (0, 0, 0);
acceleration.reset (10, 20, 30);
trace (acceleration); // output: [10, 20, 30]
```

Vector3d.getClone( )

The *getClone( )* method returns a copy of the current *Vector3d* instance:

```
Vector3d.prototype.getClone = function () {
    with (this) return new constructor (x, y, z);
};
```

This code is similar to the two-dimensional *Vector.getClone( )*, but extends it to include the z component. Also, I have used the `with` statement to optimize and shorten the code. If I didn't use `with`, this would be the code for *getClone( )*:

```
// equivalent code without "with"
Vector3d.prototype.getClone = function () {
    return new this.constructor (this.x, this.y, this.z);
};
```

As you can see, `this` is used in four places to access properties of the current object. What we can do is use the statement `with (this)` to enter the scope of `this`. The properties `constructor`, x, y, and z can thus be looked up in `this` without having the prefix specified.

N O T E : The `with` statement has some subtleties, so read its documentation carefully. In particular, you can't create new variables in the *with* scope. You can only access and modify properties and methods that already exist in that object.

In the following code example, a force vector is created and then cloned:

```
// test Vector3d.getClone()
force = new Vector3d (2, 4, 6);
forceCopy = force.getClone();
trace (forceCopy); // output: [2, 4, 6]
trace (forceCopy == force); // output: false
```

Vector3d.equals( )

The *equals( )* method checks if one *Vector3d* object has the same coordinates as another:

```
Vector3d.prototype.equals = function (v) {
    with (this) return (x == v.x && y == v.y && z == v.z)
};
```

In the following code example, a force vector is created and then cloned. Afterward, the copy is compared to the original using the *equals( )* method:

```
// test Vector3d.equals()
force = new Vector3d (2, 4, 6);
forceCopy = force.getClone();
trace (forceCopy.equals (force)); // output: true
```

Basic Operations of 3-D Vectors

Three-dimensional vectors can be manipulated arithmetically in much the same manner as 2-D vectors: addition, subtraction, multiplication, and so on. The *Vector3d* methods to perform these operations are similar to the two-dimensional Vector methods. Because of this, the methods are quite straightforward, so we'll run through them quickly.

Vector3d.plus( )

The *plus( )* method adds one vector to another, taking a *Vector3d* object as a parameter and adding it to the current object:

```
Vector3d.prototype.plus = function (v) {
    with (this) {
        x += v.x;
        y += v.y;
        z += v.z;
    }
};
```

Again, I'm using a `with` statement to shorten the code.

The following example shows how *Vector3d* objects can be used in dynamic animation by adding vectors together:

```
// test Vector3d.plus()
position = new Vector3d (1, 1, 1);
velocity = new Vector3d (2, 1, 3);
```

```
position.plus (velocity);
trace (position);  // output: [3, 2, 4]
```

First, a *Vector3d* called `position` is created to represent a point in 3-D space. Then, a `velocity` object is created. The point is moved, or translated, by adding `velocity` to `position`, using the *plus( )* method. This process is explained further in Chapter 8. As you can see, this code is fairly simple and compact because of its object-oriented nature. Though there are six numbers involved, the addition itself is performed in one line of code. Imagine, instead, having six separate variables for the numbers, which would have to be added together in six lines of code. It starts getting messy rather quickly, and that's just one addition. The vector approach is cleaner and more organized.

NOTE: The *Vector3d.plus( )* method will accept any object with *x, y,* and *z* properties, e.g., {x:3, y:2, z:0}.

Vector3d.plusNew( )

The *plusNew( )* method adds two vectors and returns the sum as a new *Vector3d* object:

```
Vector3d.prototype.plusNew = function (v) {
    return new this.constructor (this.x + v.x,
                                 this.y + v.y,
                                 this.z + v.z);
};
```

The following code example is similar to the preceding one for *Vector3d.plus( )*. However, with *plusNew( )*, an additional vector `newPosition` is created, which stores the sum of `position` and `velocity`:

```
// test Vector3d.plusNew()
position = new Vector3d (1, 1, 1);
velocity = new Vector3d (2, 1, 3);
newPosition = position.plusNew (velocity);
trace (newPosition);  // output: [3, 2, 4]
```

Vector3d.minus( )

The *minus( )* method subtracts one vector from another, taking a *Vector3d* object as a parameter and subtracting it from the current object:

```
Vector3d.prototype.minus = function (v) {
    with (this) {
        x -= v.x;
        y -= v.y;
        z -= v.z;
    }
};
```

The following code example shows how two points could be subtracted from one another to find the x, y, and z distances between them:

```
// test Vector3d.minus()
farPoint = new Vector3d (10, -6, 5);
nearPoint = new Vector3d (6, -2, 0);
farPoint.minus (nearPoint);
trace (farPoint);   // output: [4, -4, 5]
```

Vector3d.minusNew( )

The *minusNew( )* method subtracts two vectors and returns the difference as a new *Vector3d* object:

```
Vector3d.prototype.minusNew = function (v) {
    with (this) return new constructor (x - v.x,
                                        y - v.y,
                                        z - v.z);
};
```

The following code example demonstrates how the displacement between two points can be found, using vectors and the *minusNew( )* method:

```
// test Vector3d.minus()
farPoint = new Vector3d (10, -6, 5);
nearPoint = new Vector3d (6, -2, 0);
displacement = farPoint.minusNew (nearPoint);
trace (displacement);   // output: [4, -4, 5]
```

Vector3d.negate( )

The *negate( )* method reverses the direction of a *Vector3d* object:

```
Vector3d.prototype.negate = function () {
    with (this) {
        x = -x;
        y = -y;
        z = -z;
    }
};
```

After being modified by *negate( )*, the vector is the same length as before, but is rotated 180 degrees.

In this code example, a `direction` vector is created and reversed with the *negate( )* method:

```
// test Vector3d.negate()
direction = new Vector3d (3, -6, -9);
direction.negate();
trace (direction); // output: [-3, 6, 9]
```

Vector3d.negateNew( )

The *negateNew( )* method returns a new *Vector3d* object that faces opposite the current one:

```
Vector3d.prototype.negateNew = function () {
    with (this) return new constructor (-x, -y, -z);
};
```

In the following example, a `towards` vector is created, with a *z* component of –20. The vector points out of the screen, towards the camera. Then a new `away` vector, pointing in the opposite direction, is derived by using the *negateNew( )* method on `towards`.

```
// test Vector3d.negateNew()
towards = new Vector3d (0, 0, -20);
away = towards.negateNew();
trace (away); // output: [0, 0, 20]
```

Vector3d.scale( )

The *scale( )* method takes a *Vector3d* object as a parameter and adds it to the current object:

```
Vector3d.prototype.scale = function (s) {
    with (this) {
        x *= s;
        y *= s;
        z *= s;
    }
};
```

Here is a code example that shows how a force of tension can be doubled with the *scale( )* method:

```
// test Vector3d.scale()
tensionForce = new Vector3d (3, -1, 0);
tensionForce.scale (2);
trace (tensionForce);   // output: [6, -2, 0]
```

Vector3d.scaleNew( )

The *scaleNew( )* method returns a new, scaled *Vector3d* object:

```
Vector3d.prototype.scaleNew = function (s) {
    with (this) return new constructor (x * s, y * s, z * s);
};
```

This example is similar to the previous one, scaling a tension force by a factor of 2. This code, however, creates a new force vector with the *scaleNew( )* method, as shown next:

```
// test Vector3d.scaleNew()
tensionForce = new Vector3d (3, -1, 0);
strongerForce = tensionForce.scaleNew (2);
trace (strongerForce);   // output: [6, -2, 0]
```

Vector3d.getLength( )

The *Vector3d.getLength( )* method calculates and returns the length of the vector. If the vector is treated as a point, the result of *getLength( )* is also the point's distance from the origin (0, 0, 0).

```
Vector3d.prototype.getLength = function () {
    with (this) return Math.sqrt (x*x + y*y + z*z);
};
```

In the *getLength( )* method, the Pythagorean Theorem is extended to three dimensions: the x, y, and z components are squared and added, and *Math.sqrt( )* takes the square root.

In the following example, the speed of a velocity vector is calculated by finding its length:

```
// test Vector3d.getLength()
velocity = new Vector3d (3, 4, 0);
speed = velocity.getLength();
trace (speed); // output: 5
```

As I mentioned in Chapter 4, speed is the magnitude of velocity, which is a vector quantity. Velocity may be represented by several numbers, and has a direction. Speed, meanwhile, is a scalar quantity, and is specified by one number.

Vector3d.setLength( )

We can give a *Vector3d* object a new length. If the vector is used as a 3-D point, this is also a way to set its distance from the origin (0, 0, 0).

```
Vector3d.prototype.setLength = function (len) {
    var r = this.getLength();
    if (r) this.scale (len / r);
    else this.x = len;
};
```

NOTE: Upon comparison, you may notice that the internal code of *Vector3d.setLength( )* is exactly the same as *Vector.setLength( )*, (see Chapter 4).

Here's a code example which shows how *setLength( )* can be used to set a velocity vector to a new speed:

```
// test Vector3d.setLength()
velocity = new Vector3d (3, 4, 0);
trace (velocity.getLength()); // output: 5
// set a new speed, in the same direction
velocity.setLength (10);
// check the new speed of the velocity vector
trace (velocity.getLength()); // output: 10
trace (velocity); // output: [6, 8, 0];
```

First, a `velocity` vector is created with the components [3, 4, 0]. In the next line of code, the vector's length is found to be 5, using the *getLength( )* method. The vector is then given a new length of 10, using the *setLength( )* method. The length is verified with *getLength( )*, and found to be 10. Finally, we see that the components of the vector have been changed to [6, 8, 0]. Notice that each number has doubled in size.

Vector Products

There are two different ways to multiply 3-D vectors. The dot product produces a single-dimensional number, while the cross product produces a vector.

The Dot Product

The dot product is also called *scalar multiplication*, because it produces a scalar number. The dot product of 3-D vectors is similar to that of 2-D vectors. In mathematical terms, it looks like this:

if $A = [x_A, y_A, z_A]$ and $B = [x_B, y_B, z_B]$,

$$A \cdot B = x_A x_B + y_A y_B + z_A z_B$$

The only difference in the 3-D dot product is that the z components are multiplied and added to the total.

The dot product can also be found by multiplying the lengths of both vectors by the cosine of the angle between them:

$$A \cdot B = |A| \, |B| \, \cos\theta$$

As explained in Chapter 4, the vertical lines | | around a vector denote its absolute value, or magnitude. This equation is identical to the one for 2-D vectors. We'll use it later to find the angle between two vectors. The dot product is also useful for finding the projection of one vector onto another, which I won't discuss here.

Vector3d.dot( )

The *Vector3d.dot( )* method calculates the dot product of two vectors. This 3-D method extends its *Vector* counterpart to include the z component in the calculation:

```
Vector3d.prototype.dot = function (v) {
    with (this) return x * v.x + y * v.y + z * v.z;
};
```

In the following example, the dot product is taken of two vectors v and w:

```
// test Vector3d.dot()
v = new Vector3d (2, 0, 1);
w = new Vector3d (3, 5, 4);
trace ( v.dot (w) ); // output: 10
```

Calculated manually, the dot product of these two vectors is $2 \times 3 + 0 \times 5 + 1 \times 4 = 6 + 0 + 4 = 10$.

The Cross Product

The cross product is also called *vector multiplication*, because it produces a vector. This is the mathematical definition of the cross product:

if $A = [x_A, y_A, z_A]$ and $B = [x_B, y_B, z_B]$,

$A \times B = [x_C, y_C, z_C]$

where:

$x_C = y_A z_B - y_B z_A$

$y_C = z_A x_B - z_B x_A$

$z_C = x_A y_B - x_B y_A$

When you cross two 3-D vectors, you get a third 3-D vector. What makes the cross product interesting is that the resulting vector is perpendicular to the first two vectors. In other words, the cross product produces a *normal* vector to the other two vectors. Figure 5-2 shows vectors *a* and *b*, and their cross product *c*.

Vector *a* lies along the x-axis, and *b* along the y-axis. Their cross product, *c,* lies along the z-axis, which is at 90 degrees to the other axes.

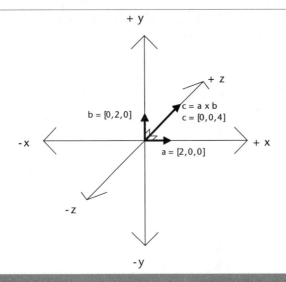

FIGURE 5-2

The cross product c = a × b of vectors *a* and *b*

If you reverse the order of the cross product, the resulting vector will point in the opposite direction. In mathematical terms, it looks like this:

$$\boldsymbol{A} \times \boldsymbol{B} = -\boldsymbol{B} \times \boldsymbol{A}$$

Figure 5-3 shows the result of a cross product in reverse order.

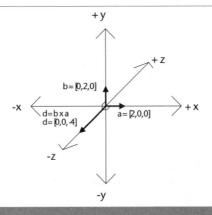

FIGURE 5-3

The reversed cross product d = b × a of vectors *a* and *b*

The cross product vector **d** points along the negative z-axis, in the opposite direction of **c** in Figure 5-2. In other words, **d** = -**c**.

There's one final feature of the cross product. Remember that the dot product was related to *cos* θ, as shown here:

A·B = | **A** | | **B** | *cos* θ

You'll notice that the cross product has a similar relationship, except that it involves *sin* θ instead of *cos* θ:

|**A**×**B**| = | **A** | | **B** | *sin* θ

In plain English, this equation says that the magnitude of the cross product of **A** and **B** is equal to the magnitude of **A**, multiplied by the magnitude of **B**, multiplied by the sine of the angle between them. Although the importance of this relationship may not be obvious, I have included it for the sake of completeness.

The cross product is useful wherever you need to find a surface normal, a common task in 3-D graphics rendering. The surface normal is often used to perform backface culling and lighting calculations. These are possible in ActionScript, but I don't have the space to discuss them here. If you have a background in 3-D graphics programming, you should be able to work out culling and lighting in ActionScript using a combination of *Vector3d* methods.

Vector3d.cross( )

The *cross( )* method calculates the cross product of two 3-D vectors, returning the resulting vector:

```
Vector3d.prototype.cross = function (v) {
    with (this) {
        var cx = y * v.z - z * v.y;
        var cy = z * v.x - x * v.z;
        var cz = x * v.y - y * v.x;
        return new constructor (cx, cy, cz);
    }
};
```

Using this method, the notation **a** × **b** is equivalent to a.cross(b) in ActionScript.

Here's an example of taking the cross product of two vectors:

```
a = new Vector3d (2, 0, 0);
b = new Vector3d (0, 2, 0);
c = a.cross (b);
trace (c); // output: [0, 0, 4]
d = b.cross (a);
trace (d); // output: [0, 0, -4]
```

First, vectors a and b are defined, lying on the x and y axes, respectively. A new vector c is set to the cross product a × b. Tracing c reveals that it lies along the z-axis, which is perpendicular to the x and y axes. Thus, c is perpendicular to vectors a and b. Finally, the cross product of a and b is taken in the reverse order: b × a. The resulting vector is stored as d. We see that d, with coordinates [0, 0, -4], also lies along the z-axis, but in the opposite direction of c.

The Angle Between Vectors

Finding the angle between two vectors is virtually the same in three dimensions as it is in two dimensions. The equations and ActionScript methods are identical.

The Equation to Find the Angle

To review, the dot product of two vectors can be defined like so:

$$\mathbf{A} \cdot \mathbf{B} = |\mathbf{A}| \, |\mathbf{B}| \cos \theta$$

If we rearrange to solve for θ, we get this equation:

$$\theta = \cos^{-1} \left(\frac{\mathbf{A} \cdot \mathbf{B}}{|\mathbf{A}| \, |\mathbf{B}|} \right)$$

Finding the angle between vectors **A** and **B** involves the following steps:

1. Finding the dot product of **A** and **B**
2. Dividing by the length of **A**
3. Dividing by the length of **B**
4. Taking the inverse cosine of the result

Vector3d.angleBetween( )

The *angleBetween( )* method for *Vector3d* uses the same code as the 2-D Vector class:

```
Vector3d.prototype.angleBetween = function (v) {
    var dp = this.dot (v);
    var cosAngle = dp / (this.getLength() * v.getLength());
    return Math.acosD (cosAngle);
};
```

I'm using my custom function, *Math.acosD( ),* to return the angle in degrees instead of radians.

NOTE: If either of the two vectors has a length of zero, *angleBetween( )* will return a value of NaN — not a number — resulting from a division by zero in the code. The result makes sense: mathematically, you can't define an angle between these two vectors. Think of a normal vector as a *line* extending from the origin, and a zero-length vector as a *dot* on the origin. How can you measure the angle between a dot and a line? You simply can't — the concept doesn't apply in this special situation.

In the following example, *Vector3d.angleBetween( )* is used to find the angle between two forces acting on an object. One vector represents a force pulling the object to the right. Another vector represents the force of wind pushing towards the screen (the negative-z direction):

```
// test Vector3d.angleBetween()
pullForce = new Vector3d (4, 0, 0);
windForce = new Vector3d (0, 0, -3);
theta = pullForce.angleBetween (windForce);
trace (theta); // output: 90
```

As expected, the angle between the two forces is 90 degrees.

Projecting Onto the Viewing Plane

We experience the real world in both two and three dimensions. We move through space in three dimensions. However, we can see our world in two dimensions. The eye captures a two-dimensional image and sends it to the brain for interpretation. We are able to infer the three-dimensional positions and sizes of objects by interpreting many different cues in the two-dimensional image. Why do closer objects appear larger and distant objects smaller? This effect occurs because the light from the objects is focused through the eye's lens and projected onto the retina, producing a 2-D image.

To create scripted 3-D graphics in Flash, we want to mimic the light projection process. First, we define three-dimensional points with *Vector3d* objects. Then, we project them onto a viewing screen to produce two-dimensional points. If we use the correct equations, we can produce a convincing 3-D effect.

Vector3d.getPerspective( )

The *getPerspective( )* method starts the projection process by calculating and returning the perspective ratio needed to scale an object correctly:

```
Vector3d.prototype.getPerspective = function (viewDist) {
    if (viewDist == undefined) viewDist = 300;
    return viewDist / (this.z + viewDist);
};
```

Because of perspective, the apparent size of an object is inversely proportional to its distance from the viewpoint. Points with large z values are farther away, and appear smaller on the screen. Thus, the perspective ratio returned by *getPerspective( )* will be small for these objects. Conversely, closer points will have smaller z values, but larger perspective values, and thus, a larger screen size.

The parameter `viewDist` controls the viewing distance of the projection. Large values of `viewDist` produce an image in which there is little size difference between close and distant objects. Small values of `viewDist` produce more of a "fisheye" effect, distorting the image like a peephole. If `viewDist` is not specified, a default value of 300 is chosen, which gives a natural-looking perspective.

In the following code example, the perspective ratio is calculated for the `pointA` vector:

```
// test Vector3d.getPerspective()
pointA = new Vector3d (50, 20, 40);
pers = pointA.getPerspective();
trace (pers); // output: 0.862068965517241
```

The resulting perspective ratio `pers` is approximately 0.86. This means that an object residing at `pointA`'s coordinates will appear at 86 percent of its actual size.

By itself, the *getPerspective( )* method does not change the *Vector3d* object. It merely returns a number: a perspective ratio. However, we can take this number and pass it to other functions to change the scale of objects or points projected onto the screen.

Vector3d.persProject( )

The *persProject( )* method performs a perspective projection on a 3-D point. It converts (x, y, z) coordinates to a 2-D location (x, y) on the screen:

```
Vector3d.prototype.persProject = function (p) {
    with (this) {
        if (p == undefined) p = getPerspective();
        x *= p;
        y *= p;
        z = 0;
    }
};
```

The perspective ratio p is passed in as an argument. If it is missing, p is automatically calculated by calling the *getPerspective( )* method. The projection is performed by multiplying the x and y components by p, and setting the z component to zero. We can ignore z from now on, since the vector has essentially been flattened into two dimensions, a point on the screen. We can now use the x and y coordinates to plot a graphical representation of the 3-D object. An example involving 3-D particles follows later in this chapter.

In the following example, a vector pointA is created and projected onto the screen:

```
// test Vector3d.persProject()
pointA = new Vector3d (50, 20, 40);
pointA.persProject();
trace (pointA); // output: [44.118, 17.647, 0]
```

In this example, no argument is passed to *persProject( )*, so the perspective is automatically calculated internally.

Vector3d.persProjectNew( )

The *persProjectNew( )* method operates like *persProject( )*, but creates and returns a new object containing the projected points:

```
Vector3d.prototype.persProjectNew = function (p) {
    with (this) {
```

```
            if (p == undefined) p = getPerspective();
            return new constructor (p * x, p * y, 0);
    }
};
```

In the following example, a vector `pointA` is created. Its perspective ratio is calculated with the *getPerspective( )* method and stored in the variable `pers`. Then the point is projected onto the screen:

```
// test Vector3d.persProjectNew()
pointA = new Vector3d (50, 20, 40);
pers = pointA.getPerspective();
screenA = pointA.persProjectNew (pers);
trace (screenA); // output: [44.118, 17.647, 0]
```

With this approach, the original point and the projected point are stored as two independent objects: `screenA` and `pointA.`, respectively. I prefer to use this method when plotting 3-D graphics. In the particle example later in this chapter, you will see that I use the *persProjectNew( )* method in this manner.

3-D Rotation

There are two fundamental tasks in rendering 3-D graphics: projection and rotation. We have already learned how to project points onto the screen. Now we will see how to rotate points in 3-D space. Rotating an object around its center gives us a full appreciation of its 3-D qualities because we can view it from all angles. Rotation around the x, y, and z axes can be done separately or together. I have created *Vector3d* methods that can rotate around one axis at a time, or in combination, for efficiency.

X-axis Rotation

If you've ever ridden on a Ferris wheel, you've experienced x-axis rotation. It is a circular movement around a line horizontal to the viewpoint. Figure 5-4 shows the direction of x-axis rotation.

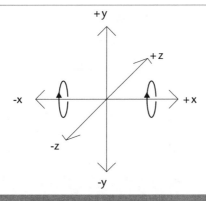

X-axis rotation

Vector3d.rotateX( )

The *rotateX( )* method takes an angle in degrees and rotates the vector around the x-axis:

```
Vector3d.prototype.rotateX = function (angle) {
    with (Math) {
        var ca = cosD (angle);
        var sa = sinD (angle);
    }
    with (this) {
        var tempY = y * ca - z * sa;
        var tempZ = y * sa + z * ca;
        y = tempY;
        z = tempZ;
    }
};
```

Here's a code example:

```
// test Vector3d.rotateX()
p = new Vector3d (1, 4, 7);
p.rotateX (180);
trace (p); // output: [1, -4, -7]
```

NOTE: When you rotate a 3-D point around the x-axis, the x coordinate does not change.

Vector3d.rotateXTrig( )

The *rotateXTrig( )* method performs the same rotation as *rotateX( )*, but takes different parameters. Instead of passing the angle of rotation, you pass the cosine and sine of the angle:

```
Vector3d.prototype.rotateXTrig = function (ca, sa) {
    with (this) {
        var tempY = y * ca - z * sa;
        var tempZ = y * sa + z * ca;
        y = tempY;
        z = tempZ;
    }
};
```

Why would we want to perform rotations this way? The reason for this alternative approach is optimization. Suppose you had a 3-D object composed of 40 points, and you want to perform an x-rotation of that object by 30 degrees. Each point has to be individually rotated by 30 degrees. You could just use the *rotateX( )* method on each vector. However, this is not very efficient. Inside *rotateX( )*, the sine and cosine of 30 degrees is calculated. Since these values are the same for all 40 points, the calculation is repeated 40 times, needlessly. What we can do instead, is calculate the sine and cosine of 30 degrees *first*, then pass them to the *rotateXTrig( )* method. In my testing, this more efficient approach resulted in a 20 percent increase in frame rate.

The following example shows how this process works. First, a new point p is created. Then the cosine and sine for 180 degrees are calculated, and stored in the variables `cosAngle` and `sinAngle`. These values are passed to the *rotateXTrig( )* method of p, causing it to rotate by 180 degrees about the x-axis.

```
// test Vector3d.rotateXTrig()
p = new Vector3d (1, 4, 7);
cosAngle = Math.cosD (180);
sinAngle = Math.sinD (180);
p.rotateXTrig (cosAngle, sinAngle);
trace (p); // output: [1, -4, -7]
```

Again, *Math.cosD( )* and *Math.sinD( )* are my custom functions. You could easily use the standard *Math.cos( )* and *Math.sin( )* instead. For instance, you could specify the rotation angle using π radians instead of 180 degrees, like this:

```
cosAngle = Math.cos (Math.PI);
sinAngle = Math.sin (Math.PI);
```

Y-axis Rotation

To keep with the carnival motif, if you've ever ridden on a merry-go-round, you've experienced y-axis rotation. It is a circular movement around a line vertical to the viewpoint. Figure 5-5 shows the direction of y-axis rotation.

Vector3d.rotateY( )

The *rotateY( )* method takes an angle in degrees and rotates the vector around the y-axis:

```
Vector3d.prototype.rotateY = function (angle) {
    var ca = Math.cosD (angle);
    var sa = Math.sinD (angle);
    var tempX = this.x * ca + this.z * sa;
    var tempZ = this.x * -sa + this.z * ca;
    this.x = tempX;
    this.z = tempZ;
};
```

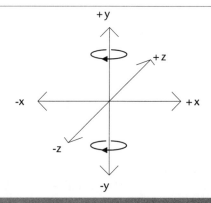

FIGURE 5-5

Y-axis rotation

Here's a code example:

```
// test Vector3d.rotateY()
p = new Vector3d (1, 4, 7);
p.rotateY (180);
trace (p); // output: [-1, 4, -7]
```

NOTE: The y coordinate does not change during a y-axis rotation.

Vector3d.rotateYTrig( )

The *rotateYTrig( )* method performs the same rotation as *rotateY( )*, but instead of passing the angle of rotation, you pass the cosine and sine of the angle:

```
Vector3d.prototype.rotateYTrig = function (ca, sa) {
    with (this) {
        var tempX = x * ca + z * sa;
        var tempZ = x * -sa + z * ca;
        x = tempX;
        z = tempZ;
    }
};
```

Here's a code example for *rotateYTrig( )*:

```
// test Vector3d.rotateYTrig()
p = new Vector3d (3, -8, 5);
cosAngle = Math.cosD (90);
sinAngle = Math.sinD (90);
p.rotateYTrig (cosAngle, sinAngle);
trace (p); // output: [5, -8, -3]
```

Z-axis Rotation

If you've ever watched a hamster running in its little wheel, you have witnessed z-axis rotation. It is a circular movement around a line coming out from the viewpoint. Figure 5-6 shows the direction of z-axis rotation.

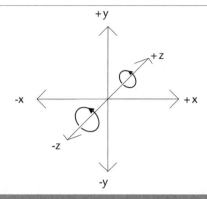

Z-axis rotation

Vector3d.rotateZ( )

The *rotateZ( )* method takes an angle in degrees and rotates the vector around the z-axis:

```
Vector3d.prototype.rotateZ = function (angle) {
    with (Math) {
        var ca = cosD (angle);
        var sa = sinD (angle);
    }
    with (this) {
        var tempX = x * ca - y * sa;
        var tempY = x * sa + y * ca;
        x = tempX;
        y = tempY;
    }
};
```

This example creates a 3-D point and rotates it around the z-axis by 180 degrees:

```
// test Vector3d.rotateZ()
p = new Vector3d (1, 4, 7);
p.rotateZ (180);
trace (p); // output: [-1, -4, 7]
```

NOTE: The *z* coordinate does not change during a z-axis rotation.

Vector3d.rotateZTrig( )

The *rotateZTrig( )* method uses the following code to rotate the vector:

```
Vector3d.prototype.rotateZTrig = function (ca, sa) {
    with (this) {
        var tempX = x * ca - y * sa;
        var tempY = x * sa + y * ca;
        x = tempX;
        y = tempY;
    }
};
```

This example uses *rotateZTrig( )* to rotate a point around the z-axis by 45 degrees:

```
// test Vector3d.rotateZTrig()
p = new Vector3d (6, 1, 4);
cosAngle = Math.cosD (45);
sinAngle = Math.sinD (45);
p.rotateZTrig (cosAngle, sinAngle);
trace (p); // output: [3.536, 4.95, 4]
```

Vector3d.rotateXY( )

If you want to rotate a *Vector3d* object around the x and y axes at the same time, you can use the *rotateXY( )* method:

```
Vector3d.prototype.rotateXY = function (a, b) {
    with (Math) {
        var ca = cosD (a), sa = sinD (a);
        var cb = cosD (b), sb = sinD (b);
    }
    with (this) {
        // x-axis rotation
        y = y * ca - z * sa;
        var rz1 = y * sa + z * ca;
        // y-axis rotation
        z = x * -sb + rz1 * cb;
```

```
        x = x * cb + rz1 * sb;
    }
};
```

This example shows how to create a point and rotate it 45 degrees along the x and y axes:

```
// test Vector3d.rotateXY()
p = new Vector3d (8, 0, 0);
p.rotateXY (45, 45);
trace (p); // output: [5.657, 0, -5.657]
```

Vector3d.rotateXYTrig( )

The *rotateXYTrig( )* method rotates around two axes using precalculated sine and cosine values:

```
Vector3d.prototype.rotateXYTrig = function (ca, sa, cb, sb) {
    with (this) {
        // x-axis rotation
        var rz = y * sa + z * ca;
        y = y * ca - z * sa;
        // y-axis rotation
        z = x * -sb + rz * cb;
        x = x * cb + rz * sb;
    }
};
```

See similar preceding methods such as *rotateXTrig( )* for usage examples.

Vector3d.rotateXYZ( )

If you want to rotate a *Vector3d* object around all three axes at once, you can use the *rotateXYZ( )* method:

```
Vector3d.prototype.rotateXYZ = function (a, b, c) {
    with (Math) {
        var ca = cosD (a), sa = sinD (a);
        var cb = cosD (b), sb = sinD (b);
        var cc = cosD (c), sc = sinD (c);
    }
    with (this) {
        // x-axis rotation
        var ry = y * ca - z * sa;
```

```
        var rz = y * sa + z * ca;
        // y-axis rotation
        var rx = x * cb + rz * sb;
        z = x * -sb + rz * cb;
        // z-axis rotation
        x = rx * cc - ry * sc;
        y = rx * sc + ry * cc;
    }
};
```

As you can see, full three-axis rotation is an involved procedure, invoking three sine calculations, three cosines, and twelve multiplications. I have optimized this method for performance wherever I can, eliminating unnecessary operations. For example, since the sines and cosines are used repeatedly, I store them in variables so they don't have to be recalculated.

This example shows how to create a point and rotate it 45 degrees along all three axes:

```
// test Vector3d.rotateXYZ()
p = new Vector3d (8, 0, 0);
p.rotateXYZ (45, 45, 45);
trace (p); // output: [4, 4, -5.657]
```

Vector3d.rotateXYZTrig( )

The *rotateXYZTrig( )* method returns a new *Vector3d* object that has been rotated around all three axes:

```
Vector3d.prototype.rotateXYZTrig = function (ca, sa, cb, sb, cc, sc) {
    with (this) {
        // x-axis rotation
        var ry = y * ca - z * sa;
        var rz = y * sa + z * ca;
        // y-axis rotation
        var rx = x * cb + rz * sb;
        z = x * -sb + rz * cb;
        // z-axis rotation
        x = rx * cc - ry * sc;
        y = rx * sc + ry * cc;
    }
};
```

Again, similar preceding methods, such as *rotateXTrig( )*, for usage examples.

Plotting 3-D Particles

We now have a *Vector3d* class which encapsulates 3-D entities, with methods that provide a powerful and convenient means of manipulating these entities. A *Vector3d* object contains pure 3-D information: three numbers. Its abstract nature is beneficial because it allows the class to be used in many different scenarios.

However, it may not be obvious how to apply *Vector3d* in Flash in a practical manner. It's nice to have three numbers *x, y,* and *z,* but we want to do something *visual* with them. What we need is a way to connect *Vector3d* data to graphical elements—in Flash, that means movie clips.

The Particle3d Class

I created a custom ActionScript class called *Particle3d*. This is a template for an object that contains both 3-D coordinates and graphics. A *Particle3d* object is not itself a movie clip. It is a code object, which can attach and manipulate a movie clip by reference, like a remote control. Here is the code for the *Particle3d* constructor:

```
_global.Particle3d = function (x, y, z, timeline, mcID, depth) {
    this.position = new Vector3d (x, y, z);
    this.timeline = timeline;
    this.mc = this.attachGraphic (mcID, depth);
    this.scale = 100;
    this.render();
}
```

Here's how the constructor function operates. First, a new *Vector3d* is created to represent the particle's 3-D location:

```
this.position = new Vector3d (x, y, z);
```

The x, y, and z arguments are copied to the new *Vector3d* instance, which is stored in the this.position property.

In the next line of code, a property this.timeline is created:

```
this.timeline = timeline;
```

This is a reference to the movie clip which contains this particular *Particle3d* object.

The next step is to attach a movie clip from the library:

```
this.mc = this.attachGraphic (mcID, depth);
```

The `mcID` and `depth` arguments are passed to the *attachGraphic( )* method, and a reference to the new instance is returned. The reference is then stored in the property `this.mc`, which is hereafter used like a remote control to change the particle's appearance. The inner workings of the *attachGraphic( )* method will be explained shortly.

In the next line, the `scale` property is initialized to 100. This is the "real size" of the object, which is independent of how large or small it may appear in the viewport. And finally, the *render( )* method is called to project an initial view of this 3-D object onto the screen.

The following example shows how to call the *Particle3d* constructor:

```
pointA = new Particle3d (50, -30, 20, this, "dot", 1);
```

Looking at the parameters passed to the constructor, we see that the *Particle3d* object is given an initial position of [50, -30, 20]. The timeline controlled by the object is `this`, the current movie clip, in which this code resides. The next parameter "dot" names the linkage ID of the movie clip in the library that will be used to represent the particle. And in the final parameter, the particle is given a depth of 1.

Once a *Particle3d* instance is initialized, you can play with it by changing the object's `position` property. You can call its *Vector3d* methods, like *plus( )* or *rotateXY( )*, and then call the particle's *render( )* method to update the screen. In the following example, `pointA` is rotated 5 degrees about the x-axis, and then rendered:

```
pointA.position.rotateX (5); // rotate the position vector
pointA.render(); // update the screen
```

Animation can be easily produced by putting this code in a frame loop (as we will see in the Particle Wall example).

Particle3d.attachGraphic( )

The *attachGraphic( )* method creates a new movie clip instance to represent the particle. Here is the code:

```
Particle3d.prototype.attachGraphic = function (mcID, depth) {
    return this.timeline.attachMovie (mcID,
                                      mcID + "_" + depth,
                                      depth);
};
```

The first parameter, `mcID`, specifies the linkage ID for the library symbol, while the `depth` parameter controls the layering of the new movie clip instance. Both parameters are passed to *attachMovie( )*, which attaches the graphic to the movie clip referenced by `this.timeline`. The attached clip is given a name combining `mcID` and `depth`, and a reference to it is returned from the function.

NOTE: In Flash MX, the *MovieClip* methods *attachMovie( )*, *duplicateMovieClip( )*, and *createEmptyMovieClip( )* return references to the movie clips they create. Since this is not mentioned in the Flash manual, this could be considered an undocumented feature.

Particle3d.render( )

The *render( )* method updates the particle's visual representation to match its current status. Here is its code:

```
Particle3d.prototype.render = function () {
    var pos = this.position;
    var pers = this.position.getPerspective();
    this.screenPos = pos.persProjectNew (pers);
    with (this.mc) {
        _x = this.screenPos.x;
        _y = -this.screenPos.y;
        _xscale = _yscale = this.scale * pers;
        swapDepths (100000 - pos.z * 100)
    }
};
```

First, the perspective factor `pers` is found using the *getPerspective( )* method of the vector `this.position`. The `pers` value is passed to the *persProjectNew( )* method, which calculates the projection of `this.position` onto the screen. This projected vector is stored in `this.screenPos`. Having a *z* component of 0, `this.screenPos` is essentially a two-dimensional vector, and represents a point on the two-dimensional screen.

The last section of *render( )* manipulates the particle's movie clip `this.mc`. First, the scope is set to that movie clip using `with (this.mc)`. The clip is then moved to new _x and _y coordinates. Since `this.screenPos` stores Cartesian coordinates, the y value is flipped before being assigned to _y. Then the size of `this.mc` is changed to give the appearance of depth. New values of _xscale and _yscale are calculated by multiplying the `this.scale` property by the perspective factor `pers`.

And finally, z-sorting is implemented by using *swapDepths( )*. The z coordinate of `this.position` determines the depth of the particle. When *z* is larger, the point is farther away, and should appear behind closer objects. In Flash's stacking system, graphics at higher depth numbers obscure lower ones. Thus, the z value must be subtracted from a large number to achieve the desired layering. Also, since the z value is a decimal number, but depth numbers are all integers, it helps to scale z (by a factor of 100 in this case). This avoids a z-sorting glitch where objects that are close together change depths erratically.

Example: the Particle Wall

To test the *Particle3d* class, I set up a simple example movie that creates a wall of particles. The idea is to arrange movie clips in rows and columns, defining a rectangular grid, and have it rotated in three dimensions by the mouse. Figure 5-7 shows how the particle wall appears during an x-axis rotation, and Figure 5-8 shows the particle wall during a y-axis rotation.

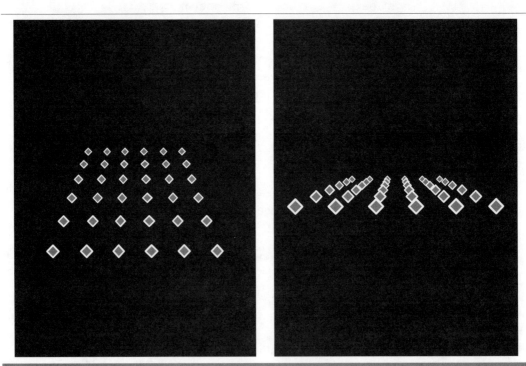

FIGURE 5-7

The particle wall rotating around the x-axis

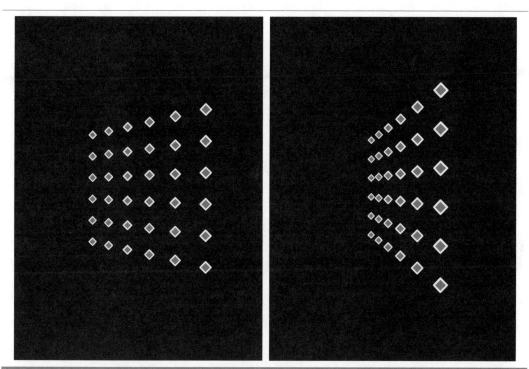

FIGURE 5-8

The particle wall rotating around the y-axis

Setup

First of all, we need to include our code libraries. The *Particle3d* class depends on the *Vector3d* class, which in turn uses my custom trigonometric degrees functions. I've included all three libraries in the first frame of the main timeline with this code:

```
#include "trig_functions_degrees.as"
#include "vector3d_class.as"
#include "particle3d_class_simple.as"
```

Also, I created a *viewport* movie clip to hold the animation, for two reasons. First, I try not to have many movie clips directly on the _root timeline, just as I don't like individual files in the root folder of my hard drive. Second, the *viewport* clip allows me to position my (0, 0) point, the origin, in the middle of the screen. This movie is 400×300, so the *viewport* movie clip is placed at (200, 150). The *viewport* clip doesn't contain any graphics at design-time, just code. But we'll attach other clips to it at run time.

The getWallPoints( ) Function

Inside viewport, I have a *functions* layer containing two functions. The first one is *getWallPoints( )*, which creates an array of points defining a wall:

```
function getWallPoints (width, height, xDivisions, yDivisions) {
    var x, y, z;
    var pts = new Array();
    var depth = 0;
    for (var i=0; i <= xDivisions; i++) {
        for (var j=0; j <= yDivisions; j++) {
            x = width * (i / xDivisions - .5);
            y = height * (j / yDivisions - .5);
            z = 0;
            pts.push (new Particle3d (x, y, z, this, "dot", depth++));
        }
    }
    return pts;
};
```

The *getWallPoints( )* function takes three arguments. The `width` and `height` parameters define the dimensions of the wall, while the `divisions` argument controls the number of sections in the wall, and thus, the number of points that define it. A wall with two divisions will have three points along each edge, and contain a total of nine points.

Two `for` loops, one nested within the other, place the particles in rows and columns. The algorithm to space out the particles evenly, I found by trial and error:

```
x = width * (i / divisions - .5);
y = height * (j / divisions - .5);
z = 0;
```

This arranges the objects in a nice grid on the *xy* plane. I could have played with the z value, but left it at zero to produce a flat wall.

Once the x, y, and z coordinates have been chosen for a particular point, a new *Particle3d* object is created to represent it visually:

```
pts.push (new Particle3d (x, y, z, this, "dot", depth++));
```

The *Particle3d* constructor is passed six arguments, the first three being the coordinates. The fourth parameter is a reference to the timeline which contains the particle; in our case, it is this movie clip. The next parameter is the symbol ID of the movie clip to attach. I created one called "dot" and set its export linkage in the library. And finally, the depth parameter is passed and incremented in one step, giving each movie clip its own unique depth. When the nested for loops have finished executing, the pts array is complete, and is returned in the final line of the function.

Initializing the Wall

With the *getWallPoints( )* function set up, the particle wall itself is created with a single line of code:

```
wall = getWallPoints (200, 200, 4, 6);
```

The wall variable is now an array of *Particle3d* objects. For this example, I created a square wall, 200 × 200. I chose four divisions horizontally, and six divisions vertically, which translates to 5 × 7 = 35 points in total. Figure 5-9 shows how the particle wall looks from a straight-on view.

Now that we've created the particle wall, we need to rotate it.

The arrayRotateXY( ) Function

In our array of *Particle3d* objects, each particle can be individually rotated by manipulating its position vector property, and then re-rendering:

```
particleA.position.rotateXY (angleX, angleY);
particleA.render();
```

In this example, we call the *rotateXY( )* method of particleA.position, then the *render( )* method of particleA. to update the screen. If we want

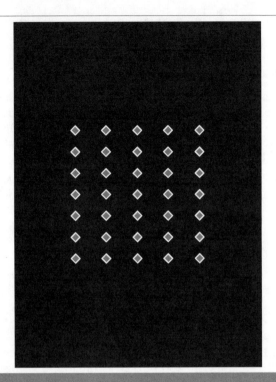

FIGURE 5-9

The particle wall from a stright view

to rotate the whole array of particles, though, we need to loop through the array and call the methods on each element in turn.

This kind of task is best encapsulated in a function, so I created *arrayRotateXY( )*, which rotates any array of *Particle3d* objects around the x and y axes:

```
function arrayRotateXY (particleArr, angleX, angleY) {
    var i = particleArr.length;
    while (i--) {
        particleArr[i].position.rotateXY (angleX, angleY);
        particleArr[i].render();
```

```
    }
}
```

The angleX and angleY parameters are given in degrees here. Don't worry if the style of the while loop in this code is unfamiliar to you. I could have used a standard for loop instead, counting forwards like this:

```
for (var i=0; i < particleArr.length; i++) {
```

This is the type of loop you most often see in ActionScript. However, the backwards while loop I used is more efficient; it eliminates unnecessary lookups and comparisons of variables.

With *arrayRotateXY( )*, we have an easy way to rotate the entire wall of particles. Now we just need to animate it.

Animating with onEnterFrame

Creating animation with frame loops is a joy in Flash MX. You simply define a function, assign it to the this.onEnterFrame property of a movie clip, and you're off to the races. In our case, we want to call our *arrayRotateXY( )* function every frame. I created an anonymous function that calls the rotation function, and assigned it to the *onEnterFrame( )* handler, as shown next:

```
this.onEnterFrame = function () {
      this.arrayRotateXY (wall, _ymouse / 20, _xmouse / 20);
};
```

Inside the event handler function *onEnterFrame( )*, we call arrayRotateXY( ) and pass it three parameters. The first is our array of particles: wall. The other two arguments are the angles of rotation about the x and y axes. Through experimentation, I decide I like the feel of having the *x* angle controlled by _ymouse, and the *y* angle controlled by _xmouse. Dividing the mouse coordinates by 20 gives a good range of rotation speed.

Conclusion

In this chapter, we've built upon previous math concepts and extended vectors into the third dimension. We now have a powerful and object-oriented code library, which can be used in various 3-D graphics projects. We've also looked at a simple example of how to connect the *Vector3d* class to visual elements, thereby creating a rotating, interactive 3-D object. In the next chapter, we'll complete our foundational series of concepts by exploring event-based programming principles and Flash MX's new event model.

Chapter 6

Event-Based Programming

You may have heard that Flash MX has a "new event model." What does this mean? This chapter will show you how events in Flash 5 can be handled in new ways in Flash MX. The new event model allows you to create scripted animation much more easily, using clean, object-oriented code. This new style is similar to handlers in JavaScript and Java. If you have invested time learning event handlers in any of these systems, your knowledge will transfer over well. In any case, I think you'll find that the event model in MX event model makes more sense than in Flash 5, and has many practical advantages.

Flash 5's Event Model

Let's start with a quick review of the event model as it was before MX. Flash 5 gives us these movie clip events:

- ❯ *enterFrame*
- ❯ *load*
- ❯ *unload*
- ❯ *mouseDown*
- ❯ *mouseUp*
- ❯ *mouseMove*
- ❯ *keyDown*
- ❯ *keyUp*
- ❯ *data*

These movie clip events are accessed by defining clip event handlers. The `onClipEvent` handler is placed on a movie clip instance, and this is the general syntax:

```
onClipEvent (event) {
    // code
}
```

Flash 5 has events for buttons as well:

> ❯ *press*

> ❯ *release*

> ❯ *releaseOutside*

> ❯ *rollOver*

> ❯ *rollOut*

> ❯ *dragOver*

> ❯ *dragOut*

> ❯ *keyPress*

Button events have their own event handlers, which are similar to those for movie clips. This is the general syntax for button event handlers:

```
on (event) {
    // code
}
```

The main drawback with event handlers in Flash 5 is that you have to attach the code to the outside of a movie clip or button instance. This gives rise to several problems:

> ❯ You can't access `onClipEvent` handlers inside the movie clip in question.

> ❯ You can't directly change or disable the event handlers once the movie is running.

> ❯ You can't attach a movie clip from the library with *attachMovie( )*, and then assign `onClipEvent` handlers to it.

There are various workarounds for these issues, often involving empty movie clips inside other ones, but they can be cumbersome. Thankfully,

Flash MX has a new event model that allows us to work with events much more easily, and in an object-oriented fashion.

Flash MX's Event Model

In Flash MX, an event handler is simply a method of the movie clip or button. For example, the handler for the *onEnterFrame* event for a movie clip mc is mc.onEnterFrame. You can create a frame loop for mc simply by assigning a function to mc.onEnterFrame. The other event handlers introduced in Flash MX are functions as well.

Suppose you have a movie clip named ball that you want to spin with ActionScript. In Flash 5, you would attach the following code to the outside of ball:

```
// code on "ball" instance
onClipEvent (enterFrame) {
    this._rotation += 5;
}
```

This script causes the movie clip's rotation to increase by five degrees every frame. Notice that you can't stop the frame loop from inside the movie clip. Once spinning, always spinning.

In Flash MX's new event model, you can put the code inside the symbol itself. This is how you would do the same thing as shown previously:

```
// code inside "ball" symbol
this.onEnterFrame = function () {
    this._rotation += 5;
};
```

The advantage of this approach is that you can change this.onEnterFrame at any time. If you want the ball to spin the other way, you can change the event handler to a new function:

```
this.onEnterFrame = function () {
    this._rotation -= 5;
};
```

To stop the frame loop altogether, simply delete this.onEnterFrame:

```
delete this.onEnterFrame;
```

Button and Movie Clip Events in Flash MX

In MX, buttons are now true objects, similar to movie clips in many respects. All buttons created at author-time become instances of the *Button* class at run time. Here is the complete list of events for buttons:

❯ *Button.onDragOut*

❯ *Button.onDragOver*

❯ *Button.onKeyDown*

❯ *Button.onKeyUp*

❯ *Button.onKillFocus*

❯ *Button.onPress*

❯ *Button.onRelease*

❯ *Button.onReleaseOutside*

❯ *Button.onRollOut*

❯ *Button.onRollOver*

❯ *Button.onSetFocus*

All of the standard Flash 5 button events have MX equivalents, except for *KeyPress*. There are also new event handlers for focus: *onSetFocus* and *onKillFocus*.

Here is the complete list of movie clip events in Flash MX:

❯ *MovieClip.onData*

❯ *MovieClip.onDragOut*

❯ *MovieClip.onDragOver*

❯ *MovieClip.onEnterFrame*

❯ *MovieClip.onKeyDown*

❯ *MovieClip.onKeyUp*

❯ *MovieClip.onKillFocus*

❯ *MovieClip.onLoad*

❯ *MovieClip.onMouseDown*

❯ *MovieClip.onMouseMove*

❯ *MovieClip.onMouseUp*

> *MovieClip.onPress*

> *MovieClip.onRelease*

> *MovieClip.onReleaseOutside*

> *MovieClip.onRollOut*

> *MovieClip.onRollOver*

> *MovieClip.onSetFocus*

> *MovieClip.onUnload*

Notice that movie clips can now receive button events like *onPress* and *onRollOver*. This means you no longer have to use *hitTest( )* with the *onMouseDown* event to determine if a particular movie clip was clicked, as was done in Flash 5.

Example: MX Glide

MX Glide is a simple example of how to use the new event handlers in Flash MX. I used several movie clip events (*onEnterFrame, onMouseDown, onMouseUp*) as well as some button events (*onPress, onRelease, onRollOver*). You can interact with the ball (see Figure 6-1) using the mouse in different ways. Notice how each event creates a different response.

FIGURE 6-1

An MX Glide screenshot

The "glide" is a common Flash technique that is used to create an ease-out. With a simple bit of code, you can slide a movie clip to a point, making it gradually slow down and stop. In our case, we will make the movie clip glide towards the mouse position. This produces a "chasing" effect when you hold down the mouse and move rapidly.

Here is the core animation function, *glideToMouse( )*:

```
function glideToMouse () {
    this._x += (_parent._xmouse - this._x) * .2;
    this._y += (_parent._ymouse - this._y) * .2;
}
```

The *glideToMouse( )* function finds the horizontal and vertical distances between the movie clip and the mouse position. For example, the horizontal distance is found with _parent._xmouse - this._x. Then the code moves the current movie clip a fraction of that distance towards the mouse—in our case, one fifth (0.2) of the distance.

To start the glide, we create a frame loop by setting the *onEnterFrame* event handler to our gliding function:

```
this.onEnterFrame = this.glideToMouse;
```

Now the *glideToMouse( )* function will be executed once per frame. Notice that here, glideToMouse does not have parentheses ( ) because it is not being *called* in this code. Rather, the function is being *assigned* to the *onEnterFrame* handler. From now on, the *onEnterFrame* handler will call *glideToMouse( )* every frame, automatically.

If we want to stop the glide, we use this simple code:

```
delete this.onEnterFrame;
```

Deleting this.onEnterFrame causes no function to be executed by the event handler, effectively stopping the frame loop.

Now that we know how to start and stop the glide, we connect the mouse event handlers to those commands:

```
this.onMouseDown = function () {
    this.onEnterFrame = this.glideToMouse;
};

this.onMouseUp = function () {
    delete this.onEnterFrame;
};
```

The result: when the mouse button is pressed down, the gliding frame loop is started. When the mouse button is released, the frame loop is stopped.

The last four event handlers inside the ball movie clip are for the button events *onRollOver*, *onPress*, *onRelease*, and *onReleaseOutside*:

```
this.onRollOver = function () {
    this._rotation += 30;
};

this.onPress = function () {
    this._xscale = this._yscale = 120;
};

this.onRelease = function () {
    this._xscale = this._yscale = 100;
};

this.onReleaseOutside = this.onRelease;
```

I kept the commands in each event handler quite simple:

> ❯ The *onRollOver* handler rotates the movie clip by 30 degrees.

> ❯ The *onPress* handler scales the movie clip to 120%.

> ❯ The *onRelease* handler returns the movie clip to 100% scale.

> ❯ The *onReleaseOutside* handler is set to the *onRelease* handler.

You can play around with the event handlers to create different interactions. For example, you could try making the ball fade out on roll over, and fade back in on roll out. Or for an extra challenge, you could define several different behavior functions, similar to *glideToMouse( )*, and randomly assign them to onEnterFrame each time the mouse is pressed.

In Flash MX, the choice is yours—you can use either the old or new approaches to handling events. The Flash 5 event handlers onClipEvent and on are still available, and they aren't deprecated. There are a few situations where the old handlers are still necessary—onClipEvent (load) comes to mind. Nevertheless, because the new event model has so many advantages, I recommend using the Flash MX syntax as much as possible. After a while, you will probably find that your movie clips are more self-contained and your code is more object-oriented as you use the new event handlers.

Listeners

We earlier learned about event handlers, which are the cornerstone of the MX event model. The other main feature of the new event model is listeners. Listeners utilize event handlers, but go beyond them, allowing for more powerful programming structures.

To understand listeners, you first need to understand the difference between time-based and event-based programming. Time-based programming is like buying a magazine from the store every month, whereas event-based is like having it delivered to your door. Let's explore this analogy further.

Time-Based Programming

In time-based programming, an object has to keep checking other objects for changes that may have occurred. This is like buying your favorite magazine from the store every month. You have to check periodically to see if the new issue has arrived. If you want your shiny new mag as soon as it's available, you'll have to check quite often at the end of the month.

In object-oriented terms, imagine that you are represented by a movie clip named me. This movie clip has to check the month property of the magazine object. The magazine belongs to the newsstand, which belongs to the store. Suppose the magazine is *wiredMag*, and April is the next issue. The code to check the newsstand would look something like this:

```
// code inside the me movie clip
// check the newsstand for the April issue
if (store.newsstand.wiredMag.month == 4) {
    this.buy (store.newsstand.wiredMag);
    this.read (store.newsstand.wiredMag);
}
```

> ❱ The me object finds the magazine by navigating the hierarchy of store | newsstand | magazine.

> ❱ The month property of magazine is compared with the number of the new month (4 for April).

> ❱ If the magazine is the new April issue, the person calls its own actions, *this.buy( )* and *this.read( )*, to grab the magazine.

This code covers one check of the newsstand. How would we do this repeatedly? We can easily set up a frame loop with the `onEnterFrame` handler, with this code:

```
// code inside the me movie clip
// check the newsstand for the April issue
// once per frame
this.onEnterFrame = function () {
    if (store.newsstand.wiredMag.month == 4) {
        this.buy (store.newsstand.wiredMag);
        this.read (store.newsstand.wiredMag);
        delete this.onEnterFrame;
    }
};
```

I encased the code in a function and assigned it to `this.onEnterFrame`, causing it to be executed once per frame. I also added one other line of code:

```
delete this.onEnterFrame;
```

This stops the frame loop right after buying the magazine. Since you have the new issue, you don't need to keep checking for it. But what about the month after that? It won't be long before you'll have to start another loop to check for the new issue again.

Surely there's a more efficient way to do this. After all, checking the newsstand time and again would get tiresome after a while. How many months would it take before you decided to just subscribe to the magazine? Because of this, subscriptions are at the heart of event-based programming and listeners.

Event-Based Programming

When you move from time-based to event-based programming, there is a shifting of responsibility. In event-based programming, it's no longer your job to keep checking for new events. Instead, you tell another object to subscribe you to its events. This object is the event source, and you are a listener. You *listen* for events from the event source.

In our example, the magazine company is the event source—let's call it `wiredCo`. When you buy a `wiredMag` subscription, you become a listener for events from `wiredCo`. As a result, you need to give it your address so it knows where to contact you when an event occurs.

The code to subscribe to `wiredCo` events looks like this:

```
// code inside the me movie clip
// subscribe to wiredCo events
wiredCo.addListener (this);
```

This short piece of code achieves the following results:

> ❭ The `wiredCo` event source object is contacted, and asked to add you as a listener, using its *addListener( )* method.

> ❭ Your address is sent to `wiredCo` by passing the reference `this`.

> ❭ The `wiredCo` object stores your address in its internal list of subscribers.

> ❭ When an event occurs, `wiredCo` will look up the addresses of its subscribers and sends each one a message. This is called event broadcasting.

Now that you've subscribed to an event source as a listener, you need to decide how you're going to handle incoming events. The event that `wiredCo` uses happens to be called *onNewMag*. Thus, you need to set up a method with the same name. This *onNewMag( )* function is called an event handler. We define it with the following code:

```
// code inside the me movie clip
// define an event handler
this.onNewMag = function (mag) {
    this.read (mag);
};
```

As a result, the following has been accomplished:

1. The `wiredCo` object will invoke the *onNewMag( )* method when that event occurs.

2. It passes one argument, `mag`, an object representing the magazine.

3. The `mag` object is passed to the *this.read( )* method.

That's it—now you can sit back and let the magazines come to you automatically. This is quite a nice arrangement. Once you've (a) defined event handler(s) and (b) subscribed as a listener, you don't have to do any more work. The system is in place, and the event source is in control.

NOTE: It's a good idea to define event handlers first *before* subscribing as a listener, since you want to be ready in case the event comes in immediately.

Listening to MX Objects

Flash MX has several built-in objects and classes that can act as event sources: *Key, Mouse, Stage, Selection,* and *Textfield.* Each has an *addListener( )* method, which subscribes a listener for events from that object. Table 6-1 summarizes the event subscription methods for each of these.

In MX, movie clips are automatically subscribed to *Key* and *Mouse* events. For example, a movie clip's *onMouseDown( )* event handler is automatically called when the mouse is pressed. However, this isn't the case for custom code objects. However, you can make an object listen to the mouse by using *Mouse.addListener( ).* Here is a code example you can try:

```
// make a code object listen for Mouse events
obj = new Object();
obj.onMouseDown = function () { trace ("obj received mouseDown"); };
obj.onMouseUp = function () { trace ("obj received mouseUp"); };
obj.onMouseMove = function () { trace ("obj received mouseMove"); };
Mouse.addListener (obj);
```

As you move and click the mouse, you can see the results of the interaction in the output window, as the code object `obj` reacts to the mouse events. Movie clips listen to mouse events automatically, but code objects must have *Mouse.addListener( )* invoked on them in order to start listening to these events.

Example: Listening to a TextField

Text fields in MX are instances of the *TextField* class. They are much more powerful than in Flash 5. Among other things, a *TextField* can broadcast

Event Subscription Method	Result
`Key.addListener (obj)`	subscribes `obj` to *onKeyDown* and *onKeyUp* events
`Mouse.addListener (obj)`	subscribes `obj` to *onMouseDown, onMouseMove,* and *onMouseUp* events
`Selection.addListener (obj)`	subscribes `obj` to the *onSetFocus* event
`Stage.addListener (obj)`	subscribes `obj` to the *onResize* event
`myTextField.addListener (obj)`	subscribes `obj` to *onChanged* and *onScroller* events from `myTextField`

TABLE 6-1

The addListener( ) Methods of Built-in Event Sources

events to listeners. Figure 6-2 is a screenshot of a simple demonstration of this. The triangle movie clip is affected when the text field is changed or scrolled.

The text field is on the main timeline, and has an instance name of *infoText*. The triangle movie clip's response to *infoText* is produced by these few lines of code:

```
// code inside triangle movie clip
this.onChanged = function () {
    this._yscale += 10;
};

this.onScroller = function () {
    this._rotation += 10;
};

_parent.infoText.addListener (this);
```

Here again, we see the two steps for subscribing to events: defining event handler(s) and subscribing as a listener.

In this case, there are two event handlers, because there are two events coming from the text field: *onChanged* and *onScroller*. Let's look first at the *onChanged* event handler:

```
this.onChanged = function () {
    this._yscale += 10;
};
```

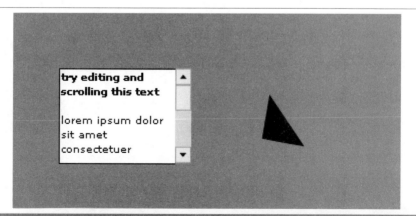

FIGURE 6-2

A text field broadcasting events to a movie clip

With this setup, the *onChanged* event causes the movie clip to stretch vertically—whenever you type in the text field.

```
this.onScroller = function () {
    this._rotation += 10;
};
```

The *onScroller* event handler, meanwhile, is called when the text field is scrolled, prompting the triangle to rotate by 10 degrees.

With the event handlers in place, the last step is to subscribe the movie clip to the text field's events:

```
_parent.infoText.addListener (this);
```

The *infoText* object adds the movie clip as a listener, and we're all set.

One-to-Many Broadcasting

The preceding example is purposely quite simple: one object listens to one other object. However, event-based programming shows its true prowess when you have multiple objects listening. An object can listen to more than one event source. Conversely, an event source can broadcast to many listeners. Figure 6-3 shows the modified example, with multiple triangle listeners.

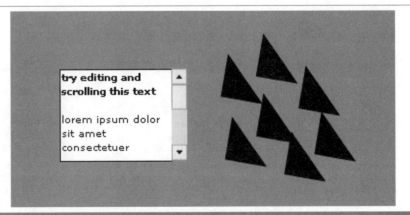

FIGURE 6-3

Broadcasting text field events to multiple listeners

It takes a mere ten seconds to turn the first example into this one. The triangle and its code are nicely self-contained, so you can just throw more copies onto the stage. Each instance will automatically register itself with *infoText* as a listener. As a result, when the *onChanged* and *onScroller* events occur, the text field notifies all of the triangles.

This is an example of one-to-many broadcasting with listeners. The core concept is not really that complicated, but it is extremely powerful. Event-based programming has revolutionized the way I program in ActionScript. I now think much more in terms of events, and responding to them. Increasingly, I'm making my own event sources, using custom classes. For now, get familiar with the different event sources supplied in Flash MX, listed in the earlier table. In the next section, we'll look at how you can create your own event sources, which can add listeners and broadcast messages.

Built-In Event Sources

We saw previously that various built-in Flash objects are event sources. For instance, the *Mouse* object broadcasts the events *onMouseDown, onMouseUp,* and *onMouseMove*. The *Mouse* object has *addListener( )* and *removeListener( )* methods, which subscribe objects to its events. A listening object should have event handler methods, such as *onMouseDown( ),* which respond to the events emanating from *Mouse.*

Digging Deeper

At this point, we may ask: how does *Mouse* broadcast its events? And is it possible for us to broadcast our own events in the same manner?

It turns out that *Mouse* has a semi-hidden, undocumented method called *broadcastMessage( ).* We can verify this with the following code:

```
trace (typeof Mouse.broadcastMessage); // output: function
```

There is also an array hidden in *Mouse,* called _listeners:

```
trace (Mouse._listeners instanceof Array); // output: true
```

The preceding code shows that Mouse._listeners is an instance of the *Array* class. Whenever you add a listener to *Mouse,* it is stored in Mouse._listeners. We can test this by adding _level0 as a listener, as in the following code:

```
Mouse.addListener (_level0);
trace (Mouse._listeners); // output: _level0
```

Here we see that `Mouse._listeners` contains one element: a reference to the movie clip _level0.

The *Key*, *Selection*, and *Stage* objects also add listeners and broadcast events. If we do similar detective work on them as with *Mouse*, we find these objects have the same hidden features:

```
trace (typeof Key.broadcastMessage); // output: function
trace (Key._listeners instanceof Array); // output: true
// same results can be found for Selection and Stage
```

Core Capabilities of Event Sources

Let's generalize from these results. If a built-in object *obj* is an event source, it has the following methods and properties:

1. *obj.addListener( )*

2. *obj.removeListener( )*

3. *obj.broadcastMessage( )*

4. `obj._listeners`

   This makes perfect sense. After all, an event source needs to do four key things:

1. Subscribe an object

2. Unsubscribe an object

3. Send a message to all subscribers

4. Keep a list of subscribers

   These four behaviors correspond to the three methods and one property listed previously. But just how do the built-in event sources gain these capabilities? Read on.

ASBroadcaster

Flash detectives on the *Flashcoders* list discovered an undocumented global object called *ASBroadcaster*. You can dig it up yourself with this snippet of code:

```
ASSetPropFlags (_global, null, 8, 1);
for (var i in _global) trace (i);
```

This will spit out an intriguing list of objects and functions like *NetStream*, *MMSave*, and yes, *ASBroadcaster*.

NOTE: The *ASSetPropFlags( )* command is another undocumented feature, which is used here to "unhide" an object's properties. For more information, see the Flashcoders Wiki page: http://chattyfig.figleaf.com/flashcoders-wiki/index.php?ASSetPropFlags.

We can list all of *ASBroadcaster*'s methods and properties with this code:

```
ASSetPropFlags (ASBroadcaster, null, 8, 1);
for (var i in ASBroadcaster) trace (i);
```

This list is then sent to the Output window:

```
// ASBroadcaster properties and methods
initialize
removeListener
addListener
broadcastMessage
prototype
__proto__
constructor
```

The last three properties on the preceding list are standard issue for objects, but the first four look interesting. We have *addListener( )* and *removeListener( )*, as well as a new method *initialize( )*. What might *ASBroadcaster.initialize( )* do?

Initializing an Event Source

To answer that last question, let's try *ASBroadcaster.initialize( )* on a generic object, and see what happens.

```
obj = new Object();
ASBroadcaster.initialize (obj);
```

Did the makeup of the object change at all? We can list its properties with a for..in loop:

```
for (var i in obj) trace (i); // output: [nothing]
```

Hmm... It appears that `obj` has no properties. Or does it? Let's try our *ASSetPropFlags( )* trick to unearth any properties that might be trying to hide:

```
ASSetPropFlags (obj, null, 8, 1);
for (var i in obj) trace (i);
```

We get this output:

```
_listeners
removeListener
addListener
broadcastMessage
__constructor__
constructor
__proto__
```

NOTE: The hidden __constructor__ property is one of the more exotic undocumented features. I discuss its role in Flash MX inheritance in Chapter 2.

Those first four properties are exactly what we want to see:

1. _listeners

2. removeListener

3. addListener

4. broadcastMessage

Apparently, *ASBroadcaster.initialize( )* has bestowed upon `obj` the four key characteristics of an event source. In a superhero movie, this would be the scene where an unsuspecting, ordinary guy is bitten by some sort of mutant/radioactive animal and gains that animal's powers.

In a similar way, we can "bite" objects with *ASBroadcaster.initialize( )* to transform them from mild-mannered milquetoasts into powerful, event-radiating über-objects. It just takes one line of code:

```
ASBroadcaster.initialize (obj);
```

Now we can start adding and removing listeners, which we have already learned how to do. But what about sending the events—how does that work?

Broadcasting Events

An ActionScript event source uses its *broadcastMessage( )* method (copied from *ASBroadcaster*) to notify its listeners of events. The following is the syntax for *broadcastMessage( )*:

```
obj.broadcastMessage (handlerName[, arg1, arg2, ..., argn]);
```

The `handlerName` parameter is a string that names the listener's event handler method, such as "onMouseDown" or "onKeyUp." The *broadcastMessage( )* method loops through all the listeners in the `_listeners` array, and calls the event handler for each. The other parameters `arg1`, `arg2`, and so on are optional arguments you can pass to the listener's event handler.

For example, suppose we have a `mouth` event source. It broadcasts a "speak" event, passing a "words" string as a parameter. The event would be sent like this:

```
mouth.broadcastMessage ("onSpeak", "hey you");
```

If we have an `ear` object listening for events from `mouth`, it would have an *onSpeak( )* event handler:

```
ear.onSpeak = function (words) {
    trace (words); // output: hey you
};
```

Here is the complete code for this small broadcasting scenario:

```
mouth = new Object();
ASBroadcaster.initialize (mouth);

ear = new Object();
```

```
ear.onSpeak = function (message) {
    trace (message);
};


mouth.addListener (ear);
mouth.broadcastMessage ("onSpeak", "hey you");
```

The following constitutes the steps in the preceding code:

1. Create the event source object: `mouth`

2. Initialize the event source with *ASBroadcaster.initialize( )*

3. Create a listener object: `ear`

4. Add an event handler: *onSpeak( )*

5. Register the listener: *mouth.addListener( )*

6. Broadcast the event: *mouth.broadcastMessage( )*

These six steps comprise the basic process of creating an event source and listeners, and broadcasting events.

The NewsFeed Event Source

Let's look at an example of a custom, object-oriented event source. Event sources will often be custom objects that belong to a class. For example, text fields are instances of the *TextField* class, and are event sources. (As mentioned previously, text fields broadcast *onChanged* and *onScroller* events.)

We will design a *NewsFeed* class—a template for a simple event source. Other objects can receive the news feed by subscribing as listeners. When a news item comes in, the news feed sends a headline, short summary, and a URL to each subscriber. The feed also sends a reference to itself, so the listener knows the source of the news.

NewsFeed Constructor

As usual, the code for the class begins with the constructor. The *NewsFeed* constructor is simple:

```
_global.NewsFeed = function (name) {
    this.name = name;
};
```

We stick the constructor in `_global` for easy access. The function's one parameter, `name`, is a string. We copy `name` into the `this.name` property of the news feed object. Next, we'll add methods to give *NewsFeed* objects some abilities.

NewsFeed.toString( )

It's useful to code a custom *toString( )* method, which returns a string representation of the object:

```
NewsFeed.prototype.toString = function () {
    return this.name;
};
```

Now the name of the news feed will be returned when we use *trace( )* on the object. This will come into play later.

N O T E :   Without this custom *toString( )*, a *trace( )* on a *NewsFeed* instance would return [object Object].

Initializing with ASBroadcaster

To turn an object into an event source, we use *ASBroadcaster.initialize( )* on it. With a class, the question is, what is the proper object to operate on? Should we initialize each instance? If so, that would mean putting *ASBroadcaster* in the constructor, as in the following code:

```
// hypothetical constructor
_global.NewsFeed = function (name) {
    this.name = name;
    ASBroadcaster.initialize (this);
};
```

This would do the job. The *NewsFeed* instance would gain the `_listeners` array and the three methods *addListener( )*, *removeListener( )*, and *broadcastMessage( )*. However, this isn't very efficient—each instance has its own copy of the methods. An ActionScript class should be designed to keep common methods in the prototype object.

What we can do instead is initialize the prototype object itself this way:

```
ASBroadcaster.initialize (NewsFeed.prototype);
```

Notice that this code is executed *outside* the constructor. Thus, it is run once per class, not once per instance. It adds three methods to `NewsFeed.prototype`. Our class now has the following methods:

> *NewsFeed.prototype.toString( )*

> *NewsFeed.prototype.addListener( )*

> *NewsFeed.prototype.removeListener( )*

> *NewsFeed.prototype.broadcastMessage( )*

NOTE: As Casper Schuirink has discovered, this approach—`ASBroadcaster.initialize` (`Class.prototype`)—is used by Flash internally when it first sets up the *TextField* class.

Revising the Constructor

As a result of the *ASBroadcaster.initialize( )* operation, we also have a `_listeners` array in `NewsFeed.prototype`. Unlike the methods for adding and removing listeners, we don't want to share this `_listeners` property among the instances. We want each individual news feed to have its *own* list of subscribers. So each object should have its own `_listeners` array.

Thus, we need to modify the *NewsFeed* constructor to declare a `_listeners` array for the instance:

```
_global.NewsFeed = function (name) {
    this.name = name;
    this._listeners = new Array();
};
```

Now each news feed will maintain its own array of listeners. As a result, the `_listeners` property in `NewsFeed.prototype`, created automatically by *ASBroadcaster.initialize( )*, will simply be overridden and ignored.

The NewsFeed.sendNews( ) Method

We're finally ready to broadcast something. We could let the end user (the ActionScript developer) call the *broadcastMessage( )* directly as a *NewsFeed* method. However, it would be more convenient (and encapsulated) to wrap *broadcastMessage( )* in a customized *sendNews( )* method:

```
NewsFeed.prototype.sendNews = function (headline, summary, url) {
    this.broadcastMessage ("onNews", this, headline, summary, url);
};
```

The method is passed three arguments. The `headline`, `summary`, and `url` arguments are all strings. Internally, *sendNews( )* broadcasts the news item to the *onNews* handlers of the listeners, using *broadcastMessage( )*. It passes four parameters to *onNews( )*: the three supplied arguments, and `this`, a reference to the news feed object itself.

Here is an example of how we would call the *sendNews( )* method:

```
myNewsFeed.sendNews ("The End is Near", "Magma will cover the Earth",
"http://drevil.com");
```

A listener's *onNews( )* event handler would look like this:

```
myListener.onNews = function (source, headline, summary, url) {
    // do something with the news
};
```

The *onNews( )* methods of different listeners will follow this basic structure. However, their responses to the news can vary greatly, as we'll see.

Setting Up the System

As we saw previously, there are six basic steps for creating an event-based system in ActionScript:

1. Create the event source object

2. Initialize the event source with *ASBroadcaster.initialize( )*

3. Create a listener object

4. Define event handlers for the listener

5. Register the listener

6. Broadcast the event

We have already covered Step 2 on the list—initializing the event source. But it has only been done at the class level. We need to create an instance.

Creating the Event Source Object

Next, we create the event source object, an instance of our *NewsFeed* class. Let's create a feed for the *National Press* this way:

```
natPress = new NewsFeed ("National Press");
```

Why don't we run a quick test of the *NewsFeed.toString( )* method by tracing the object:

```
trace (natPress); // output: "National Press"
```

The name of the news feed is returned, so it appears the method is functioning correctly.

Creating Listener Objects

We'll create two listener objects for this example, with the following code:

```
NABC = new Object();
AICN = new Object();
```

NABC and AICN are two news services that use stories from the *National Press* news feed.

For this example, these listeners will start as simple, generic objects. In a real project, it would be beneficial to have objects defined by a particular class, having a variety of properties and methods. To keep things simple here, we'll add just one method to each object, and no properties.

Defining Event Handlers

For Step 4, each listener needs an *onNews( )* handler to respond to the news feed's messages. We have already decided that the event will be sent with four parameters: source, headline, summary, and url. Therefore, we can start out the handler methods like this:

```
NABC.onNews = function (source, headline, summary, url)
AICN.onNews = function (source, headline, summary, url)
```

Thus, both event handlers receive the same information. However, each listener will format the news with its own template. NABC delivers its news in a calm style:

```
NABC.onNews = function (source, headline, summary, url) {
    trace ("----- NABC News -----");
    trace ("> " + headline + " <");
    trace (summary);
    trace (">> " + url);
```

```
    trace ("[via " + source + "]");
    trace ("--");
};
```

AICN, on the other hand, likes to spice up the headlines a little:

```
AICN.onNews = function (source, headline, summary, url) {
    trace ("///// Ain't It Crazy News /////");
    trace ("Unbelievable!!");
    trace (headline + "!!!");
    trace (source + " reports: '" + summary + "'");
    trace ("Read the rest of the incredible story here:");
    trace (url);
    trace ("//");
};
```

Registering the Listeners

With the listeners and their event handlers created, we move to Step 5—registering them with the event source:

```
natPress.addListener (NABC);
natPress.addListener (AICN);
```

NABC and AICN are now listening to events from natPress. If we check the natPress._listeners array, we can view our objects:

```
trace (natPress._listeners);
```

Broadcasting the Event

We're finally at the sixth and final step—triggering the event to send the news. The *NewsFeed.sendNews( )* method we defined takes three arguments: headline, summary, and url. We call *natPress.sendNews( )* and pass strings for each of these:

```
natPress.sendNews ( "Marcosoft buys Murkimedia",
    "After months of secret negotiations, Marcosoft absorbs its chief rival",
    "http://www.marcosoft.com" );
```

The two listeners respond immediately, sending this text to the Output window:

```
----- NABC News -----
> Marcosoft buys Murkimedia <
After months of secret negotiations, Marcosoft absorbs its chief rival
>> http://www.marcosoft.com
[via National Press]
--
///// Ain't It Crazy News /////
Unbelievable!!
Marcosoft buys Murkimedia!!!
National Press reports: 'After months of secret negotiations, Marcosoft
absorbs its chief rival'
Read the rest of the incredible story here:
http://www.marcosoft.com
//
```

As an exercise, you can try creating your own listener and event handler, with a different template for the news.

Conclusion

There are many possible approaches to creating event sources. This section has shown, through a simple example, how to design an object-oriented event source, using a class and *ASBroadcaster*. As you apply these concepts in your own projects, the elegance of event-based programming will hopefully result in faster implementation and cleaner code. I use this approach increasingly in my work, as you'll see in later chapters.

Part III

Dynamic Visuals

Chapter 7

Motion, Tweening, and Easing

Things moving. Isn't that what drew most of us to Flash? Motion is deep in Flash's genetic code. The Timeline animation tools haven't changed much over the various versions of Flash. But in Flash 4 and 5, and now MX, the growing capabilities of ActionScript have provided powerful and creative new ways of making things move. In this chapter, we'll explore the concepts of motion, tweening, and easing. We'll develop a thorough understanding of these ideas, and then look at how to realize them in ActionScript. That said, it's time to get in touch with our motions.

Concepts of Motion

I have spent quite some time thinking about motion as it applies to programmatic animation. This is something that comes from my philosophy training—analyzing a concept to break it into definitive components. More specifically, the issue is this: what constitutes *a motion*—an identifiable instance of motion—from a programmer's point of view? To keep it simple, I decided to restrict my consideration to *one-dimensional* motion, at least initially. I came up with this definition: a motion is *a numerical change in position over time*. Breaking this down even further, we see that there are three key components of a motion: position, time, and beginning position.

> **Position**   A motion has a unique numerical value—its *position*—at any point in time. When the value of the position changes, there is movement.

> **Time**   A motion occurs over *time*. Typically, time is measured in positive numbers. In my mind, it makes sense to standardize motion time by starting it at zero, like a shuttle launch. After that, a motion's time property ticks away like its own personal stopwatch.

❯ Beginning Position A motion has to start somewhere. From our perspective, the motion starts at the moment in time we start observing it—in other words, when time is zero. Thus, we define *beginning position* as the motion's position when time is zero.

More on Position

By *position*, I don't mean merely *physical* position. For our purposes, *position* can be any numerical quantity. It could be something visual like the movie clip properties _x, _xscale, or _alpha. It could also be a variable representing money, temperature, music volume, or population density.

To be more specific, the *position* quantity should be a real number that is *one-dimensional*. In other words, position has a *scalar*, not a *vector* value, as discussed in Chapter 4. The number can be positive, negative, or zero, a decimal or an integer. In visual terms, we should be able to locate the quantity on a number line, either to the left or right of zero, or at zero itself. Figure 7-1 shows two positions on a number line, at –2 and 1.

NOTE: In contrast to real numbers, there are *imaginary numbers*, which essentially consist of a real number multiplied by *i*, the square root of -1. There are also *complex numbers*, which are two-dimensional. Each complex number is the sum of a real and an imaginary number.

Of course, we find motions in higher dimensions. We are most familiar with two- and three-dimensional movement in our world. However, a multi-dimensional position can usually be broken down into several one-dimensional positions. The Flash stage is a two-dimensional space, through which movie clips travel. A simple diagonal tween may look like one motion, but really it's a combination of changes in _x and _y, which are independent from each other. By contrast, _width and _xscale are not independent—changing one affects the other. Thus, they are not separate dimensions, but different aspects of the same dimension.

NOTE: Consider the fact that a movie clip has many numerical visual properties: _x, _y, _xscale, _yscale, _rotation, and _alpha. Consequently, you could say that an animated movie clip is moving through *six-dimensional space*. If you're interested in learning more about higher dimensions, I recommend the books *Flatland* and *The Mathematical Tourist*.

FIGURE 7-1

Positions p1 and p2 on a number line

It's important to realize that, from a programming perspective, the position of a motion is numerical *by necessity*. Any quantity that can be said to be *moving*, you should be able to represent with a number. For instance, suppose a string variable contains a single letter, and is "moving" through the letters of the alphabet—first it's "A," a second later it's "B," and so on. The quantity in question, letters, is not natively numeric. However, we know that there is a specific order to the symbols: B follows A as surely as 2 follows 1. It is possible to place the letters in order on a number line. We can easily correlate the letters of the alphabet with numbers; in fact, the ASCII codes have already done this. Thus, we can treat the changing letters as a numerical motion.

Position as a Function of Time

The aspect of time is crucial to motion—things change *over time*. Nothing can move in "zero time," or be in two places at once (although quantum theory may have some strange exceptions to this rule). In other words, a position needs time to change, and it can have only one value at a specific point in time.

Because position and time have this one-to-one relationship, we can say that *position is a function of time*. This means that, given a specific point in time, we can find one, and only one, corresponding position. In mathematical terms:

where p = position, t = time:

$p = f(t)$

In ActionScript, we can implement mathematical functions literally with—you guessed it—functions. Notice the similarity between the following code and the preceding math notation:

```
f = function (time) {
    return 2 * time;
};
// test f()
t = 12;
p = f(t);
trace (p); // output: 24
```

In comes the time, out goes the position. Since an ActionScript function can only return one value, we can see the importance of the one-to-one relationship between time and position. Later in the chapter, we'll look at my tweening functions, which provide meaningful and predictable relationships between position and time.

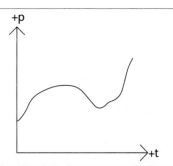

FIGURE 7-2

Graph of a motion's position over time

NOTE: In a sense, a function can have many values at once if you pack an object with properties and return the object. However, what is returned from the function is still one value—an object reference.

Motion as a Graph

Time is one-dimensional, and for this discussion, we are keeping position one-dimensional as well. Position can be represented on a number line, and time can be displayed on another number line. If we put these two number lines at right angles to each other, we have a Cartesian graph (discussed in Chapter 3). The standard practice is to put *time* along the x-axis, and the *function of time* (*position* in our case) on the y-axis.

With this setup, we can visually represent a motion by plotting points on the graph. Instead of (*x*, *y*), we have (*p*, *t*) coordinates. Figure 7-2 shows a graph of a possible motion.

Static Tweens in Flash

The word "tween" is derived from "between." The term comes from traditional animation, where the work is split between keyframes and tween frames. Some of the animators would draw the keyframes, and others, perhaps those with less talent or seniority, would do the grunt work of filling in the gaps with tween frames.

The concept transfers well to Flash. On the Timeline, a designer can define keyframes, and tell Flash to do the mundane work of tweening between them. I call these *Timeline* tweens. You define them at author-time, on the Timeline, and Flash "hard-codes" that motion into the SWF. You can't change these tweens at run-time, so I also call them *static* or *author-time* tweens. The converse would be *dynamic*, *run-time*, *ActionScript* tweens, which we'll explore later in the chapter.

You may be interested to know that author-time tweens actually don't exist in a SWF file. I once thought that Flash stores the keyframes in the SWF and then calculates the tween on the fly. I discovered, however, that this is not the case. When you publish your movie, Flash simply keyframes the entire tween. You can verify this by comparing the file sizes of SWFs with the same movement, one with a tween, the other with keyframes. Try an experiment by following these steps:

1. Start with a new movie.

2. Create an empty movie clip symbol.

3. Drag the movie clip from the library to the stage to create a keyframe on frame 1.

4. Insert a keyframe on frame 5.

5. Move the movie clip to a new position on frame 5.

6. Create a Timeline tween between frames 1 and 5.

7. Turn SWF compression off in the Publish Settings.

8. Test the movie (CTRL-ENTER). The SWF should be about 104 bytes.

9. Now keyframe the entire tween by selecting all of the frames and pressing F6.

10. Test the movie. The SWF has the same file size.

As you can see, author-time tweens have no advantage, in terms of file size, over keyframes. There is also no difference in processor usage between timeline tweens and keyframes.

Shape tweens are a different story. Through testing, I found that the transition frames in a shape tween *are* calculated on-the-fly—not pre-rendered in the SWF. As a result, you can increase the length (in frames) of a shape tween without seeing much increase in file size. If you convert a shape tween to keyframes, however, you will likely see an increase in file size if the shapes are sufficiently complex. I ran a test on a shape tween between two dense scribble shapes. With ten frames in the tween, the SWF file size was 38 KB. However, after keyframing the ten frames and clearing the shape tween setting, the same animation became 258 KB! The other end of the stick is that shape tweens are more demanding on the CPU than are motion tweens, as the intermediary curves must first be calculated and then rendered.

Dynamic Tweening in ActionScript

I have often heard ActionScript programmers express their desire to "break free of the Timeline," especially when it comes to animation. Timeline tweens are static and stolid. You're stuck with whatever endpoints and easing you define in the authoring tool.

Once you begin working with ActionScripted motion, however, a whole world of possibilities opens up. You can produce interactive, dynamic motion that seems smoother and more alive than Timeline tweens. Often, this involves using principles of physics to create bounce and acceleration, which we'll discuss in Chapter 8. In the remainder of this chapter, though, we'll explore a variety of ways to dynamically tween in ActionScript.

The Standard Exponential Slide

The most well-known technique of ActionScripted tweening is what I call the *standard exponential slide*. (It's tempting to coin a tacky acronym like *SES*, but I'll abstain.) The slide is a movement towards a destination that gradually slows to a stop—an ease-out. The slide is exponential because the speed can be represented with an equation that depends on a changing exponent. Later in the chapter, we will look at this equation. You may recognize the slide technique in the following code:

```
// a standard exponential slide
this.onEnterFrame = function () {
    var distance = this.destinationX - this._x;
    this._x += distance / 2;
};
```

At my first FlashForward conference, I remember hearing the concept of this slide explained by three different speakers. The idea is simply that you move a fraction of the distance—say one-half—to your destination in each unit of time. For instance, if you need to move a total of ten feet, you could move five feet, then 2.5 feet, then 1.25, then .625, and so on.

The ancient Greek philosopher Zeno explored this idea in one of his famous paradoxes: if you have to move halfway each time, you never actually reach your destination. (Zeno had a decent point, at least until quantum theory showed that space is not infinitely divisible.) In Flash, though, you soon get "close enough," that is, within a pixel of your destination, or until you've exceeded the available decimal places of floating-point numbers (at which point 9.9999... turns into 10).

All in all, the standard exponential slide is a dynamic ease-out motion easily generated with a tiny amount of ActionScript. This, of course, is why you see it everywhere. However, I grew dissatisfied with this technique, for several reasons. First of all, you can only do ease-out, not ease-in. Also, the motion is aesthetically different from Flash's own eased tweens. Compared to a Timeline tween with ease-out, the slide moves "too fast" in the beginning, then "too slow" towards the end.

Furthermore, you can't directly find the tween's position for a given time. For instance, you have no way of knowing exactly where the moving object will be when ten frames have elapsed. Each frame's position is dependent on the previous frame. Consequently, you have to run the whole process from the beginning to get to a specific point in time. There's no easy way to jump to an arbitrary frame in the tween.

Lastly, you can't directly specify the duration of the tween. The formula doesn't let you make the tween, say, 20 frames in length. Basically, "it gets there when it gets there." You can change the acceleration factor to speed up the process or slow it down, but it takes trial and error to get a tween of the desired duration.

Noticing these shortcomings, I made it my mission to find an alternative to the standard exponential slide. I wanted tweens and easing that would give more control to the ActionScript developer. But first, more analysis was needed.

Key Components of a Tween

A tween can be defined as *an interpolation from one position to another*. Thus, a tween fits our earlier definition of a motion—a change in position over time. Tweens are a subset of motions, just as diamonds are a subset of gems. As such, tweens and motions share the three essentials of *position*, *time*, and *beginning position*. In addition, tweens have two other essential characteristics: *duration* and *final position*.

Duration

A tween has to end. It has to take "less than an eternity" to reach its destination. In other words, a tween must have a *duration* that is less than infinity, but greater than zero.

NOTE: By contrast, a generic motion doesn't necessarily have a finite duration. For instance, a circular orbit is a motion that never ends. A motion without a duration is definitely not a tween.

Final Position

A tween fills in the gap between two keyframe positions, getting you "from Point A to Point B." Point A is the *beginning position*—something all motions have. Point B, meanwhile, is the *final position*, an essential component of a tween.

NOTE: It's also possible to replace final position with *change in position,* which is simply the difference between Point A and Point B. For example, you can either say, "start at 10 and go to 15," or you can say, "start at 10 and go forward by 5." Final position is an *absolute* coordinate, whereas change in position is a *relative* coordinate.

Tweening Functions

Naturally, there are different ways to implement tweening in ActionScript. However, having boiled tweens down to their essence, I believe that my code captures the key elements—no more, no less.

The purpose of a tweening function is to *deliver a position for a specific time, given the tween's essential characteristics.* These characteristics are beginning position, final position, and duration.

In terms of structure, we have five quantities to incorporate into the function. Position is the one that is spit out the back end. The other four items are fed to the function as parameters. A tweening function should have this approximate structure, then:

```
getTweenPosition = function (time, begin, final,
duration) {
    // calculate position here
    return position;
};
```

Alternatively, *change in position* could be used instead of *final position*, in which case, the function would look like this:

```
getTweenPosition = function (time, begin, change,
duration) {
    // calculate position here
    return position;
};
```

With my tweening functions, I found that I could optimize the code a bit more if I used *change*. I also decided to store the functions in the *Math* object, to make them globally accessible. My tweening functions have this format:

```
Math.tweenFunc = function (t, b, c, d) {
    // calculate and return position
};
```

NOTE: I shortened the parameter names to one letter for speed. Variables with longer names take longer to look up than variables with short names, because of the interpreter's internal hashing procedure. I heard this from Gary Grossman, the creator of ActionScript. Timing tests run by members of the Flashcoders list have also confirmed the difference in speed.

As for the actual calculation of the tween's position—that's where things get interesting. We are now ready to explore specific equations that interpolate between two points in diverse ways.

Linear Tweening

"The shortest path between two points is a straight line"—so goes the saying. When you want to move from Point A to Point B, a linear tween is the simplest path, mathematically speaking. This tween has constant velocity throughout; there is no acceleration. In Flash, a Timeline tween with an easing of zero is a linear tween.

Graph

When you graph a linear tween over time, it comes out as a straight line. That's why I call it a "linear" tween. Figure 7-3 shows the graph of a linear tween's position over time.

In this chapter, the tweening graphs I use are all "normalized" in a particular way. Both axes—*position* and *time*—are plotted between standard values of 0 and 1. Of course, in real-world situations, position and time range between many different values. For instance, a tween may move a total of 120 pixels in 30 frames. If we graphed this motion, the position axis would be displayed between 0 and 120, and time would range from 0 to 30. However, we can easily stretch our original normalized (0 to 1) graph to match this new graph. All it takes is simple multiplication: 30 horizontally by 120 vertically.

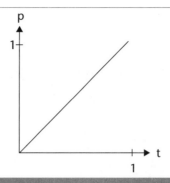

FIGURE 7-3

Graph of a linear tween's position over time

The equation for the graph in Figure 7-3 is quite simple:

$p(t) = t$

This is the basic $y = x$ equation for a diagonal line that most of us learned in high school math. If the time is 0.6, the position is also 0.6.

As the graph stands, the slope of the line (rise over run) is 1: position (the rise) changes by 1 over the course of the tween, and so does time (the run). This is the normalized form of the equation, though, with values ranging from 0 to 1. If we take the example tween mentioned earlier, where position changes by 120, and the duration is 30, the slope is different:

slope = rise / run
slope = change in position / duration
slope = 120 pixels / 30 frames
slope = 4 pixels / frame

In this case, the slope is 4 pixels per frame. The slope of the line is also the velocity of the motion. A different tween covering 240 pixels in 30 frames would have a velocity of 8 pixels per frame. It moves faster than the first tween and its graph has a steeper slope.

We can generalize these results to come up with a standard equation for a linear tween, given the change in position and duration. We know that that velocity is constant during a linear tween, just as the slope is constant. Thus, we can find the tween's position at a particular time by simply multiplying velocity by time:

$p(t) = t \times v$

To take a real-life example, suppose your car's velocity is 60 miles per hour:

$v = 60$

If you've been driving two hours, how many miles have you covered? This is easy to work out in your head, but let's do the math explicitly:

$t = 2$
$p(t) = t \times v$
$p(2) = 2 \times 60$
$p(2) = 120$

We know that velocity equals change over duration, so we can replace v with c divided by d:

let c = change in position and d = duration
$v = c / d$
$p(t) = t \times v$
$p(t) = t \times (c / d)$

One last thing: remember that a tween has a beginning position. So far, we've assumed that the beginning position is zero. However, this often isn't the case. In terms of the car example, suppose you start 10 miles out of town, then drive at 60 mph for 2 hours. You'll end up 130 miles from the town (120 + 10).

We can incorporate the beginning position into our equation, simply by adding it at the end:

let b = beginning position
$p(t) = t \times (c / d) + b$

NOTE: The preceding equation is a form of the "slope-y-intercept" equation for a line: $y = mx + b$. Here, the variable m is the slope, and b is the y-intercept, the point where the line crosses the y-axis.

ActionScript Function

The code for our linear tween function follows the earlier equation closely:

```
Math.linearTween = function (t, b, c, d) {
    return c*t/d + b;
};
```

Four parameters enter the function—time, beginning position, change in position, and duration—and the corresponding position is returned.

Implementing a Tween with a Function

How do we actually use a tweening function? It's a matter of setting up the key properties of a tween, and feeding them into the function. First, we decide which property we want to set in motion. The _x property of a movie clip will do nicely to start. Tweening _x will produce a horizontal motion.

Then we need to choose the parameters of the tween. Where will it start, where will it finish, and how long will it take? We then establish these quantities in begin, finish, and duration properties inside the movie clip:

```
this.begin = 100;
this.finish = 220;
this.duration = 30;
```

This tween will start at 100 pixels and end up at 220, over the course of 30 frames. Looking ahead, we know that the tweening function requires the *change* in position, rather than the *final* position itself. So we might as well add a change property:

```
this.change = this.finish - this.begin;
```

A tween's time starts at zero, so let's initialize it as another property:

```
this.time = 0;
```

To produce animation, we need a frame loop. This calls for an *onEnterFrame( )* handler for the movie clip:

```
this.onEnterFrame = function () {
    // do tweening stuff
};
```

Now we have to figure out what code to put in the frame loop. What properties change over the course of the tween? Our first three properties, begin, change, and duration, don't vary. It is time and position that change during the tween. We'll have time track the number of frames that have elapsed. Thus, it should be incremented every frame:

```
this.onEnterFrame = function () {
    this.time++;
};
```

The other changing property is position. How do we get the position as time flies by? We call upon our tweening function, which takes four tween parameters and returns the position. So we could call it like this:

```
this.position = Math.linearTween (this.time, this.begin,
    this.change, this.duration);
this._x = this.position;
```

We can make this more straightforward by assigning the position value directly to the _x property:

```
this._x = Math.linearTween (this.time, this.begin,
    this.change, this.duration);
```

We can shorten this even further by using the with statement:

```
with (this) {
    _x = Math.linearTween (time, begin, change,
duration);
}
```

Setting the scope to this eliminates the need to reference each of the properties with the "this" prefix.

Now we can put the tweening function inside the *onEnterFrame( )* handler to produce animation, with the following code:

```
this.onEnterFrame = function () {
    with (this) {
        _x = Math.linearTween (time, begin, change, duration);
    }
    this.time++;
};
```

The position is calculated, then time is incremented by one. We can simplify a bit by incremented time in the same step as passing it to the function:

```
this.onEnterFrame = function () {
    with (this) {
        _x = Math.linearTween (time++, begin, change, duration);
    }
};
```

Putting all of our code together, we have this:

```
this.begin = 100;
this.finish = 220;
this.change = this.finish - this.begin;
this.duration = 30;
this.time = 0;
this.onEnterFrame = function () {
    with (this) {
        _x = Math.linearTween (time++, begin, change, duration);
    }
};
```

At this point, you can stick this code into a movie clip and try it out. It should work—for the most part. There will be one small problem, however: the tween won't end. For the animation to work, we need to stop when the tween's time is up. If the time is greater than the duration, we should stop the frame loop by deleting the *onEnterFrame( )* handler. By adding one line of code to perform this check, our tween is finished:

```
// a linear tween in _x
this.begin = 100;
this.finish = 220;
this.change = this.finish - this.begin;
this.duration = 30;
this.time = 0;
this.onEnterFrame = function () {
    with (this) {
        _x = Math.linearTween (time++, begin, change, duration);
        if (time > duration) delete this.onEnterFrame;
    }
};
```

In this code, you can replace `Math.linearTween` with another tweening function to produce a different style of tween. Thankfully, all my tweening functions have the same structure, making them easily interchangeable. We'll look at the different flavors of tweening and easing later in the chapter. But first, let's return to our discussion of linear motion.

Aesthetics of Linear Motion

I'll be honest—I don't care much for linear tweens. They look stiff, artificial, mechanical. You mostly see unaccelerated motion in machinery. An automated factory is chock-full of linear tweens—robotic arms, conveyor belts, assembly lines. It is extremely difficult for humans to move in a linear fashion. Breakdancers who do "robot"-style moves have achieved their linearity with much practice. In this sense, you could say Michael Jackson is the master of the linear tween.

So, there are some legitimate uses of linear tweens. If you're animating robots or breakdancers, they're perfect. For most other things, though, linear motion can look downright ugly. I have often come across animations where the author obviously threw down some keyframes and tweened between them without applying any easing. It drives me nuts.

I don't know how much the average person picks up on the naturalness or falsity of motion in Flash movies, but in 3-D animation, people certainly are quick to say when the movement "looks totally fake," even when the object texture is photorealistic. For example, in *Star Wars Episode II: Attack of the Clones*, there is some excruciatingly bad animation in the scene where Anakin is trying to ride one of the "Naboo cows." It's something most adults would notice, I think.

I have a theory that the mind is constantly interpreting an object's motion in order to *infer the forces* acting on it. When an object accelerates in an unnatural way, the brain picks up on it and says, "that's not possible with real-world forces." In real life, suppose you saw a ball roll to the right at a constant speed, then abruptly roll to the left at a faster speed. You would think to yourself, "Something must have hit it"—*even if you didn't see a collision*. Similarly, when an object switches from one linear tween to another, there is an instantaneous change in velocity, like the ball changing direction suddenly. When I see this, I *feel* like the object has been jerked by an invisible chain, or bounced off an unseen wall. But when I can't see a chain or a wall, the "cognitive dissonance" drives me crazy. "It's not supposed to move that way!" I protest. It takes some easing to calm me down.

Easing

Easing is acceleration, a change in speed. In this chapter, I focus on easing as the transition between the states of *moving* and *not-moving*. When an object is moving, it has a velocity of some magnitude. When the object is not moving, its velocity is zero. How does the velocity change—what does the acceleration look like?

In the real world, velocity doesn't suddenly jump from one value to another. Sometimes it looks that way, for instance, when you hit a baseball with a bat. Even here, though, the change isn't instantaneous. If you watch the collision in super-slow motion, you can see the ball gradually slowing to a stop, and actually deforming around the bat. Then, the ball accelerates in the direction of the bat's swing and flies off. There is a deceleration to a speed of zero, then an acceleration in the other direction—two instances of easing.

Aesthetics of Eased Motion

Most movements in nature have some kind of easing. Organic processes typically involve forces (which we'll discuss in detail in Chapter 8). If the forces aren't in balance, acceleration is produced. Our minds make this connection between acceleration and force intuitively. When we see the velocity of an object gradually changing, we infer that some force is steadily pushing or pulling it. As a result, animation usually looks more natural and fluid when it follows similar rules.

Elevators are great examples of the importance of easing. Imagine riding in an elevator that didn't start or stop moving with any easing. You press the button to go to the twentieth floor. The elevator doors close, then the whole thing suddenly jerks upwards, throwing you to the floor. Getting back to your feet, you watch the numbers: eighteen… nineteen… *ding!* Your body flies straight upwards. As the doors open, you frantically try to pull your head out of the ceiling. Too late! The elevator flies back down to the first floor, and suddenly you're weightless.

This is a facetious example, to be sure. But I literally feel "jerked around" in a similar way when I watch animation without proper easing. Let's look at three general categories of easing: ease-in, ease-out, and ease-in-out.

Ease-In

Start slow and speed up—that's an *ease-in*. With author-time tweens, an easing value of -100 produces an ease-in. In my Flash 4 days, when I majored in Timeline tweens, I nearly always used easing values of either 100 or -100. In general, I don't find less-than-100 percent easing very useful. Therefore, from this point on, I will use "easing" to mean 100 percent easing.

If we graph the position of an ease-in tween over time, we arrive at a curve like the one in Figure 7-4. With easing, we get a curve. Without easing, we get a line as in Figure 7-3.

Remember that the slope of a graph corresponds to velocity. The tween curve starts out horizontal—a slope of zero. Thus, at $t=0$, the velocity is

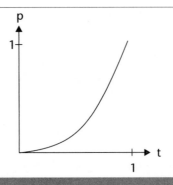

Graph of an ease-in tween

zero—a dead stop. Over time, the graph gradually becomes steeper and the velocity increases.

NOTE: Ease-in and ease-out are reversed in Flash from what they are in many other animation programs. In 3-D animation software, for instance, an ease-in slows down at the end of the tween, not the beginning.

Ease-Out

The inverse of an ease-in is an *ease-out*, where the motion starts fast and slows to a stop. A Timeline ease-out tween has an easing value of 100. Take a look at the ease-out curve in Figure 7-5.

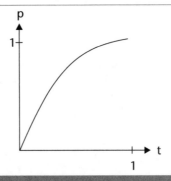

Graph of an ease-out tween

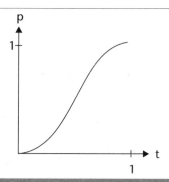

FIGURE 7-6

Graph of an ease-in-out tween

The graph starts out steep but levels off, becoming horizontal at the end of the tween. The velocity starts out at some positive value and steadily decreases to zero.

Ease-In-Out

The third category of easing is my favorite. An ease-in-out is a delicious half-and-half combination, like a vanilla-chocolate swirl ice cream cone. The first half of the tween is an ease-in; the second half, an ease-out. The curve of the ease-in-out, shown in Figure 7-6, is quite lovely (and bears more than a passing resemblance to a certain product logo).

I use in-out easing pervasively because it produces the most natural-looking motion. Think about how a real-world object might move from one point of rest to another. The object accelerates from a standstill, then slows down and comes to a stop at its destination. Elevators, for example, use in-out easing.

Unfortunately, Flash doesn't have in-out easing for author-time tweens. When I do Timeline animation, I am forced to create each ease-in-out with two tweens. As you can imagine, this is a real pain to maintain when I have to modify the animation. Every time I change an endpoint of the overall tween, I have to redo the two half-tweens. I had hoped to find an ease-in-out option in Flash MX, but alas, it was not to be.

Varieties of Eased Tweens

Thankfully, with ActionScripted motion, the possibilities are endless. With the right mathematics and code, we can define all manner of tweens with ease (pun intended).

Quadratic Easing

Flash's Timeline tweens use something called *quadratic easing*—which could actually be termed "normal" easing. The word *quadratic* refers to the fact that the equation for this motion is based on a squared variable, in this case, t^2:

$$p(t) = t^2$$

NOTE: I always wondered why the term *quad*-ratic (the prefix means "four") is used to describe equations with a degree of two (x^2). While writing this chapter, I finally looked it up in the dictionary (RTFD, you might say). I discovered that *quad* originally referred to the four sides of a square. Thus, a *squared* variable is *quadratic*.

I used the quadratic easing curve earlier in Figure 7-4. It's actually half a parabola. Here it is again, for reference purposes, in Figure 7-7.

Here's the quadratic ease-in ActionScript function:

```
Math.easeInQuad = function (t, b, c, d) {
    return c*(t/=d)*t + b;
};
```

Recall that t is time, b is beginning position, c is the total change in position, and d is the duration of the tween.

This equation is more complex than the linear tween, but it's the simplest of the equations that implement easing. Basically, I normalize t by dividing it by d. This forces t to fall between 0 and 1. I multiply t by itself to produce quadratic curvature in the values. Then I scale the value from a

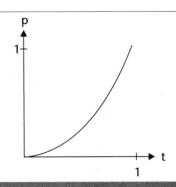

FIGURE 7-7

Graph of quadratic easing

normalized one to the desired output, by multiplying by c. I finish off the position calculation by adding the initial offset b, then returning the value.

NOTE: The t /=d bit in the preceding code is an optimization technique. This compound operator lets you divide and reassign t, *and* use its value in further operations, all in one step. The Flash Player uses a stack-based virtual machine that has four "registers" or memory locations reserved for holding data temporarily. Information can be stored and retrieved much faster from a register than from a variable, but registers are rarely used in Flash-generated bytecode. However, in-line syntax like p = (t/=d) * t is compiled to bytecodes that use one of the registers to temporarily store a value during the calculation, speeding up the process. (A special thanks goes to Tatsuo Kato for first applying this technique to my code.)

The following code is the quadratic ease-out function:

```
Math.easeOutQuad = function (t, b, c, d) {
    return -c * (t/=d)*(t-2) + b;
};
```

The original quadratic curve needed to be massaged a bit to get it where I wanted it. I multiplied *c* by -1 to flip the curve vertically. I also had to play with the value of *t* to shift the curve into place.

Now, here's the quadratic ease-in-out function:

```
Math.easeInOutQuad = function (t, b, c, d) {
    if ((t/=d/2) < 1) return c/2*t*t + b;
    return -c/2 * ((--t)*(t-2) - 1) + b;
};
```

I've combined the in and out code into one function—two half-tweens fused together. You may notice several divisions by 2 in the code. I did this to scale the equations to half their normal size, since each equation covers half of the time span. The ease-in equation governs the tween until half the time has elapsed, after which the ease-out equation takes over. Between the equation-switching and some additional curve-shifting, the code became increasingly cryptic—but beautifully so.

Cubic Easing

A cubic equation is based on the power of three.

$$p(t) = t^3$$

A cubic ease is a bit more curved than a quadratic one. Figure 7-8 shows the graph of a tween with a cubic ease-in.

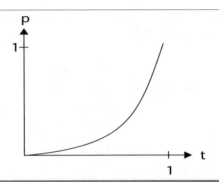

FIGURE 7-8

Graph of cubic easing

The following displays the cubic easing functions:

```
Math.easeInCubic = function (t, b, c, d) {
    return c * Math.pow (t/d, 3) + b;
};


Math.easeOutCubic = function (t, b, c, d) {
    return c * (Math.pow (t/d-1, 3) + 1) + b;
};


Math.easeInOutCubic = function (t, b, c, d) {
    if ((t/=d/2) < 1)
        return c/2 * Math.pow (t, 3) + b;
    return c/2 * (Math.pow (t-2, 3) + 2) + b;
};
```

You'll notice I used the *Math.pow( )* function here to raise numbers to the third power. In the first cubic easing function, for instance, I calculated $(t/d)^3$ like this:

```
Math.pow (t/d, 3)
```

Alternatively, I could cube this quantity by multiplying it by itself:

```
(t/=d) *t*t
```

However, once you get into higher exponents, it's faster to just call *Math.pow( )* to perform the multiplication.

Quartic Easing

A quartic equation is based on the power of four:

$$p(t) = t^4$$

The quartic ease, shown in Figure 7-9, puts just a bit more bend in the curve. A cubic ease, though more pronounced than a quadratic ease, still feels fairly natural. It's at the quartic level that the motion starts to feel a bit "other-worldly," as the acceleration becomes more exaggerated.

Here are the quartic easing functions:

```
Math.easeInQuart = function (t, b, c, d) {
    return c * Math.pow (t/d, 4) + b;
};


Math.easeOutQuart = function (t, b, c, d) {
    return -c * (Math.pow (t/d-1, 4) - 1) + b;
};


Math.easeInOutQuart = function (t, b, c, d) {
    if ((t/=d/2) < 1)
        return c/2 * Math.pow (t, 4) + b;
    return -c/2 * (Math.pow (t-2, 4) - 2) + b;
};
```

The code is similar in structure to the cubic functions, only with *Math.pow( )* raising t to the fourth power now and some adjusted curve shifting.

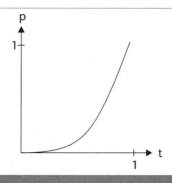

FIGURE 7-9

Graph of quartic easing

Quintic Easing

Quintic easing continues the upward trend, raises time to the fifth power:

$$p(t) = t^5$$

Quintic is a fairly pronounced curve, as Figure 7-10 shows. The motion starts out quite slow, then becomes quite fast. The curvature of the graph is close to that of exponential easing, discussed later in the chapter.

Putting all of the t^n ease curves on the same graph makes for an interesting comparison, as shown in Figure 7-11.

Here are the quintic easing functions:

```
Math.easeInQuint = function (t, b, c, d) {
    return c * Math.pow (t/d, 5) + b;
};

Math.easeOutQuint = function (t, b, c, d) {
    return c * (Math.pow (t/d-1, 5) + 1) + b;
};

Math.easeInOutQuint = function (t, b, c, d) {
    if ((t/=d/2) < 1)
        return c/2 * Math.pow (t, 5) + b;
    return c/2 * (Math.pow (t-2, 5) + 2) + b;
};
```

This concludes the t^n easing equations. We will now look at some other mathematical operations that can produce easing curves.

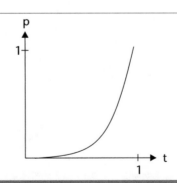

FIGURE 7-10

Graph of quintic easing

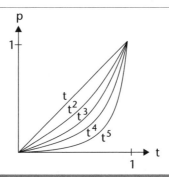

FIGURE 7-11

Graphs of t, t^2, t^3, t^4, and t^5 easing

Sinusoidal Easing

A sinusoidal equation is based on a sine or cosine function. Either one produces a *sine wave*—a periodic oscillation of a specific shape. This is the equation on which I based the easing curve:

$$p(t) = \sin(t \times \pi/2)$$

In the ActionScript implementation, two of the sinusoidal easing functions use cosine instead, but only to optimize the calculation. Sine and cosine functions can be transformed into each other at will. You just have to shift the curves along the time axis by one-quarter of a cycle (90 degrees or $\pi/2$ radians).

Sinusoidal easing is quite gentle, even more so than quadratic easing. Figure 7-12 shows that its path doesn't have a lot of curvature. Much of the curve resembles a straight line angled at 45 degrees, with just a bit of a curve to it.

Here are the sinusoidal easing functions:

```
Math.easeInSine = function (t, b, c, d) {
    return c * (1 - Math.cos(t/d * (Math.PI/2))) + b;
};


Math.easeOutSine = function (t, b, c, d) {
    return c * Math.sin(t/d * (Math.PI/2)) + b;
};


Math.easeInOutSine = function (t, b, c, d) {
    return c/2 * (1 - Math.cos(Math.PI*t/d)) + b;
};
```

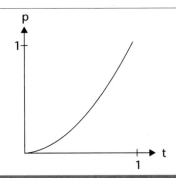

FIGURE 7-12

Graph of sinusoidal easing

Exponential Easing

I based my exponential functions on the number 2 raised to a multiple of 10:

$$p(t) = 2^{10(t-1)}$$

Of all the easing equations in this chapter, this one took me the longest to find. Part of the challenge is that the slope for an ease-in curve should be zero at $t=0$. An exponential curve, however, never has a slope of zero. I ended up giving the curve a very small slope that was "close enough" to zero. (If you plug $t=0$ into the preceding equation, you get 2^{-10}, which is 0.0009765625.)

Exponential easing has a lot of curvature, as shown in Figure 7-13.

The following shows the exponential easing functions:

```
Math.easeInExpo = function (t, b, c, d) {
    return c * Math.pow(2, 10 * (t/d - 1)) + b;
};


Math.easeOutExpo = function (t, b, c, d) {
    return c * (-Math.pow(2, -10 * t/d) + 1) + b;
};


Math.easeInOutExpo = function (t, b, c, d) {
    if ((t/=d/2) < 1)
        return c/2 * Math.pow(2, 10 * (t - 1)) + b;
    return c/2 * (-Math.pow(2, -10 * --t) + 2) + b;
};
```

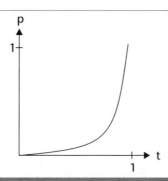

FIGURE 7-13

Graph of exponential easing

The exponential ease-out function *Math.easeOutExpo( )* produces essentially the same motion as the standard exponential slide discussed earlier. However, with my approach, you have precise control over the duration of the tween, and can jump to any point in time without running the tween from the starting point.

Circular Easing

Circular easing is based on the equation for half of a circle, which uses a square root (shown next).

$$p(t) = 1 - \sqrt{1 - t^2}$$

The curve for circular easing is simply an arc (the quarter-circle shown in Figure 7-14), but it adds a unique flavor when put into motion. Like quintic

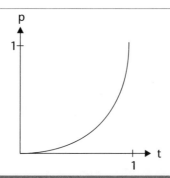

FIGURE 7-14

Graph of circular easing

and exponential easing, the acceleration for circular easing is dramatic, but somehow it seems to happen more "suddenly" than the others.

Here are the circular easing functions:

```
Math.easeInCirc = function (t, b, c, d) {
    return c * (1 - Math.sqrt(1 - (t/=d)*t)) + b;
};

Math.easeOutCirc = function (t, b, c, d) {
    return c * Math.sqrt(1 - (t=t/d-1)*t) + b;
};

Math.easeInOutCirc = function (t, b, c, d) {
    if ((t/=d/2) < 1)
        return c/2 * (1 - Math.sqrt(1 - t*t)) + b;
    return c/2 * (Math.sqrt(1 - (t-=2)*t) + 1) + b;
};
```

This concludes the tweening functions for this chapter. Like an ice cream stand, we have eight flavors of tweening: linear, quadratic, cubic, quartic, quintic, sinusoidal, exponential, and circular. Obviously, additional types of tweening are possible. All it takes is some kind of equation that takes the four essential parameters—time, beginning position, change, and duration—and calculates an appropriate position.

Introducing the Tween Class

Remember the process we went through earlier in the chapter to produce a dynamic tween? This was the resulting code:

```
// a linear tween in _x
this.begin = 100;
this.finish = 220;
this.change = this.finish - this.begin;
this.duration = 30;
this.time = 0;
this.onEnterFrame = function () {
    with (this) {
        _x = Math.linearTween (time++, begin, change, duration);
        if (time > duration) delete this.onEnterFrame;
    }
};
```

The code works well, but it's a bit unwieldy to type it all out whenever we want to create a dynamic tween. I developed a *Tween* class to simplify dynamic ActionScript movement, encapsulating the necessary elements for a tween. Using *Tween*, I can replace the preceding code with just one line:

```
x_twn = new Tween (this, "_x", Math.tweenLinear, 100, 220, 30);
```

The *Tween* instance x_twn handles the movement deftly, automatically starting and stopping the movement and keeping track of the time in its own internal clock. Soon, we'll examine the inner workings of the *Tween* class and learn how it manages the necessary details. But first, let's look at its superclass, *Motion*.

The Motion Class

I abstracted a lot of animation functionality into a *Motion* class. *Motion* is the superclass for several classes, one of which is *Tween* (another is the *MotionCam* class, discussed in Chapter 13). We'll look first at the *Motion* class, and then the *Tween* class.

The Motion Constructor

The constructor for the *Motion* class has a fair bit of code:

```
_global.Motion = function (obj, prop, begin, duration, useSeconds) {
    this.setObj (obj);
    this.setProp (prop);
    this.setBegin (begin);
    this.setPosition (begin);
    this.setDuration (duration);
    this.setUseSeconds (useSeconds);
    this._listeners = [];
    this.addListener (this);
    this.start ();
};
```

This isn't as complicated as it looks. Most of the code has to do with initializing properties. We'll step through it a bit at a time.

First off, we have five arguments that enter the function. Table 7-1 lists and describes the arguments for the *Motion* constructor.

Parameter	Type	Sample Value	Description
obj	object reference	mc	The object containing the affected property
prop	string	"_x"	The name of the property that will be controlled by the motion
begin	number	20	The starting position of the motion
duration	number	30	The length of time of the motion, in either frames or seconds; if the parameter is undefined or 0, the duration is infinity
useSeconds	Boolean	true	A flag asking whether to use seconds instead of frames; defaults to false

TABLE 7-1

Arguments for the *Motion* Constructor

The next three lines initialize the first three properties—obj, prop, and begin—by calling their respective setter methods:

```
this.setObj (obj);
this.setProp (prop);
this.setBegin (begin);
```

Since the motion's position should start at the specified beginning position, we set the position to begin as well:

```
this.setPosition (begin);
```

Then, the last two constructor arguments, duration and useSeconds, are passed to their respective setter methods:

```
this.setDuration (duration);
this.setUseSeconds (useSeconds);
```

Next, we declare a _listeners array property. This is required to support event broadcasting.

```
this._listeners = [];
```

A *Motion* object broadcasts custom events, like *onMotionStarted* and *onMotionChanged*. The *ASBroadcaster* object is used to enable *Motion* as an event source, as outlined in Chapter 6. The *ASBroadcaster.initialize( ) method* is invoked on the prototype after the constructor, as we'll see shortly.

The next step is to make the *Motion* instance listen to itself:

```
this.addListener (this);
```

As a result of this code, a *Motion* receives its own events. This means we can not only add other objects as listeners for *Motion* events, we can also use the *Motion*'s own event handlers as callbacks for the events.

If this seems confusing, think of a more familiar class: *TextField*. A *TextField* instance works with events in much the same way as a *Motion*. One of the *TextField* event handlers is *onChanged( )*. A text field can register listeners, all of which can respond to this event with their *onChanged( )* event handlers. However, the text field *itself* responds to the event with its own *onChanged( )* handler. Thus, we could say that a text field listens to its own events. In the *TextField* constructor, the text field adds itself as a listener, with the equivalent of this code:

```
this.addListener (this);
```

This is exactly what I have done in the *Motion* constructor. I've simply mimicked the process by which the *TextField* class handles events. I did this in order to provide maximum flexibility. Some people may want to use listeners; others will prefer simple callbacks on the *Motion* object itself. The choice is yours.

You may be wondering how I know what's inside the *TextField* constructor. The truth is, I don't know the exact code, but I have other evidence that the text field adds itself as a listener. If you create a new text field and check its _listeners property, you'll find it already has an object in it. The length of the _listeners array is 1, as the following code demonstrates:

```
tf = new TextField();
trace (tf._listeners.length); // output: 1
```

Furthermore, the first listener in the array—the object in the first index— is the text field itself, as the following code proves:

```
trace (tf._listeners[0] == tf); // true
```

The *Motion* constructor has one last task to perform. The function concludes by starting the *Motion* from the beginning:

```
this.start();
```

Now the *Motion* instance moves automatically each frame, because, as we'll see, the *start( )* method enables the object's *onEnterFrame( )* handler.

Public Methods

Adding methods is my favorite part of building a class. It's like I've created a basic shell for a gadget, and now I get to add buttons and features.

I start by defining a temporary shortcut variable, MP, to *Motion's* prototype object:

```
var MP = Motion.prototype;
```

Now I can define methods in MP, and it's the same as defining them in Motion.prototype, only with shorter code.

We want *Motion* to be an event source, so we call *AsBroadcaster.initialize( )* on its prototype to empower it to that end (see Chapter 6), using the following code:

```
AsBroadcaster.initialize (MP);
```

Now let's look at the public methods that let the ActionScript user manipulate *Motion* objects.

Motion.start( )

The *start( )* method causes the *Motion* to play from the beginning:

```
MP.start = function () {
    this.rewind();
    MovieClip.addListener (this);
    this.broadcastMessage ("onMotionStarted", this);
};
```

First, the *rewind( )* method is called to send the *Motion* to its beginning point in time:

```
this.rewind();
```

Then, the object is added as a listener for *MovieClip* events:

```
MovieClip.addListener (this);
```

The *Motion* instance now receives an *onEnterFrame* event for each frame, which causes its *onEnterFrame( )* method to execute automatically. (We'll see later that *onEnterFrame( )* calls the *nextFrame( )* method.)

The last line broadcasts the *onMotionStarted* event, which invokes the *onMotionStarted( )* methods of both the *Motion* instance and its subscribed listeners. A reference to this, the current object, is sent in the broadcast as an argument. This allows listeners to know which object is sending the event.

Motion.stop( )

The *stop( )* method causes the *Motion* to quit moving on its own. Here's the code:

```
MP.stop = function () {
    MovieClip.removeListener (this);
    this.broadcastMessage ("onMotionStopped", this);
};
```

The first line uses the *MovieClip.removeListener( )* method to deactivate the *onEnterFrame( )* handler, stopping the frame loop. As a result, the *Motion* instance no longer moves each frame. The second line broadcasts the *onMotionStopped* event to subscribed listeners. Again, a reference to this is sent in the broadcast as an argument.

Motion.resume( )

The *resume( )* method causes the *Motion* object to play automatically. Unlike the *start( )* method, however, *resume( )* proceeds from the *Motion's* current time instead of from the beginning.

```
MP.resume = function () {
    this.fixTime();
    MovieClip.addListener (this);
    this.broadcastMessage ("onMotionResumed", this);
};
```

The first line calls *fixTimer( )* to make the necessary adjustments when in timer-based mode (useSeconds is true). When a *Motion* is paused, the value of *getTimer( )* keeps increasing. When the *Motion* starts playing again, the *fixTime( )* method finds the new timer offset to use for the internal time.

The second line calls *MovieClip.addListener( )*, causing the *Motion* instance to receive *onEnterFrame* events. The last line broadcasts the *onMotionResumed* event to subscribed listeners, which can react accordingly with their *onMotionResumed( )* event handlers.

Motion.rewind( )

The *rewind( )* method sends the *Motion* back to its beginning point in time. Here is the code for it:

```
MP.rewind = function (t) {
    this.$time = (t == undefined) ? 1 : t;
    this.fixTime();
};
```

The first line validates the incoming t argument, which specifies a starting offset. If t isn't specified, a default value of 1 is chosen; otherwise, the $time property is set to the value of t. I'm using a dollar sign ($) in the property name to signify that it has a corresponding time getter/setter property, which we'll discuss later in the chapter. This is merely a personal naming convention I settled on.

Lastly, *fixTime( )*, a private method, is called to adjust the internal time-tracking offset. We'll look at *fixTime( )* later in the chapter in the "Private Methods" section.

NOTE: When *rewind( )* is called publicly, that is, by ActionScript outside the *Motion* instance, the t parameter isn't necessary. The parameter is used only by the *Motion.setTime( )* method internally in a special case where the *Motion* instance loops in timer-based mode.

Motion.fforward( )

The *fforward( )* method "fast-forward" the *Motion* instance to its end point. Over the course of the *Motion*, time moves between zero and the duration. Thus, the endpoint of the *Motion* is simply where the current time equals the duration. The method's code is straightforward:

```
MP.fforward = function () {
    this.setTime (this.$duration);
    this.fixTime();
};
```

The time is set to the *Motion*'s duration, and then adjusted with the private *fixTime( )* method.

Motion.nextFrame( )

The *nextFrame( )* method advances the time of the *Motion* by one frame. The code is built to accommodate the two different time modes—timer-based and frame-based:

```
MP.nextFrame = function () {
    if (this.$useSeconds) {
        this.setTime ((getTimer() - this.startTime) / 1000);
    } else {
        this.setTime (this.$time + 1);
    }
};
```

The `if` statement checks the `$useSeconds` property. If it is `true`, the *Motion* is in timer-based mode. In that case, the value of *getTimer( )* is checked against the internal offset `this.startTime`, and divided by 1000 to convert it to seconds. This value is passed to the *setTime( )* method.

If the *Motion* is in frame-based mode, the time value is simply increased by one.

NOTE: Although *nextFrame( )* is a public method, you probably won't need to call it directly in most situations, as it is called automatically by the *onEnterFrame( )* handler.

Motion.prevFrame( )

The *prevFrame( )* method sets the *Motion* back in time by one frame. Here's the code:

```
MP.prevFrame = function () {
    if (!this.$useSeconds) this.setTime (this.$time - 1);
};
```

The *prevFrame( )* method is designed to work only with frame-based motion. It's quite difficult to go backwards when you're using timer-based motion, because *getTimer( )* is always moving *forward*. Consequently, there is an `if` statement to check the `$useSeconds` property. If the property is `true`, the *Motion* instance is timer-based, and so the rest of the code is not allowed to execute. If `$useSeconds` is false, the *Motion* is frame-based, and thus, the time is decreased by 1 to go to the previous frame.

NOTE: When a *Motion* is playing automatically, the *nextFrame( )* method is called each frame by *onEnterFrame( )*. Thus, you should call the *stop( )* method before calling *prevFrame( )*. Otherwise, the calls to *prevFrame( )* and *nextFrame( )* will effectively cancel each other out in each frame.

Motion.onEnterFrame( )

One of the best features of *Motion* objects is that they can run themselves. As we saw earlier, the *start( )* method uses *MovieClip.addListener( )* to subscribe the object to *onEnterFrame* events. All we really need the *onEnterFrame( )* handler to do is advance the *Motion* to the next frame. Thus, its code is very simple:

```
MP.onEnterFrame = MP.nextFrame;
```

We just assign a reference to the *nextFrame( )* method straight across to *onEnterFrame( )*.

Motion.toString( )

The *toString( )* method provides a custom string representation of the object. I chose the three main *Motion* properties to put in the string—prop, time, and position:

```
MP.toString = function () {
    return "[Motion prop=" + this.prop + " t=" + this.time +
        " pos=" + this.position + "]";
};
```

This method is useful primarily for debugging purposes. When we trace a *Motion* object, its *toString( )* method is called automatically, sending a string to the Output window. In the following code example, a *Motion* is created and traced:

```
motionX = new Motion (this, "_x", 90, 20, false);
trace (motionX);
// output: [Motion prop=_x t=0 pos=90]
```

Getter/Setter Methods

The getter and setter methods of a class are public methods that provide an interface to its properties. The *Motion* class has quite a few getter and setter methods.

Motion.getPosition( )

The *getPosition( )* method is an empty placeholder function:

```
MP.getPosition = function (t) {
    // calculate and return position
};
```

Nevertheless, *getPosition( )* is the most crucial *Motion* method. Its purpose is to return the position of the *Motion* at a specified time.

If that is the case, then why is the *getPosition( )* function empty? It's what you might call an *abstract* method. It defines the interface—the external structure—of the method, but doesn't specify how the method is implemented. It is intended to be overridden in either an instance or a subclass of *Motion*. We'll see how this is done when we look at the *getPosition( )* method of the *Tween* class, which overrides *Motion.getPosition( )*.

Motion.setPosition( )

The *setPosition( )* method changes the position of the *Motion*. The following shows the code for the *setPosition( )* method:

```
MP.setPosition = function (p) {
    this.$prevPos = this.$pos;
    this.$obj[this.$prop] = this.$pos = p;
    this.broadcastMessage ("onMotionChanged", this, this.$pos);
};
```

First, the previous position is stored in a separate property this.$prevPos. This value can be retrieved through the *getPrevPos( )* method. Next, the incoming p parameter is assigned to the this.$pos property, and then to the controlled property referenced by this.$obj[this.$prop]. For instance, if the *Motion* controls the _alpha of a movie clip ball, this.$obj[this.$prop] translates to ball["_alpha"], which is the same as ball._alpha. Again, I'm using dollar signs in these property names because they have corresponding getter/setter properties, defined later.

Lastly, the *onMotionChanged* event is broadcast to the *Motion's* listeners. This causes each listener's *onMotionChanged( )* handlers to be invoked and passed two arguments: the current *Motion* object and its position. Remember that the *Motion* object listens to itself, so its own *onMotionChanged( )* handler is called here.

Motion.getPrevPos( )

At times, we may want to compare a *Motion's* current position with the previous frame's. For example, we may need to draw a line between the two points or calculate the *Motion's* velocity. The *getPrevPos( )* method retrieves this value for us. Here's the code:

```
MP.getPrevPos = function () {
    return this.$prevPos;
};
```

Motion.setTime( )

The purpose of the *setTime( )* method is quite simple: to change the current time of the *Motion*. The implementation, though, is a bit involved, as the method's code shows:

```
MP.setTime = function (t) {
    this.prevTime = this.$time;
```

```
    if (t > this.duration) {
        if (this.$looping) {
            this.rewind (t - this.$duration);
            this.broadcastMessage ("onMotionLooped", this);
        } else {
            this.stop();
            this.broadcastMessage ("onMotionFinished", this);
        }
    } else if (t < 0) {
        this.rewind();
    } else {
        this.$time = t;
    }
    this.update();
};
```

I've spent many hours on this method alone, rethinking and restructuring the code time and again. There are a number of conditions to check with nested `if..else` statements. If the new time is greater than the duration, the *Motion* needs to be stopped, and an *onMotionFinished* event broadcasted to listeners. The exception is that if the *Motion* is set to loop, it should rewind and broadcast a *onMotionLooped* event instead.

If the new time t is less than zero, the *Motion* is rewound. And if by some chance t is actually in the correct range and makes it through the sieve of conditionals, the *Motion*'s time is set to the value of t. The *update( )* method is called after all this, to bring the *Motion*'s position in line with the new time.

Motion.getTime( )

The *getTime( )* method is straightforward, returning the current time stored in the internal $time property:

```
MP.getTime = function () {
    return this.$time;
};
```

Motion.setBegin( ) and getBegin( )

The *setBegin( )* method defines the starting position of the *Motion*, and the *getBegin( )* method returns it. Their code is minimal:

```
MP.setBegin = function (b) {
    this.$begin = b;
};
```

```
MP.getBegin = function () {
    return this.$begin;
};
```

Motion.setDuration( ) and getDuration( )

The *setDuration( )* method defines the length of time of the *Motion*, in either frames or seconds. Here's the method's code:

```
MP.setDuration = function (d) {
    this.$duration = (d == null || d <= 0) ? Infinity : d;
};
```

I perform a simple validation here with an abbreviated if statement (the ternary operator). This is the logic in plain terms: If the d parameter is missing, negative, or zero, the *Motion* is given an infinite duration. Otherwise, the duration is set to the value of d.

The *getDuration( )* method returns the *Motion*'s duration in a straightforward manner:

```
MP.getDuration = function () {
    return this.$duration;
};
```

Motion.setLooping( ) and getLooping( )

By default, when a *Motion*'s time is up, it stops automatically. However, you can set a looping flag that causes the *Motion* to go back to the beginning instead, repeating the same movement *ad infinitum*.

The *setLooping( )* and *getLooping( )* methods provide access to the looping property. Their code is simple:

```
MP.setLooping = function (b) {
    this.$looping = b;
};
```

```
MP.getLooping = function () {
    return this.$looping;
};
```

Other Getter/Setter Methods

The remaining getters and setters are simple methods. They change or retrieve their respective properties without any special validation—for now, that is. The point of getter and setter methods is that they force the user to invoke a method in order to access a property. In other words, the changing of a property (or retrieval) is intercepted by a function, which can execute other code to verify or modify the data. A property may not require any validation or other associated code at first. However, you may change your class later on, and find you need to mediate access to certain properties. If you've been using getter and setter methods all along, you can just update the code in the methods and not need to change any code outside the class. All in all, although getter and setter methods may seem like overkill, they are a good practice in general for OOP projects.

The following code lists the remaining getter and setter methods:

```
MP.setObj = function (o) {
    this.$obj = o;
};
MP.getObj = function () {
    return this.$obj;
};

MP.setProp = function (p) {
    this.$prop = p;
};
MP.getProp = function () {
    return this.$prop;
};

MP.setUseSeconds = function (useSecs) {
    this.$useSeconds = useSecs;
};
MP.getUseSeconds = function () {
    return this.$useSeconds;
};
```

Private Methods

In full-fledged object-oriented programming languages like C++ and Java, private methods are accessible only to code in the same object. In ActionScript, you can't hide an object's methods from the outside environment. However, you will sometimes have methods that *should* only be used internally by the object, ideally. In these cases, it's good practice to leave comments in the code indicating that these particular methods are "private." This basically means, "you can access these methods, but you shouldn't need to, so please don't." Using private methods is like walking into a restaurant's kitchen to grab your meal: you can do it, but it's better to leave it to the waiter.

In the *Motion* class, I have two private methods: *fixTime( )* and *update( )*. They encapsulate tasks that other methods depend on.

Motion.fixTime( )

The *Motion.fixTime( )* method solves a particular problem I ran into with the *resume( )*, *rewind( )*, and *fforward( )* methods. With the *Motion* in timer-based mode (that is, when useSeconds is true and *Motion* is calculated with *getTimer( )*), the time needs to be "fixed" when these three methods are called. It was difficult to find the solution to this obscure obstacle, and it is likewise difficult to explain its importance. In any case, here is the code:

```
MP.fixTime = function () {
    if (this.useSeconds)
        this.startTime = getTimer() - this.$time*1000;
};
```

First, the useSeconds property is checked. If it is true, the startTime property is set to the current *getTimer( )* value minus the current time. Since the *Motion*'s time is stored in seconds, and *getTimer( )* and startTime are in milliseconds, this.$time is multiplied by 1000. It's really the startTime property that is corrected by *fixtime( )*—it is synchronized with the current time. If startTime is already in sync, it won't be affected by the method.

Motion.update( )

The private method *update( )* updates the *Motion*'s targeted property to reflect the position at the current time. Here's the code:

```
MP.update = function () {
    this.setPosition (this.getPosition (this.$time));
};
```

The current time is passed to the *getPosition( )* method, which calculates and returns the position. This is then passed to the *setPosition( )* method, which changes the targeted property.

Getter/Setter Properties

With the getter and setter methods defined, we might as well link them to getter/setter properties, with the following code:

```
with (MP) {
    addProperty ("obj", getObj, setObj);
    addProperty ("prop", getProp, setProp);
    addProperty ("begin", getBegin, setBegin);
    addProperty ("duration", getDuration, setDuration);
```

```
addProperty ("useSeconds", getUseSeconds, setUseSeconds);
addProperty ("looping", getLooping, setLooping);
addProperty ("prevPos", getPrevPos, null);
addProperty ("time", getTime, setTime);
addProperty ("position",
             function() { return this.getPosition(); },
             function(p){ this.setPosition (p); } );
}
```

Because we have a consistent naming convention for the getter and setter methods, the parameters for the *addProperty( )* commands are straightforward. The name of the property comes first, as a string—"duration" for example. Then we pass a reference to the getter function, and finally, the setter function—for instance, *getDuration( )* and *setDuration( )*. In the case of the prevPos property, there is no setter function (it doesn't make sense to *set* this property from outside the object), so we put null instead of a setter function reference.

I used the with statement in conjuction with *Object.addProperty( )* to shorten the code and eliminate redundancy. If I don't use with, the code looks like this:

```
MP.addProperty ("obj", MP.getObj, MP.setObj);
MP.addProperty ("prop", MP.getProp, MP.setProp);
// etc.
```

Since everything in this situation belongs to MP (Motion.prototype), we might as well set the scope to MP using with:

```
with (MP) {
    addProperty ("obj", getObj, setObj);
    addProperty ("prop", getProp, setProp);
// etc.
}
```

The one oddity in this litany of properties is the position property. The code looks a bit different:

```
addProperty ("position",
             function() { return this.getPosition(); },
             function(p){ this.setPosition (p); } );
```

Because the *getPosition( )* method is designed to be overridden, we don't want to connect the `position` getter/setter property *directly* to the current *getPosition( )*. Instead, we use anonymous wrapper functions to look up the methods dynamically. Without the mediation of these wrapper functions, the `position` getter/setter property would not work properly in subclasses of *Motion*.

Finishing Off

Now that the methods have been defined, the MP variable is no longer needed. Thus, it is deleted this way:

```
delete MP;
```

The code for the *Motion* class is finished. We send a message to the Output window to celebrate:

```
trace (">> Motion class loaded");
```

The Tween Class

I have worked on the *Tween* and *Motion* classes off and on for almost a year, spending upwards of 80 hours on them. I originally had just a *Tween* class, but after a while, I saw that other types of motion, such as physics or recorded motion, shared much of the same infrastructure. I abstracted the overlapping functionality out of the *Tween* class and into the *Motion* superclass. We have seen how *Motion* objects keep track of time, position, movement, and other matters. Now we'll look at how the *Tween* class builds on top of this and provides a convenient, object-oriented framework for ActionScripted motion tweens.

The Tween Constructor

Once again, our exploration of a class begins with the constructor. Here's the code for the *Tween* constructor:

```
_global.Tween = function (obj, prop, func,
    begin, finish, duration, useSeconds) {
    this.superCon (obj, prop, begin, duration, useSeconds);
    this.setFunc (func);
    this.setFinish (finish);
};
```

Parameter	Type	Sample Value	Description
obj	object reference	this	The object containing the property to be tweened
prop	string	"_x"	The name of the property to tween
func	function reference	Math.easeInQuad	A tweening function used to calculate the position
begin	number	100	The starting position of the tween
finish	number	220	The finishing position of the tween
duration	number	0	The length of time of the tween, in either frames or seconds
useSeconds	Boolean	true	A flag specifying whether to use seconds instead of frames

TABLE 7-2

Arguments for the *Tween* Constructor

The constructor has seven arguments which are summarized and described in Table 7-2.

The first line of the constructor passes five of the seven arguments to the *Motion* superclass constructor:

```
this.superCon (obj, prop, begin, duration, useSeconds);
```

The remaining two arguments, `func` and `finish`, are passed to the appropriate setter methods:

```
this.setFunc (func);
this.setFinish (finish);
```

That's all there is to the *Tween* constructor; it's actually quite simple. Although seven arguments may seem like a lot, five of them are handled by the superclass, and the other two are taken care of by straightforward methods.

Immediately after the constructor, inheritance is established between the *Tween* and *Motion* classes:

```
Tween.extend (Motion);
```

This sets up the prototype chain so that *Tween*'s prototype inherits everything from *Motion*'s prototype; its methods in particular. Speaking of which, it's time to give our *Tween* class some methods of its own.

Public Methods

As usual, I define a temporary shortcut to the class prototype, in the following code:

```
var TP = Tween.prototype;
```

Because the *Tween* class inherits a number of public methods from *Motion*, it doesn't need too many more. I thought of two new public methods that would be useful, though I will probably think of more in the future.

Tween.continueTo( )

Wouldn't it be nice to have an easy way to string together several movements? For instance, you may want to tween a clip's _alpha to 80, then tween to 40 immediately after. The *continueTo( )* method lets you point a *Tween* to a new destination with a simple command. Here is its code:

```
TP.continueTo = function (finish, duration) {
    this.setBegin (this.getPosition());
    this.setFinish (finish);
    if (duration != undefined)
        this.setDuration (duration);
    this.start();
};
```

First, the current position of the *Tween* becomes its new starting point:

```
this.setBegin (this.getPosition());
```

Then, the incoming `finish` argument becomes the new finishing point of the *Tween*:

```
this.setFinish (finish);
```

The method also gives you the option of setting a new duration. If the duration argument is defined, the *Tween* is changed accordingly:

```
if (duration != undefined)
    this.setDuration (duration);
```

Lastly, the *Tween* is started from its new beginning point:

```
this.start();
```

The following code example shows how to use *continueTo( )* in conjunction with the *onMotionFinished( )* handler to produce a continuous string of eased movements:

```
// test Tween.continueTo()
// "ball" is an existing movie clip instance
x_twn = new Tween (ball, "_x", Math.easeInOutCirc, 20, 70, 25);
```

```
x_twn.onMotionFinished = function () {
    this.continueTo (this.position + 50);
};
```

This code causes the ball movie clip to start at a position (20, 0), and move to (70, 0) over 25 frames, using circular in-out easing. When x_twn finishes by reaching its destination, the *onMotionFinished* event is fired automatically. This invokes x_twn's callback method *x_twn.onMotionFinished( )*, which causes the *Tween* to "continue to" the point 50 pixels to the right of its current position. When this new destination is reached, the *onMotionFinished* event fires again, which defines a new destination, and so on. The process repeats indefinitely, but it can be stopped either by calling the *x_twn.stop( )* method or by deleting the *x_twn.onMotionFinished( )* handler.

Tween.yoyo( )

Here's a fun method—*yoyo( )*:

```
TP.yoyo = function () {
    with (this) {
        continueTo (getBegin(), getTime());
    }
};
```

The *yoyo( )* method sends the *Motion* back towards its starting point, using the *continueTo( )* method. The current time is passed as the second parameter. This ensures that the trip backward takes the same amount of time as the trip forward. For example, if a *Tween* has a duration of 60 frames, but the *yoyo( )* method is called 25 frames into it, the *Tween* will return to its starting point in 25 frames.

Here is a code example that produces a nice down-up yo-yo motion with easing:

```
// test Tween.yoyo()
// "ball" is an existing movie clip instance
y_twn = new Tween (ball, "_y", Math.easeOutQuad, 40, 180, 20);
y_twn.onMotionFinished = function () {
    this.setFunc (Math.easeInQuad);
    this.yoyo();
    delete this.onMotionFinished;
};
```

First, a *Tween* object is created to control the _y property of the ball movie clip, taking it from 40 to 180 pixels vertically in a 20-frame time span. The *Tween.onMotionFinished( )* handler is then assigned a few actions that will execute when the *Tween* finishes:

1. The tweening function is changed from an ease-out to an ease-in. A real yo-yo starts out fast at the top and slows to a stop at the bottom— an ease-out. It then speeds up as it rises, stopping suddenly at the top—an ease-in.

2. The *Tween.yoyo( )* method is called to swap the start and end points of the *Tween*.

3. The *onMotionFinished( )* handler is deleted because we want it to only execute once. If you eliminate this step, the ball will oscillate indefinitely.

Getter/Setter Methods

The *Tween* class adds three getter/setter properties: func, change, and finish. We first define the getter/setter methods for these, then connect them to the properties with *Object.addProperty( )* (illustrated later in the "Getter/Setter Properties" section of this chapter). But first, we take care of the all-important *getPosition( )* method.

Tween.getPosition( )

The *getPosition( )* method returns the position of the *Tween* at a certain time, and overrides the superclass method *Motion.getPosition( )* (which is an empty function by default). Here's the code:

```
TP.getPosition = function (t) {
    if (t == undefined) t = this.$time;
    with (this) return $func (t,
                                $begin,
                                $change,
                                $duration);
};
```

In the first line, if a specific time is not given through the t argument, the current time is chosen. Next, the properties for the time, beginning position, change in position, and duration are passed to the easing function. The resulting value is returned from the method.

Tween.setFunc( ) and getFunc( )

The *setFunc( )* and *getFunc( )* methods govern the `func` getter/setter property, represented internally by the `$func` property. My tweening functions are ideal candidates for `func`, although you can define your own, as long as they conform to the same basic structure and arguments (`t`, `b`, `c`, and `d`).

Here's the code for the methods:

```
TP.setFunc = function (f) {
    this.$func = f;
};

TP.getFunc = function () {
    return this.$func;
};
```

Tween.setChange( ) and getChange( )

The *setChange( )* and *getChange( )* methods mediate access to the `change` property, which stores the change in position from the beginning of the *Tween* to the end.

NOTE: In mathematical function terminology, you could call the change of a tween its *range*, and its duration the tween's *domain*.

The code for these methods is straightforward:

```
TP.setChange = function (c) {
    this.$change = c;
};

TP.getChange = function () {
    return this.$change;
};
```

Tween.setFinish( ) and getFinish( )

The `finish` getter/setter property governs the finishing position of the *Tween*. It is implemented a little differently than previous properties. The value of `finish` *per se* is not stored as its own property. Rather, it is defined in terms of the `change` property. The two are interdependent: you can't modify `finish` without modifying `change`. Thus, I only maintain one internal property—for `change`, calculating `finish` as needed. I chose `change` because my tweening functions use a change argument (rather than a finish argument).

You can see in the following code how a specified value for finish is converted into the equivalent change value:

```
TP.setFinish = function (f) {
    this.$change = f - this.$begin;
};
```

The beginning position is subtracted from the finishing point to yield the change in position.

Likewise, the *getFinish( )* method calculates the finish value on the fly by adding change to begin:

```
TP.getFinish = function () {
    return this.$begin + this.$change;
};
```

Getter/Setter Properties

The *Tween* class inherits the nine getter/setter properties of the *Motion* superclass. It also adds three more getter/setter properties—func, change, and finish—with the following code:

```
with (TP) {
    addProperty ("func", getFunc, setFunc);
    addProperty ("change", getChange, setChange);
    addProperty ("finish", getFinish, setFinish);
}
```

Some people will prefer getter/setter properties; others will choose to call the methods directly. It's a matter of personal preference. Personally, I use the methods most of the time; it's slightly faster than calling the getter/setter property, which causes the run-time interpreter to look up the method for you.

Finishing Off

With the constructor, methods and properties defined, our *Tween* class is complete. It's time to clean up by deleting the shortcut variable TP and sending a message to the Output window, with the last bit of code:

```
delete TP;
trace (">> Tween class loaded");
```

Conclusion

In this chapter, we have looked at dynamic motion from a particular angle—where there is one definite position for a given time. We dissected the concept of easing and looked at several examples of easing curves and functions. These concepts are encapsulated in a practical manner in the *Motion* and *Tween* classes. In the next chapter, we'll look at motion produced by a different process—physics animation.

Chapter 8

Physics

T

o understand physics is to understand how the physical world works. In this chapter, we'll look at several core principles of physics—velocity, acceleration, force—and the relationships between them. We'll explore some specific forces, such as friction, elasticity, and gravity, and how they can be calculated and incorporated into dynamic animation. Lastly, we'll discuss wave physics and a custom *WaveMotion* class to encapsulate customizable oscillation.

Kinematics

Mechanics is the section of physics concerned with the action of forces on physical objects and the resulting motion. There are three main areas within mechanics: statics, kinetics, and kinematics. Statics deals with forces in equilibrium, whereas kinetics governs accelerated motion produced by unbalanced forces. Kinematics, meanwhile, deals with pure motion, without regard to the force or mass involved. We will look at some concepts from kinematics in this section, then some kinetics in the Force section later on.

Position

In this chapter, we'll focus on kinematics in two dimensions, which we'll name x and y. Thus, *position* in our current discussion is a two-dimensional vector quantity, containing x and y components. The *Vector* class we explored in Chapter 4 serves our purposes nicely here. We can declare a two-dimensional position object by creating a *Vector* instance, as in the following code:

```
// position as a 2-D vector
pos = new Vector (2, 5);
```

As we progress through the chapter, we'll use this basic syntax many times over to create vectors for a variety of physics concepts, such as displacement, velocity, acceleration, and force.

NOTE: Kinematics can be extended to three or more dimensions without too much difficulty. In fact, once you're comfortable with implementing kinematics in ActionScript with the two-dimensional *Vector* class, you will find that many of the operations transfer to the *Vector3d* class (see Chapter 5) quite easily. I deliberately use *polymorphism* (see Chapter 2) in designing the two vector classes, so that their methods provide a closely matching interface.

Displacement

Displacement is a *change of position*. Put another way, displacement is the difference *between* two positions. When the positions are vectors, the displacement is also a vector. You can find the displacement vector between two positions by subtracting one position vector from the other. Figure 8-1 shows two points on a graph and the displacement vector between them.

We have two points: A at (2, 3) and B at (4, 2). We also have two corresponding vectors: a = [2, 3] and b = [4, 2]. The displacement vector d is calculated by subtracting b from a. Figure 8-1 shows this graphically, but here is how the process works mathematically:

a = [2, 3]

b = [4, 2]

let d be the displacement between a and b

$d = b - a$

d = [4 − 2, 2 − 3]

d = [2, −1]

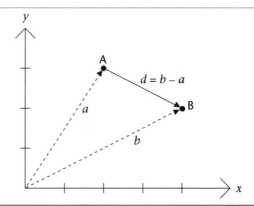

FIGURE 8-1

Finding the displacement vector d between points A and B

Transferring this process to ActionScript, our *Vector* class makes it easy to create position vectors and subtract them. The following code example demonstrates this process of finding the displacement vector between two positions:

```
// finding displacement vector
pointA = new Vector (2, 3);
pointB = new Vector (4, 2);
disp = pointB.minusNew (pointA);
trace (disp);   // output: [2, -1]
```

First, we create two position vectors, pointA and pointB. To find the displacement from pointA to pointB, we subtract the first from the second. Using the capabilities of our *Vector* class, we call the *minusNew( )* method of pointB, to subtract pointA and return the difference as a new vector disp.

Distance

Though closely related, *displacement* and *distance* are two separate things. Distance is a one-dimensional quantity, while displacement can have two or more dimensions. Put another way, distance is scalar, and displacement is vector. In the preceding code example, the displacement between pointA and pointB is [2, –1]. If we were to calculate the distance, we'd find that it is the square root of 5, or approximately 2.236. You can confirm this with a Pythagorean function, such as *Math.distance( )* from Chapter 3. Or, as we see in the following code, the *length* of the disp vector is the same value:

```
// continuing previous example
trace (disp.getLength()); // output: 2.23606797749979
```

This is not a coincidence. The distance between two points is always equal to the *length of the displacement vector* between them. Thus, if you have a displacement vector between two positions, and you want to find the distance "as the crow flies," call the *getLength( )* method on that *Vector*:

```
// finding distance from displacement
disp = new Vector (3, 4);
distance = disp.getLength();
trace (distance); // output: 2.23606797749979
```

Velocity

Velocity is the *change of position over time*. Put another way, it is the *ratio between displacement and time*. Velocity is also a vector quantity, with two dimensions in our current context.

When we're creating scripted animation, we usually don't want to *find* the velocity of an object by tracking its position. Rather, we need to *define* a velocity, and have the object's position automatically follow from that. For instance, when you play the *Asteroids* arcade game, you don't have direct control over the position of the space ship. All you can do is affect the ship's velocity, which in turn affects the position. To use another example, think about the difference between mice and joysticks. A mouse controls the cursor's *position* directly, but a joystick controls the *velocity* of the cursor. With real-world objects, it's usually easier to control velocity than position, which is why many remote controls use joysticks.

Movement with Constant Velocity

When an object has a constant velocity both vertically and horizontally, it moves in a straight line. Here is a code example that demonstrates a simple approach to moving a movie clip with constant velocity:

```
// movement with constant velocity
pos = new Vector (0, 0);
vel = new Vector (1, 2);
this.onEnterFrame = function () {
    pos.plus (vel);
    this._x = pos.x;
    this._y = pos.y;
};
```

First, the *Vector* objects `pos` and `vel` are declared to represent the object's position and velocity. The initial position is (0, 0) and the initial velocity is down-and-to-the-right. Then, a frame loop is created with the *onEnterFrame( )* handler. Each frame, the velocity is added to the position, using the *Vector.plus( )* method. Lastly, the x and y components of the position are rendered to the screen by assigning them to the _x and _y properties of the movie clip.

NOTE: The preceding example uses the Flash coordinate system. If you want to use Cartesian coordinates, simply replace `this._y = pos.y` with `this._y = -pos.y`. This inverts the y component of the position before assigning it to _y.

Movement with Random Velocity

Having done constant velocity, let's look at an example of motion involving a changing velocity, in the following code:

```
// movement with random velocity
pos = new Vector (200, 200);
vel = new Vector (0, 0);
this.onEnterFrame = function () {
    vel.reset (random(9)-4, random(9)-4);
    pos.plus (vel);
    this._x = pos.x;
    this._y = pos.y;
};
```

The structure is much the same as the previous example. First, we define pos and vel *Vector* objects. Then, in an *onEnterframe( )* handler, we add vel to pos and render pos to the screen. The extra step added here is this line of code:

```
vel.reset (random(9)-4, random(9)-4);
```

For each frame, a new velocity vector is chosen, which is then used to move the object. The x and y values of vel are random integers between –4 and 4. This gives the object an erratic wandering effect motion.

Movement with Mouse-Controlled Velocity

Our next code example shows how a movie clip's velocity can be controlled interactively with the mouse:

```
// mouse-controlled velocity
pos = new Vector (200, 200);
vel = new Vector (0, 0);
this.onEnterFrame = function () {
    vel.reset (this._xmouse / 10,
               this._ymouse / 10);
    pos.plus (vel);
    this._x = pos.x;
    this._y = pos.y;
};
```

This script is identical to the previous example except for one line of code:

```
vel.reset (this._xmouse / 10,
            this._ymouse / 10);
```

Instead of random numbers, the mouse coordinates are used to supply new values for the vel *Vector*. Since the _xmouse and _ymouse properties used here are relative to the moving object, the object moves toward the mouse.

Speed

Speed and velocity have a relationship similar to that between distance and displacement. Velocity is vector and multidimensional, but speed is scalar and one-dimensional. Furthermore, speed is the *length* of a velocity vector, and is also called the *magnitude* or *absolute value* of velocity. Remember that a vector has both magnitude and direction. When you take away the directional aspect of velocity, you're left with its magnitude—speed.

Here is a code example that demonstrates how to find the speed of a velocity vector:

```
vel = new Vector (3, 4);
speed = vel.getLength();
trace (speed); // output: 5
```

Just as we did to find the distance of a displacement vector, we call the *getLength( )* method to find the absolute value of the velocity vector—the speed.

Acceleration

Acceleration is the *rate of change of velocity*. Since velocity is the rate of change of position, we can also say that acceleration is the *rate of change of the rate of change of position*. A car's speedometer shows its velocity at any given time. When the car accelerates, the needle on the speedometer changes as the velocity changes. The faster the needle moves, the greater the acceleration. Acceleration is also a vector quantity, with magnitude and direction.

Let's take a look at three scripts that demonstrate how to manipulate acceleration in dynamic motion. In a similar approach to the three preceding velocity examples, we'll examine acceleration that is constant, random, and mouse-controlled.

Movement with Constant Acceleration

The following code shows simple dynamic movement with constant acceleration:

```
// movement with constant acceleration
pos = new Vector (0, 0);
vel = new Vector (0, 0);
accel = new Vector (1, 0);
this.onEnterFrame = function () {
    vel.plus (accel);
    pos.plus (vel);
    this._x = pos.x;
    this._y = pos.y;
};
```

First, three *Vector* instances are created to represent position, velocity, and acceleration. Then in an *onEnterFrame( )* handler, acceleration is added to velocity, and velocity is added to position, which is then rendered. That's all there is to it.

The object starts at a standstill, then moves increasingly faster to the right. You can play around with the initial values of the pos, vel, or accel vectors to produce different animations. For instance, you can define a velocity that points left, as in the following code:

```
vel = new Vector (-12, 0);
```

This causes the object to initially move to the left, but slow to a stop and then accelerate to the right.

Movement with Random Acceleration

Our next code example demonstrates random acceleration:

```
// movement with random acceleration
pos = new Vector (200, 200);
vel = new Vector (0, 0);
accel = new Vector (0, 0);
this.onEnterFrame = function () {
    accel.reset (random(5)-2, random(5)-2);
    vel.plus (accel);
    pos.plus (vel);
```

```
        this._x = pos.x;
        this._y = pos.y;
};
```

This is similar to the random velocity example, except that here, the values of `accel.x` and `accel.y` are random integers between –2 and 2. This script produces a wandering motion, but it looks different from the random velocity wandering.

NOTE: This is actually an example of Brownian motion, wherein an object experiences randomly changing forces (and thus acceleration) from different directions. We'll look more closely at Brownian motion in Chapter 11.

Movement with Mouse-Controlled Acceleration

Lastly, here is a script in which the acceleration is controlled with the mouse:

```
// mouse-controlled acceleration
pos = new Vector (200, 200);
vel = new Vector (0, 0);
accel = new Vector (0, 0);
this.onEnterFrame = function () {
    accel.reset (this._xmouse / 100,
                 this._ymouse / 100);
    vel.plus (accel);
    pos.plus (vel);
    this._x = pos.x;
    this._y = pos.y;
};
```

Force

A force is simply a push or a pull in some direction. Without force, nothing in the physical world would change, and thus, nothing would happen. From a certain perspective, life can be seen as just a process of moving bits of matter around.

You may have heard that matter consists mostly of empty space. This is true; an atom is composed of a nucleus and orbiting electrons, separated by a relatively huge expanse, whose proportions can be seen as similar to those of our own solar system. If this is the case, how can objects that are 99.9999 percent empty push each other around? Or how can a rope support my weight when its atoms aren't even touching each other? Actually, it's the *electromagnetic force* between the atoms' electrons that's responsible for the "illusion of solidity" we experience. Besides gravity, all of the forces we experience in our macroscopic world, including friction, tension, magnetism, and electricity, are a result of electromagnetic force.

NOTE: The other two fundamental forces in physics besides gravity and the electromagnetic force are the strong and weak nuclear forces. They operate at the level of the atom, therefore we don't experience them directly. However, the nuclear forces keep us from dematerializing into oblivion.

Force is a vector quantity, with magnitude and direction. It influences motion by causing acceleration, as Newton made clear in the 1600s. Newton is most famous for his discoveries in gravitation, but his Laws of Motion are a work of genius in their own right.

Newton's First Law of Motion

One of the foundational laws of mechanics is that an acceleration—a change in velocity—doesn't just *happen*. If an object's velocity changes, there must have been a force that acted upon it. This is, in fact, Newton's *First Law of Motion*, which is often stated like this:

"An object at rest tends to stay at rest, and an object in motion tends to stay in motion with the same speed and in the same direction unless acted upon by an unbalanced force."

Newton's First Law is also called the *Law of Inertia*. Inertia is an object's *resistance to change in its velocity*. If a rock isn't moving, it won't start moving until some unbalanced force acts upon it. Conversely, if the rock *is* moving, it won't speed up or slow down unless a force, such as friction or gravity, acts upon it.

In outer space, objects experience very little friction, and can travel long distances without losing much speed at all. As a result, we can send probes across the solar system to spy on other planets, sailing millions of miles on inertia.

Net Force

Newton's First Law of Motion mentions an *unbalanced force*, which can also be called the *net force*. One object can have several forces acting on it simultaneously, in different directions. In a game of tug-of-war, a rope has two main forces pulling on it, in opposite directions. If the teams are evenly matched, the forces will cancel each other out, and the rope won't move. If the forces are unbalanced, though, the rope will move towards the stronger team. Thus, the difference between the two forces is the net force.

In a system where several forces are pushing or pulling on an object, we calculate the net force by adding up all of the force vectors for that object. If the net force is zero, the object will stay at the same velocity. However, if the net force is something other than zero, the object will accelerate in the direction of the net force vector.

In the following code example, three forces are defined, and then added together to find the net force:

```
// declare force vectors
forceA = new Vector (2, 0);
forceB = new Vector (-3, 2);
forceC = new Vector (0, 1);
// sum the forces
forceNet = new Vector (0, 0);
forceNet.plus (forceA);
forceNet.plus (forceB);
forceNet.plus (forceC);
trace (forceNet); // [-1, 3]
```

In this approach, a zero vector `forceNet` is created, and then the three force vectors are added to it, one by one. The *x* components total –1 (2 – 3 + 0), and the *y* components add up to 3 (0 + 2 + 1).

We can shorten this process by using the *Vector.plusNew( )* method, which adds two vectors and creates the sum vector in one step:

```
// sum the forces (shortcut)
forceNet = forceA.plusNew (forceB);
forceNet.plus (forceC);
trace (forceNet); // [-1, 3]
```

The `forceA` vector is added to `forceB`, and the result is assigned to `forceNet`. Adding `forceC` to `forceNet` completes the process of finding the net force.

NOTE: In situations where you need to add together many forces, say five or more, it is more efficient to code your own addition procedure that bypasses the *Vector.plus( )* method. This will typically involve putting the vectors into an array, looping through the array, adding up the *x* and *y* components in their own variables, and storing the result in a new *Vector*.

Newton's Second Law of Motion

We know from Newton's First Law that a net force action on an object causes it to accelerate. We also know how to calculate the net force on an object, by adding up the forces. But *how much* acceleration does the force cause—what kind of numerical relationship is there? Experience tells us that if you push a light object and a heavy object with the same force, the light object will accelerate more. It seems that the mass of an object affects the acceleration.

Newton's *Second Law of Motion* describes the relationship between net force, mass, and acceleration:

"The acceleration of an object as produced by a net force is directly proportional to the magnitude of the net force, in the same direction as the net force, and inversely proportional to the mass of the object."

To state this another way, more net force means more acceleration, and more mass means less acceleration.

Newton's Second Law can be expressed mathematically with this equation:

$f = ma$

Here, *a* is the object's acceleration, *f* is the net force acting on it, and *m* is the object's mass. This equation is often seen rearranged in this form:

$a = f / m$

This form of the equation shows us how to find the acceleration of an object, when we know its mass and the net force acting on it. You simply take the net force and divide it by the mass. Suppose the net force is [8, 0] (a magnitude of 8 pointing to the right), and the mass is 2. We calculate the acceleration like so:

f = [8, 0]
m = 2
a = f / m
a = [8, 0] / 2
a = [4, 0]

We find that the acceleration vector is [4, 0]—in the same direction as the force vector, as we would expect.

Suppose we apply the same force [8, 0] to a heavier object, with a mass of 4. The resulting acceleration would be

f = [8, 0]

m = 4

a = f / m

a = [8, 0] / 4

a = [2, 0]

The heavy object's acceleration is [2, 0]—half of the acceleration of the lighter object. Thus, we see the relationship between mass and acceleration: When the mass is doubled, the acceleration is halved.

Force-Driven Motion in Flash

To produce convincing dynamic motion in Flash, based on forces, we want to start with forces and end up with an object's new position, calculated automatically. To accomplish this, we use what we have learned so far about velocity, acceleration, and so on. To quickly review: Forces on an object combine to produce a net force. The net force produces an acceleration. Acceleration changes the velocity of the object. Velocity changes the position of the object. The order is this: forces | net force | acceleration | velocity | position.

In an ActionScript implementation of this process, there are six identifiable steps:

1. Calculate the forces acting on an object.
   The force vectors can be calculated any way you like. Later in the chapter, we'll see how to calculate forces like gravity and elasticity. For now, we'll represent this step with this generalized ActionScript:

   ```
   // define forces
   forceA = new Vector (1, 2);
   forceB = new Vector (3, 4);
   ```

2. Add the forces to find the net force.
   Earlier in the chapter, we saw this procedure for finding the net force:

   ```
   // find the net force
   forceNet = forceA.plusNew (forceB);
   ```

3. Find the acceleration due to the force.

Remember our equation for acceleration:

a = f / m

In ActionScript, we divide the net force vector by the object's mass:

```
// find acceleration
// mass is previously defined
accel = forceNet.scaleNew (1 / mass);
```

Sometimes the mass of the moving objects isn't significant to the animation. You can actually ignore mass by pretending that an object is a particle with a mass of 1. In this case, the acceleration equation becomes a bit simpler:

a = f / m

m = 1

a = f / 1

a = f

When the mass is 1, acceleration is equal to the net force. Thus, the ActionScript to find acceleration would look like this instead:

```
// find acceleration
accel = forceNet;
```

In most of my animations, the mass of the objects isn't important to me, so I assume the mass is 1 and simply skip step 3 altogether.

4. Add acceleration to velocity.
    The velocity vector is changed by the acceleration vector:

```
// find new velocity
// vel is previously defined
vel.plus (accel);
```

5. Add velocity to position.
    This is similar to the previous step, except we're now changing position:

```
// find new position
// pos is previously defined
pos.plus (vel);
```

6. Move the object to the new position.

Generally, this means setting the _x and _y properties of a movie clip to the *x* and *y* components of the position vector:

```
// update movie clip position
mc._x = pos.x;
mc._y = pos.y;
```

As I mentioned in Chapter 3, I sometimes prefer to use traditional Cartesian coordinates, rather than Flash's screen coordinates. In which case, I flip the y-axis by multiplying the vector's *y* component by –1:

```
// using Cartesian coordinates
mc._x = pos.x;
mc._y = -pos.y;
```

The preceding six steps give you a general procedure for working from forces to dynamic motion. So far, we've been working in a perfect universe—one where there is no resistance to slow us down. To produce more realistic motion, however, we need to bring friction into the picture.

Friction

Friction is a reaction to movement—a force that acts in the opposite direction of an object's motion. When you try to push a couch across the floor, the carpet starts pushing back, with friction force. If your force is stronger than the carpet's friction force, the net force will be able to get the couch moving.

Notice that friction is a *reactive* force. It doesn't spontaneously push objects on its own—friction arises as a response to movement. For instance, when a couch sits undisturbed, no friction is acting on it. When you try to move it, though, a force of friction resists you. When two solid objects are in contact with each other, there are two main types of friction: kinetic and static.

Kinetic Friction

Kinetic friction is also called sliding friction. When a hockey puck slides across the ice, there is a force of friction that gradually slows it down. The magnitude of the friction basically remains constant. Consequently, the deceleration of the puck is constant. This is the same acceleration as a quadratic ease-out.

The amount of friction depends on how much perpendicular force (also called *normal force*) is pushing the surfaces against each other. A heavy object will have more friction than a light object on the same ice, because there is a greater force of gravity pulling it against the ice.

Here is the equation for kinetic friction in its common form:

$$f_k = \mu_k N$$

In this equation, f_k is the force of kinetic friction, μ_k is the coefficient of kinetic friction, and N is the magnitude of the normal force pushing the two surfaces together. The value of μ_k (μ is pronounced "miu") is generally between 0 and 1. The higher the coefficient's value, the more friction is produced proportionate to the normal force.

If you want to use kinetic friction in a Flash animation that isn't a strict physics simulation, it will be easiest to just assign a value directly to f_k, without worrying about the coefficient and normal force. You can even skip straight to assigning a value to the friction's *acceleration*, rather than the friction's *force*. For instance, the "proper" and longer way would be to find a value for the friction force, then use the $f = ma$ equation to find the acceleration, as in the following example:

$f_k = 10$

$a = f / m$

$m = 5$

$a = 10 / 5$

$a = 2$

However, you can just decide that the acceleration due to friction will be a certain value, and assign it directly, ignoring the object's mass:

$a = 2$

Once you have the acceleration due to kinetic friction, the process to implement it is a bit involved (at least compared to simplified fluid friction, which we'll look at shortly). The following ActionScript provides an example of this procedure:

```
// calculation of kinetic friction in one dimension
velX = 0;
kFrictionAccel = .8;

this.onEnterFrame = function () {
    velX += accelX;
    accelX = 0;
    if (velX > 0) {
        velX = Math.max (0, velX - kFrictionAccel);
```

```
    } else if (velX < 0) {
        velX = Math.min (0, velX + kFrictionAccel);
    }
    this._x += velX;
};

this.onMouseDown = function () {
    accelX = 15;
};
```

When this example is run, the object is stationary until a mouse click produces an acceleration. At that point, the object briefly accelerates, but the force of kinetic friction slows it to a stop.

The logic of the code is this: If the horizontal velocity is greater than zero (that is, if the object is moving to the right), the kinetic friction acceleration is the opposite way—in the negative direction (to the left). In that case, the velocity should be reduced by the amount of the friction acceleration (velX – kFrictionAccel).

However, friction must not *change the direction* of the velocity. In other words, if velX is originally positive, it must not be allowed to become negative after subtracting kFrictionAccel. Friction slows the object's velocity down to zero, but doesn't cause it to move in the opposite direction. Thus, I use the *Math.max( )* and *Math.min( )* functions to ensure that the subtraction doesn't cross the zero line.

Static Friction

When an object is stationary on a surface, static friction is possible. Static friction is usually stronger than kinetic friction, which explains why it's often harder to get something moving than to keep it moving.

A stationary object doesn't budge until you push it hard enough. Then it suddenly breaks free and starts sliding. A sled, when stationary, can stay put on a snowy hill. The force of gravity is pulling on it, but the force of friction between the snow and the sled is strong enough to match it. The two forces are equal, and in opposite directions, so they cancel each other out, and the sled does not accelerate. However, if you give the sled a little push, the extra force overcomes the force of static friction, and the sled begins to accelerate.

The important thing to remember about static friction is that it only comes into play when the two objects in question *aren't moving* relative to each other. Once the surfaces in contact start sliding past each other, though, the friction is now kinetic friction, which usually has a weaker force than static friction.

Here is the equation for static friction:

$$f_s = \mu_s N$$

In this equation, f_s is the force of static friction, μ_s is the coefficient of static friction, and N is the magnitude of the normal force pushing the two surfaces together. The value of μ_s is generally between 0 and 1. The higher the coefficient's value, the more friction is produced proportionate to the normal force.

To date, I haven't used static friction in any animations, though I am tempted to now, having written about it. The logic for the implementation is simple:

1. Check that the object in question is stationary (speed is 0).

2. Calculate the net force acting on the object.

3. Calculate the force of static friction acting on the object.

4. If the net force is less than the force of static friction, do nothing.

5. Otherwise, accelerate the object accordingly.

Fluid Friction

So far, we've looked at friction between solid objects. A fluid, on the other hand, is either a gas or a liquid. We most commonly encounter fluid friction as we move through water and air. The faster an object moves through a fluid, the greater the force of fluid friction. For example, when you drive a car, you encounter more air resistance when you drive faster.

Producing an accurate simulation of fluid friction requires a number of complex equations. When we aren't so concerned with physical accuracy, though, in dynamic Flash animations, we can use an approximation to produce a nice friction effect. We can use this general principle: *Higher speed means more loss of speed due to friction*. In other words, the speed lost is *relative* to the speed itself.

In numerical terms, relative quantities often translate into percentages. For instance, sales tax is a percentage: the more you buy, the more you pay in tax. Fluid friction, then, is like a tax on velocity. It can be defined as a *percentage of velocity lost per unit of time*. In Flash, the basic unit of time is the frame. So in practical terms, we can quantify fluid friction as *a percentage of velocity lost per frame*.

For example, a force of friction may cause an object's speed to decrease by ten percent each frame. If the object starts with a speed of 100, the next frame would be 90 (100 – 10). In the next frame, the speed decreases by 9 (10% of 90) to 81. The next drop is by 8.1 to 72.9, and so on.

The following code example shows how this effect can be achieved in ActionScript:

```
// calculation of fluid friction in one dimension
velX = 0;
fluidFriction = .07;
this.onEnterFrame = function () {
    velX += accelX;
    accelX = 0;
    velX *= (1 - fluidFriction);
    this._x += velX;
};
this.onMouseDown = function () {
    accelX = 15;
};
```

This script is similar to the preceding kinetic friction example. There are two differences, the first being the declaration of the friction variable:

```
fluidFriction = .07;
```

Fluid friction is defined as a percentage; in this case, seven percent of the velocity is lost each frame. The other difference is the one line of code where the friction affects the velocity:

```
velX *= (1 - fluidFriction);
```

This reduces `velX` by the percentage specified in `fluidFriction`. In our case, the subtraction `1 - fluidFriction` yields .93. Multiplying the velocity by .93 has the effect of reducing it by seven percent.

As you can see, the code for fluid friction is simpler and faster than for kinetic friction. I use fluid friction most of the time, the most notable exception being the Axis Interactive v2 site (www.axis-media.com), where I used kinetic friction for the floating main menu.

If your primary concern is the speed of execution, use fluid friction. If you're looking for physical accuracy, use kinetic friction where objects are rolling or sliding, and use fluid friction where objects are moving through liquid, gas, or space (which usually has a bit of gas). Comparing the two types of friction to tweens, kinetic friction produces a quadratic ease-out, whereas fluid friction results in an exponential ease-out (see Chapter 7 for more details).

Gravitation in Space

Between any two objects, there is a force of gravity—even between two specks of dust. It's only when you have a lot of matter clumped together, though, that the force of gravity accumulates enough to be noticeable, as it is around planets and stars.

This is the classical Newtonian formula for gravitation between two masses:

$$F_g = \frac{Gm_1m_2}{r^2}$$

F_g is the magnitude of the force of gravity, while m_1 and m_2 are bodies of mass. G is the gravitational constant 6.67×10^{11} Nm^2/kg^2, and r is the distance between the centers of the two masses.

The force of gravity, F_g, is *directly proportional* to the amount of mass involved. If you double one of the masses, m_1 or m_2, the force of gravity doubles. If you double both masses, there is four times as much mass as before, and thus, four times the gravity.

On the other hand, there is an inverse square relationship between force and distance. When the distance r between the two masses doubles, the gravity between them *decreases* to a quarter of the original force. Conversely, if the masses move closer together by half the original distance, the force of gravity increases four-fold.

In Flash, we are primarily concerned with effect, not physical accuracy. As such, we don't have to use the official gravitational constant G. We don't even have to include the masses of the two objects in the calculation if we don't feel it's necessary.

What's important is this principle: Between two objects, there is a gravitational force whose strength varies with the distance r between them, in an inverse-square relationship. What we can do then is specify the strength of gravitation between the two objects, find the distance r, and divide the strength value by r^2 to find the force of gravity.

Let's look at an example of how to implement gravitation in ActionScript. First, here is the complete code:

```
// gravitation around a mouse-clicked point
this.pos = new Vector (150, 100);
this.vel = new Vector (5, 0);
this.accel = new Vector (0, 0);
this.friction = 0;

// gravity properties
```

```
this.anchor = new Vector (250, 200);
this.strength = 5000;

this.doForce = function () {
    // calculate gravity force
    this.netForce = this.pos.minusNew (this.anchor);
    var r = this.netForce.getLength();
    this.netForce.setLength (-this.strength / (r*r));
};

this.move = function () {
    // calculate new position
    this.vel.plus (this.netForce);
    this.vel.scale (1 - this.friction);
    this.pos.plus (this.vel);
    // render position
    this._x = this.pos.x;
    this._y = this.pos.y;
};

this.onEnterFrame = function () {
    this.doForce();
    this.move();
};

this.onMouseDown = function () {
    this.anchor.reset (this._parent._xmouse,
                       this._parent._ymouse);
};
```

This code should be placed inside a movie clip that has a visible graphic, like a ball. Be sure to include the *Vector* class (*vector_class.as*) as well. When this example is running, you can click with the mouse to cause the movie clip to orbit around that spot. Let's look at the code in more detail.

The first section of code declares the main vectors, for position, velocity, acceleration, and friction:

```
this.pos = new Vector (150, 100);
this.vel = new Vector (5, 0);
this.accel = new Vector (0, 0);
this.friction = 0;
```

These are familiar from our discussions earlier in the chapter. Next, two properties specific to gravity are declared:

```
this.anchor = new Vector (250, 200);
this.strength = 5000;
```

The `anchor` *Vector* is the point on the stage that the moving object will orbit around. The `strength` property specifies how strong the force of gravity is between the anchor point and the moving object. Feel free to try different values for `strength` and see the effect it has on the animation.

The next item is the *doForce( )* method, which has this code:

```
this.doForce = function () {
    // calculate gravity force
    this.netForce = this.pos.minusNew (this.anchor);
    var r = this.netForce.getLength();
    this.netForce.setLength (-this.strength / (r*r));
};
```

This is where the net force is calculated. The first line of code finds the displacement vector between the anchor point and the position vector by subtracting one from the other:

```
this.netForce = this.pos.minusNew (this.anchor);
```

I'm actually involving `this.netForce` here because the net force vector will be *parallel* to the displacement vector. Thus, I can point the `netForce` *Vector* in the correct *direction*, and then change its *magnitude*—its length—in the code that follows:

```
var r = this.netForce.getLength();
this.netForce.setLength (-this.strength / (r*r));
```

The first line finds the *distance* r between the anchor and the object's position by finding the length of the displacement vector, which is actually `this.netForce` at the moment. (Remember our discussion on displacement vs. distance earlier in this chapter.) Finally, the `netForce` *Vector* is given the correct length according to the inverse-square relationship defined in the gravitation equation.

Now that we know the net force, we just need to translate it into velocity and motion. The *move( )* method handles that process with the following code:

```
this.move = function () {
    // calculate new position
    this.vel.plus (this.netForce);
    this.vel.scale (1 - this.friction);
    this.pos.plus (this.vel);
    // render position
    this._x = this.pos.x;
    this._y = this.pos.y;
};
```

This procedure should be familiar from our earlier examples. Acceleration is added to velocity, which is scaled back by friction and then added to position. The position is then rendered to the screen. In this example, the net force is added directly to the velocity in place of acceleration, because the net force is equal to the acceleration.

With the hard work out of the way, we create a simple frame loop to drive the animation:

```
this.onEnterFrame = function () {
    this.doForce();
    this.move();
};
```

For each frame, the *onEnterFrame( )* handler calls the *doForce( )* method to calculate a new net force, then the *move( )* method to animate the object accordingly.

Finally, the mouse interactivity is defined using the *onMouseDown( )* event handler:

```
this.onMouseDown = function () {
    this.anchor.reset (this._parent._xmouse,
                       this._parent._ymouse);
};
```

Whenever the mouse button is pressed, the location of the anchor *Vector* is set to the mouse coordinates. This is a simple example of how to simulate gravitation between objects in space. Next, we'll look at how gravity operates in a more down-to-earth context.

Gravity Near a Surface

On earth, we experience gravity as a constant force, which acts on the vertical axis only. Gravity actually defines our vertical axis for us. What direction is *down*? The force of gravity pulls us toward the center of the earth. Thus, *down* is simply the direction to the center of the earth. This direction also happens to be perpendicular to the surface of the earth.

With gravitation in space between two objects, the mass of each affects the resulting forces of gravity and acceleration. With objects on earth's surface, however, the acceleration due to gravity is basically the same for different sizes of objects.

Several centuries ago in a famous experiment, Galileo dispelled the notion that heavier objects fall faster by dropping two cannonballs of different weights from the Leaning Tower of Pisa. The cannonballs were dropped at the same time, and hit the ground at the same time. The earth is so massive in comparison to these objects that the force of gravity between the earth and a heavy cannonball is virtually identical to the gravity between the earth and a lighter cannonball.

NOTE: The only reason a feather doesn't fall as quickly as a stone is air resistance. In a vacuum, however, the two would fall at the same speed.

Because surface gravity is a constant acceleration along just the vertical dimension, it is easy to implement in our ActionScript motion process. We define the acceleration of gravity at the start of the movie, and then feed it into the calculations in a straightforward manner.

The following code example shows an implementation of surface gravity:

```
// accelerated fall due to surface gravity
this.pos = new Vector (this._x, this._y);
this.vel = new Vector (0, 0);
this.friction = 0;

// gravity properties
this.gravAccel = new Vector (0, .5);

this.move = function () {
    // calculate new position
    this.vel.plus (this.gravAccel);
```

```
        this.vel.scale (1 - this.friction);
        this.pos.plus (this.vel);
        // render position
        this._x = this.pos.x;
        this._y = this.pos.y;
    };


this.onEnterFrame = function () {
    this.doForce();
    this.move();
};


this.onMouseDown = function () {
    this.pos.reset (this._parent._xmouse,
                    this._parent._ymouse);
    this.vel.reset (0, 0);
};
```

When this script is run, each click of the mouse places the movie clip at a new position, where it accelerates in a freefall. In the *onMouseDown( )* handler, the position vector `this.pos` is set to match the mouse coordinates, and the velocity vector `this.vel` is reset to zero.

The object's acceleration is governed by the gravity acceleration property `this.gravAccel`, defined near the beginning of the script as the vector [0, .5], which points downward. From that point on, we use the same process as in the preceding examples to translate the acceleration into dynamic motion.

Elasticity

We encounter the physics of elasticity in many places: stretching a rubber band, jumping on a trampoline, even putting on underwear. When you stretch an elastic object, you feel a force pulling back, resisting you. This is the force of elasticity, or the elastic force.

Not all materials are elastic; some will simply break apart if you pull on them. But some materials can be stretched, allowing the molecules to slide away from each other. As this happens, the atoms still have an attraction to each other, via the electromagnetic force (one of the four fundamental forces). This is where the elastic force comes from.

State of Rest

An elastic object is in a state of equilibrium when at rest. However, the object can be stretched away from that state of equilibrium. The farther you stretch it, the more elastic force develops.

There is a direct relationship between the stretching displacement and the amount of elastic force. For instance, if you stretch an elastic band by one inch and get a certain amount of force, you would get twice that force by stretching it two inches. Keep in mind, too, that an elastic system is always seeking a state of rest.

Hooke's Law

Remember that math is essentially about relationships, which it describes with equations. As we have seen, the relationship between stretching displacement and force is fairly straightforward. Consequently, it has a simple equation:

$$F = -kd$$

This is known as *Hooke's Law*. In general terms, the equation says that the force of elasticity is directly proportional to the stretching displacement.

NOTE: Robert Hooke discovered this equation in the 1600's. He was a colleague of Sir Isaac Newton.

The F variable in the equation is the amount of elastic force. The d variable, meanwhile, is the stretching displacement. In physics, d is usually given in meters, and F in *Newtons* (the metric unit of force). In Flash animations, though, we usually don't need to worry about units.

The Elasticity Constant

The k quantity in Hooke's Law is the elasticity constant. This is a positive number that indicates the "tautness" of the elastic material and lies between 0 and 1. The larger k is, the stiffer the elastic substance is.

For example, a thick rubber band has a larger k than a thin rubber band. As a result, the thick rubber band generates more elastic force when you stretch it. Put another way, you have to apply more force to the thick rubber band to stretch it the same amount as the thin one.

The Direction of the Elastic Force

Why is there a negative sign in the equation $F = -kd$? The reason is that the elastic force operates in the *opposite direction* of the stretching displacement. Suppose you hook an elastic band on something and stretch it out to the right. The elastic force tries to pull your hand the other way, to the left. Thus, if your stretching displacement is positive, the elastic force is negative, and vice versa.

The ActionScript Implementation

```
// elasticity around a mouse-clicked point
this.pos = new Vector (this._x, this._y);
this.vel = new Vector (0, 0);
this.accel = new Vector (0, 0);
this.friction = .1;

// elasticity properties
this.anchor = new Vector (150, 100);
this.tautness = .25;

this.doForce = function () {
    // calculate elasticity force
    this.netForce = this.pos.minusNew (this.anchor);
    this.netForce.scale (-this.tautness);
};

this.move = function () {
    // calculate new position
    this.vel.plus (this.netForce);
    this.vel.scale (1 - this.friction);
    this.pos.plus (this.vel);
    // render position
    this._x = this.pos.x;
    this._y = this.pos.y;
};
```

```
this.onEnterFrame = function () {
    this.doForce();
    this.move();
};

this.onMouseDown = function () {
    this.anchor.reset (this._parent._xmouse,
                           this._parent._ymouse);
};
```

First, the standard vectors for position, velocity, and acceleration are declared, along with a fluid friction of 10%. Then two properties specific to elasticity are declared: the anchor *Vector* this.anchor and the elasticity constant this.tautness.

The anchor point is initially set to (150, 100), but this is reset to the mouse coordinates with each mouse-click. The movie clip is pulled toward the anchor point, picking up speed and overshooting it, then returning and overshooting again—back and forth it oscillates, as friction gradually slows it to a stop.

The key method in the script is *doForce( )*, where the elasticity is calculated:

```
this.doForce = function () {
    // calculate elasticity force
    this.netForce = this.pos.minusNew (this.anchor);
    this.netForce.scale (-this.tautness);
};
```

Remember that the equation for the elastic force is Hooke's Law: $F = -kd$. The stretching displacement d is found by subtracting the anchor vector from the position vector, in the first line of code:

```
this.netForce = this.pos.minusNew (this.anchor);
```

The this.netForce property now stores the displacement vector that points from the movie clip to the anchor point that is the source of the elastic force.

The second line of code performs the $-kd$ multiplication, using the *Vector.scale( )* method:

```
this.netForce.scale (-this.tautness);
```

The netForce *Vector* now stores the force of elasticity.

The remaining methods, *move( )*, *onEnterFrame( )*, and *onMouseDown( )*, have exactly the same code as in the earlier example for gravitation in space.

Wave Motion

Many things oscillate, employing a motion that is cyclical and periodic. Graphs of their positions over time produce a sine wave, as shown in Figure 8-2.

Sinusoidal waves, such as this one, can be based on either a sine or cosine function. This particular equation is based on sine:

$P = \sin(t)$

Here, *t* is an angle in radians. There are 2π radians in a circle, and likewise, it takes 2π radians for the sine wave to make a complete cycle. Looking at the graph, you can see the wave crossing the x-axis just past 3. This is the halfway point of the cycle, which corresponds to 3.1415... radians or 180 degrees. The curve returns to its original point and restarts the cycle at 6.2832... radians (2π), or 360 degrees.

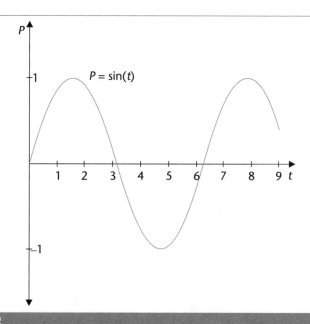

FIGURE 8-2

A standard sine wave

Amplitude

Amplitude is the magnitude of a wave's oscillation. Amplitude is also defined as the maximum displacement of the wave from the center position in either direction. By default, the sine wave has an amplitude of 1. Figure 8-3 shows two sine waves with different amplitudes. The reference wave $P = \sin(t)$ goes twice as high and twice as low as the other wave, $P = .5 \times \sin(t)$.

In general, the effect of amplitude on the wave function is captured in the following equation:

$$P = amp \times \sin(t)$$

The *amp* quantity scales the entire sine function to yield a new amplitude.

Frequency

Frequency is the wave's rate of oscillation. Multiplying the t parameter in the $\sin(t)$ equation changes the frequency of the wave. Figure 8-4 compares the $\sin(t)$ wave with $\sin(2t)$.

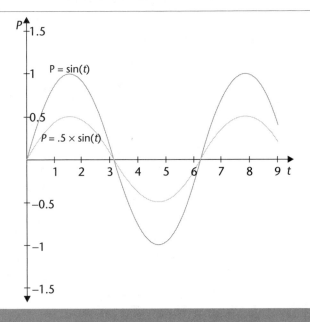

FIGURE 8-3

Changing the amplitude of the sine wave

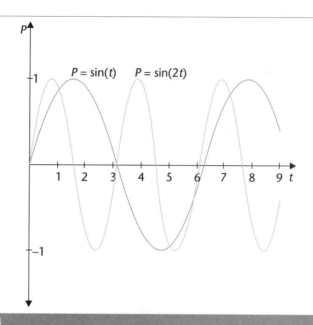

Changing the frequency of the sine wave

As you can see, multiplying *t* by 2 doubles the frequency. Likewise, multiplying *t* by .5 would halve the frequency. The following equation states this relationship in general terms:

$P = \sin(2\pi \times freq \times t)$

How did π find its way into the equation? The sin(*t*) function repeats itself every 2π radians (360 degrees), which means that the wave has a natural frequency of $1/(2\pi)$. Consequently, if we want to give the wave a new frequency, we must first multiply *t* by 2π to normalize its frequency to 1 ($1/(2\pi) \times 2\pi = 1$), and then multiply by the frequency.

NOTE: In physics, frequency is usually measured in Hertz (Hz), which corresponds to one cycle per second. Sounds, for instance, travel in waves that have frequencies specified in Hertz. The human ear can hear sounds between about 20 Hz and 20,000 Hz.

Period

Period is the length of time it takes for the wave to go through one oscillation, and is closely related to frequency. The two properties are inverses of each other, as expressed in the following simple equations:

period = 1 / freq

freq = 1 / period

If you divide the number 1 by the frequency, you get the period, and if you divide 1 by the period, you get the frequency. For example, if you have an object that oscillates four times a second, its frequency is 4 Hz, but its period is .25 seconds.

If we replace *freq* in our previous sine wave equation with 1/*period*, we have the following function:

$P = \sin(2\pi \times t/period)$

The period of a wave is independent of its amplitude—you can change the period without changing the amplitude, and vice versa. However, period and frequency are linked, and cannot be changed independently of one another, since they are two aspects of the same quality of waves.

Time Shift

The time shift variable in the wave equation moves the wave left or right on the horizontal time axis, as shown in Figure 8-5. As you can see, subtracting 1 from *t* with sin(*t* – 1) shifts the curve to the right by 1. Conversely, adding 1 with sin(*t* + 1) would shift the wave to the left.

Time shift is closely related to *phase shift*, which also moves the curve along the time axis. However, phase shift is specified slightly differently— in terms of an angle. For example, two waves might be said to be "out of phase by 90 degrees" (which is actually true of the sin(*t*) and cos(*t*) functions).

Offset

The offset variable in the wave equation moves the wave up or down on the vertical position axis, as shown in Figure 8-6. The offset defines the center point of the wave. By default, the offset is zero, so the wave oscillates above and below the time axis, where position is zero. In Figure 8-6, however, the function *P* = sin(*t*) + .5 has an offset of .5, so its center point of oscillation is shifted up to .5 on the vertical axis.

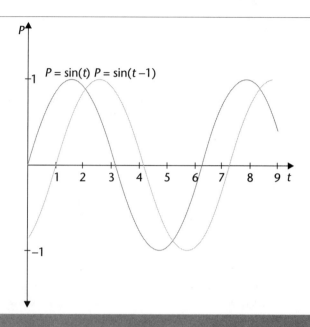

FIGURE 8-5

Changing the time shift of the sine wave

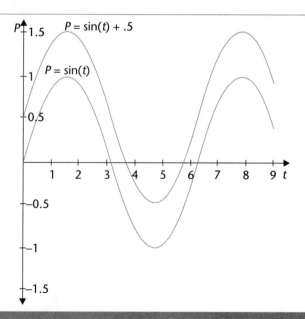

FIGURE 8-6

Changing the offset of the sine wave

The Wave Equation

We can incorporate these wave properties into a single wave equation, as shown here:

$$P_w = amp \times \sin[(t - shift) \times 2\pi \,/\, period] + offset$$

Here's the ActionScript implementation as the function *Math.wave( )*:

```
Math.wave = function (t, amp, period, timeShift, offset) {
    return amp *
        Math.sin ((t-timeShift) * (2*Math.PI) / period)
        + offset;
};
```

The *Math.wave( )* function provides a convenient interface for calculating an oscillating motion. You can just pick the intuitive properties of the wave, pass them to the function, and receive the current value of the wave, without having to worry about the calculations.

The WaveMotion Class

I developed a *WaveMotion* class to encapsulate oscillation and allow easy manipulation of wave properties. *WaveMotion* extends the *Motion* class (discussed in the previous chapter). As a subclass, *WaveMotion* inherits the methods and properties of *Motion*, and adds new ones. Consequently, the code for the *Motion* class must be included first in your movie in order for *WaveMotion* to work properly. ActionScript has little in the way of error checking. In particular, it won't verify that the superclass code is in place when it compiles the subclass code. I wrote my own little test, a line of code that checks for the existence of the *Motion* superclass:

```
if (typeof _global.Motion != 'function')
    trace (">> Error: superclass missing - Motion");
```

This code simply determines whether the superclass constructor is a function, and traces an error message to the Output window if this is not the case. The next steps are to declare the *WaveMotion* constructor, define the class inheritance, and then add methods to the class prototype.

The WaveMotion Constructor

Remember that the *Motion* constructor takes five properties: obj, prop, begin, duration, and useSeconds. I added two wave properties to the *WaveMotion* constructor: amp and period. Amplitude and period are the two most crucial properties of a wave, giving its oscillation a size and speed.

The following shows the code for the *WaveMotion* constructor:

```
_global.WaveMotion = function (obj, prop, begin,
    amp, period, duration, useSeconds) {
    this.superCon (obj, prop, begin, duration,
useSeconds);
    this.setOffset (begin);
    this.setAmp (amp);
    this.setPeriod (period);
};
```

The seven parameters enter the function. Five of them are shipped off to the superclass constructor, using the *superCon( )* method (discussed in Chapter 2). Then, I initialize the offset, amp, and period properties with their respective setter methods.

Next, I cause *WaveMotion* to inherit methods from *Motion* with the *extend( )* method (discussed in Chapter 2):

```
WaveMotion.extend (Motion);
```

After coding the constructor and inheritance, we start attaching methods to the class prototype. I often create a temporary shortcut variable to the prototype object to shorten the code a bit:

```
var WMP = WaveMotion.prototype;
```

From here on, the variable WMP will be used in place of WaveMotion .prototype.

WaveMotion.getPosition( )

The *getPosition( )* method is the cornerstone of any *Motion* subclass. This is the place where we define the relationship between time and position. The *getPosition( )* method is actually blank in the Motion class, because it is intended to be overridden with your own function, either in a *Motion* instance or in a *Motion* subclass.

With the *WaveMotion* class, we use our wave equation:

```
WMP.getPosition = function (t) {
    if (t == undefined) t = this.$time;
    return this.$amp *
        Math.sin ((t-this.$timeShift) * (2*Math.PI) / this.$period)
        + this.$offset;
};
```

WaveMotion Getter/Setter Methods

WaveMotion.setAmp( ) and *getAmp( )* control the amplitude of the wave:

```
WMP.setAmp = function (a) {
    if (a != undefined) this.$amp = a;
};
```

```
WMP.getAmp = function () {
    return this.$amp;
};
```

You'll notice that the setter function does a small validation on the data. It only changes the amplitude if the incoming parameter is defined.

WaveMotion.setPeriod( ) and *getPeriod( )* control the period of the wave this way:

```
WMP.setPeriod = function (p) {
    if (p != undefined) this.$period = p;
};
```

```
WMP.getPeriod = function () {
    return this.$period;
};
```

The *setPeriod( )* method validates the data in the same way as as*setAmp( )*. *WaveMotion.setFreq( )* and *getFreq( )* change and return the frequency of the wave:

```
WMP.setFreq = function (f) {
    this.setPeriod (1 / f);
};
```

```
WMP.getFreq = function () {
    return 1 / this.getPeriod();
};
```

You'll notice these methods function differently from the other getters and setters. Unlike amplitude and period, frequency isn't stored as a property within the *WaveMotion* object. Instead, frequency is converted to the corresponding period, and the wave is changed to that period. As mentioned before, period and frequency are the inverse of each other. Thus, you take the reciprocal of frequency (1 / f) to find the period.

The *WaveMotion.setTimeShift( )* and *getTimeShift( )* methods shift the wave along the time dimension:

```
WMP.setTimeShift = function (t) {
    if (t != undefined) this.$timeShift = t;
};
```

```
WMP.getTimeShift = function () {
    return this.$timeShift;
};
```

In a similar way, *setOffset( )* and *getOffset( )* move the wave, but along the *position* dimension:

```
WMP.setOffset = function (f) {
    if (f != undefined) this.$offset = f;
};
```

```
WMP.getOffset = function () {
    return this.$offset;
};
```

I added one more setter method for convenience *WaveMotion.setWavePhysics( )* lets you set the four main properties of the wave in one step:

```
WMP.setWavePhysics = function (amp, period, timeShift, offset) {
    this.setAmp (amp);
    this.setPeriod (period);
    this.setTimeShift (timeShift);
    this.setOffset (offset);
};
```

WaveMotion Getter/Setter Properties

With getter and setter methods defined, we can now define getter/setter properties using Flash MX's *addProperty( )* method.

```
with (WMP) {
    addProperty ("amp", getAmp, setAmp);
    addProperty ("offset", getOffset, setOffset);
    addProperty ("period", getPeriod, setPeriod);
    addProperty ("freq", getFreq, setFreq);
    addProperty ("timeShift", getTimeShift,
setTimeShift);
}
```

To finish off, I clean up by deleting the temporary variable WMP:

```
delete WMP;
```

Then I send a simple message to the Output window to signal that the class code has been loaded:

```
trace (">> WaveMotion class loaded");
```

Using WaveMotion

Here's an example of how to create a *WaveMotion* instance:

```
waveX = new WaveMotion (this, "_x", 200, 80, 2, 0, true);
```

If you place this code in the first frame of a movie clip, it will start oscillating horizontally at 2 seconds per cycle, while centered at 200 pixels on the x-axis. It will oscillate indefinitely if left alone. Table 8-1 lists and describes arguments for the *WaveMotion* constructor.

With the *WaveMotion* instance created, the specified movie clip oscillates automatically. What we can do now is modify the parameters of the wave while the movie is running. For example, we can add this bit of code, which steadily increases the amplitude of the wave:

```
this.onEnterFrame = function () {
    waveX.amp++;
};
```

Parameter	Type	Value	Description
obj	reference	this	The object to affect
prop	string	"_x"	The name of the property to oscillate
begin	number	200	The center point of the wave
amp	number	80	The size of the wave's oscillation
period	number	2	The length of time it takes to complete one oscillation
duration	number	0	The length of time it takes before the motion stops; a value of 0 results in an infinite duration
useSeconds	Boolean	true	A flag asking whether to use seconds and timer-based motion (instead of frame-based)

TABLE 8-1

Parameters for the *WaveMotion* constructor

As the `amp` property of the `waveX` object is increased, the object gradually swings over a greater and greater range.

We can modify this a bit to give us more direct control over the amplitude of the wave.

```
this.onEnterFrame = function () {
    waveX.setAmp (this._parent._ymouse);
};
```

NOTE: In the preceding code, I used the *setAmp( )* method to change the amplitude. I could have used the `amp` property instead, as I did in the first example, but I wanted to demonstrate both approaches. The `amp` property can be more convenient, but the *setAmp( )* method is more direct, and probably a bit faster to execute.

Here is another code example, that controls two wave properties at once with the mouse position:

```
this.onEnterFrame = function () {
    waveX.setAmp (this._parent._ymouse);
    waveX.setOffset (this._parent._xmouse);
};
```

As before, the amplitude of the wave is controlled by the mouse's vertical position. But now the wave offset corresponds to the mouse's horizontal position. This causes the wave's oscillation to stay centered horizontally on the mouse cursor.

Conclusion

Physics is a fascinating discipline to study. We have learned a few of its classic principles: velocity, acceleration, force, and the relationships between them. We have also explored some specific forces, such as friction, elasticity, and gravity, and how they can be calculated and incorporated into dynamic animation. Lastly, we've looked at some wave physics, and a custom *WaveMotion* class designed to encapsulate customizable and easily controllable oscillation. After two intense chapters on scripted motion (via tweening and physics), we will turn to the area of color in the next chapter.

Chapter 9

Coloring with ActionScript

ntroduced in Flash 5, the *Color* class gave us just a few basic methods: *setRGB( )*, *getRGB( )*, *setTransform( )*, and *getTransform( )*. Since the *Color* class hasn't changed any for Flash MX (it still consists of the same four methods), you may be wondering why I've devoted a whole chapter to dynamic color. Good question.

The color programming contained in this chapter won't be found in the manual. What follows is an extensive collection of custom methods (written by yours truly) that allows you to manipulate colors in ActionScript more intuitively. For instance, let's say you want to change a graphic's brightness percentage, or tint it with a color (like the Properties Inspector), yet do it dynamically. The *Color* class doesn't have methods that allow you to do this directly, like *setBrightness( )* or *setTint( )*. However, this chapter shows you how to extend the *Color* class to give you intuitive control over the color of movie clips.

Solid Coloration

Let's start with what I call "solid" or "opaque" coloration. This color treatment is equivalent to tinting by 100 percent, replacing the original colors of the movie clip with a single, solid color. The *Color.setRGB( )* and *getRGB( )* methods deal with solid coloration, whereas *setTransform( )* and *getTransform( )* implement color transformations that are usually more complex.

Color.setRGB( )

Color.setRGB( ) sets a targeted movie clip to a specified solid color. Since the *setRGB( )* method is well-documented, I won't bother repeating what's printed in the manual.

The following is a code example demonstrating how to target a movie clip and change its color:

```
// test Color.setRGB()
col = new Color (mc);
col.setRGB (0x0000FF);
```

In this example, the parameter for *setRGB( )* is 0x0000FF. If you've worked in HTML at all, you'll recognize 0000FF as the color blue, in hexadecimal format. What's important to realize, however, is that 0x0000FF is a *number* literal, not a string. A string literal would be enclosed in quotes. The prefix 0x indicates that digits are in base 16, hexadecimal. The number 255 in base 10 is exactly the same value as 0x0000FF. This can be demonstrated with the following code:

```
trace ( 0x0000FF ); // output: 255
trace ( 0x0000FF - 255 ); // output: 0
```

More than a few people have been confused by this, so let me reiterate: the number you pass to *setRGB( )* does not have to be defined in hex, it simply has to be a number between 0 and 16,777,215 (inclusive). You can just as easily use the code col.setRGB (255) to color a movie clip blue. If you want to define a color with a hex string like "0000FF", you'll need to convert the string to a number first, before passing it to *setRGB( )*. Later in this chapter, we'll look at a custom function *setRGBStr( )*, which accepts a hex string parameter.

NOTE: The number 16,777,215 is equal to $2^{24} - 1$. In hex, that's 0xFFFFFF. The *Color* class uses 24-bit RGB color, with eight bits each for red, green, and blue. The Flash Player also uses eight bits internally to control the alpha channel.

MovieClip.setRGB( )

A *Color* object can only target a movie clip, and frankly, changing a movie clip's color can often seem like a hassle. After all, you first have to create a *Color* object, point it to the movie clip, and then call its methods. To help, I've developed several shortcuts you can use to eliminate some of these steps. The first (we'll see many throughout this chapter) is a custom *MovieClip* method that wraps around a *Color* method. It's shown in the following code:

```
MovieClip.prototype.setRGB = function (col) {
    (new Color(this)).setRGB (col);
};
```

The *MovieClip.setRGB( )* method accepts a parameter `col` and passes it to the *setRGB( )* method of a *Color* object, using a syntax that may look a little strange:

```
(new Color(this)).setRGB (col);
```

What's happening here is that I'm creating an *anonymous Color* object, and calling its method in the same line of code. The anonymous object is automatically disposed of (garbage collected) some time after the method finishes executing.

I could have used this code instead:

```
var c = new Color (this);
c.setRGB (col);
```

This accomplishes the same thing as before, but not as efficiently. Since I only need the *Color* object temporarily, I might as well use the shorter approach.

With *MovieClip.setRGB( )* defined, I can change the color of a movie clip in one step:

```
// test MovieClip.setRGB()
mc.setRGB (0xFF0000);
```

This replaces the following "standard" procedure, which involves creating a *Color* object manually:

```
// standard procedure for setRGB()
c = new Color (mc);
c.setRGB (0xFF0000);
```

Color.getRGB( )

The *Color.getRGB( )* method returns the current solid color applied to the target movie clip. The color is given as a 24-bit number between 0 and 16,777,215 (or 0xFFFFFF).

MovieClip.getRGB( )

The *MovieClip.getRGB( )* method wraps around the *Color.getRGB( )* method, allowing you to retrieve the current color in one step:

```
MovieClip.prototype.getRGB = function () {
    return (new Color(this)).getRGB();
};
```

So far, we've looked at the standard *setRGB( )* and *getRGB( )* methods of the *Color* class. We have also defined parallel methods for *MovieClip*, which wrap around these two methods.

Color.setRGBStr( )

The standard *Color.setRGB( )* method accepts a number as a parameter, which specifies the color. However, we may want to specify the color as a string instead, which gives the number in hexadecimal. For instance, suppose you had some colors stored in hex in an XML document, and you wanted to read them dynamically. XML information always starts out as text, so the color string would need to be parsed into a number.

The *parseInt( )* function is the easiest way to perform this task. By default, it converts strings to numbers in base 10; however, you can specify other bases for *parseInt( )* to use. Hexadecimal numbers use base 16. Thus, we can convert a simple hex string to a number with this syntax:

```
parseInt (hexStr, 16)
```

Here are some examples of hex numbers being converted to base 10:

```
trace ( parseInt ("A", 16) ); // output: 10
trace ( parseInt ("F", 16) ); // output: 15
trace ( parseInt ("FF", 16) ); // output: 255
```

Now that we know how to perform the string-to-number conversion, we can write a method for the *Color* class:

```
Color.prototype.setRGBStr = function (hexStr) {
    hexStr = hexStr.substr (-6, 6);
    this.setRGB (parseInt (hexStr, 16));
};
```

The last line should look familiar. It uses *parseInt( )* to convert the hex string to a decimal number, then it passes the number to the *Color.setRGB( )* method. But what about the line before that?

I added a step which validates the incoming hexStr argument. I've heard people ask how they can use a color hex string in a variety of formats. The string could be "0xRRGGBB", "#RRGGBB" following HTML syntax, or just "RRGGBB". The easiest approach is simply to grab the last six digits of the hex string. This way, it doesn't matter what prefix you use. In the first line of the *setRGBStr( )* method, I use the *String.substr( )* method to extract the digits:

```
hexStr = hexStr.substr (-6, 6);
```

The first parameter, -6, starts the new slice six characters from the *end* of `hexStr`. The second parameter, meanwhile, extracts the six characters to the right of that starting point.

MovieClip.setRGBStr( )

The *MovieClip.setRGBStr( )* method allows you to color a movie clip using a hex string. It wraps around the corresponding *Color* method:

```
MovieClip.prototype.setRGBStr = function (hexStr) {
    (new Color(this)).setRGBStr (hexStr);
};
```

This *MovieClip* method eliminates the need to create a *Color* object manually.

In the following code example, the current movie clip is turned to a solid yellow color:

```
this.setRGBStr ("FFFF00");
```

A different prefix for the string will work as well, for example:

```
this.setRGBStr ("#FFFF00");
```

Color.getRGBStr( )

The *Color.getRGB( )* method will tell you the color of a movie clip that has been solid colored with the *Color* class. The color returned, however, is given as a decimal number. The following *Color.getRGBStr( )* method allows you to find the color as a string instead, in hex format:

```
Color.prototype.getRGBStr = function () {
    var hexStr = this.getRGB().toString (16);
```

```
        var toFill = 6 - hexStr.length;
        while (toFill--) hexStr = "0" + hexStr;
        return hexStr.toUpperCase();
};
```

The first step in this procedure is to convert the RGB number from base 10 to base 16. The *Number.toString( )* method can accept the base, or *radix*, as an argument, and produce the appropriate string. Thus, we call the *Color.getRGB( )* method and immediately convert the result to a base 16 string:

```
var hexStr = this.getRGB().toString (16);
```

Unfortunately for our purposes, this approach doesn't always produce six digits. If the color is solid blue, the hex string should be 0000FF. This is equivalent to a decimal value of 255. However, *toString( )* converts 255 to just ff:

```
trace ( (255).toString (16) ); // output: ff
```

Thus, we need to fill in the rest of the string with zeroes. The next two lines of code accomplish this:

```
var toFill = 6 - hexStr.length;
while (toFill--) hexStr = "0" + hexStr;
```

I optimized this little while loop as much as possible.
The last step is to convert the string to uppercase before returning it:

```
return hexStr.toUpperCase();
```

The function's output is now standardized to the RRGGBB form.

MovieClip.getRGBStr( )

The *MovieClip.getRGBStr( )* method allows you to retrieve the hex color of a colored movie clip as a hex string. It wraps around the corresponding *Color* method, as shown next:

```
MovieClip.prototype.getRGBStr = function () {
    return (new Color(this)).getRGBStr();
};
```

This *MovieClip* method eliminates the need to create a *Color* object manually.

In the following code example, the current movie clip is colored a solid blue using the *MovieClip.setRGB( )* method. Then, the color is checked in both hex and decimal format:

```
// test MovieClip.getRGBStr()
// color the movie clip blue
this.setRGB (0x0000FF);
// check the hex string
trace ( this.getRGBStr() ); // output: 0000FF
// check the equivalent decimal value
trace ( this.getRGB() ); // output: 255
```

Color.setRGB2( )

Colors are often specified in separate red, green, and blue numbers, each between 0 and 255. The built-in *Color* methods don't allow us to color movie clips with separated RGB values. However, we can write a custom method which gives us three parameters:

```
Color.prototype.setRGB2 = function (r, g, b) {
    this.setRGB (r << 16 | g << 8 | b);
};
```

I believe Branden Hall first wrote this method. The code makes creative use of two bitwise operators. The << operator shifts bits to the left by a specified number of digits, which has the effect of multiplying a number by powers of two. For example:

```
trace (5 << 1); // 10
trace (5 << 2); // 20
```

A color is represented by 24 bits, eight each for red, green, and blue. The bits are arranged like this:

```
rrrrrrrr gggggggg bbbbbbbb
```

The bits of the g argument for *setRGB2( )* look like this:

```
00000000 00000000 gggggggg
```

However, we want the green bits to be in the middle, like this:

```
00000000 gggggggg 00000000
```

Thus, we use the << operator to shift g eight bits to the left:

```
g << 8
```

Similarly, we shift the red component r, moving it 16 bits instead:

```
r << 16
```

This produces the following bit arrangement for r:

```
rrrrrrrr 00000000 00000000
```

Now that the bits are in their proper positions, we can add them together to create one 24-bit number. We accomplish this with the bitwise OR operator, | (pipe):

```
r << 16 | g << 8 | b
```

Lastly, we pass this combined value to the *setRGB( )* method:

```
this.setRGB (r << 16 | g << 8 | b);
```

MovieClip.setRGB2( )

The *MovieClip.setRGB2( )* method allows you to solid-color a movie clip using separate red, green, and blue components:

```
MovieClip.prototype.setRGB2 = function (r, g, b) {
    (new Color(this)).setRGB2 (r, g, b);
};
```

This *MovieClip* method wraps around the corresponding *Color* method, eliminating the need to create a *Color* object manually.

In the following code example, the current movie clip is colored a solid magenta with the *MovieClip.setRGB2( )* method:

```
// test MovieClip.setRGB2()
this.setRGB2 (255, 0, 255);
```

Magenta is a combination of red and blue values. We produce a full magenta by specifying 255 red, 0 green, and 255 blue.

Color.getRGB2( )

We can find the color of a solid-colored movie clip with the *Color.getRGB( )* method. However, this is given as a decimal number between 0 and 16,777,215. This is certainly better than nothing, but perhaps we could find a more convenient format.

The *Color.getRGB2( )* method allows you to find the separate red, green, and blue components of a solid-colored movie clip. Here is the code:

```
Color.prototype.getRGB2 = function () {
    var t = this.getTransform();
    return {r:t.rb, g:t.gb, b:t.bb};
};
```

The function returns an object containing r, g, and b properties, each lying between 0 and 255.

The method begins by finding the current transform values of the *Color* object. A local variable t is created to hold them:

```
var t = this.getTransform();
```

The variable t is now an object containing eight properties, whose relevant properties here are the color offsets rb, gb, and bb. These correspond exactly to the RGB components of the current solid color. Thus, we copy these values into a new anonymous object, giving it r, g, and b properties, then return the object:

```
return {r:t.rb, g:t.gb, b:t.bb};
```

A lot happens in this one line of code.

When we call the *getRGB2( )* method, we need to assign the result of the function to a variable:

```
// col is an existing Color object
rgb = col.getRGB2();
```

Now the variable rgb is an object, containing the properties r, g, and b. Each of these is a number, ranging between 0 and 255.

MovieClip.getRGB2( )

The *MovieClip.getRGB2( )* method allows you to find the red, green, and blue components of a solid-colored movie clip method:

```
MovieClip.prototype.getRGB2 = function () {
    return (new Color(this)).getRGB2();
};
```

This *MovieClip* method eliminates the need to create a *Color* object manually.

In the following code example, the current movie clip is colored solid magenta with the *MovieClip.setRGB( )* method. Then, the individual color components are retrieved with *MovieClip.getRGB2( )*:

```
// test MovieClip.getRGB2()
// color the movie clip magenta
this.setRGB (0xFF00FF);
// check color components
rgb = this.getRGB2();
trace ( rgb.r ); // output: 255
trace ( rgb.g ); // output: 0
trace ( rgb.b ); // output: 255
```

Color Transforms

Flash provides the *Color.setTransform( )* and *getTransform( )* methods to implement complex color manipulations. Let's look at how these built-in capabilities work.

Color.setTransform( )

The *Color.setTransform( )* method takes one argument, an object. This color transform object can contain up to eight properties, listed in Table 9-1.

Property Name	Definition
ra	red percentage
ga	green percentage
ba	blue percentage
rb	red offset
gb	green offset
bb	blue offset
aa	alpha percentage
ab	alpha offset

TABLE 9-1

Color Transform Object Properties

In my work, I don't generally call *Color.setTransform( )* directly. Taken at face value, it is not the most intuitive function. However, *setTransform( )* is quite powerful, if you know what values to give the eight transform properties. I have spent a significant amount of time finding equations and code that translate familiar concepts like *brightness* and *tint* into values that can be used by *setTransform( )*. These custom functions will be presented as *Color* and *MovieClip* methods throughout the remainder of this chapter.

MovieClip.setColorTransform( )

The *MovieClip.setColorTransform( )* method is a wrapper function that allows you to set the color transform directly from the movie clip, without creating a *Color* object yourself:

```
MovieClip.prototype.setColorTransform = function (trans) {
    (new Color(this)).setTransform (trans);
};
```

Color.getTransform( )

The *Color.getTransform( )* method returns a color transform object that contains the six properties listed in Table 9-1. As with *setTransform( )*, I rarely use *getTransform( )* directly. Instead, I employ my own methods which I call *getTransform( )*.

MovieClip.getColorTransform( )

The *MovieClip.getColorTransform( )* method is a wrapper function that allows you to set the color transform directly from the movie clip, without creating a *Color* object yourself:

```
MovieClip.prototype.getColorTransform = function () {
    return (new Color(this)).getTransform();
};
```

Resetting to Original Color

After changing a movie clip's color dynamically, how do we return it to its original appearance? When a *Color* object is first created, it starts with default color transform values, listed in Table 9-2. Red, green, and blue are at 100 percent of their normal values, and are not offset by any amount.

Color.reset( )

The *Color.reset( )* method returns the color transform to these default values:

```
Color.prototype.reset = function () {
    this.setTransform ({ra:100, ga:100, ba:100,
                        rb:0, gb:0, bb:0});
};
```

Color Transform Property	Value
ra	100
ga	100
ba	100
rb	0
gb	0
bb	0
TABLE 9-2	

Default Values of the Color Transform Properties

An anonymous object is created to hold the transform values. It is passed to the *setTransform( )* method to apply the transform and return the movie clip's colors to normal.

MovieClip.resetColor( )

The *MovieClip.resetColor( )* method is a convenient way to quickly reset a movie clip's color:

```
MovieClip.prototype.resetColor = function () {
    (new Color(this)).reset();
};
```

I used a method name of "resetColor" instead of "reset," because a movie clip has many other properties that could conceivably be reset.

In the following example, a movie clip is colored, then restored to normal:

```
// test MovieClip.resetColor()
this.setRGB (0xCCCCCC);
this.resetColor();
```

Controlling Brightness

In my Flash 4 days, I enjoyed changing the appearance of symbols with alpha, brightness, and tint effects. Over time, I found myself gravitating more and more towards changes in brightness. Some of this was for aesthetic reasons. In particular, the Axis Interactive site (axis-media.com) I worked on had a distinctly "heavenly" feel, which lent itself to brightness tweens. Many graphical elements transitioned between their natural color and pure white.

Another motivation was graphical performance. If you're animating over a solid white background, an alpha fade and a brightness tween look the same. However, the alpha change is more processor-intensive, because the colors of two objects are mixed together. This realization led me to change alpha to brightness tweens wherever it was possible to do so without changing the appearance of the animation.

With Flash 5, my focus shifted from static timeline animations to dynamic ActionScript-driven movement. The new *Color* object allowed me to modify a movie clip's colors dynamically. However, it did not provide a straightforward way to change brightness. After a while, I decided that there must be a way to set brightness using specific color transform properties. I played around with the Flash 5 Effect Panel (replaced in Flash

MX by the Properties Inspector) to try to decipher how the colors were being transformed. I would set a brightness value for the symbol instance, then switch to the Special section of the color settings and see what values were there. Eventually, through trial and error, I worked it out. I found a numerical relationship between the brightness percentage and the color percentages and offsets, and code that would perform the conversion. From this came the *Color.setBrightness( )* and *getBrightness( )* methods.

Color.setBrightness( )

The *Color.setBrightness( )* method changes the brightness of a targeted movie clip:

```
Color.prototype.setBrightness = function (bright) {
    var trans = this.getTransform();
    with (trans) {
        ra = ga = ba = 100 - Math.abs (bright);
        rb = gb = bb = (bright > 0)
                        ? bright * (256/100) : 0;
    }
    this.setTransform (trans);
};
```

The `bright` parameter is a percentage between -100 and 100. Positive values brighten the graphic, and negative values darken it. A value of 100 turns the graphic completely white, and -100 turns it black.

MovieClip.setBrightness( )

The *MovieClip.setBrightness( )* method is a shortcut to setting the brightness of a movie clip:

```
MovieClip.prototype.setBrightness = function (bright) {
    (new Color(this)).setBrightness (bright);
};
```

The following code example shows how to brighten and darken a movie clip:

```
// test MovieClip.setBrightness()
// brighten
mc.setBrightness (50);
// darken
mc.setBrightness (-50);
```

```
// normal
mc.setBrightness (0);
```

Color.getBrightness( )

Once the brightness of a movie clip has been set, either through the
Properties Inspector or with code, is it possible to retrieve the brightness
value? Yes it is, using a custom *Color.getBrightness( )* method:

```
Color.prototype.getBrightness = function () {
    var trans = this.getTransform();
    with (trans) return rb ? 100 - ra : ra - 100;
};
```

The function returns a value between -100 and 100.

The *getBrightness( )* method will only work if the brightness has been set
properly beforehand. If this is the case, the red, green, and blue percentages
will be equal, as will the red, green, and blue offsets. As a result, I check just
one color, red in this case, to determine the brightness value.

There is usually some rounding error when you set and retrieve the
brightness. This is due to the fact that Flash actually stores the color
percentages internally as eight-bit values. This means that a given number
between 0 and 100 is mapped to an integer between 0 and 255. This also
happens with the _alpha property. If you set _alpha to a specific number,
you probably won't find the same number when you trace _alpha
immediately following.

NOTE: This rounding error can become a problem during slow dynamic tweens—for example, the value can get
"stuck" if it doesn't change by a large enough amount. The solution is to maintain the value in a separate variable,
incrementing it and then applying it to the color property to update the display.

MovieClip.getBrightness( )

MovieClip.getBrightness( ) is yet another *MovieClip* wrapper method for a
Color method:

```
MovieClip.prototype.getBrightness = function () {
    return (new Color(this)).getBrightness();
};
```

The following example shows how to change the brightness of a movie
clip and then check the brightness value:

```
// test MovieClip.getBrightness()
mc.setBrightness (70);
trace ( mc.getBrightness() ); // output: 70.3125
```

This example shows the rounding error mentioned earlier.

Brightness Offset

Back in my Flash 4 days, I distinctly remember stumbling upon Irene Chan's work at www.eneri.net. It made quite an impression on me. To this day, I love aesthetic styles that exude "quiet confidence," as I call it. One of the most striking visual features of eneri.net was the way the bitmaps would brighten. There seemed to be a sort of "dilation" effect, where the bright areas of the graphic would expand and eventually take over the rest of the image. It was as if my pupil was dilating and letting in too much light. I was mystified by the effect. At first, I thought that perhaps Irene was fading between two different images. But the effect seemed too smooth for that to be the case. It wasn't until later, when I read Irene's chapter in the book *New Masters of Flash*, that I understood how this effect was achieved.

The brightness we're used to seeing in Flash moves a graphic towards white or black by a certain percentage. Since normal brightness involves a percentage, it is, in a sense, *relative*. By contrast, we can also brighten movie clips in an *absolute* manner. This is done by using an *offset* rather than a percentage. This is not merely a theoretical point—this approach to brightness produces a different aesthetic effect. Increasing the brightness *offset* was what produced the hypnotic dilation effect seen on eneri.net.

Although I focus here on changing the brightness offset with code, you can set it manually on a symbol instance, using the Properties Inspector. You can't set the brightness offset in the Brightness section, however. To do this, you have to set the red, green, and blue offsets, in the Special section, giving them positive values equal to each other. The offsets push the image's colors up towards white. This effect shows up most dramatically when you apply it to a bitmap.

Color.setBrightOffset( )

The *Color.setBrightOffset( )* method pushes a movie clip's colors towards white or black by an absolute amount:

```
Color.prototype.setBrightOffset = function (offset) {
    var trans = this.getTransform()
    with (trans) rb = gb = bb = offset;
```

```
    this.setTransform (trans);
};
```

The `offset` argument is a number between -255 and 255. Positive values push colors towards white; negative values towards black.

MovieClip.setBrightOffset( )

The *MovieClip.setBrightOffset( )* method wraps around the *Color.setBrightOffset( )* method:

```
MovieClip.prototype.setBrightOffset = function (offset) {
    (new Color(this)).setBrightOffset (offset);
};
```

In the following example, a movie clip's brightness offset is manipulated in positive and negative directions:

```
// test MovieClip.setBrightOffset()
// brighten
mc.setBrightOffset (140);
// darken
mc.setBrightOffset (-140);
// normal
mc.setBrightOffset (0);
```

NOTE: Brightness offset is independent of percentage brightness—in other words, setting one does not affect the other. Consequently, you can achieve some interesting effects by darkening with a percentage and then brightening by an offset, or *vice versa*.

Color.getBrightOffset( )

Similar to the *Color.getBrightness( )* method, *Color.getBrightOffset( )* returns the value previously set by the *setBrightOffset( )* method:

```
Color.prototype.getBrightOffset = function () {
    return this.getTransform().rb;
};
```

We assume that the three color offsets are equal. Thus, we pick one offset, red in this case, and return it as the brightness offset. *Color.getBrightOffset( )* returns a number between -255 and 255.

MovieClip.getBrightOffset( )

The *MovieClip.getBrightOffset( )* method wraps around the corresponding method *Color.getBrightOffset( )*:

```
MovieClip.prototype.getBrightOffset = function () {
    return (new Color(this)).getBrightOffset();
};
```

The *MovieClip.getBrightOffset( )* method returns a number between -255 and 255.

Tinting

Another staple effect for tweens is tinting. As with brightness, tinting was a Flash 4 design-time effect that I wanted to achieve dynamically, using Flash 5 code. I figured out how to tint with the *Color* object shortly after I conquered brightness. The two are related—brightness is the same as tinting with white or black.

Color.setTint( )

The *Color.setTint( )* method tints the targeted movie clip with a color according to a certain percentage:

```
Color.prototype.setTint = function (r, g, b, percent) {
    var ratio = percent / 100;
    var trans = {rb:r*ratio, gb:g*ratio, bb:b*ratio};
    trans.ra = trans.ga = trans.ba = 100 - percent;
    this.setTransform (trans);
};
```

The parameters of *setTint( )* correspond to a tint you might define in the Properties Inspector. The r, g, and b arguments fall between 0 and 255, and percent should be between 0 and 100. I kept the red, green, and blue components separate for convenience.

NOTE: You can actually use negative values for r, g, b, and percent if you like. These produce some interesting "non-standard" effects.

MovieClip.setTint( )

The *MovieClip.setTint( )* method is an easy way to tint a movie clip with a color, as shown in the following code:

```
MovieClip.prototype.setTint = function (r, g, b, percent) {
    (new Color(this)).setTint (r, g, b, percent);
};
```

Color.getTint( )

The *Color.getTint( )* method is the inverse of *setTint( )*. It retrieves the tint color and percentage that was previously defined:

```
Color.prototype.getTint = function () {
    var trans = this.getTransform();
    var tint = {percent: 100 - trans.ra};
    var ratio = 100 / tint.percent;
    tint.r = trans.rb * ratio;
    tint.g = trans.gb * ratio;
    tint.b = trans.bb * ratio;
    return tint;
};
```

The method returns an object that contains r, g, b, and `percent` properties.

MovieClip.getTint( )

The following code exhibits the *MovieClip* version of getTint( ), and returns an object that contains *r, g, b,* and percent properties:

```
MovieClip.prototype.getTint = function () {
    return (new Color(this)).getTint();
};
```

Tint Offset

Tint offset is quite similar to the brightness offset. In both cases, you push colors around by an absolute amount. With tint, however, the offset is separated into red, green, and blue components.

Color.setTintOffset( )

The *Color.setTintOffset( )* method enables you to set a tint offset defined by red, green, and blue components:

```
Color.prototype.setTintOffset = function (r, g, b) {
    var trans = this.getTransform();
    with (trans) { rb = r; gb = g; bb = b; }
    this.setTransform (trans);
};
```

The r, g, and b arguments lie between -255 and 255. The tint offset is somewhat related to the brightness offset. For example, if you set the three tint offset arguments to the same value, say 120, the effect is the same as setting the brightness offset to 120.

MovieClip.setTintOffset( )

The code that follows shows the *MovieClip* version of *setTintOffset( )*:

```
MovieClip.prototype.setTintOffset = function (r, g, b) {
    (new Color(this)).setTintOffset (r, g, b);
};
```

In the following example, a movie clip has its red values decreased by 90 units and its green increased by 40:

```
// test MovieClip.setTintOffset()
mc.setTintOffset (90, 40, 0);
```

Color.getTintOffset( )

The *Color.getTintOffset( )* is similar to the *getRGB2( )* method—so similar, in fact, that it has the same internal code:

```
Color.prototype.getTintOffset = function () {
    var t = this.getTransform();
    return {r:t.rb, g:t.gb, b:t.bb};
};
```

MovieClip.getTintOffset( )

Here is the *MovieClip* version of *getTintOffset( )*:

```
MovieClip.prototype.getTintOffset = function () {
    return (new Color(this)).getTintOffset();
};
```

Inverting Colors

For the longest time, I didn't use the color offsets in the Special area of the Properties Inspector. I hardly noticed the offsets, in fact, until I learned how Irene Chan used them to create her brightness dilation effect. After that, I played with them quite a bit. One day I discovered, by accident, that it was possible to create a negative image using the Properties Inspector. By setting the color percentages to the minimum value, and the color offsets to their maximums, I could invert all the colors. Black traded places with white, red with cyan, green with magenta, and blue with yellow. I used my findings to create several *Color* methods that invert colors of images.

Color.invert( )

The *Color.invert( )* method performs a straightforward color inversion:

```
Color.prototype.invert = function () {
    var trans = this.getTransform();
    with (trans) {
        ra = -ra;
        ga = -ga;
        ba = -ba;
        rb = 255 - rb;
        gb = 255 - gb;
        bb = 255 - bb;
    }
    this.setTransform (trans);
};
```

The colors of the targeted movie clip are flipped to their opposites on the color wheel. If the graphic has been previously tinted or brightened with a *Color* object, this is taken into account.

For example, suppose you have a movie clip containing a blue circle. If its colors are inverted at this stage, the circle will become yellow. However, if the movie clip is set to 100 percent brightness, either with the Properties Inspector or ActionScript, it will be a solid white color. Targeting this movie clip with a *Color* object and calling *Color.invert( )* will turn it into a black circle.

MovieClip.invertColor( )

The *MovieClip.invertColor( )* method is a wrapper for *Color.invert( )*, as shown next:

```
MovieClip.prototype.invertColor = function () {
    (new Color(this)).invert();
};
```

I called the *MovieClip* method invertColor( ) to avoid ambiguity (since there are other movie clip properties that could conceivably be inverted).

Color.setNegative( )

The *Color.setNegative( )* method works a little differently from *Color.invert( )*, allowing you to invert an image by a specific percentage. Here is the code:

```
Color.prototype.setNegative = function (percent) {
    var t = {};
    t.ra = t.ga = t.ba = 100 - 2 * percent;
    t.rb = t.gb = t.bb = percent * (255/100);
    this.setTransform (t);
};
```

The percent argument is a number between 0 and 100. A value of 100 gives a full negative effect, as you would get with the *Color.invert( )* method.

MovieClip.setNegativeColor( )

The *MovieClip.setNegativeColor( )* method is a wrapper for *Color.setNegative( )*:

```
MovieClip.prototype.setNegativeColor = function (percent) {
    (new Color(this)).setNegative (percent);
};
```

I called the *MovieClip* method setNegativeColor( ) to avoid any confusion, since there are other movie clip properties that could be negative.

Color.getNegative( )

The *Color.getNegative( )* method is the inverse of *setNegative( )*. It returns the current negative color percentage, as shown next:

```
Color.prototype.getNegative = function () {
    return this.getTransform().rb * (100/255);
};
```

The returned value is a number between 0 and 100.

MovieClip.getNegativeColor( )

The *MovieClip.getNegativeColor( )* method is a wrapper for *Color.getNegative( )*:

```
MovieClip.prototype.getNegativeColor = function () {
    return (new Color(this)).getNegative();
};
```

Again, the returned value is a number between 0 and 100.

Individual Solid Colors

The built-in *Color.setRGB( )* method lets us do solid coloring of movie clips. I wrote some methods which split apart solid coloring into separate methods for red, green, and blue.

setRed( )

The *Color.setRed( )* method is similar to the *setRGB( )* method. Both color an image opaquely, as if it was tinted by 100 percent. However, the *setRed( )* method allows you to control the red component of the color independently. Here is the code for the method:

```
Color.prototype.setRed = function (amount) {
    var t = this.getTransform();
    this.setRGB (amount << 16 | t.gb << 8 | t.bb);
};
```

In the preceding code, the amount argument is a number between 0 and 255. Keep in mind, too, that setting the red component of a movie clip does not affect the green or blue components.

The *MovieClip.setRed( )* method wraps around the corresponding *Color* method in this manner:

```
MovieClip.prototype.setRed = function (amount) {
    (new Color(this)).setRed (amount);
};
```

setGreen( )

The setter methods for green follow the same pattern as for red:

```
Color.prototype.setGreen = function (amount) {
    var t = this.getTransform();
    this.setRGB (t.rb << 16 | amount << 8 | t.bb);
};

MovieClip.prototype.setGreen = function (percent) {
    (new Color(this)).setGreen (percent);
};
```

setBlue( )

The following are the setter methods for the third color component, blue:

```
Color.prototype.setBlue = function (amount) {
    var t = this.getTransform();
    this.setRGB (t.rb << 16 | t.gb << 8 | amount);
};

MovieClip.prototype.setBlue = function (percent) {
    (new Color(this)).setBlue (percent);
};
```

getRed( )

The *getRed( )* method performs the inverse of *setRed( )*, returning the red component of the color applied to the target movie clip. Here is the method's code:

```
Color.prototype.getRed = function () {
    return this.getTransform().rb;
};
```

The following is the *MovieClip* companion method:

```
MovieClip.prototype.getRed = function () {
    return (new Color(this)).getRed();
};
```

getGreen( )

The getter methods for green follow the same pattern as for red:

```
Color.prototype.getGreen = function () {
    return this.getTransform().gb;
};
```

```
MovieClip.prototype.getGreen = function () {
    return (new Color(this)).getGreen();
};
```

getBlue( )

To finish things off, the following shows the getter methods for blue:

```
Color.prototype.getBlue = function () {
    return this.getTransform().bb;
};
```

```
MovieClip.prototype.getBlue = function () {
    return (new Color(this)).getBlue();
};
```

Adding Color Properties to MovieClip

Movie clips have built-in properties like _x, _alpha, and _rotation. They behave similarly to variables, storing numerical quantities. When you set one of these properties to a new value, the appearance of the movie clip is changed. For instance, you set the _rotation property like so:

```
this._rotation = 30;
```

This not only changes the _rotation property, but causes the movie clip to rotate slightly. Somehow, the Flash Player detects when the value of _rotation has changed, and sends a command to its internal renderer to update the display. Properties like _rotation are called *getter/setter properties*. When the property values are accessed or changed, getter or setter methods are called automatically.

The *Color* class doesn't have getter/setter properties. Rather, visual changes are always executed by calling methods, like *setRGB( )*. In dynamic animation, it can be more difficult to work with methods than properties.

For instance, it is a simpler process to set up a tween when you can use a getter/setter property. To move a movie clip horizontally, we can just increment the _x property:

```
this._x += 10;
```

Or, we can set up a *Tween* object for the _x property, as discussed in Chapter 7:

```
xTwn = new Tween (this, "_x", Math.easeOutQuad, 0, 300, 25);
```

This code defines a tween, xTwn, that will move the current movie clip horizontally between 0 and 300, over 25 frames, using a quadratic ease-out.

Unfortunately, when it comes to color, there are no _red, _green, or _blue properties that we can use in a similar fashion—incrementing or tweening directly. We could define properties with these names, but on their own, they would not call the *Color* methods and change the display. However, a new feature in Flash MX allows us to construct our own getter/setter properties. The *Object.addProperty( )* command links a property to getter and setter methods, allowing for some creative programming possibilities, as we'll see next.

MovieClip._red, _green, and _blue

While writing this chapter, I refined previous *Color* methods I had developed, and created some new ones. In doing this, an idea suddenly came to me of using all these *setXXX( )* and *getXXX( )* methods as getters and setters for movie clip properties. I'm always motivated by making things convenient for the ActionScript developer. *Color* methods like *setBrightness( )* and *setRed( )* certainly accomplished that, but how wouldn't _brightness or _red properties be even better? I did some experimenting with *Object.addProperty( )*, and sure enough, the idea worked!

Here's the syntax for *Object.addProperty( )* in general:

```
myObject.addProperty (prop, getFunc, setFunc)
```

In the preceding code, the prop parameter is the name of the property, given as a string. The getFunc argument, meanwhile, is a function that will be called whenever prop is read, returning a value representing prop. Lastly, the setFunc parameter is the setter function, which receives a new value for prop and takes appropriate action.

Here's how the *Object.addProperty( )* syntax works for defining a _red property:

```
MovieClip.prototype.addProperty ("_red",
    MovieClip.prototype.getRed, MovieClip.prototype.setRed);
```

First of all, the object that is gaining a new property is MovieClip.prototype, because I want all movie clips to inherit this property. Hence, *addProperty( )* is called as a method of MovieClip.prototype. The name of the property is "_red", naturally. The getter and setter functions are ones we have already discussed in this chapter: *MovieClip.prototype.getRed( )* and *MovieClip.prototype.setRed( )*.

This code can be shortened a bit. Since MovieClip.prototype is called three times, we can tighten things up by using the with statement, like so:

```
with (MovieClip.prototype) {
    addProperty ("_red", getRed, setRed);
}
```

This is much easier to read, as long as we remember that addProperty, getRed, and setRed are in the scope of MovieClip.prototype. In general, it's best to put the property and the getter and setter functions together in the same object.

With the property defined, we can now manipulate _red the same way we would _x or _alpha. We can increment it directly this way:

```
this._red += 2;
```

Or, we can set up a *Tween* object for _red:

```
redTwn = new Tween (this, "_red", Math.easeInOutCubic,
255, 0, 70);
```

This code defines a tween `redTwn` that changes the solid red color component of the movie clip from 255 to 0, over 70 frames, using a cubic ease-in-out.

A _green property can be set up in the same manner:

```
with (MovieClip.prototype) {
    addProperty ("_green", getGreen, setGreen);
}
```

Likewise for _blue:

```
with (MovieClip.prototype) {
    addProperty ("_blue", getBlue, setBlue);
}
```

We now have three color properties that can be used in conjunction to easily change the solid coloration of movie clips.

MovieClip._rgb

The _red, _green, and _blue properties control the individual RGB components of solid coloration. But what if we want to pick a specific color and set it directly, using a property? We can actually just use the built-in *Color* methods *getRGB( )* and *setRGB( )*. They are set up perfectly for this—they give and receive a single number, between 0 and 16,777,215. The code to add an _rgb property is quite simple:

```
with (MovieClip.prototype) {
    addProperty ("_rgb", getRGB, setRGB);
}
```

Here's a fun little example of how to use _rgb:

```
// inside a movie clip
this.onEnterFrame = function () {
    this._rgb = Math.floor (Math.random() * 16777216);
};
```

This code turns a movie clip a random solid color on each frame. The value of *Math.random( )* (between 0 and 0.99999…) is multiplied by 16,777,216 to produce a random number between 0 and 16,777,215.99999…. This number is then rounded down to the nearest integer with *Math.floor( )*, producing an integer between 0 and 16,777,215. This value, representing one of all possible colors in 24-bit color, is lastly assigned to the _rgb property.

MovieClip._brightness

A _brightness movie clip getter/setter property can also be defined with this approach:

```
with (MovieClip.prototype) {
    addProperty ("_brightness",
                    getBrightness, setBrightness);
}
```

The valid values of _brightness lie between –100 and 100.

Here is an example of a _brightness *Tween*, taking a movie clip from all-dark to all-light in 40 frames:

```
brightTwn = new Tween (this, "_brightness",
    Math.easeInOutQuad, -100, 100, 40);
```

MovieClip._brightOffset

Lastly, we define a _brightOffset movie clip property in this manner:

```
with (MovieClip.prototype) {
    addProperty ("_brightOffset", getBrightOffset,
                    setBrightOffset);
}
```

Here, the valid values of _brightOffset lie between –255 and 255, since it is an offset, not a percentage (as discussed earlier in this chapter).

The following code takes `_brightOffset` from a mostly-light 200 to a mostly-dark –200 in 80 frames:

```
brightOffsetTwn = new Tween (this, "_ brightOffset",
    Math.easeOutQuart, 200, -200, 80);
```

Conclusion

In this chapter, we have seen that a score of useful programming tools can be built on four simple *Color* methods. We now have an extensive code library for dynamic color programming. Movie clips can be easily brightened, darkened, tinted, and inverted. The *Color* API has been extended to the *MovieClip* class, allowing us to save coding time by performing color operations directly from clips themselves. There are many other *Color* extensions possible—for example, methods that use the HSB or CMYK color models. I encourage you to explore these areas further, gleaning custom methods from others in the Flash community or writing your own. I have also created additional *Color* methods and properties, such as *setRedPercent( )* and `_redPercent`, which, given space considerations, we can't discuss here. Look for them, though, in the code accompanying this book.

Now that we know how to dynamically color existing images, it's time to learn how to create vector graphics from scratch—in our next chapter.

Chapter **10**

Drawing with ActionScript

One of the most exciting new features of Flash MX is the ability to create graphics with ActionScript. No longer do we have to resort to cheap tricks to generate dynamic graphics. Say goodbye to the old duplicated movie clips with 100×100 diagonal lines and skewed triangles.

In the first section of the chapter, I will run through the eight commands of the Shape Drawing API, commenting on each. Then we'll spend the bulk of the chapter extending these to create a powerful custom API for more complex shapes, including triangles, rectangles, polygons, and cubic Beziers.

The Shape Drawing API

The *Shape Drawing API*, as it's referred to in the documentation, exposes the Flash Player's internal drawing capabilities to the ActionScript programmer. API stands for Application Programming Interface, and is a common term in computer programming. An API is generally a collection of commands that gives a developer access to specific functionality.

The Shape Drawing API is comprised of eight commands:

❱ *moveTo( )*

❱ *lineTo( )*

❱ *lineStyle( )*

❱ *curveTo( )*

❱ *beginFill( )*

❱ *beginGradientFill( )*

❱ *endFill( )*

❱ *clear( )*

These functions are methods of the *MovieClip* class. This makes sense, because drawing always occurs in some movie clip. You can draw in an empty movie clip or in one that contains design-time graphics. However, dynamically drawn graphics are always rendered first in each frame. Thus, they appear *underneath* design-time graphics in the same movie clip.

The drawing methods are intentionally basic. They are meant to mirror the simple drawing commands of the Flash Player. All of the vector graphics you see in a Flash movie are produced with simple lines and quadratic curves.

This chapter is focused on ways to extend the capabilities of the Drawing API, not simply repeat the Flash manual's contents. As such, I'll comment on the built-in methods only briefly, before moving on to custom code.

MovieClip.moveTo( )

The *moveTo( )* method moves the drawing cursor to a new location. This is its syntax:

```
mc.moveTo (x, y);
```

The x and y arguments are coordinates local to the movie clip that contains the drawing.

One subtlety of the *moveTo( )* command is that it starts a new subpath. Think about how you write words by hand. When you lift your pen, that's like a *moveTo( )* command—starting a new subpath. A simple word like "and" can be written in one subpath. However, the word "the" requires two subpaths, because you have to cross the "t." The subpath concept comes up later with the *endFill( )* method.

MovieClip.lineTo( )

The *lineTo( )* method draws a line to a specified location using the current fill and line style. This is its syntax:

```
mc.lineTo (x, y);
```

The x and y arguments are coordinates local to the movie clip that contains the drawing. The line begins at the current location of the drawing cursor. If we want the line to begin somewhere else, we first have to move to that point with *moveTo( )*, then call *lineTo( )*.

MovieClip.lineStyle( )

The *lineStyle( )* method sets the current stroke style for the Shape Drawing API:

```
mc.lineStyle (thickness, rgb, alpha);
```

The thickness parameter specifies the width of the stroke in points. If a thickness of zero is specified, a hairline stroke is drawn. If `thickness` is undefined, no stroke is drawn at all.

NOTE: A hairline stroke is a special setting that draws a line about a pixel thick, no matter what the scale factor of the movie is. When you have a normal stroke width, such as two points, the line appears thicker as you zoom into the movie. The appearance of a hairline stroke, however, doesn't change. This is the same behavior as with manually created lines.

The `rgb` and `alpha` arguments are optional parameters. The `rgb` value is a standard 0xRRGGBB color number (see Chapter 9 for more details on color). The `alpha` parameter specifies the opacity of the color. The value of `alpha` can range between 0 and 100, and it defaults to 100 if unspecified.

MovieClip.curveTo( )

The *curveTo( )* method draws a quadratic Bezier curve. Resembling a parabola, a quadratic Bezier is defined by three points, as shown in Figure 10-1.

There are two anchor points (*a* and *c*) and one control point (*b*). The anchor points are the endpoints of the curve, while the control point influences the curve between them. The curve starts at the first anchor point, and heads toward the control point. At the same time, it starts curving toward the second anchor point. As a result, the path doesn't touch the control point.

The *curveTo( )* method uses this syntax:

```
mc.curveTo (controlX, controlY, anchorX, anchorY);
```

The four parameters are coordinates for two points within the movie clip. The `controlX` and `controlY` arguments are the coordinates of the control point, and `anchorX` and `anchorY` are the coordinates of the second anchor point. That takes care of two points, but what about the third one, the first anchor point? The current location of the drawing pen is used as the first anchor point. This is set by *moveTo( )*.

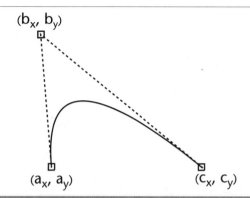

A quadratic Bezier curve defined by points a, b, and c

MovieClip.beginFill( )

The *beginFill( )* method sets the current fill for the drawing commands. This is its syntax:

```
mc.beginFill (rgb, alpha);
```

The `rgb` parameter is a standard 0xRRGGBB color number. If `rgb` is undefined, the fill is empty. The `alpha` argument is optional. It can range between 0 and 100, and `alpha` defaults to 100 if undefined. The fill will also need to be eventually closed off using the *endFill( )* command.

MovieClip.beginGradientFill( )

The *beginGradientFill( )* method sets a gradient fill to be used by the drawing commands. This is the most complex method in the Shape Drawing API, taking five arguments:

```
mc.beginGradientFill (fillType, colors, alphas, ratios, matrix);
```

The `fillType` argument defines the style of gradient with a string—either "linear" or "radial." A gradient creates a fade between two or more colors. These are specified by `colors`, which is an array of 0xRRGGBB color numbers. The next argument `alphas` is also an array, this time with alpha values which correspond to the colors in the `colors` array. The `ratios` argument is an array of color distributions. Each value in the array lies between 0 and 255. The color distribution value defines the percentage of the width where the color is sampled at 100 percent.

The `matrix` argument is an object that contains transformation properties. There are two types of matrices, which are described briefly in the ActionScript Dictionary. The "box" type is fairly straightforward, using coordinates much like the "relative-coordinate rectangle" which is discussed later in this chapter in the section, "Rectangles." The other matrix type is a 3×3 transformation matrix, which is much more complex, conferring the ability to skew a gradient. (Personally, I don't use gradients much, because it's far too easy to end up with something ugly. Producing an attractive gradient with code is difficult. So, good luck—you're on your own with this one.)

MovieClip.endFill( )

The *endFill( )* method finalizes a fill for a dynamically drawn shape:

```
mc.endFill();
```

It will affect whatever lines and curves you have drawn since calling *beginFill( )* or *beginGradientFill( )*.

The *endFill( )* method will also close off a subpath for you. Every time you call *moveTo( )*, a new subpath is started. Suppose you begin a fill, move to a point, and draw two lines. If you then close the fill, the subpath will automatically be closed and filled, forming a triangle. Here is some code to illustrate:

```
// closing a subpath
this.beginfill (0xCCFF00, 40);
this.moveTo (20, 30);
this.lineTo (120, 200);
this.lineTo (220, 30);
this.endFill();
```

The *endFill( )* command causes a line to be drawn from the last point (220, 30) to the first point of the subpath (20, 30).

It's a good idea to close a fill in the same frame it was opened. Otherwise, strange artifacts may appear in the image on some systems. (Of course, those who have a preference for chaos may consider this an "undocumented feature.")

MovieClip.clear( )

The *clear( )* method removes all dynamically drawn shapes in the current movie clip. If not cleared, graphics will pile on top of each other, and may slow the Flash Player to a crawl if too much builds up. Its syntax is as simple as it gets:

```
mc.clear();
```

The *clear( )* command also removes the current line style.

Animation and Dynamic Drawing

The Shape Drawing API can be used to create static images. But, being Flashers, we're not content to let graphics just sit there—we want to animate! There are two main approaches to animating dynamically drawn graphics, which I'll call *movie clip animation* and *shape animation*. They are similar to motion tweening and shape tweening, respectively, and the two approaches complement one another.

Movie Clip Animation

The first approach is an extension of our existing animation skills. We start by filling a movie clip with graphics using the Shape Drawing API. Then we can treat it as just another movie clip, whose properties we can manipulate to produce animation. We can move it around with the _x and _y properties, stretch it with _xscale, _yscale, _width, and _height, spin it with _rotation, and fade it with _alpha. In other words, once the insides are drawn, we can manipulate the container using all of the tweening and animation techniques of Chapters 7 and 8.

Here is a quick example to illustrate this approach. A vertical line is drawn within the current movie clip, then the movie clip slides to the right:

```
// movie clip animation of a vertical line
this.lineStyle (2, 0x0000FF);
this.lineTo (0, 200);
this.onEnterFrame = function () {
    this._x += 10;
};
```

With this code in the first frame of a movie clip, the drawing commands are called just once. After the line has been drawn, a frame loop is created using the onEnterFrame handler. The loop increases the _x property by 10 pixels every frame, moving the movie clip steadily to the right.

This "movie clip animation" with code is analogous to motion tweening on the timeline by hand. Think of how you would create this simple line animation manually. You would draw a vertical line inside a symbol, then motion tween the symbol on the timeline. However, you could produce the same animation with shape tweening, and this has a parallel in code: shape animation.

Shape Animation

Movie clip animation manipulates the container, but shape animation changes the graphics *inside* the container. We use the drawing commands to plot different shapes from frame to frame. Since the shapes will pile up over time, we clear the graphics from the previous frame before drawing the new frame. In other words, we call the *clear( )* method at the beginning of the frame, then use the other drawing commands.

Let's return to our simple example of a vertical line sliding to the right. How could we produce the same animation without affecting the movie clip properties? We'll draw the line dynamically, between different points in each frame. This will be a bit more involved because we'll have to keep track of the line's endpoints ourselves. Here's how it works out in ActionScript:

```
// shape animation of a vertical line
this.startX = 0;
this.onEnterFrame = function () {
    this.clear();
    this.lineStyle (2, 0x0000FF);
    this.startX += 10;
    this.moveTo (this.startX, 0);
    this.lineTo (this.startX, 200);
};
```

We start by initializing the startX variable to zero. Then a frame loop is created with onEnterFrame. At the beginning of each frame, the dynamically drawn graphics are cleared with *this.clear( )*. Since the *clear( )* command removes the line style, we set it again with *this.lineStyle( )*. The horizontal position moves by 10 pixels every frame, so we increase this.startX by 10. Now to draw the line, we move to the new starting point, at which _x equals this.startX, and _y equals zero. Finally, we use *lineTo( )* to draw a line to the point 200 pixels directly beneath.

This example is incredibly basic, I know, and the animation is not very exciting. The point I'm trying to make is that this is a different type of animation, produced by redrawing the shape itself, rather than moving the movie clip containing the shape. This is analogous to using a shape tween on the timeline instead of a motion tween.

Drawing Common Shapes

The eight commands in the Shape Drawing API are intentionally basic. It's up to us developers to build levels of complexity on top of them. There are many common shapes we can draw with just the *moveTo( )*, *lineTo( )*, and *curveTo( )* methods. We can encapsulate shape-drawing procedures in our own methods, working from simple shapes to complex ones.

Lines

The *lineTo( )* command draws a line to a point. However, it doesn't let us specify the *starting point* of the line—it always begins at the current drawing location. This isn't too difficult to work around. If we want to draw a line between (*x1, y1*) and (*x2, y2*) in a movie clip mc, we can use these two commands:

```
mc.moveTo (x1, y1);
mc.lineTo (x2, y2);
```

However, drawing a line is such a simple operation that it feels unnecessary to have to type two lines of code. Wouldn't it be easier to encapsulate the commands into a new function?

I added a *drawLine( )* method to the *MovieClip* class that draws a line between two points:

```
MovieClip.prototype.drawLine = function (x1, y1, x2, y2) {
    this.moveTo (x1, y1);
    this.lineTo (x2, y2);
};
```

I simply took the *moveTo( )* and *lineTo( )* commands and placed them in the most logical place—the *MovieClip* prototype. Now we can tell any movie clip to draw a line within itself, using this syntax:

```
mc.drawLine (x1, y1, x2, y2);
```

Now suppose we have two points represented as *Vector* objects. How would we draw a line between them with *MovieClip.drawLine( )*? The following example shows how to create two *Vectors* and pass their properties to *drawLine( )*:

```
a = new Vector (2, 2);
b = new Vector (0, 9);
mc.drawLine (a.x, a.y, b.x, b.y);
```

This procedure isn't too difficult. But I always ask myself, "Is this as convenient as it could possibly be?" I would like to be able to just pass two point objects to a function and have it draw a line between them. I wrote another method *MovieClip.drawLinePts( )* for this purpose:

```
MovieClip.prototype.drawLinePts = function (p1, p2) {
    this.moveTo (p1.x, p1.y);
    this.lineTo (p2.x, p2.y);
};
```

This method is similar to *drawLine( )*. However, it accepts two arguments instead of four. The line is defined by point objects p1 and p2, as shown in Figure 10-2.

Both p1 and p2 should contain x and y properties, which are numbers. The objects could be instances of our *Vector* class from Chapter 4. Here's an example of creating two *Vector* objects and passing them directly to the *drawLinePts( )* method:

```
a = new Vector (20, 100);
b = new Vector (90, 0);
mc.drawLinePts (a, b);
```

However, any object with x and y properties will do. We can create ordinary objects with coordinates and pass them to *drawLinePts( )*, as the following example demonstrates:

```
a = {x:20, y:100};
b = {x:90, y:0};
mc.drawLinePts (a, b);
```

The point objects a and b are created with the object literal syntax (the braces). They contain the same coordinate data as our previous example with *Vector* objects. Passing these objects to *drawLinePts( )* works exactly the same as before. Creating generic point objects is sometimes preferable to creating instances of a custom class like *Vector*. The object literal code is

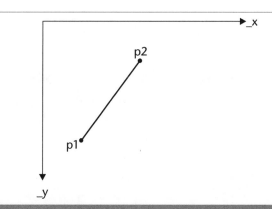

FIGURE 10-2

A line defined by points p1 and p2

faster and shorter than calling the *Vector* constructor; however, you lose the benefit of the *Vector* methods for rotation, translation, and so on. In any case, these custom drawing methods are flexible enough to work with both incarnations.

Triangles

The simplest connected two-dimensional shape is the triangle. A generic triangle is defined by three points, which are connected with three lines. Given this, we can easily draw a generic triangle using the *MovieClip.drawTri( )* method:

```
MovieClip.prototype.drawTri = function (p1, p2, p3) {
    with (this) {
        moveTo (p1.x, p1.y);
        lineTo (p2.x, p2.y);
        lineTo (p3.x, p3.y);
        lineTo (p1.x, p1.y);
    }
};
```

The arguments p1, p2, and p3 are point objects that define the corners of the triangle, as shown in Figure 10-3.

The internal procedure of this method is straightforward. Begin by moving to the first point. Then, draw lines to the second and third points,

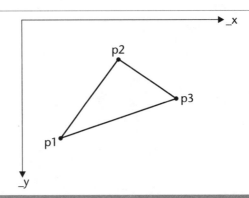

A triangle defined by points p1, p2, and p3

and back to the first point. I decided to use point object arguments, instead of numbers, for this method. It's easy to create an alternate method that takes numbers instead. However, this would result in six arguments instead of three: x1, y1, x2, y2, x3, and y3. In general, if a drawing method requires three or more points, I use point object arguments instead of numbers, for convenience.

NOTE: I used the `with` statement in the above method to make the code slightly shorter and faster. The drawing commands will all execute in the context of `this`, so it makes sense to temporarily change the scope using `with`.

The following code example shows how to create three points and draw a triangle between them:

```
// test MovieClip.drawTri()
this.lineStyle (4, 0x0000FF, 60);
a = {x:20, y:100};
b = {x:90, y:0};
c = {x:200, y:50};
this.drawTri (a, b, c);
```

Does *drawTri( )* create a solid triangle, or an outlined one? That's for you to decide—outside this particular method. I deliberately left the fill and stroke unchanged in *drawTri( )*, allowing you to use it with all possible combinations of the two. My drawing methods all use the current fill and stroke, defined with *beginFill( )*, *beginGradientFill( )*, or *lineStyle( )*.

NOTE: You may also notice that I didn't use the *endFill( )* method in *drawTri( )*. I debated, for a while, whether to include *endFill( )*, and eventually decided it'd be best not to force it on the user. There are situations where you may want to draw several triangles in succession before ending the fill. For example, you can get interesting "negative space" effects if these triangles overlap. Your options are open: you can begin a fill before calling *drawTri( )*, and then either end the fill or draw more graphics.

Quadrilaterals

A quadrilateral is any closed shape with four sides. Squares, rectangles, parallelograms, and rhombi are all quadrilaterals. We will create methods to draw rectangles later on, but right now, we're working from the general to the specific. My *drawQuad( )* method can draw a generic quadrilateral using the current fill and stroke:

```
MovieClip.prototype.drawQuad = function (p1, p2, p3, p4) {
    with (this) {
        moveTo (p1.x, p1.y);
        lineTo (p2.x, p2.y);
        lineTo (p3.x, p3.y);
        lineTo (p4.x, p4.y);
        lineTo (p1.x, p1.y);
    }
};
```

The arguments p1, p2, p3, and p4 define the four corners of the quadrilateral, as shown in Figure 10-4.

The code is quite similar to *drawTri( )*, merely extending it from three points to four. Again, I have used point objects instead of individual numbers, thus reducing a potential eight arguments to four.

The following code example shows how to create four points and draw a quadrilateral between them:

```
// test MovieClip.drawQuad()
this.beginfill (0x00CC22, 40);
this.lineStyle (2, 0x330000);
a = {x:0, y:20};
b = {x:10, y:80};
c = {x:100, y:120};
d = {x:150, y:0};
this.drawQuad (a, b, c, d);
this.endFill();
```

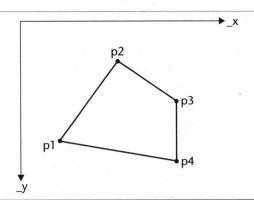

FIGURE 10-4

A quadrilateral defined by points p1, p2, p3, and p4

Rectangles

A rectangle is any four-sided shape that contains four 90-degree angles. Think about the different ways you could describe a rectangle with numbers. You could define it with two corner points—for example, one corner at (0, 0), the other at (5, 10). This could be called *absolute* coordinates. Alternatively, you could start with a corner point, but give the rectangle's width and height—*relative* coordinates. Or, you could give the rectangle's center point instead, along with its height and width—*centered* coordinates. I think all of these approaches are useful in different situations. For convenience, I created rectangle drawing methods for all three coordinate styles—absolute, relative, and centered.

MovieClip.drawRect( )

The *drawRect( )* method draws a rectangle defined by two corner points—in other words, absolute coordinates:

```
MovieClip.prototype.drawRect = function (x1, y1, x2, y2) {
    with (this) {
        moveTo (x1, y1);
        lineTo (x2, y1);
        lineTo (x2, y2);
        lineTo (x1, y2);
        lineTo (x1, y1);
    }
};
```

The four arguments are numbers which define the corner points (x1, y1) and (x2, y2), as shown in Figure 10-5.

The internal drawing procedure is straightforward. After moving the drawing cursor to the first corner, four lines are drawn—two horizontal, two vertical.

NOTE: I decided to use number variables here instead of point objects because the function has only four parameters.

In the following code example, a rectangle is drawn between two corner points using the *drawRect( )* method:

```
// test MovieClip.drawRect()
this.beginFill (0x33DD00, 60);
this.drawRect (10, 10, 240, 150);
this.endFill();
```

MovieClip.drawRectRel( )

Sometimes it is more convenient to define a rectangle using width and height—relative coordinates, as Figure 10-6 illustrates.

The *drawRectRel( )* method draws a rectangle defined by its starting point and its width and height:

```
MovieClip.prototype.drawRectRel = function (x, y, width, height) {
    this.drawRect (x, y, x + width, y + height);
};
```

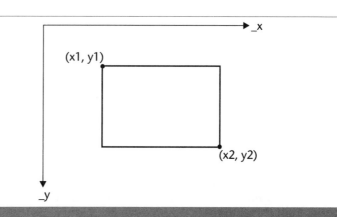

FIGURE 10-5

A rectangle defined by corners (x1, y1) and (x2, y2)

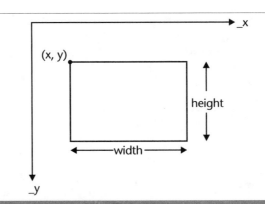

FIGURE 10-6

A rectangle defined by corner (x, y), width, and height

As you can see, *drawRectRel( )* is just a wrapper method for *drawRect( )*. It converts relative coordinates to absolute coordinates, and passes them to *drawRect( )* to carry out the actual drawing procedure.

In the following code example, a 20×30 rectangle is drawn, with its corner point at (60, 60):

```
// test MovieClip.drawRectRel()
this.beginFill (0x0000FF, 40);
this.drawRectRel (60, 60, 20, 30);
this.endFill();
```

MovieClip.drawRectCent( )

Suppose you want to draw a rectangle of a certain size, but centered at a certain point. Figure 10-7 shows the dimensions of a centered rectangle.

The *MovieClip.drawRectCent( )* method draws a rectangle defined by a center x and y, and a width and height:

```
MovieClip.prototype.drawRectCent = function (x, y, w, h) {
    this.drawRect (x - w/2, y - h/2, x + w/2, y + h/2);
};
```

Again, this is a wrapper method for our base rectangle drawing method *drawRect( )*. This time, centered coordinates are converted to absolute coordinates by shifting them up and left by half of the width and height, respectively.

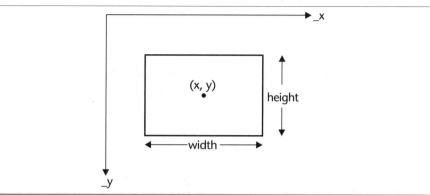

A rectangle defined by center (x, y), width, and height

In the following code example, a 70×10 rectangle is drawn, with its center point at (150, 100):

```
// test MovieClip.drawRectCent()
this.lineStyle (2, 0x00FF00);
this.drawRectCent (150, 100, 70, 10);
```

Squares

A square is a special case of a rectangle—one with equal width and height. Consequently, we can use our existing rectangle drawing methods to draw squares, rather than recoding the entire procedure.

MovieClip.drawSquare( )

The *drawSquare( )* method plots a square of a certain width, starting at the specified corner point:

```
MovieClip.prototype.drawSquare = function (x, y, width) {
    this.drawRect (x, y, x + width, y + width);
};
```

The x and y arguments specify the top-left corner of the square. The width parameter determines how far the square extends from there. Notice that we're using *drawRect( )* to draw a rectangle which has an equal width and height.

In the following code example, a 50×50 square is drawn, with its corner point at (250, 10):

```
// test MovieClip.drawSquare()
this.lineStyle (2, 0x00FF00);
this.drawSquare (250, 10, 50);
```

MovieClip.drawSquareCent( )

The *drawSquareCent( )* method plots a square centered at a specific point:

```
MovieClip.prototype.drawSquareCent = function (x, y, width) {
    var r = width / 2;
    this.drawRect (x - r, y - r, x + r, y + r);
};
```

Centered coordinates are converted to absolute coordinates by shifting them up and left by half of the width.

I could have coded this method differently, calling *drawRectCent( )* instead, as the following code shows:

```
// alternative code approach
MovieClip.prototype.drawSquareCent = function (x, y, width) {
    this.drawRectCent (x, y, width, width);
};
```

However, this approach is less efficient, since *drawRectCent( )* itself calls another function—*drawRect( )*. I decided to call *drawRect( )* directly from *drawSquareCent( )*, eliminating the extra step.

The following code example draws a 90×90 square, centered at (20, 80):

```
// test MovieClip.drawSquareCent()
this.beginFill (0x3300DD, 30);
this.drawSquareCent (20, 80, 90);
this.endFill();
```

Dots

Unlike Director, Flash does not allow you to plot individual pixels—only vector shapes and bitmaps. However, we can simulate a dot by drawing a tiny square. Here is the *drawDot( )* method:

```
MovieClip.prototype.drawDot = function (x, y) {
    this.drawRect (x - .5, y - .5, x + .5, y + .5);
};
```

This draws a one-pixel-wide square, centered on the current point. When the Flash Player is in high quality mode, the dot will hardly show up, because of anti-aliasing. High quality mode anti-aliases on a 4×4 grid. As a result, the colors of pixels around the tiny square are mixed into it, making it appear smaller. On the other hand, medium quality mode anti-aliases on a 2×2 grid, and low quality doesn't anti-alias at all. Our dot will look most like a real pixel in low quality mode.

The following code draws a dot at (130, 100):

```
// test MovieClip.drawDot()
this.beginFill (0x00CC00);
this.drawDot (130, 100);
this.endFill();
```

N O T E :   It's also possible to draw a dot with a very short line, say half a pixel long or less. This produces a rounded shape instead of a square one.

Polygons

A polygon is any closed two-dimensional shape composed of straight lines. When people think of polygons, they often picture regular polygons like pentagons, which have equal sides. For now, we're dealing with polygons in the most general sense. A generic polygon can have any number of sides, of any length. The *drawPoly( )* method draws a generic polygon, based on a collection of points:

```
MovieClip.prototype.drawPoly = function (pts) {
    this.moveTo (pts[0].x, pts[0].y);
    var i = pts.length;
    while (i--) this.lineTo (pts[i].x, pts[i].y);
};
```

The single argument, `pts` is an array of point objects, each point containing x and y properties. The task of *drawPoly( )* is to connect these points with lines, in the order they are given. There could be three points in the `pts` array or 300—however many, they will all be used. Figure 10-8 shows a polygon based on a five-point array.

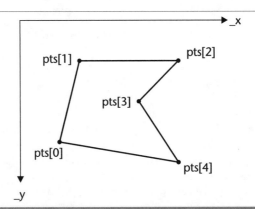

A polygon defined by an array of points

The procedure begins by moving the drawing pen to the first point in the list. Then, a line is drawn to the last point, the second-to-last, and so on, back to the first point. I decided to go backwards through the array so that I could use a highly optimized `while (i--)` loop. Forwards or backwards—the direction doesn't really matter, as long as the drawing pen ends up back at the first point. It's actually important that the drawing pen finishes at the first point, not any other point, in order for other drawing commands to carry on from the correct location.

In the following code example, 50 random points are generated, and used to draw a polygon:

```
// test MovieClip.drawPoly()
// create an array of random points
var pts = [];
var numPoints = 50;
while (numPoints--) {
    pts.push ({x:Math.random()*300, y:Math.random()*300});
}
// draw polygon with the points
this.beginFill (0x339933);
this.drawPoly (pts);
```

Regular Polygons

A regular polygon is a polygon with equal angles and sides. For example, a pentagon, as it's usually pictured, has five equal sides and angles. Regular polygons also possess rotational symmetry. For example, if you rotate a regular pentagon 72 degrees (360 / 5), it looks exactly the same.

The *drawRegPoly( )* method draws a regular polygon:

```
MovieClip.prototype.drawRegPoly = function (x, y, r, numPts, rotation) {
        var angle = (rotation - 90) * (Math.PI/180);
        var pts = [];
        var dAngle = 2 * Math.PI / numPts;
        var cos = Math.cos, sin = Math.sin;
        this.moveTo (r*cos(angle) + x, r*sin(angle) + y);
        while (numPts--) {
            angle += dAngle;
            this.lineTo (r*cos(angle) + x, r*sin(angle) + y);
        }
};
```

The x and y arguments define the center of the polygon, while the r parameter specifies the radius from the center to one of the polygon's corners, as shown in Figure 10-9.

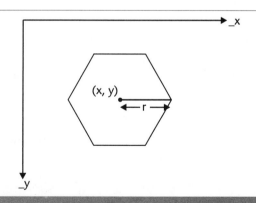

FIGURE 10-9

A regular polygon with center (x, y) and radius r

The `numPts` parameter determines the number of points (and sides) of the polygon. For example, `numPts` would be eight for an octagon. The last parameter, `rotation`, turns the polygon by an angle (given in degrees).

I'll make some general comments on the code for *drawRegPoly( )* without going into the nitty-gritty details of the algorithm. The internal procedure is similar to the code for the *drawPoly( )* method:

> move to the starting point

> loop through a number of points, drawing a line to each one

> finish at the starting point

The difference here is that the points are generated according to a specific formula. Trigonometry is used to space the points evenly around a circle of a specific radius. If you are skilled with polar coordinates by now, you may recognize some of the math, involving sine and cosine, from Chapter 3.

The following code draws a regular pentagon of radius 90, centered at (100, 100) and rotated by 15 degrees:

```
this.beginFill (0xFF0000, 70);
this.drawRegPoly (100, 100, 90, 5, 15);
this.endFill();
```

Ellipses

An ellipse cannot be exactly drawn with any type of Bezier curve. However, it can be approximated reasonably well with eight quadratic Bezier curves. In fact, this is what Flash does in the authoring tool. Try this: create an ellipse and then select it with the Subselect tool. You'll notice that there are eight nodes and eight curve segments.

NOTE: Most illustration programs use cubic Beziers instead of quadratics (see the comparison discussion later in this chapter). An ellipse can be approximated decently with four cubic Beziers. Thus, an ellipse in Adobe Illustrator, for example, has four nodes—one for each cubic Bezier.

There are several different methods to draw circles and ellipses available in the Flash community. They all basically use eight *curveTo( )* commands, and rely on trigonometry or pre-calculated numbers to determine the appropriate control points of the quadratic Beziers.

However, the internal implementation isn't as important as the code interface. An ellipse is most commonly defined by a center point (x, y), a horizontal radius, and a vertical radius, as Figure 10-10 illustrates.

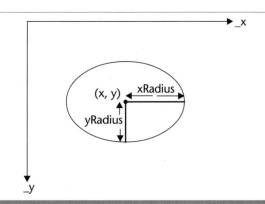

An ellipse defined by (x, y), xRadius, and yRadius

As you can see, an ellipse is defined by four numbers, and thus, a corresponding drawing method takes four parameters, as shown in the following code:

```
// adapted from Casper Schuirink's drawCircle() method
MovieClip.prototype.drawOval = function (x, y, rx, ry) {
    this.moveTo (x+rx, y);
    this.curveTo (rx+x, 0.4142*ry+y, 0.7071*rx+x, 0.7071*ry+y);
    this.curveTo (0.4142*rx+x, ry+y, x, ry+y);
    this.curveTo (-0.4142*rx+x, ry+y, -0.7071*rx+x, 0.7071*ry+y);
    this.curveTo (-rx+x, 0.4142*ry+y, -rx+x, y);
    this.curveTo (-rx+x, -0.4142*ry+y, -0.7071*rx+x, -0.7071*ry+y);
    this.curveTo (-0.4142*rx+x, -ry+y, x, -ry+y);
    this.curveTo (0.4142*rx+x, -ry+y, 0.7071*rx+x, -0.7071*ry+y);
    this.curveTo (rx+x, -0.4142*ry+y, rx+x, y);
};
```

I took Casper Schuirink's circle-drawing method and modified it to create ellipses.

The following code example draws an ellipse centered at (80, 100):

```
this.drawOval (80, 100, 25, 15);
```

It is 50 pixels wide and 30 pixels high because its x-radius is 25 and its y-radius is 15.

Circles

A circle is a special case of an ellipse—one that has equal horizontal and vertical radii. As such, a *drawCircle( )* method can simply call the *drawOval( )* method, as the following code demonstrates:

```
MovieClip.prototype.drawCircle = function (x, y, r) {
    this.drawOval (x, y, r, r);
};
```

The following code example draws a 100-pixel-wide circle (radius of 50), centered at (150, 100):

```
this.drawCircle (150, 100, 50);
```

Finding the Pen Location

One significant drawback of the Shape Drawing API is that there is no easy way to find the current location of the drawing pen—no built-in command to find the last point used by a *moveTo( )*, *lineTo( )*, or *curveTo( )* operation. It's crucial to know this information in order to draw certain shapes. A solution is to overwrite some of the built-in drawing methods with custom methods. This is similar to call-forwarding with phone numbers. A call to *curveTo( )* will be redirected to a custom function, which will call the built-in *curveTo( )*, and then set variables for the pen coordinates.

MovieClip._xpen and _ypen Properties

We're going to be using `MovieClip.prototype` quite a lot in the code that follows. So first, I'll define a shortcut variable:

```
MCP = MovieClip.prototype;
```

The MCP variable now points to the same object as `MovieClip.prototype`. We can now call MCP any place we would normally call `MovieClip.prototype`. This will shorten our code and save a bit of file space.

The first step in overwriting a built-in method is to save a backup of the original. I store the built-in method in a backup variable:

```
MCP.f6lineTo = MCP.lineTo;
```

Now `MovieClip.prototype` contains a method *f6lineTo( )*, which is simply the built-in *lineTo( )* under another name.

Next, I redefine the *lineTo( )* method with a custom function:

```
MCP.lineTo = function (x, y) {
    with (this) {
        f6lineTo (x, y);
        _xpen = x;
        _ypen = y;
    }
};
```

This new method first calls the old, built-in method, passing the x and y arguments. Then the movie clip's _xpen and _ypen properties are set to the x and y coordinates, respectively.

Now, after calling *lineTo( )*, you can find the coordinates of the drawing pen by checking the _xpen and _ypen properties, as shown in this code example:

```
this.lineTo (123, 246);
trace (this._xpen); // output: 123
trace (this._ypen); // output: 246
```

We can use the same procedure to redefine *curveTo( )*:

```
MCP.f6curveTo = MCP.curveTo;
MCP.curveTo = function (cx, cy, ax, ay) {
    with (this) {
        f6curveTo (cx, cy, ax, ay);
        _xpen = ax;
        _ypen = ay;
    }
};
```

MovieClip._xpenStart and _ypenStart Properties

The built-in *MovieClip.moveTo( )* method starts a new subpath each time it is called (as previously discussed). It would be useful to store the coordinates for the point where a new subpath was started. This allows us to more easily close a subpath after drawing a number of lines or curves.

I overwrote the built-in *moveTo( )* with a custom function that sets custom _xpenStart and _ypenStart properties. It also changes _xpen and _ypen, of course, as the following code shows:

```
// previously defined: MCP = MovieClip.prototype;
MCP.f6moveTo = MCP.moveTo;
MCP.moveTo = function (x, y) {
    with (this) {
        f6moveTo (x, y);
        _xpen = _xpenStart = x;
        _ypen = _ypenStart = y;
    }
};
```

We also need to redefine *MovieClip.clear( )*, since that command resets the drawing pen to (0, 0). Here is the code:

```
MCP.f6clear = MCP.clear;
MCP.clear = function () {
    with (this) {
        f6clear();
        _xpen = _ypen = _xpenStart = _ypenStart = 0;
    }
};
```

Initializing the Properties

For each movie clip, the drawing pen starts at (0, 0). Thus, we will give our custom properties a default value of zero:

```
// previously defined: MCP = MovieClip.prototype;
MCP._xpen = MCP._ypen = MCP._xpenStart = MCP._ypenStart = 0;
```

By setting the properties to zero in `MovieClip.prototype`, every movie clip will inherit the values.

Lastly, we can use the undocumented function *ASSetPropFlags( )* to hide our custom methods from `for..in` loops:

```
ASSetPropFlags (MCP, null, 1);
```

ASSetPropFlags( ) is a useful little function that was hidden for the longest time, but is quickly becoming popular among ActionScripters. It can be used to hide or unhide properties from `for..in` loops, and also protect/ unprotect them from being deleted or changed. See http://chattyfig .figleaf.com/flashcoders-wiki/index.php?ASSetPropFlags for a full rundown of its options.

Cubic Beziers

If you've created vector graphics in programs like Adobe Illustrator or Macromedia Freehand, you are familiar with Bezier curves. What you may not know is that there are different types of Beziers. The curves you normally use to design graphics are *cubic* Beziers. However, some programs, including Flash, use *quadratic* Beziers.

Quadratic vs. Cubic Beziers

Cubic Bezier curves are more complex than quadratic Beziers, both in appearance and underlying mathematics. Quadratic Beziers have one control point, whereas cubic Beziers have two, as shown in Figure 10-11.

Also, a cubic Bezier can change direction in the middle of the curve. For example, it can curve clockwise, then counterclockwise, between its endpoints. A quadratic Bezier cannot change direction between its nodes. It either curves clockwise, counterclockwise, or not at all.

CPU Performance

Quadratic Beziers can be calculated much more quickly than cubic Beziers.

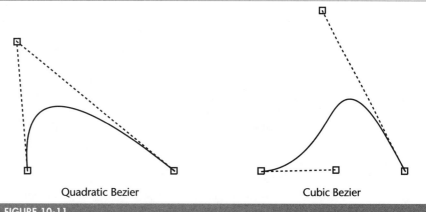

Quadratic Bezier   Cubic Bezier

FIGURE 10-11

Quadratic vs. cubic Bezier curves

Quadratic means that the underlying equations are based on a power of two (x^2), whereas *cubic* corresponds to a power of three (x^3).

Here is the standard form of the quadratic Bezier equation:

$$P(t) = (1-t)^2 a + 2t(1-t)b + t^2 c$$

$P(t)$ is the position of the curve at time t, and a, b, and c are the values of the control points. This equation governs one dimension, or axis, only. For a two-dimensional curve, you need two $P(t)$ equations—one for x, one for y.

Here is the standard equation for a cubic Bezier:

$$P(t) = (1-t)^3 a + 3t(1-t)^2 b + 3t^2(1-t)c + t^3 d$$

In a cubic Bezier, there are four control points: *a*, *b*, *c*, and *d*. Perhaps these equations give you some idea of the difference in complexity between quadratic and cubic curves. Cubic Bezier equations allow for more complex curves, but at a computational cost.

It is possible to have Bezier curves in higher degrees: x^4 (quartic Bezier), x^5 (quintic Bezier)—as high as you want to go. However, the equations for higher-order Beziers become so complex that they are rarely used in a practical setting.

Beziers in Fonts

You may have heard that Type 1 fonts are superior to TrueType fonts. Perhaps this seems self-evident, since the former is made by Adobe, and the latter, by Microsoft. Without surrendering to such bias, I can say that the rumor is true—Type 1 fonts are superior, at least in terms of *curve accuracy*. The reason is that Type 1 fonts use cubic Beziers, whereas TrueType fonts use quadratic Beziers. Thus, if you have a font in both Type 1 and TrueType, the latter will be an approximation of the former. Each cubic Bezier will be "simulated" by one or more quadratics in the TrueType font.

To be fair, Microsoft used quadratic Beziers for a reason—to optimize for speed. TrueType's simpler curves render more quickly on the screen. Do you remember the speeds of CPUs when TrueType was introduced? At the time, I used Windows 3.1 and TrueType on my 12MHz, 16-bit 286—without a floating-point coprocessor. I don't think my machine was ready for on-the-fly cubic Bezier fonts at that point, but it was able to handle quadratics.

Flash's Use of Quadratic Beziers

Flash uses quadratic Beziers pervasively. They allow quick vector rendering in the Flash Player, and quadratics also allow special drawing operations in the authoring tool, like vector erasing.

Though you can use cubic Beziers in the Flash authoring tool, cubics are actually turned into quadratic Beziers as soon as you finish editing them. Try it for yourself.

1. Draw a single s-shaped Bezier with the Pen tool.

2. Rotate it with the Free Transform tool.

3. Select it with the Subselect tool.

You'll find that several nodes have been added. There are probably seven nodes instead of the original two.

Approximating a Cubic Bezier with Quadratics

If you import vector art from other illustration software into Flash, the curves are most likely cubic Beziers. Flash will approximate each cubic with one or more quadratic curves. You may have noticed that extra nodes are added to your art. Flash does a pretty good job with the approximation, though, so the difference in the final appearance is negligible.

The cubic-to-quadratic approximation is done outside of the SWF file, because a SWF can contain only quadratics. In other words, Flash performs the approximation calculations at design-time, not run time. Flash MX can load JPEG data at run time, but there is no way to import and display cubic Bezier data in the same manner. You can't use *loadMovie( )* on an EPS or SVG file, and there is no command to draw cubic Beziers—*curveTo( )* only plots quadratics.

If Flash can convert cubics to quadratics within the authoring tool, isn't it theoretically possible to run a similar algorithm in the Flash Player? There are two difficulties here: finding an algorithm, and getting it to run fast enough to be useful. ActionScript executes *much* slower than C++, which was used to build Flash. As for the algorithm, I don't know exactly how Flash performs its approximation.

However, I did some research into the math involved, and developed my own cubic-approximation algorithm. Based on the coordinates for two control points and two anchor points, a "virtual cubic" is rendered with carefully calculated *curveTo( )* commands. I based my technique on deCasteljau's algorithm, which recursively subdivides a cubic Bezier into smaller cubics. (Flash's built-in approximation probably uses a similar approach, though I don't know for sure.) A nice feature of deCasteljau's algorithm is that it gets progressively more accurate. This means you can decide how precise the curve needs to be, and stop subdividing when you're satisfied.

It is also possible to render a cubic Bezier with many small, straight line segments. People have done this in Flash 5, in fact. However, this approach is not very efficient, and the resulting curve doesn't look as good as a quadratic approximation. Similarly, a circle approximated with 100 straight lines would take longer to draw and wouldn't look as good as one rendered with eight quadratic curves.

Cubic Bezier Drawing Methods

I developed several methods for cubic Bezier plotting. At the core is one function that draws the Bezier curve by calling itself recursively. I also created several wrapper methods, which accept different types of parameters and pass them to the cubic function. This is similar to my approach with the rectangle methods: create several methods to maximize convenience. The code that implements the Bezier drawing is too long and complex to discuss here, but let's look at how the methods are utilized.

MovieClip.drawBezier( )

The *drawBezier( )* method draws a cubic Bezier curve with this syntax:

```
mc.drawBezier (x1, y1, x2, y2, x3, y3, x4, y4, tolerance)
```

The first eight arguments of *drawBezier( )* are numbers that define four points—two anchor and two control points. The curve begins at (x1, y1) and ends at (x4, y4). The two control points, which influence the shape of the curve, are located at (x2, y2) and (x3, y3).

The `tolerance` parameter controls the accuracy of the curve. When the tolerance is smaller, a more accurate curve is drawn. However, the curve will probably be more complex, composed of more quadratic segments. When the tolerance is high, the cubic Bezier will be rendered more quickly, but less accurately. This means you can draw stationary graphics with high accuracy, but animate with lower accuracy and higher speed. The algorithm is quite flexible in this way. The `tolerance` parameter is approximately equivalent to pixel accuracy. For instance, when `tolerance` is 2, the curve will be accurate to within two pixels, more or less.

The following code draws a filled shape composed of two cubic Bezier curves:

```
// test MovieClip.drawBezier()
this.beginFill (0x0000DD);
this.drawBezier (0, 0, 100, 0, 0, 100, 300, 300, 2);
this.drawBezier (300, 300, 200, 300, 100, 200, 0, 0, 2);
this.endFill();
```

MovieClip.drawBezierPts( )

The *drawBezierPts( )* method draws a cubic Bezier curve with this syntax:

```
mc.drawBezierPts (p1, p2, p3, p4, accuracy)
```

This method operates much like *drawBezier( )*, but uses point objects as parameters instead of individual coordinates.

This code example shows how to create four points and pass them to *drawBezierPts( )* to draw a cubic Bezier:

```
// test MovieClip.drawBezierPts()
this.lineStyle (4, 0xCCCCCC);
a = {x:100, y:20};
b = {x:0, y:80};
c = {x:150, y:0};
d = {x:10, y:200};
this.drawBezierPts (a, b, c, d, 2);
```

Of course, you can also create *Vector* objects for the points, and then pass them to *drawBezierPts( )*.

MovieClip.curveToCubic( )

The *curveToCubic( )* method draws a cubic Bezier curve with a slightly different approach. It is similar to the *curveTo( )* command—it uses the current drawing location as the first point of the curve. Here is the syntax:

```
mc.curveToCubic (x1, y1, x2, y2, x3, y3, tolerance)
```

The following code shows how to move to a point and plot a cubic curve to another point:

```
// test MovieClip.curveToCubic()
this.lineStyle (2, 0x33DD77);
this.moveTo (60, 40);
this.curveToCubic (100, 0, 0, 100, 250, 30, 2);
```

MovieClip.curveToCubicPts( )

The *curveToCubicPts( )* method operates much like the *curveToCubic( )* method. The difference is that it uses three point objects instead of six numbers:

```
mc.curveToCubicPts (p1, p2, p3, tolerance)
```

The following code example shows how to create three points and use them to draw a cubic Bezier with *curveToCubicPts( )*:

```
// test MovieClip.curveToCubicPts()
this.lineStyle (4, 0x0000FF, 60);
this.moveTo (60, 20);
a = {x:20, y:100};
b = {x:90, y:0};
c = {x:200, y:50};
this.curveToCubicPts (a, b, c);
```

Conclusion

Through this chapter, we have begun to see the possibilities of Flash MX's Shape Drawing API. The eight basic commands given to us, once understood, can form the basis of sophisticated custom shape drawing commands. This chapter concludes the theoretical section of the book. We have explored object-oriented design, math, events, motion, physics, color, and now drawing. With these hefty tools under our belt, we're in good shape to deconstruct some projects in the following chapters.

Part IV

Case Studies

Chapter 11

Aurora Borealis

One of the phrases I remember from my youth is "ionization of the stratosphere." It's been stuck in my head since I heard it from a friend of the family, an Alaskan gold miner who knew a little bit about everything. Someone asked him what caused the northern lights, and he immediately replied, "Ionization of the stratosphere." Why this information made an indelible imprint on my brain, I don't know.

I grew up in northern British Columbia, Canada. The town of Quesnel isn't in the Arctic Circle, and I never did learn how to build an igloo, but we did see the northern lights once in a while. So ghostlike and eerie—shapeshifting color swatches from every part of the color wheel suspended miles in the air. At the time, I had no idea that one day, I would create my own interpretation of the northern lights, the aurora borealis, in something called "Flash," and have it seen by people all over the world.

Evolution of the Concept

The first incarnation of Aurora Borealis was a self-propelling swirl in a little animation for *A Maze of Grace*, a theatrical dance production I was involved in. (I was in up to my eyeballs that year—playing keyboards for the show's live band, building the web site, and even dancing hip-hop and tap in a few numbers.) The animation was monochromatic—a fading white gradient over an icy blue-green duotone. Looking at a piece of it, it reminded me of the northern lights. It wasn't long before I decided to make it interactive, then dynamically colored.

The movement of the aurora particles is based on the concept of *Brownian* motion. Brownian motion has nothing to do with the digestive process. Rather, it describes an erratic, zigzag movement in microscopic particles. It was first observed in 1827 by the English botanist Robert Brown, who was investigating the suspension of microscopic pollen particles in an aqueous solution. He thought the movement must be due to the live pollen. However, pollen grains that had been stored for a century moved in the same way as the live ones. What could possibly be moving these particles?

This motion was explained a generation later by Maxwell and Einstein. It's due to the invisible water molecules hitting the visible particles and moving them a bit. Since the particles are hit continuously from all sides, they move in a random fashion.

You can explore a simple example of Brownian motion with a "random walk." Toss a coin, and step forward if heads, back if tails... see where you end up. If you flip another coin to determine whether you step left or right, your Brownian motion becomes two-dimensional. You become a randomly-wandering particle, tracing a jagged path behind you.

The PhysicsParticle Class

After programming physics-based motion for a while, I noticed a number of common steps in the process. For instance, there are usually acceleration, velocity, position, and friction quantities which govern the motion of objects, as we saw in Chapter 8. I took my approach to physics animation and generalized it into a reusable class. The *PhysicsParticle* class encapsulates the process by which physical forces move a particle. For our purposes, a *particle* is defined as a representation of a physical object with negligible mass. I also created a *Force* class which collaborates with the *PhysicsParticle* class. I then rewrote my Aurora Borealis code to make use of both. We will first look at the *PhysicsParticle* and *Force* classes, then see how they are used in the context of Aurora Borealis.

Constructor

The following shows how a *PhysicsParticle* object is created:

```
p = new PhysicsParticle (this, 0, 0, "_x", "_yscale");
```

These are actually the parameters I use for the Aurora particles. The *PhysicsParticle* constructor function has five arguments, which are summarized in Table 11-1.

Here's the code for the *PhysicsParticle* constructor:

```
_global.PhysicsParticle = function (target, x, y, xProp, yProp) {
    this.$target = target;
    this.$pos = new Vector (x, y);
    this.$vel = new Vector (0, 0);
    this.accel = new Vector (0, 0);
```

```
        this.$friction = new Vector (0, 0);
        this.setXYProps (xProp, yProp);
        this.forces = {};
        MovieClip.addListener (this);
    };
```

As with most of my classes, the constructor function is assigned to the `_global` object to make it easily accessible anywhere in the movie.

First, the `target` argument, a movie clip reference, is assigned to the `$target` property:

```
this.$target = target;
```

This allows the *PhysicsParticle* instance to access and control the movie clip that represents it visually.

N O T E :   With this approach, the movie clip needs to exist *first*, before creating a *PhysicsParticle* instance to control it. I took a different approach with the *Particle3d* class in Chapter 5. There, I have the *Particle3d* instance create a new movie clip using *attachMovie( )*. There are advantages and disadvantages to each approach; I wouldn't say that one is definitely superior to the other. An entirely different approach involves *Object.registerClass( )*, which I use in Chapter 13 with the *FractalBranch* class.

Next, I initialize the position vector $pos:

```
this.$pos = new Vector (x, y);
```

The x and y arguments are fed directly to the *Vector* constructor to create a new object with those coordinates. As in other chapters, I'm using a naming

Parameter	Type	Sample Value	Description
`target`	Movie clip reference	`mc`	The movie clip that represents the particle visually
`x`	Number	`150`	The initial x position of the particle
`y`	Number	`40`	The initial y position of the particle
`xProp`	String	`"_xscale"`	(Optional) The name of the property to link to the x component of the position; this defaults to "_x" if the parameter is omitted
`yProp`	String	`"_rotation"`	(Optional) The name of the property to link to the y component of the position; this defaults to "_y" if the parameter is omitted
TABLE 11-1			

Parameters for the *PhysicsParticle* Constructor

convention where properties that are associated with getter/setter properties are named with a dollar sign ($).

Three more vectors are needed—for velocity, acceleration, and friction:

```
this.$vel = new Vector (0, 0);
this.accel = new Vector (0, 0);
this.$friction = new Vector (0, 0);
```

These are all initialized to [0, 0]. Notice that the particle defaults to frictionless mode. This can be changed with the *PhysicsParticle.setFriction( )* method though, as we'll see later.

NOTE: I initially had a scalar value for friction — one number instead of a vector. However, I realized there are often situations where you need the ability to define different degrees of friction along the horizontal and vertical axes. For instance, a box on the ground has a small degree of vertical friction considering there is only air above it, but encounters a great deal more horizontal friction due to the ground.

A *PhysicsParticle* object moves because of forces acting on it. These forces are stored in a `forces` property:

```
this.forces = {};
```

The `forces` property is an object, created by the empty brackets (object literal syntax). I could have used `new Object( )` instead, but the brackets execute slightly faster, and require less typing.

The final step in the constructor is to empower the object to receive *onEnterFrame* events, by subscribing to *MovieClip* (see Chapter 6):

```
MovieClip.addListener (this);
```

NOTE: The *MovieClip.addListener( )* command will not work unless the infrastructure code in the core_setup.as file has been included first. *MovieClip* doesn't have the inherent power to add listeners like *Mouse* does. Therefore, we have to give that capability to *MovieClip* with custom code.

Public Methods

With the constructor defined, it's time to add methods to the class prototype, which is `PhysicsParticle.prototype` in this case. To shorten the code, I define an abbreviated variable that stores this object reference:

```
var PPP = PhysicsParticle.prototype;
```

Now when methods are assigned to PPP, they actually get attached to PhysicsParticle.prototype.

PhysicsParticle.addForce( )

To get a *PhysicsParticle* instance to accelerate, we must add a force to it, using the *addForce( )* method. Here is the code for the method:

```
PPP.addForce = function (id_str, force_obj) {
    this.forces[id_str] = force_obj;
    force_obj.setParent (this);
};
```

The second argument, force_obj, is an instance of the *Force* class. We'll look at that class and how to instantiate it later in the chapter. For now, just know that it is a *Force* object that you will have already created, and are now applying to the particle.

The first argument, id_str, is a string that gives the force a unique identifier. This ID is used to index the force in the this.forces object, using the following line of code:

```
this.forces[id_str] = force_obj;
```

For instance, suppose we index a force under the ID "gravity." The preceding line of code would then be equivalent to this:

```
this.forces["gravity"] = force_obj;
```

Thereafter, we can access the gravity force within the object using either this.forces["gravity"] or this.forces.gravity.

The last line of code in the method tells the force object to remember its connection to the current particle:

```
force_obj.setParent (this);
```

A force will often need to access its parent particle in order to recalculate its value. For instance, an elastic force changes as the particle moves toward or away from the anchor point (like stretching a rubber band). Later, we'll look at the *Force.setParent( )* method and see how an instance of the *Force* class checks the position of its parent particle.

PhysicsParticle.removeForce( )

The *removeForce( )* method disengages a force from the particle. The code is simple:

```
PPP.removeForce = function (id_str) {
    delete this.forces[id_str];
};
```

The ID string is used to look up and delete the force from the `forces` object.

For example, if a *PhysicsParticle* instance, `myParticle`, has a force with an ID of "gravity," we can remove it with this code:

```
myParticle.removeForce ("gravity");
```

NOTE: The way the `delete` operator works is that it will delete an object if no other references to that object exist in the movie. The deletion works by "dereferencing" the object, releasing its memory location so it can be subsequently used by other variables. If multiple references to the object exist, deleting one of them will not free up the memory. However, if no references remain, that memory space will be freed up by the "garbage collector" (a background process in the Flash Player) when it has a moment to spare.

Getter/Setter Methods

There are several methods in the *PhysicsParticle* class that change or retrieve various quantities, such as position and friction.

PhysicsParticle.setPosition( ) and getPosition( )

The *setPosition( )* and *getPosition( )* methods provide access to the position vector, changing the location of the particle. Here is the code for the methods:

```
PPP.setPosition = function (x, y) {
    this.$pos.reset (x, y);
};

PPP.getPosition = function () {
    return this.$pos;
};
```

You shouldn't have to set the particle's position manually very often. The *PhysicsParticle* class is designed to calculate the position dynamically, based on forces acting on the particle, and move it automatically.

PhysicsParticle.setVelocity( ) and getVelocity( )

The *setVelocity( )* and *getVelocity( )* methods provide access to the velocity vector, changing the rate at which the particle is moving. Here is the code for these methods:

```
PPP.setVelocity = function (x, y) {
    this.$vel.reset (x, y);
};

PPP.getVelocity = function () {
    return this.$vel;
};
```

PhysicsParticle.setFriction( ) and getFriction( )

The *setFriction( )* and *getFriction( )* methods provide access to the friction vector, controlling the rate at which velocity is lost over time. Friction is stored as a two-dimensional vector, allowing independent control over the horizontal and vertical components of friction.

For example, a skater on ice experiences a certain degree of friction as she moves horizontally across the ice. If she jumps into the air, her vertical movement is impacted by a different friction—air resistance—which is much less noticeable than the ice's friction. In other words, the horizontal component of the friction acting on the skater "particle" is much greater than the vertical component. Consequently, the friction vector for this situation might be something like [.03, .001].

Here is the code for the *setFriction( )* method:

```
PPP.setFriction = function (fx, fy) {
    if (fy == undefined) fy = fx;
    this.$friction.reset (fx, fy);
};
```

The parameters `fx` and `fy` represent the percentage of velocity lost due to friction per frame. Thus, they should be decimal numbers between 0 and 1. For example, a 3 percent loss would be represented by the number .03.

I use a bit of validation in this method, as seen in the first line of code:

```
if (fy == undefined) fy = fx;
```

If the second argument `fy` is missing, it is assumed the friction is the same in both directions—horizontal and vertical. Thus, the value of `fx` is copied to `fy`. The *getFriction( )* method returns the friction vector with the following code:

```
PPP.getFriction = function () {
    return this.$friction;
};
```

PhysicsParticle.setXYProps( )

Normally, a *PhysicsParticle* object will control the _x and _y properties of a movie clip. However, these defaults can be overridden with the *setXYProps( )* method. I decided to use one method to set both xProp and yProp, because they are closely linked. Here is the code:

```
PPP.setXYProps = function (xp, yp) {
    this.xProp = (xp == undefined) ? "_x" : xp;
    this.yProp = (yp == undefined) ? "_y" : yp;
};
```

I included some validation here, using the shortcut if-then syntax (also known as the *ternary conditional operator*). The logic is simple: if the argument (xp) is undefined, then the property (xProp) is assigned a default value ("_x"). Otherwise, the supplied argument (xp) is used. In the Aurora Borealis animation, I use _yscale for the yProp property instead of _y.

Private Methods

There are three private methods for *PhysicsParticle*: *move( )*, *render( )*, and *onEnterFrame( )*. Being private, they are not supposed to be called from outside the *PhysicsParticle* instance.

PhysicsParticle.move( )

The *move( )* method is responsible for getting the particle to its new location for the current point in time. It adds up all the forces acting on the particle, calculates the corresponding acceleration, velocity, and position, and moves the particle accordingly. The code for this method is a bit lengthy:

```
PPP.move = function () {
    var fx, fy, val;
    var fs = this.forces;
    for (var i in fs) {
        if (!fs[i].live()) {
            delete fs[i];
```

```
        } else {
            fx += (val=fs[i].getValue()).x;
            fy += val.y;
        }
    }
    this.accel.reset (fx, fy);
    var v = this.$vel;
    v.plus (this.accel);
    v.x *= (1 - this.$friction.x);
    v.y *= (1 - this.$friction.y);
    this.$pos.plus (v);
    this.render();
};
```

First, some local variables are declared:

```
var fx, fy, val;
```

The `fx` and `fy` variables will be used to store the components of the *net force* acting on the particle. They are initialized to zero.

The next section of code loops through the `this.forces` object and adds up the x and y components of the forces. First, I declare a local variable, `fs`, which points to `this.forces`:

```
var fs = this.forces;
```

This step is for purposes of optimization. It is quicker for the Flash run-time interpreter to look up `fs` than `this.forces`, and we need to access `this.forces` several times in the code that follows.

Next, I use a `for..in` loop to iterate over the properties of the forces object:

```
for (var i in fs) {
    if (!fs[i].live()) {
        delete fs[i];
    } else {
        fx += (val=fs[i].getValue()).x;
        fy += val.y;
    }
}
```

Inside this loop, fs[i] is used to access individual forces. For instance, if there is a force with an ID of "elastic," that force is located at fs["elastic"] (which is a shortcut to this.forces["elastic"]). At some point in the for..in loop, the iterator variable i will equal "elastic," and thus, fs[i] will equal fs["elastic"].

As each force is accessed, its *live( )* method is called:

```
if (!fs[i].live()) {
```

There is a full explanation of *Force.live( )* later in the chapter, but to sum it up, the method decreases the force's life by one frame and updates its value. The *live( )* method also returns a Boolean value: either true if the force is still alive, or false if the force is dead.

The if statement checks the return value of *live( )*. If it is false, the force is deleted since it is dead:

```
if (!fs[i].live()) {
    delete fs[i];
```

The exclamation mark in the preceding code inverts the returned value of the method, from true to false and vice versa. If *live( )* is false, then "it's true" that the force is dead. Alternatively, I could have coded the if condition like this:

```
if (fs[i].live() == false)
```

I chose the shorter way, though, because it executes faster.

If, on the other hand, the force is still alive, then its value is added to the net force, as in the following code:

```
} else {
    fx += (val=fs[i].getValue()).x;
    fy += val.y;
}
```

There's a lot going on in the first line of the else clause:

```
fx += (val=fs[i].getValue()).x;
```

Let's break it down bit by bit.

The current force is indexed by fs[i]. The value of that force is accessed with fs[i].getValue( ). The x component of that value is at fs[i].getValue().x. So to add the x component of the current force to the running total, the code is:

```
fx += fs[i].getValue().x;
```

Now the y component of the force needs to be accessed as well. We could just repeat the same syntax, replacing x with y, as in the following code:

```
fy += fs[i].getValue().y;
```

However, this involves redundant steps of looking up i, then fs[i], then calling fs[i].getValue(), and finally finding y. The *getValue( )* method returns an object reference. Why don't we store that reference in a local variable—in the process of looking up x—and reuse it for y? The code could look like this:

```
val = fs[i].getValue();
fx += val.x;
fy += val.y;
```

The reference to the value vector is stored in the local variable val, and used to look up x and y. This is more optimized, but we can go one step better.

It's possible to combine the first two lines of the previous code into one, assigning the reference to val and using it at the same time. The following code is the result of this optimization:

```
fx += (val=fs[i].getValue()).x;
fy += val.y;
```

NOTE: I used separate variables fx and fy, instead of a single *Vector* object, to speed up the execution of this code. As much as I like to use the *Vector* methods to add vectors, they introduce additional overhead that needs to be optimized out sometimes, especially in performance-critical loops.

At this point in the *move( )* method, the x and y components of the various forces acting on the particle have been totaled to find the net force. It doesn't really matter how many forces are acting on a particle; what counts is the net force that results. There could be ten massive forces pushing from various angles, but if they cancel each other out, the particle will not accelerate. The next step is to take the net force and turn that into the appropriate acceleration, velocity, and position for the particle at the current point in time.

First of all, the acceleration vector this.accel is changed to match the net force, defined by fx and fy:

```
this.accel.reset (fx, fy);
```

We saw in Chapter 8 that acceleration equals force divided by mass:

$$a = f / m$$

However, with a particle, we assume that the mass is simply 1. Thus, acceleration is exactly equal to the mass:

$$a = f / 1$$
$$a = f$$

Consequently, the net force on the particle becomes its exact acceleration.

The next stage is to calculate a new velocity vector, which is stored in the `this.$vel` property. Since we'll be accessing this property several times, a local variable pointing to it helps speed up the code execution.

```
var v = this.$vel;
```

NOTE: Generally speaking, each dot in a path (for example, `this.a.b.c`) represents an additional two bytecodes (a *push* operation and a *getMember* lookup) for the Flash Player's run-time interpreter to perform. Looking up the reference `this.a.b.c` takes eight bytecodes, versus two bytecodes to look up just `c`. If you're interested in intense low-level ActionScript optimization, learn the FLASM program, available at http://flasm.sourceforge.net. I learned a tremendous amount about ActionScript by playing with FLASM.

To find the new velocity, we add the acceleration to the current velocity with this code:

```
v.plus (this.accel);
```

Remember that `v` points to the `this.$vel` *Vector*. We call its *plus( )* method to add the `this.accel` *Vector* to `v`.

This velocity must now lose a little bit to friction in the next two lines of code:

```
v.x *= (1 - this.$friction.x);
v.y *= (1 - this.$friction.y);
```

This calculation is explained in Chapter 8. Basically, if `$friction.x` is .03, 1 - `$friction.x` is .97. Multiplying by .97 (97 percent) is the same as subtracting 3 percent.

The velocity calculations are over. Now we can find the new position of the particle by adding the velocity to the previous position:

```
this.$pos.plus (v);
```

The acceleration, velocity, and position of the particle are now up-to-date. All that is left is to update the visuals by calling the *render( )* method:

```
this.render();
```

We will examine *render( )* shortly.

PhysicsParticle.onEnterFrame( )

The *onEnterFrame( )* method is an event handler. It is simply pointed to the *move( )* method:

```
PPP.onEnterFrame = PPP.move;
```

This sets up the *PhysicsParticle* object to call its *move( )* method automatically every frame. Since the ActionScript user shouldn't need to change this, I included *onEnterFrame( )* with the private methods.

PhysicsParticle.render( )

The *render( )* method updates the visual representation of the particle, bringing it in sync with the position vector. You shouldn't have to invoke *render( )* directly, as it is called at the end of the *move( )* method. Here is the code:

```
PPP.render = function () {
    with (this) {
        $target[xProp] = pos.x;
        $target[yProp] = pos.y;
    }
};
```

I used a `with` statement to shorten and speed up the code. Otherwise, this is what the code would look like:

```
PPP.render = function () {
    this.$target[this.xProp] = this.pos.x;
    this.$target[this.yProp] = this.pos.y;
};
```

As you can see, the `with` statement eliminates six occurrences of `this`, which means six fewer things for the run-time interpreter to look up as the code executes.

The `$target` property points to the movie clip that represents the particle. The `xProp` and `yProp` properties store the names of the object's properties being controlled. By default, `xProp` is "`_x`", and `yProp` is "`_y`". Consequently, the preceding code would be equivalent to the code that follows:

```
$target["_x"] = pos.x;
$target["_y"] = pos.y;
```

This can also be written with the following syntax, which may be more familiar:

```
$target._x = pos.x;
$target._y = pos.y;
```

The _x and _y properties of the movie clip are being changed to the x and y properties of the position vector. This is the default scenario. If, on the other hand, `xProp` were `_xscale`, and `yProp` were `_rotation`, the code would be equivalent to the following:

```
$target._xscale = pos.x;
$target._rotation = pos.y;
```

Getter/Setter Properties

For convenience, I created four getter/setter properties for the *PhysicsParticle* class, associating them with previously defined methods with the following code:

```
with (PPP) {
    addProperty ("target", getTarget, setTarget);
    addProperty ("position", getPosition, null);
    addProperty ("velocity", getVelocity, null);
    addProperty ("friction", getFriction, null);
}
```

You'll notice that in the last three lines of the preceding code, I pass `null` instead of a setter method (like `setPosition`). The reason is that each of these—`position`, `velocity`, and `friction`—is a *Vector* property. As such, their setter methods take *two* parameters, x and y. However, a setter method that is associated with a getter/setter property should take only *one* parameter. Thus, these particular setter methods are unsuitable for use with a getter/setter property. This doesn't stop us from using the getter methods for read access to the property, though.

Finishing Up

With all the *PhysicsParticle* methods defined, I deleted the shorcut variable PPP, and sent a message to the Output window that the class has loaded successfully:

```
delete PPP;
trace (">> PhysicsParticle class loaded");
```

This concludes the *PhysicsParticle* class. Next, we will examine an object-oriented approach to adding forces to a particle with the *Force* class.

The Force Class

A particle can have many forces acting on it. We've defined the *PhysicsParticle* class to represent the particle. Now we will construct a *Force* class to collaborate with it. As I was rewriting Aurora Borealis for Flash MX and this book, I spent some time thinking about what the essential aspects of a force would be, in terms of dynamic animation. During this process, I found it fairly challenging to figure out how to implement my ideas using an object-oriented approach. Eventually, though, I found a configuration that made sense and was easy to use, in the form of the *Force* class that we'll explore.

Probably the most essential feature of a force is that it is a vector quantity. In the task at hand, I was working in two dimensions, so a force would also be two-dimensional, with *x* and *y* components. I initially tried making my *Force* class a subclass of *Vector*, but that approach became too complicated for my liking. Consequently, I decided to make *Force* a separate class, with the *Vector* element stored in a value property. This is an example of using *composition*, a "has-a" relationship, instead of *inheritance*, an "is-a" relationship (see Chapter 2).

It also seemed useful to give a force a lifespan. I wanted to be able to define a force and then tell it to push on a particular movie clip for 20 frames, say. The force would automatically "die" after this time, ceasing to affect the clip. Or, a force could have an infinite lifespan, pulling on an object indefinitely. This life property could be specified in either frames or seconds. For simplicity, I chose frames—they are a bit simpler to work with than *getTimer( )* and absolute time in milliseconds.

Lastly, there is the aspect of a force being related to a movable object somehow. I decided that it made the most sense to allow a force to affect only one other movable object at a time. In other words, the force would have only one "parent" object. However, a movable object can have many forces acting on it.

NOTE: A *PhysicsParticle* object is a primary example of a movable object that can collaborate with a *Force* object. However, one could conceivably define other objects affected by *Force* objects.

The *Force* class is defined in the file *force_class.as*. Let's look at its ActionScript.

Constructor

The *Force* constructor is short and simple, defining the value and life properties just discussed:

```
_global.Force = function (x, y, life) {
    this.$value = new Vector (x, y);
    this.setLife (life);
};
```

A $value *Vector* object is defined, using the x and y constructor parameters. This allows you to create a *Force* object and specify its value at the same time. For example, if you wanted to define a *Force* that points to the left, you would use a negative value for x, and zero for y, as in the following example:

```
pushLeft = new Force (-8, 0);
```

The remaining constructor parameter, `life`, is a number specifying the lifespan of the force in frames. It is passed to the setter method *setLife( )*. If the `life` parameter is missing, the *Force* will be given an infinite lifespan.

Getter/Setter Methods

Before defining methods, I create a shortcut variable to `Force.prototype` called `FP`:

```
var FP = Force.prototype;
```

There are several getter and setter methods for the Force class to change properties, such as `value`, `life`, and `parent`.

Force.setValue( ) and getValue( )

The *setValue( )* method allows the user to change the value of the force. Here is the code:

```
FP.setValue = function (x, y) {
    this.$value.reset (x, y);
};
```

The method accepts x and y parameters, defining the horizontal and vertical components of the force, and passes them to the `this.value` *Vector*.

The *getValue( )* method returns a reference to the *Force*'s value, which is a *Vector* object:

```
FP.getValue = function () {
    return this.$value;
};
```

The following code example shows how to declare a *Force* object, change its value, and retrieve the new value:

```
// test Force.setValue() and getValue()
wind = new Force (0, 4, 35);
wind.setValue (-2, 1);
strength = wind.getValue();
trace (strength); // output: [-2, 1]
```

Force.setLife( ) and getLife( )

The *setLife( )* method defines the lifespan of the *Force* object. Here is the code:

```
FP.setLife = function (life) {
    this.$life = (life == undefined) ? Infinity : life;
};
```

The `life` parameter should be an integer since it specifies the lifespan in frames. The *Force* will act on its target for that amount of frames, and then expire (stop affecting it).

There is some simple validation in the preceding code. If the `life` parameter is not defined, the `this.$life` property is set to `Infinity`. This setting lets you define forces that will never expire, such as the force of gravity.

The *getLife( )* method simply returns the value of the `life` property:

```
FP.getLife = function () {
    return this.$life;
};
```

Force.setParent( ) and getParent( )

The *setParent( )* and *getParent( )* methods change or retrieve the parent object that the *Force* acts upon. This allows a *Force* to monitor the object it is affecting, and make adjustments as needed. For example, as we'll see later in the chapter, an elastic force will change its value depending on the position of its parent object.

Here is the code for *setParent( )*:

```
FP.setParent = function (p) {
    this.$parent = p;
    this.parentPos = p.getPosition();
};
```

After setting the `$parent` property, I define an additional property `parentPos` for optimization purposes. The `parentPos` property provides a reference to the position vector of the parent object, which is located with `p.getPosition( )`. Often, the `update( )` method for a *Force* will need to access its parent's position. It's faster to find the reference to that particular vector with a local object property, rather than referencing the parent's *getPosition( )* method each time. Later, we'll see how this works in the *ElasticForce.update( )* method.

The code for *getParent( )* is simple:

```
FP.getParent = function (p) {
    return this.$parent;
};
```

The method returns a reference to the parent object—usually a *PhysicsParticle*—of the *Force* instance.

Other Methods

Besides the getters and setters, there are two other methods in the *Force* class—one public, one private.

Force.live( )

The *live( )* method causes the *Force* object to "live for one frame." The following code carries this out:

```
FP.live = function () {
    if (this.$life-- <= 0) {
        return false;
    } else {
        this.update();
        return true;
    }
};
```

In plain terms, the preceding code follows this logic: "If I'm dead, return *false*; otherwise, update me and return *true*."

First, the $life property is decreased by one frame and tested against the number zero:

```
if (this.$life-- <= 0) {
    return false;
```

If this.$life is less than or equal to zero, the method returns false. In other words, if there is no life remaining, the *live( )* method returns a value that says, "It's false that I'm alive."

NOTE: I'm using what is called "post-decrement" (myVar– –) on this.life. This means the value of the variable is retrieved, then decreased by one. On the other hand, "pre-decrement" (– –myVar) decreases the variable first, *then* retrieves the value.

However, if there is some life left in the *Force* (that is, if this.$life > 0), the else clause is called:

```
} else {
    this.update();
    return true;
}
```

The *Force.update( )* method is called, and a value of true is returned from the *live( )* method, signaling that the *Force* is still alive.

Force.update( )

The purpose of *update( )* is to change the force's value. As we have just seen, the *update( )* method is called from the *live( )* method, from within the same *Force* instance. Thus, *update( )* is a private method, not needing to be called from outside the object. Here is its code:

```
FP.update = function () {
    // change force value here
};
```

By default, it is an empty function. I created *update( )* as an abstract method, which is intended to be overridden later, either in a *Force* instance or in a subclass. I used a similar strategy in Chapter 7, where I gave my *Motion* class the abstract method *getPosition( )*. We will soon see how the *ElasticForce* subclass overrides the *update( )* method.

N O T E : ActionScript doesn't give us *real* abstract methods, just as you can't have truly private properties. ActionScript doesn't check if a so-called abstract method is defined in a subclass — it's strictly voluntary. The concept is merely borrowed from more advanced OOP languages like Java for its suggestive power.

Getter/Setter Properties

Three getter/setter properties are defined—`life`, `parent`, and `value`—with the following code:

```
with (FP) {
    addProperty ("life", getLife, setLife);
    addProperty ("parent", getParent, setParent);
    addProperty ("value", getValue, null);
}
```

The `value` property is connecting only to its getter method *getValue( )*, not its setter, because it is a *Vector* property. Because the *setValue( )* method takes two parameters, `x` and `y`, it isn't suitable for use with a getter/setter property.

Finishing Up

With the *Force* class completed, we delete the shortcut variable FP and send
a message to the Output window that the class has loaded successfully:

```
delete FP;
trace (">> Force class loaded");
```

The ElasticForce Class

The *Force* class on its own is a little abstract. It's when you override the
update( ) method and/or create a subclass that things start to get interesting.
Elasticity and gravity are prime candidates for this approach. In the case
of Aurora Borealis, I created the *ElasticForce* class, a subclass of *Force*. It
encapsulates and simplifies the process of driving dynamic motion with
elastic forces. Let's take a look at the ActionScript.

    The *ElasticForce* class is defined in the file *elastic_force_class.as*. A preliminary
snippet of code checks to make sure the *Force* class is already defined:

```
if (typeof _global.Force != 'function')
    trace (">> Error: superclass missing - Force");
```

    If there is no function defined at _global.Force, an error message is
sent to the Output window to alert the user.

Constructor

The *ElasticForce* constructor isn't overly long, having four arguments and
three lines of code:

```
_global.ElasticForce = function (anchorX, anchorY, tautness, life) {
    this.superCon (0, 0, life);
    this.$anchor = new Vector (anchorX, anchorY);
    this.$tautness = tautness;
};
```

    First, some parameters are passed to the superclass constructor (*Force( )*)
with this code:

```
this.superCon (0, 0, life);
```

The parameters for the *Force( )* constructor are x, y, and life, where x and y define the value of the force. The *ElasticForce* class starts the value at [0, 0], hence the values of 0 for the x and y arguments. The life argument, on the other hand, is passed straight through.

NOTE: The *superCon( )* method is custom code that replaces the *super( )* operator, and is defined in the file *core_setup.as*. For a full discussion of *superCon( )*, see Chapter 2.

The next line defines the anchor point of the elastic force:

```
this.$anchor = new Vector (anchorX, anchorY);
```

The constructor arguments anchorX and anchorY are used to create a new *Vector* instance. This represents the anchor's 2-D position—the point that the particle is pulled towards.

Lastly, a $tautness property is defined:

```
this.$tautness = tautness;
```

The tautness argument should be a number between 0 and 1, and governs the stiffness of the force of elasticity.

Methods

The next line of code after the constructor causes the *ElasticForce* class to inherit from the *Force* class:

```
ElasticForce.extend (Force);
```

As a subclass of *Force*, *ElasticForce* inherits its methods: *setLife( )*, *setParent( )*, *live( )*, and so on.

NOTE: *extend( )* is a custom function, defined in the infrastructure file *core_setup.as*. It needs to be included first in order for the *ElasticForce* class to work properly. See Chapter 2 for more information on *Function.extend( )*.

Next, I define a shortcut variable to the class' *prototype* object:

```
var EFP = ElasticForce.prototype;
```

The *ElasticForce* class has just three methods: *setAnchor( )*, *getAnchor( )*, and *update( )*.

ElasticForce.setAnchor( ) and getAnchor( )

As we saw in Chapter 8, the anchor point of an elastic connection is where there is no elastic force. The farther the object moves away from its anchor point, the more elastic force is created, trying to pull it back in.

The *ElasticForce.setAnchor( )* and *getAnchor( )* methods give us access to the anchor point. For example, we may start with one anchor point for the force, which causes the targeted object to oscillate around that location. Then we can switch the anchor to a new location, sending the targeted object off on a new orbit.

The code for the methods is straightforward:

```
EFP.setAnchor = function (x, y) {
    this.$anchor.reset (x, y);
};

EFP.getAnchor = function () {
    return this.$anchor;
};
```

ElasticForce.setTautness( ) and getTautness( )

The *setTautness( )* and *getTautness( )* methods set and retrieve the elasticity constant, or "tautness," of the *ElasticForce*. Larger values of tautness will make the elasticity "stiffer," like having a thicker rubber band. The tautness value should be a number between 0 and 1.

The code for these methods is straightforward:

```
EFP.setTautness = function (t) {
    this.$tautness = t;
};

EFP.getTautness = function () {
    return this.$tautness;
};
```

ElasticForce.update( )

The *update( )* method calculates the appropriate force of elasticity and updates the *ElasticForce*'s value. Here is the code for the method:

```
EFP.update = function () {
    with (this) {
        $value = parentPos.minusNew ($anchor);
```

```
            $value.scale (-$tautness);
    }
};
```

This code is calculating Hooke's Law ($f = -kd$), though in a somewhat different manner than what we saw in Chapter 8. Our current approach uses *Vector* methods to perform the subtraction and multiplication on two dimensions
at the same time.

First, we find the displacement—the d in $f = -kd$. We do this by subtracting the anchor position from the particle's current position, using the *Vector.minusNew( )* method:

```
$value = parentPos.minusNew ($anchor);
```

Then we multiply the result by $-k$, the elasticity constant, to attain the force, as is done in the equation $f = -kd$. In our case, k is the $tautness property, and the multiplication is performed with *Vector.scale( )*, in the following code:

```
$value.scale (-$tautness);
```

Now the $value property stores the correct vector for the elastic force.

If we didn't use the *Vector* methods *minusNew( )* and *scale( )*, the preceding code would look like this:

```
// alternate code for update()
with (this) {
    $value.x = (parentPos.x - $anchor.x) * -$tautness;
    $value.y = (parentPos.y - $anchor.y) * -$tautness;
}
```

Getter/Setter Properties

As usual, when there are pairs of setter and getter methods, it doesn't hurt to connect them to a getter/setter property. In the *ElasticForce* class, two such properties are added, with the following code:

```
with (EFP) {
    addProperty ("tautness", getTautness, setTautness);
    addProperty ("anchor", getAnchor, null);
}
```

You'll notice that with the anchor property, I passed `null` instead of `setAnchor`. Because the *setAnchor( )* method takes two parameters, x and y, it isn't suitable for use with a getter/setter property.

Finishing Up

With the methods and properties of the *ElasticForce* class defined, we can delete the shortcut variable `EFP` and send a message to the Output window:

```
delete EFP;
trace (">> ElasticForce class loaded");
```

A Simple Example

Before we move on to Aurora Borealis, here is a short-and-quick example of how to use the *PhysicsParticle* and *ElasticForce* classes to produce dynamic animation. First, the necessary *.as* ActionScript files are included:

```
#include "core_setup.as"
#include "vector_class.as"
#include "force_class.as"
#include "elastic_force_class.as"
#include "physics_particle_class.as"
```

This code goes on the first frame of the main Timeline. The order of the `#includes` is important. The *Vector* class is dependent on the code in core_setup.as, the *Force* class is dependent on the *Vector* class, and so on.

Next, a circular movie clip with an instance name of "ball" should be placed on the Stage on the main Timeline.

Now it only takes six more lines of code on the main Timeline to create an interactive elastic system that controls the ball:

```
p = new PhysicsParticle (ball, ball._x, ball._y);
p.setFriction (.03);
eForce = new ElasticForce (200, 200, .05);
p.addForce ("elastic", eForce);

this.onMouseDown = function () {
    eForce.setAnchor (this._xmouse, this._ymouse);
};
```

As this movie plays, each mouse click changes the anchor point of the *ElasticForce*, causing the ball to oscillate around the anchor point. The small amount of friction causes the movement to decay and eventually come to rest.

Aurora FLA Code

We've taken our time looking through the *PhysicsParticle*, *Force*, and *ElasticForce* classes in detail. We've also seen a simple example showing how to put them to use. Now we're ready to see how these classes are used to produce the Aurora Borealis animation, by looking at the code in the *aurora.fla* file.

Main Timeline Code

The code on the main Timeline of the Aurora movie is all in the first frame, on two different layers. The *classes* layer contains this code:

```
#include "core_setup.as"
#include "vector_class.as"
#include "force_class.as"
#include "elastic_force_class.as"
#include "physics_particle_class.as"
```

The *core_setup.as* file contains my custom code for *Function.extend( )*, *Object.superCon( )*, and *MovieClip.addListener( )*, which I use pervasively. Each of the four classes is contained in its own *.as* file. This is a practice recommended by Macromedia and others.

The *functions* layer contains two custom functions. The first is *Math.randRangeF( )*, which returns a random number between two numbers. Here is the code:

```
Math.randRangeF = function (low, high) {
    return Math.random() * (high - low) + low;
};
```

The F in `Math.randRangeF` is for "floating-point." The function returns a floating-point number, also called a real or decimal number. (By contrast, the *random( )* function returns only integers.) If I wanted a *Math.randRangeInt( )*

function that returned a random integer between two numbers, it would be coded like this:

```
Math.randRangeInt = function (low, high) {
    return Math.floor (Math.random() * (high - low + 1) + low);
};
```

The other function in the *functions* layer is the *Color.setTint( )* method:

```
Color.prototype.setTint = function (r, g, b, percent) {
    var ratio = percent / 100;
    var trans = {rb:r*ratio, gb:g*ratio, bb:b*ratio};
    trans.ra = trans.ga = trans.ba = 100 - percent;
    this.setTransform (trans);
};
```

The *setTint( )* method, discussed in Chapter 9, will be used to color the aurora particles at run time.

The aurora Component

The *aurora* component has two component parameters: maxParticles and brownInterval. The former determines the number of particles that will comprise the aurora, with a default of 10. The brownInterval parameter specifies how often new Brownian forces are applied to the particles. At the default setting of 10, Brownian force is applied every ten frames.

The *aurora* component has one method, *init( )*, defined on its *functions* layer:

```
this.init = function () {
    for (var i=1; i < this.maxParticles; i++) {
        p.duplicateMovieClip ("p" + i, i);
    }
};
```

The *init( )* method simply creates new particles by copying the seed movie clip p. The number of particles is specified by the component parameter, maxParticles, and so a for loop repeatedly calls the *duplicateMovieClip( )* method on p. Notice that I started the incrementing variable i at 1, instead of the usual 0. I set up the conditions of the for statement so that if maxParticles is 10, for example, then *nine* new movie clips will be created, to bring the number of particles to a total of ten. The i variable would then increment through the values 1, 2, 3, 4, 5, 6, 7, 8, 9 over the course of the loop.

The only other code in the *aurora* component is on the *actions* layer, where the *init( )* method is called:

```
this.init();
stop();
```

The *aurora* movie clip contains one child movie clip—the *particle* symbol (with an instance name of "p"), which we'll look at next.

The Particle Movie Clip

For the graphical content of the *particle* movie clip, I used a thin gradient, a slice that's 2.5 pixels wide and 100 pixels long. It is a linear gradient, with a beginning color of 50 percent alpha white and an ending color of 0 percent alpha white. The white, however, will be tinted dynamically at run time to a variety of colors. The alpha in the gradient gives a nice effect, as the strips of the aurora overlap and blend with each other.

NOTE: When I have seed clips that get duplicated and stretched, I like to match one or more dimensions to 100 pixels. In Flash 5, the standard line-drawing technique involved duplicating a diagonal line movie clip, with a width and height of 100. This technique isn't necessary in Flash MX, thanks to the Shape Drawing API, but the 100 pixel dimension has stuck with me as a habit.

Particle.init( )

The *particle* movie clip has two methods defined on the *functions* layer. The first is *init( )*, naturally, which initializes the necessary properties for the particle. Here is the method's code:

```
this.init = function () {
    this.particle = new PhysicsParticle (this, 0, 0, "_x", "_yscale");
    this.particle.setFriction (.05, .05);
    this.eForce = new ElasticForce (0, 0, .002);
    this.particle.addForce ("elastic", this.eForce);
    this.col = new Color (this);
    this.t = 0;
    this.onEnterFrame = this.live;
};
```

The first line of code creates a new *PhysicsParticle* instance:

```
this.particle = new PhysicsParticle (this, 0, 0, "_x", "_yscale");
```

Looking at the constructor parameters: The particle object will control the current movie clip so this is passed as the first parameter. Next, the starting x and y coordinates are given, which are (0, 0) in this case. The final two parameters map the particle's coordinates to the _x and _yscale properties of the movie clip, rather than the default _x and _y. The particles slide sideways along _x, but they stretch vertically using _yscale.

The particle is given friction values of .05 in both directions with the next line of code:

```
this.particle.setFriction (.05, .05);
```

Now I create an *ElasticForce* object, eForce, that will act on the particle:

```
this.eForce = new ElasticForce (0, 0, .002);
```

Looking at the parameters passed to *ElasticForce* constructor in the preceding code, the force is given an initial anchor point of [0, 0] and a tautness constant of just .002—a gentle elasticity.

With the *ElasticForce* object created, I apply it to the particle using the *PhysicsParticle.addForce( )* method:

```
this.particle.addForce ("elastic", this.eForce);
```

Notice that the force doesn't apply itself to the particle. Rather, the particle takes a reference to the force and applies it to itself. This is why *addForce( )* is a method of the *particle*, not the force. (There are other possible implementations, but this is what made sense to me.) If you imagine yourself strapping on anti-gravity boots, that's like a particle attaching a force to itself.

Next, I define a *Color* object that will end up tinting the current movie clip:

```
this.col = new Color (this);
```

In the last two lines of code, a frame counter and frame loop are initialized:

```
this.t = 0;
this.onEnterFrame = this.live;
```

The this.t property will keep track of the number of frames that have elapsed, and will be used to space out Brownian motion.

Particle.live( )

The *live( )* method executes each frame, moving the particle to a new position and coloring it dynamically. It's fairly dense with code:

```
this.live = function () {
    this.eForce.setAnchor (_parent._xmouse,
_parent._ymouse);
        if (++this.t % _parent.brownInterval == 0) {
            var brownX = Math.randRangeF (-.2, .2);
            var brownYscale = Math.randRangeF (-.8, .8);
            var brownForce = new Force (brownX, brownYscale, 5);
            this.particle.addForce ("brown", brownForce);
        }
        var velX = this.particle.vel.x;
        this._xscale = velX * 100;
        this._alpha = this._width * 8;
        var r = 10 * velX * velX;
        var g = this._x * 1.5 + 120;
        var b = this._height * this._height / 300;
        this.col.setTint (r, g, b, 100);
};
```

The first line of code controls the *ElasticForce* with the mouse coordinates:

```
this.eForce.setAnchor (_parent._xmouse, _parent._ymouse);
```

This sets the anchor point of the *ElasticForce* instance to the current mouse coordinates, and causes the aurora particles to be pulled toward the cursor.

The following section of code controls the Brownian motion of the particle:

```
if (++this.t % _parent.brownInterval == 0) {
    var brownX = Math.randRangeF (-.2, .2);
    var brownYscale = Math.randRangeF (-.8, .8);
    var brownForce = new Force (brownX, brownYscale, 5);
    this.particle.addForce ("brown", brownForce);
}
```

The `if` condition in the first line causes the subsequent block of code to be executed only once every number of frames. The `brownInterval` component parameter, set in the _parent movie clip, is 10 by default, which means the subsequent code is executed once every ten frames. This is accomplished by incrementing the `this.t` property every frame, and taking the modulo of it and the `_parent.brownInterval` property. The resulting value is the remainder of a division of `this.t` by _parent.brownInterval. If brownInterval is 10, the remainder of such a division will be zero once every 10 frames.

The next three lines of code define a new Brownian force:

```
var brownX = Math.randRangeF (-.2, .2);
var brownYscale = Math.randRangeF (-.8, .8);
var brownForce = new Force (brownX, brownYscale, 5);
```

The first two lines find random values for each dimension within specific ranges. (I ended up defining a wider range for brownYscale to produce more random variation in the vertical stretching of the particles.) Then the values are used to create a new *Force* instance brownForce, which is also given a lifespan of 5 frames.

The last line of code in this section applys the new Brownian *Force* object to the particle:

```
this.particle.addForce ("brown", brownForce);
```

Now the Brownian *Force* will push on the particle for five frames and then die.

The next section of code tweaks the appearance of the particle, relating certain properties to others (_xscale to x-velocity and _alpha to _width).

First, the particle's horizontal velocity is stored in a local variable velX:

```
var velX = this.particle.vel.x;
```

The value of the x-velocity is used several times in subsequent code. Storing it in a variable allows for shorter, faster ActionScript.

The next line of code controls the _xscale of the particle movie clip:

```
this._xscale = velX * 100;
```

I wanted the aurora strips to stretch out horizontally when they moved quickly from left to right or vice versa. The preceding code ties the horizontal scale of the particle to its horizontal speed to give more of a streaking effect to the motion. The coefficient of 100 came by trial and error.

The following code relates the transparency of the clip to its width:

```
this._alpha = this._width * 8;
```

This causes the particle to fade out gradually as it gets thinner. It's a subtle effect, but try commenting out the previous line and you'll see the difference—it's not quite as smooth.

The final section of the *live( )* method governs the dynamic coloring of the particle. I tied the components of colored light—red, green, and blue—to various particle properties, including its speed, height, and horizontal position.

Red is given a relationship to the horizontal velocity of the particle `velX` with this code:

```
var r = 10 * velX * velX;
```

Squaring the variable `velX` in this manner produces a *quadratic* relationship, which has a parabolic graph (like the quadratic easing in Chapter 7). I originally tried a linear relationship between `r` and `velX`—something like `r = 50 * velX`—but it didn't produce quite the effect I wanted. I multiplied `velX` by itself to make the change in red "more drastic" as the particle moved faster. As for the coefficient of 10, I arrived at that number through trial and error.

For the next component of color, I tied green to the particle's horizontal position. As the particle moves to the right side of the screen, it becomes greener. (Keep in mind that green light mixed with red light is yellow, and green mixed with blue is cyan. Thus, if a particle is already red, adding green turns it yellow.) Here's the code that calculates the green component:

```
var g = this._x * 1.5 + 120;
```

Again, it was a matter of fumbling around with different numbers until I found something I liked. In this case, it was a linear relationship. The ideal range for a color component is between 0 and 255. Multiplying the values coming from `this._x` by 1.5 expands the range of those numbers nicely. Furthermore, the addition of 120 shifts the values up so they rise above zero often enough.

Blue, on the other hand, increases as the particle gets longer:

```
var b = this._height * this._height / 300;
```

In this case as well, I ended up choosing a quadratic relationship. It makes the blue flare up suddenly when the particle gets to a certain length. I had to shrink the squared values of `this._height` by a factor of 300 to get them to fit in the desired color range.

With the color values defined in the local variables `r`, `g`, and `b`, I can now pass them to the *Color* object `this.col`:

```
this.col.setTint (r, g, b, 100);
```

I am using my custom method*Color.setTint( )*, discussed in Chapter 9. (The code for the method must be included in the movie, of course.) The tint is set at 100 percent. (I considered making the tint parameter dynamic as well, tying it to some property of the particle, but that seemed to be going overboard.)

The code for the *particle* movie clip finishes with a simple call of the *init( )* method on the *actions* layer:

```
this.init();
stop();
```

Conclusion

In this chapter, we have built upon the physics concepts of Chapter 8 and explored their application in the *PhysicsParticle*, *Force*, and *ElasticForce* classes. We then saw how they are used to dynamically animate my Aurora Borealis experiment, a two-dimensional particle system. In our next chapter, we'll look at a three-dimensional particle system I developed to implement a snowstorm.

Chapter 12

Snowstorm

In the winter of 2001, I was asked to do a special Christmas animation for Ultrashock.com. Patrick Miko, the CEO of Ultrashock, wanted to have something fun to celebrate the season. We originally planned to have the cartoon representations of Patrick and his partner Peter Van den Wyngaert standing in the midst of a blizzard. I developed an ActionScripted particle system for this that positioned the snowflakes in a simple 3-D space and allowed the user to control the wind with mouse interaction. Ultrashock ended up using the animation for a frosty "winter menu" for the site.

Months later while planning this book, I thought that this Snowstorm animation would be a good project to deconstruct in one of the later chapters. I re-opened the files, which had been created in Flash 5, and reworked the code significantly, cleaning it up and using some new features of Flash MX, such as the new event model and the Shape Drawing API. I also turned the snowstorm into a component. In this chapter, we'll examine the code behind this animation, contained in three main entities: the *Snowflake* class, the *Snowstorm* class, and the *snowstorm* component.

The Snowflake Class

While writing this chapter, I found in a pile of old papers my original notes for Snowstorm. Before opening up Flash at all, I used three pages to "think out loud" and plan the project. On the first page, I clarified the purpose of the animation, working from general to more specific descriptions. These were some of the notes I had on the first page:

❭ snow falls at terminal velocity, so no need for y-accel.

❭ y-vel is constant (unless wind blows vertically as well)

❭ just do lateral motion—change x-vel., x-accel.

> ❭ wrapping—leaves on right, enters screen on left—same vertically
>
> ❭ gravity
>
> ❭ lots of fluid friction—reaches terminal velocity, descends slowly
>
> ❭ brownian motion
>
> ❭ randomize size
>
> ❭ wind control

These points helped me to see what capabilities I needed to provide in a custom *Snowflake* class. On the second page, I drew an initial sketch of what characteristics this class could have:

Snowflake Properties

> ❭ pos (x, y, z)—pos.z is constant
>
> ❭ vel (x, y, z)—vel.z is 0, vel.y may be constant
>
> ❭ accel (x, y, z)—accel.z is 0, accel.y may be constant
>
> ❭ size
>
> ❭ friction
>
> ❭ brown (brownian force) (x, y, z)—actually just x
>
> ❭ mc
>
> ❭ mcID
>
> ❭ brownAmp—amplitude of brown force
>
> ❭ limits object
>
> ❭ wind
>
> ❭ field

Methods

> ❭ live
>
> ❭ move
>
> ❭ render
>
> ❭ attachGraphic (mcID)
>
> ❭ setLimits (limObj)

Constructor

❭ new Snowflake (x, y, z, size, field, mcID)

On the third page of my notes, I mapped out a preliminary version of the *Snowfield* class in a similar manner. After several stages of development and revisions, the classes that I have now are noticeably different from my notes. In particular, several responsibilites have moved from the *Snowflake* to the *Snowfield* class. Nevertheless, most of the core concepts have remained in some form or another.

The *Snowflake* class is a template for a code object that represents each snowflake in the animation. A *Snowflake* instance stores a position and velocity in 3-D space, using the *Vector3d* class from Chapter 5. It also handles image rendering and movement of the flake's movie clip. The code for the *Snowflake* class is contained in the file `snowflake_class.as`.

Since the *Snowflake* class uses the *Vector3d* class, I first do a simple check that the *Snowflake* constructor exists, with this code:

```
// check for Vector3d class
if (typeof Vector3d != "function")
    trace ("Error: required class Vector3d missing");
```

If there isn't a *Vector3d( )* function, an error message is traced to the Output window.

Helper Functions

I call upon several custom functions from previous chapters to help create the snowstorm: *Math.randRangeF( )*, *MovieClip.drawRegPoly( )*, and *Color.setBrightness( )*.

Math.randRangeF( )

The custom function *Math.randRangeF( )* returns a floating-point number between two given numbers. I also use it in the Aurora Borealis animation, and discuss the function in Chapter 11. Here's the code for reference:

```
Math.randRangeF = function (low, high) {
    return Math.random() * (high - low) + low;
};
```

MovieClip.drawRegPoly( )

I include the custom drawing method *MovieClip.drawRegPoly( )*, using it to draw six-sided flakes. Because *drawRegPoly( )* relies on the custom method

MovieClip.drawPoly( ) (both are discussed in Chapter 10), I include it as well.
Here's the code for reference:

```
MovieClip.prototype.drawPoly = function (pts) {
    this.moveTo (pts[0].x, pts[0].y);
    var i = pts.length;
    while (i--) this.lineTo (pts[i].x, pts[i].y);
};


MovieClip.prototype.drawRegPoly = function (x, y,
                                            radius,
                                            numPts,
                                            rotation) {
        var angle = (-90 + rotation) * (Math.PI/180);
        var pts = [];
        var px, py;
        var dAngle = 2 * Math.PI / numPts;
        var cos = Math.cos, sin = Math.sin;
        while (numPts--) {
            angle += dAngle;
            px = radius * cos (angle) + x;
            py = radius * sin (angle) + y;
            pts.push ({x:px, y:py});
        }
        this.drawPoly (pts);
};
```

Color.setBrightness( )

I also use my custom method *Color.setBrightness( )* (discussed in Chapter 9) to
shade snowflakes, depending on their distance. Here is the code for reference:

```
Color.prototype.setBrightness = function (bright) {
    var trans = this.getTransform();
    with (trans) {
        ra = ga = ba = 100 - Math.abs (bright);
        rb = gb = bb = (bright > 0)
                        ? bright * (256/100) : 0;
    }
    this.setTransform (trans);
};
```

The Snowflake Constructor

The *Snowflake* constructor initializes the core properties of the instance, including its movie clip representation, position, and velocity. The following displays the constructor code:

```
_global.Snowflake = function (fallSpeed, timeline, depth) {
    this.mc = this.attachGraphic (timeline, depth);
    this.mcColor = new Color (this.mc);
    this.pos = new Vector3d (0, 0, 0);
    this.vel = new Vector3d (0, -fallSpeed, 0);
    this.velRot = Math.randRangeF (-10, 10);
    MovieClip.addListener (this);
};
```

The first line in the method creates a movie clip to represent the snowflake visually:

```
this.mc = this.attachGraphic (timeline, depth);
```

The *Snowflake.attachGraphic( )* method is called, and the constructor arguments `timeline` and `depth` are passed to it. We will look at *attachGraphic( )* more closely later in the chapter. Basically, the method creates a movie clip within the `timeline` clip, and returns a reference to the new clip. Back in the constructor, that reference is stored in the `this.mc` property, as shown in the preceding code.

Later on, we'll need to control the color of the movie clip. Thus, the following code defines a *Color* object targeting `this.mc`:

```
this.mcColor = new Color (this.mc);
```

Next, a 3-D position vector is intialized at [0, 0, 0]:

```
this.pos = new Vector3d (0, 0, 0);
```

A velocity vector is also initialized in the subsequent line of code:

```
this.vel = new Vector3d (0, -fallSpeed, 0);
```

The particle's speed along the X and Z axes is set to zero, but the vertical speed is set to the `fallSpeed` constructor parameter. I gave the snowflakes a constant rate of descent—this is how real snow generally falls.

One of the last aesthetic touches I put on the snowflakes was to give them a bit of a spin. The `velRot` property stores the speed of rotation, and is declared next in the constructor:

```
this.velRot = Math.randRangeF (-10, 10);
```

I used the custom function *Math.randRangeF( )* to pick a random floating-point number between –10 and 10 (see Chapter 11 for more discussion).

Lastly, *MovieClip.addListener( )* is invoked on the object to enable its *onEnterFrame( )* handler with this code:

```
MovieClip.addListener (this);
```

Listeners are discussed in Chapter 6.

Getter/Setter Methods

As usual, I set a shortcut variable SFP to point to Snowflake.prototype:

```
var SFP = Snowflake.prototype;
```

Snowflake.setXY( )

The *setXY( )* method changes the *x* and *y* components of the 3-D position vector:

```
SFP.setXY = function (x, y) {
    this.pos.x = x;
    this.pos.y = y;
    this.renderXY();
};
```

Notice that the *renderXY( )* method is called after changing the this.pos vector. This causes the snowflake's visual representation to be updated to match the new coordinates. We'll look at the *renderXY( )* method later.

Snowflake.setZ( )

The *setZ( )* method changes the snowflake's *z* coordinate, which is its distance from the viewport:

```
SFP.setZ = function (z) {
    this.pos.z = z;
    this.renderZ();
};
```

Much as before, I call another method, *renderZ( )* in this case, to update the visuals after changing coordinates.

Snowflake.setScreenX( )

There are two distinct sets of coordinates for any 3-D point represented on the screen. One set of coordinates is its position in 3-D space: [x, y, z]. The other coordinates are for the point's *projected position* on the 2-D screen: [screenX, screenY]. The *setXY( )* and *setZ( )* methods, which we've looked at, deal with the former—the 3-D coordinates.

Sometimes, however, it is useful to give a *Snowflake* a new location based on a particular point on the screen. In other words, we want to be able to move a *Snowflake* to an exact screen location, and have the corresponding 3-D coordinates set *automatically* for us.

The *setScreenX( )* method moves the *Snowflake* to a specified _x location and sets the 3-D *x* coordinate accordingly with this code:

```
SFP.setScreenX = function (x) {
    this.pos.x = (this.mc._x = x) / this.pers;
};
```

Notice that I'm changing both `this.mc._x` and `this.pos.x` in one step. Alternatively, this could be done in two lines of code:

```
this.mc._x = x;
this.pos.x = x / this.pers;
```

This is what I originally had in this method. However, I saw that I could speed up and shorten the code by using an inline optimization.

As for the equation itself, it is simply the inverse of the projection used in the *renderXY( )* method (discussed later). That code looks like this:

```
this.mc._x = this.pos.x * this.pers;
```

Using simple algebra, this can be rearranged to solve for `this.pos.x`:

```
this.pos.x = this.mc._x / this.pers;
```

Snowflake.setScreenY( )

The *setScreenY( )* method operates much like *setScreenX( )*. Here's the code:

```
SFP.setScreenY = function (y) {
    this.pos.y = -(this.mc._y = y) / this.pers;
};
```

Notice that the *y* coordinate is inverted with a negative sign (–). As discussed in Chapter 5, this is done to convert from Flash stage coordinates to Cartesian coordinates.

Snowflake.setScreenXY( )

The *setScreenXY( )* method simply combines the code of the *setScreenX( )* and *setScreenY( )* methods:

```
SFP.setScreenXY = function (x, y) {
    this.pos.x = (this.mc._x = x) / this.pers;
    this.pos.y = -(this.mc._y = y) / this.pers;
};
```

Sometimes you may want to set both coordinates at once. The *setScreenXY( )* method is convenient, and executes faster than calling two separate methods.

Snowflake.setStorm( ) and getStorm( )

A *Snowflake* object can be part of a larger *Snowstorm* object. We'll look at the *Snowstorm* class later, but in general, it allows you to easily coordinate a group of snowflakes and specify properties like friction and spatial boundaries. The *Snowflake.setStorm( )* and *getStorm( )* methods allow you to set and retrieve the this.storm property, which points to a *Snowstorm* instance. The code is quite simple:

```
SFP.setStorm = function (s) {
    this.storm = s;
};

SFP.getStorm = function () {
    return this.storm;
};
```

Private Methods

The most important and hard-working code of the *Snowflake* class is in the private methods.

Snowflake.attachGraphic( )

The snowflake needs some sort of graphical representation. The *attachGraphic( )* method creates a new movie clip and draws a hexagon inside it using the Shape Drawing API. Here's the code:

```
SFP.attachGraphic = function (timeline, depth) {
    var mc = timeline.createEmptyMovieClip ("s" + depth, depth);
    with (mc) {
        beginFill (0xFFFFFF);
        drawRegPoly (0, 0, 10, 6);
        endFill();
    }
    return mc;
};
```

The first line creates an empty movie clip, using the *MovieClip* method *createEmptyMovieClip( )*, naturally:

```
var mc = timeline.createEmptyMovieClip ("s" + depth, depth);
```

The new clip is given an appropriate instance name, using the `depth` parameter. When there are multiple *Snowflake* objects in the same movie clip, each one should be given a unique depth, so that their representative movie clips will not collide. The preceding code also stores a reference to the new clip in the local variable `mc`.

Speaking of which, we do some drawing in that new clip. A `with` statement sets the scope to `mc`, then drawing methods are called, in the following section of code:

```
with (mc) {
    beginFill (0xFFFFFF);
    drawRegPoly (0, 0, 10, 6);
    endFill();
}
```

The *beginFill( )* command sets the drawing fill to white. Then, I use my custom drawing method *MovieClip.drawRegPoly( )* to draw a regular (equal-sided) polygon (see Chapter 10). The first two arguments define the center of the polygon at [0, 0], which is the registration point of the `mc` clip. The remaining arguments give the polygon a radius of 10, and six sides, making it a hexagon. The *endFill( )* command closes off the fill properly.

NOTE: When I originally created the snowstorm in Flash 5, I attached a movie clip in the library, which contained a small white circle. With Flash MX, however, it was more fun to create a movie clip from scratch and draw a hexagon in it with the Shape Drawing API. This had aesthetic advantages, as snowflakes actually do have six sides, and now I could rotate the flakes. Also, a six-sided polygon, drawn with straight lines, is a more optimized shape than a circle, which Flash draws with eight curves.

Lastly, the movie clip reference is returned from the method:

```
return mc;
```

As mentioned previously, the code in the *Snowflake* constructor catches this returned value and stores it in the `this.mc` property.

Snowflake.move( )

The *move( )* method updates the velocity and position of the flake. Here's the code for the method:

```
SFP.move = function () {
    if (++this.t % 10 == 0) {
        this.brown = Math.randRangeF (-.2, .2);
    }
    var v = this.vel;
    v.x += this.brown + this.storm.wind;
    v.x *= 1 - this.storm.friction;
    this.pos.plus (v);
    this.rotation += this.velRot;
    this.renderXY();
};
```

The first section creates random Brownian force every 10 frames:

```
if (++this.t % 10 == 0) {
    this.brown = Math.randRangeF (-.2, .2);
}
```

In the next section, a new velocity is calculated:

```
var v = this.vel;
v.x += this.brown + this.storm.wind;
v.x *= 1 - this.storm.friction;
```

First, I set a local variable v to the `this.vel` property, to speed up access to the vector:

```
var v = this.vel;
```

Then, I increase the x component of the velocity by the Brownian force and the wind force:

```
v.x += this.brown + this.storm.wind;
```

This is a slightly compressed approach, compared to what I have previously discussed. Usually, I add forces together to find the *acceleration*, and *then* add acceleration to velocity—something like this:

```
accelX = this.brown + this.storm.wind;
vel.x += accelX;
```

However, there is no real need to have the `accelX` variable in this case, so I eliminated it to optimize the code.

The velocity calculation is concluded by reducing it because of friction:

```
v.x *= 1 - this.storm.friction;
```

The `friction` property is defined in the *Snowstorm* instance to which the flake belongs. By default, friction is set to .03 (in the component parameters for the snow storm), which means that a flake will lose three percent of its horizontal velocity each frame. Subtracting .03 from 1 yields .97, which is what v.x is multiplied by. (Multiplying a number by .97, or 97 percent, is the same as subtracting 3 percent of the number.)

The velocity vector is then added to the position vector with this code:

```
this.pos.plus (v);
```

Also, the `rotation` property is increased by the velocity of rotation:

```
this.rotation += this.velRot;
```

Lastly, since the position vector has been changed, we called the *renderXY( )* method to update the visuals:

```
this.renderXY();
```

Snowflake.onEnterFrame( )

The *move( )* method needs to be executed in each frame, so we set the *onEnterFrame( )* handler to it:

```
SFP.onEnterFrame = SFP.move;
```

Now the *Snowflake* instance is "self-running"—meaning it updates its position and animates across the screen automatically.

Snowflake.renderXY( )

When the *Snowflake* moves along the X or Y axes in 3-D space, the *renderXY( )* method is called to update the display.

```
SFP.renderXY = function () {
    var mc = this.mc;
    mc._x = this.pos.x * this.pers;
    mc._y = -this.pos.y * this.pers;
    mc._rotation = this.rotation;
    var lm = this.storm.limits;
    if (mc._y > lm.ymax) this.setScreenY (lm.ymin);
    if (mc._x > lm.xmax) this.setScreenX (lm.xmin)
        else if (mc._x < lm.xmin) this.setScreenX (lm.xmax);
};
```

First, a local variable mc is defined to point to this.mc:

```
var mc = this.mc;
```

This speeds up access to the movie clip property.

The movie clip's position and rotation are set in the next lines of code:

```
mc._x = this.pos.x * this.pers;
mc._y = -this.pos.y * this.pers;
mc._rotation = this.rotation;
```

The 3-D *x* and *y* coordinates, stored in the *Vector3d* this.pos property, are projected onto the screen, producing _x and _y coordinates. The projection is done by multiplying the 3-D coordinates by the perspective factor this.pers, which will have previously been calculated in the *Snowflake.renderZ( )* method.

The last step is to check if the *Snowflake* has moved outside its boundaries, in the final section of code. The current *Snowflake* object belongs to a *Snowstorm* object. The boundaries of the *Snowflake* are defined in a `limits` property in the *Snowstorm*. A local variable `lm` is declared to store a reference to the `limits` object, in the first line of code:

```
var lm = this.storm.limits;
```

Then the `_x` and `_y` coordinates of the *Snowflake*'s movie clip are checked against the boundaries, in the last three lines of code:

```
if (mc._y > lm.ymax) this.setScreenY (lm.ymin);
if (mc._x > lm.xmax) this.setScreenX (lm.xmin)
else if (mc._x < lm.xmin) this.setScreenX (lm.xmax);
```

In plain English, the logic in the preceding code is this:

- ❱ If the movie clip is too low on the screen, move it to the highest allowable point—the `ymin` boundary

- ❱ If the movie clip is too far right on the screen, move it to the left-most point—the `xmin` boundary

- ❱ If the movie clip is too far left on the screen, move it to the right-most point—the `xmax` boundary

Snowflake.renderZ( )

When the *z* coordinate of a *Snowflake* is changed, a number of other factors need to be updated, including the particle's size, z-order, and brightness. The *renderZ( )* method brings these aspects into coordination with the current *z* coordinate, as shown in the following code:

```
SFP.renderZ = function () {
    this.pers = this.pos.getPerspective();
    this.mc.swapDepths (Math.floor (100000 - this.pos.z * 100));
    with (this.mc) {
        _xscale = _yscale = 100 * this.pers;
    }
    this.mcColor.setBrightness (-100 * (1 - this.pers));
};
```

First, an updated perspective factor is found for the position vector `this.pos`, and stored in the `this.pers` property:

```
this.pers = this.pos.getPerspective();
```

The perspective factor determines how near objects appear larger than far objects, as shown in the next bit of code:

```
with (this.mc) {
    _xscale = _yscale = 100 * this.pers;
}
```

When a snowflake is closer, to the viewer, its perspective value increases and so does its scale. At a perspective value of 1, the movie clip will be at 100 percent scale—its original size. For more information on perspective projection, see Chapter 5.

The stacking of the flake's movie clip—the z-order—needs to be updated as well, in the following code:

```
this.mc.swapDepths (Math.floor (100000 - this.pos.z * 100));
```

Based on the *z* component of the position vector, a new position in the movie clip stack is chosen using the *MovieClip.swapDepths( )* method. This technique is also discussed in Chapter 5.

Lastly, the brightness of the movie clip is changed as in the following code:

```
this.mcColor.setBrightness (-100 * (1 - this.pers));
```

Remember that `this.mcColor` is a *Color* instance targeting the *Snowflake's* representative movie clip. I'm calling the custom method *Color.setBrightness( )* (from Chapter 9) to darken flakes dynamically, depending on their distance from the viewer. Particles that are farther away will be darker than closer ones.

The numerical values that convert `this.pers` to a brightness value came through trial and error—it took a while to find what I was looking for. In hindsight, I can see that the values of `this.pers` generally lie between 0 and 1. I wanted the brightness values to be between –100 and 0. Therefore, to map one range of values onto another, I had to invert the perspective values with a negative sign, add 1, and then scale the values by –100. The general procedure I've found for range mapping is flip (if necessary), shift, then scale. In other words, line up the ends of the ranges, and then stretch one to match the other.

The Snowstorm Class

The code for the *Snowstorm* class is contained in the file snowstorm_class.as. Since the *Snowstorm* class uses the *Snowflake* class, I do a simple check that the *Snowflake* constructor exists, with this code:

```
if (typeof Snowflake != "function")
    trace ("Error: required class Snowflake missing");
```

If there isn't a *Snowflake( )* function, an error message is traced to the Output window.

The Snowstorm Constructor

Here's the code for the constructor of the *Snowstorm* class:

```
_global.Snowstorm = function (limits, friction, fallSpeed, timeline) {
    this.limits = limits;
    this.friction = friction;
    this.fallSpeed = fallSpeed;
    this.timeline = timeline;
    this.flakes = [];
};
```

There are four constructor arguments. The first, limits, needs to be an object with six numerical properties:

) xmin

) xmax

) ymin

) ymax

) zmin

) zmax

These six properties define a boundary space that contains the storm. The first four properties, involving *x* and *y*, define boundaries for the storm in terms of *screen coordinates* (not 3-D coordinates). When a *Snowflake* moves outside of these limits on the screen, it will wrap to the opposite side. On the other hand, the zmin and zmax properties are specified in terms of the 3-D *z* coordinate (since the screen doesn't have a *z* coordinate).

The friction argument for the constructor should be a number between 0 and 1. It determines the percentage of velocity lost each frame due to friction.

(The *snowstorm* component sets the friction to .03 by default, but this is adjustable in the component parameters, which we'll discuss later in the section "The snowstorm Component.")

The third argument, `fallSpeed`, specifies the rate of descent of the flakes. (The *snowstorm* component sets the falling speed to 5 by default; this is another component parameter.) And the last argument, `timeline`, is a reference to the movie clip that will contain the movie clips for the snowflakes. As previously mentioned, each *Snowflake* instance creates a new movie clip—a child of `timeline`—which represents it visually.

Inside the constructor, each of the four arguments is copied straight into a property with the same name:

```
this.limits = limits;
this.friction = friction;
this.fallSpeed = fallSpeed;
this.timeline = timeline;
```

The last line of code creates an empty `flakes` array to store the *Snowflake* objects:

```
this.flakes = [];
```

Hereafter, as flakes are added to the storm, *Snowflake* instances will be placed in the `this.flakes` array.

Public Methods

With the constructor out of the way, it's time to give our class some methods. As usual, I set a shortcut variable SSP to point to `Snowstorm.prototype`:

```
var SSP = Snowstorm.prototype;
```

Snowstorm.addFlake( )

The *addFlake( )* method is the most complex method of the *Snowstorm* class, but the easiest to use. You just call the method without any parameters

```
myStorm.addFlake();
```

and a new snowflake will fall out of the sky. This ease of use requires a fair bit of code behind the scenes, as shown in the following:

```
SSP.addFlake = function () {
    var lm = this.limits;
    var newFlake = new Snowflake (this.fallSpeed,
```

```
                                        this.timeline,
                                        this.flakes.length);
        newFlake.setStorm (this);
        var x = Math.randRangeF (lm.xmin, lm.xmax);
        var y = lm.ymin;
        var z = Math.randRangeF (lm.zmin, lm.zmax);
        newFlake.setZ (z);
        newFlake.setScreenXY (x, y);
        this.flakes.unshift (newFlake);
};
```

First, a shortcut variable `lm` is defined to point to `this.limits`, speeding up access in subsequent code:

```
var lm = this.limits;
```

Then a new *Snowflake* instance is created, using the local properties such as `fallSpeed` and `timeline` for parameters:

```
var newFlake = new Snowflake (this.fallSpeed,
                              this.timeline,
                              this.flakes.length);
```

The new object `newFlake` is assigned to the current *Snowstorm* using its *setStorm( )* method:

```
newFlake.setStorm (this);
```

The next section of code finds a random starting point [*x, y, z*] for the *Snowflake*:

```
var x = Math.randRangeF (lm.xmin, lm.xmax);
var y = lm.ymin;
var z = Math.randRangeF (lm.zmin, lm.zmax);
```

The x and z coordinates are selected randomly within the boundaries defined by the limits object. The x value falls between `lm.xmin` and `lm.xmax`; likewise, z falls between `lm.zmin` and `lm.zmax`. The y coordinate, however, is set to the minimum allowable value `lm.ymin`, since the flakes start at the top and fall downward.

These coordinates are then passed to their respective setter methods, in the next two lines of code:

```
newFlake.setZ (z);
newFlake.setScreenXY (x, y);
```

The *Snowflake* is now in position. To finish, the instance is added to the `this.flakes` array in the last line of code:

```
this.flakes.unshift (newFlake);
```

The *Array.unshift( )* method is used to insert `newFlake` into the array.

NOTE: *Array.unshift( )* is similar to the more commonly-used *Array.push( )* method, the difference being that *unshift( )* places the new item at the beginning of the array, rather than the end. Why did I use *unshift( )* instead of *push( )*? No real reason, except for the fun of it.

Snowstorm.removeFlake( )

The *removeFlake( )* method takes the last snowflake out of the `this.flakes` array. Here's the method's code:

```
SSP.removeFlake = function () {
    return this.flakes.pop();
};
```

The last snowflake in the array is "popped" out and returned from the method. I don't actually use this method in my Snowstorm animation, but it can't hurt to have it around. It makes a nice complement to the *addFlake( )* method. I often define methods because they could *conceivably* be used in the future, even though I don't need them now.

Snowstorm.setWind( ) and getWind( )

The *setWind( )* method defines the force of wind that acts along the horizontal (X) axis, and *getWind( )* returns that quantity. Here's the code for this getter/ setter pair:

```
SSP.setWind = function (w) {
    this.$wind = w;
};

SSP.getWind = function () {
    return this.$wind;
};
```

This is a good setup for a getter/setter property. The following code connects the preceding methods to a "wind" property:

```
with (SSP) {
    addProperty ("wind", getWind, setWind);
}
```

The snowstorm FLA

So far, we have explored the potential of the *Snowflake* and *Snowstorm* classes. Now it's time to see them in action in the *snowstorm.fla* file.

The Main Timeline Code

On the main timeline of the *snowstorm* FLA, the *classes* layer contains this code:

```
#include "core_setup.as"
#include "vector3d_class.as"
#include "snowflake_class.as"
#include "snowstorm_class.as"
```

Three classes are used in this movie—*Vector3d*, *Snowflake*, and *Snowstorm*—and each resides in its own *.as* file. Their code must be included in a particular order, since there are dependencies between the classes. The *core_setup.as* file must come first, because it sets up custom code for *onEnterFrame* event broadcasting (*MovieClip.addListener( )*) and class inheritance (*Function.extend( )* and *Object.superCon( )*).

With the three classes, *Snowstorm* depends on *Snowflake*, which depends on *Vector3d*. Thus, the code for the *Vector3d* class must execute first, then the code for *Snowflake*, and finally, *Snowstorm*.

The only movie clip on the main timeline is the *snowstorm* component, which we'll look at next.

The snowstorm Component

So far, we've explored the *Snowflake* and *Snowstorm* classes, which have most of the functionality needed to produce an animated snowfall. However, we need some sort of interface to bridge the gap between the user and the classes. The *snowstorm* component fills this purpose. It provides a visual placeholder for the animation, defining a screen area for the snow. When the component movie clip itself is moved or resized, the animation's area is changed to match.

The component also exposes easy-to-use parameters to the user, allowing customization of the animation. There are four parameters for the *snowstorm* component, which are listed and described in Table 12-1.

Component Methods

Three methods are defined for the *snowstorm* component on the *methods* layer: *init( )*, *onMouseMove( )*, and *onEnterFrame( )*. They are responsible for preparing the component for animation and responding to events from the mouse and the timeline.

The init( ) Method

The *init( )* method prepares the *snowstorm* component for precipitation. Here's its code:

```
this.init = function () {
    var bleed = 10;
    var limits = {
        xmin: 0 - bleed,
        xmax: this._width + bleed,
        ymin: 0 - bleed,
        ymax: this._height + bleed,
        zmin: 0,
        zmax: this.zDepth
    };
    this.storm = new Snowstorm (limits,
                                this.friction,
                                this.fallSpeed,
                                this);
    this._xscale = this._yscale = 100;
    this.deadPreview._visible = false;
    this.onEnterFrame = this.makeFlake;
};
```

Parameter Name	Default Value	Description
maxFlakes	80	The number of snowflakes in the storm
fallSpeed	5	The rate of descent of the snowflakes
friction	.03	The amount of particle velocity lost each frame
zDepth	800	The depth of the storm along the Z-axis

TABLE 12-1

Parameters of the *Snowstorm* Component

The first section of code calculates the limits of the snowstorm, and collects them into a `limits` object:

```
var bleed = 10;
var limits = {
    xmin: 0 - bleed,
    xmax: this._width + bleed,
    ymin: 0 - bleed,
    ymax: this._height + bleed,
    zmin: 0,
    zmax: this.depth
};
```

The snowflakes will stay inside the limits of the storm, wrapping to the opposite side if they cross a boundary. These limits are defined by the dimensions of the component clip itself. For example, if you scale the component clip to 200 by 300 pixels on the stage, the snowstorm will be 200 by 300 pixels, and in the same position as the component.

I added a "bleed" factor (borrowing a term from print publication) to extend the limits outwards a bit. This is done so that the whole flake will be seen to leave the screen before wrapping to the opposite side (otherwise, a large flake would suddenly disappear while half of it was still visible).

NOTE: In print publication, a photograph that extends to the very edge of the page is called a *bleed*. Usually, the photograph will be laid out so that a bit of it is off the page, to ensure that it goes all the way to the edge when the page is trimmed. If you like, you can crop the snowstorm component by putting a mask over the animation area.

An instance of the *Snowstorm* class is created next and stored in the property `this.storm`:

```
this.storm = new Snowstorm (limits,
                            this.friction,
                            this.fallSpeed,
                            this);
```

The constructor is passed the `limits` object, the `friction` and `fallSpeed` component parameters, and `this`, a reference to the component itself.

As mentioned earlier, the user can define the dimensions of the snowstorm simply by positioning and sizing the *snowstorm* component movie clip on the stage—at design time. At run time, though, we need to return the clip to its original scale. Otherwise, the size of the snowflakes inside will be distorted. The following code returns the component to its normal size:

```
this._xscale = this._yscale = 100;
```

Then the `deadPreview` clip—which shows the user the area of the *snowstorm* component—is hidden, as it is no longer needed:

```
this.deadPreview._visible = false;
```

Lastly, a frame loop is started by setting the `this.onEnterFrame` property to the *makeFlake( )* method:

```
this.onEnterFrame = this.makeFlake;
```

The *makeFlake( )* method will be automatically called each frame (until enough snowflakes have been created).

Lastly, the *init( )* method is called on the *actions* layer of the component:

```
this.init();
stop();
```

This is the only direct call to a method in the entire component. All other code simply reacts automatically to events like *onEnterFrame* or *opMouseMove*.

The makeFlake( ) Method

The snowstorm has 80 flakes by default. The question is, how should these 80 flakes be introduced to the screen? They could appear all at once, in the same frame, but that wouldn't look very natural. Rather, the flakes should appear gradually over time, building into a storm. Consequently, we need to use a frame loop, adding new flakes frame by frame until all 80 have been created.

The *makeFlake( )* method is designed to be used in a frame loop. Here is the code:

```
this.makeFlake = function () {
    if (this.numFlakes++ < this.maxFlakes) {
        this.storm.addFlake();
    } else {
        delete this.onEnterFrame;
    }
};
```

Each time the method is called, it compares the steadily increasing `numFlakes` property with the `maxFlakes` property to see if another flake needs to be created. If so, the *addFlake( )* method of the *Snowstorm* instance is invoked. On the other hand, if there are enough flakes, the frame loop is stopped by deleting the `this.onEnterFrame` property. (The *init( )* method will have previously pointed the `this.onEnterFrame` property to the *makeFlake( )* method.)

The onMouseMove( )Handler

I made the snowstorm interactive by allowing the wind to be controlled by the mouse. It only makes sense, then, to use the *onMouseMove( )* event handler of the component to enable this interactivity:

```
this.onMouseMove = function () {
    this.storm.setWind ((this._xmouse - 200) / 200);
};
```

When the mouse moves, the *setWind( )* method of the *Snowstorm* object is called, and passed a value based on the _xmouse property. At the default dimensions, the values of _xmouse will range from 0 to 400. I subtract 200 from the values to shift them to the range –200 to 200. Then I divide by 200, squeezing the range to be between –1 and 1. The wind value doesn't *have* to be between –1 and 1; it just happens to be a good range aesthetically.

Conclusion

In this chapter, we've dissected my *Snowstorm* animation, seeing how two custom classes for snow can be combined with the *Vector3d* class and formed into a component. I hope this has shown you that even fun, experimental projects like nature simulations can be developed with clean code and object-oriented principles. In the next chapter, we'll look at an interactive fractal that uses recorded motion to dance.

Chapter 13

Fractal Dancer

I have been fascinated with fractals since high school. Fractals come in many forms and categories, but in general, they can be described as self-similar structures: shapes made up of smaller copies of the same shape, which are then made up of smaller copies, and so on. Once you know what fractals are, you start to see them everywhere—in broccoli, blood vessels, leaves, and as Mandelbrot alludes to, clouds, mountains, coastlines, bark, and lightning. I recommend, as an exercise, buying a whole head of cauliflower and just *looking* at it for a while. Not only is it composed of branches within branches, but it has spirals within spirals on top.

I've been exploring fractals on my computer since the days of my family's 286 computer, in the MS-DOS programs FractalVision and Fractint. When Flash came along, I anticipated being able to one day create my own fractals when my programming skills had sufficiently advanced. At one point, I tried to create a fractal similar to Fractal Dancer in Flash 4. It was very difficult, and I eventually gave up.

However, Flash 5 brought new hope. One of the first demos of Flash 5's new features I remember seeing was Branden Hall's rendition of the famous Koch snowflake which is actually still online at http://www.figleaf.com/development/flash5/koch.swf. This movie was also the first demonstration of recursive *attachMovie( )* operations in Flash 5.

The wall I had run up against in Flash 4 was that the action to duplicate a movie clip created new instances as *siblings* of the original movie clip, but never as children nested *inside* it. With Flash 5's *attachMovie( )*, however, I could attach a movie clip inside another instance of the same symbol. With this realization, I was soon able to grow the self-similar tree shown in Figure 13-1.

The self-similar tree in Fractal Dancer

Once I had a static structure, though, I naturally wanted to make it more dynamic and interactive. I came up with the idea of creating recursive movement within the structure, based on mouse movement. Specifically, one dimension of the mouse coordinates would control the left branches, and the other dimension would control the right branches.

The next step was inspired by Yugo Nakamura's work with recorded motion, some of which is displayed at www.yugop.com. I thought the fractal would be even more fun if users could not only interactively change its shape, but record its movement as they were doing it, and then replay it.

The FractalTree Component

Before writing this chapter, I reworked the Fractal Dancer's Flash 5 FLA significantly to improve the structure of the code and take advantage of Flash MX features. In this process, I decided to make the tree into a simple component that could be customized easily.

Component Parameters

The *FractalTree* component has several useful parameters that allow us to easily customize the fractal. The component parameters are listed in Table 13-1.

Parameter Name	Default Value
maxLevels	6
maxBranches	2
filmFrames	150

TABLE 13-1

Parameters for the *FractalTree* Component

The maxLevels parameter determines how many times a branch will sprout new branches. With a value of 2, the trunk will grow two branches and then stop. If maxLevels is 3, those two branches will each grow two branches. Thus, there would be a total of 1 + 2 + 4 = 7 branches, on three different levels. Further stages of growth will produce 8 additional branches, then 16, 32, and so on. At the default value of 6 for the maxLevels parameter, there are 1 + 2 + 4 + 8 + 16 + 32 = 63 branches.

NOTE: You can actually calculate the total number of branches for *n* levels with this formula: $b = 2^n - 1$. The tree grows exponentially, with a base of 2 in this case.

The maxBranches parameter determines the number of sub-branches that grow from a single branch. The default value is 2, but I designed the *FractalTree* component to be able to handler higher settings. In fact, you can try setting maxBranches to 3, and then changing the *poser3* layer (in the component) from a guide to a normal layer. Be warned, however—the branches multiply much more quickly. At four levels, there are already 80 branches, and at six levels (if your processor makes it that far), there will be 728 branches!

NOTE: The formula for the total number of branches for *n* levels is now: $b = 3^n - 1$. In general, the formula for an arbitrary base is $b = maxBranches^n - 1$.

The filmFrames parameter determines how many frames of mouse motion will be recorded and played back.

Methods

Three methods for the component are defined on the methods layer: *init( )*, *onMouseDown( )*, and *onMouseUp( )*.

The init( ) Method

The *init( )* method initializes the *FractalTree* component. Here is its complete code:

```
this.init = function () {
    this.posers = [];
    for (var i=1; i <= this.maxBranches; i++) {
        this.posers[i] = this["poser"+i];
        this.posers[i]._visible = false;
    }
    this.xCam = new MotionCam (this.x_txt, "text", this.filmFrames);
    this.xCam.setActor (_level0, "_xmouse");
    this.xCam.setLooping (true);

    this.yCam = new MotionCam (this.y_txt, "text", this.filmFrames);
    this.yCam.setActor (_level0, "_ymouse");
    this.yCam.setLooping (true);
};
```

First, I create a `posers` array:

```
this.posers = [];
```

This array will store references to the "poser" movie clips in the *FractalTree* component. These are the two branches that have been placed at angles to the trunk. Their position, rotation, and scale determine the shape of the tree. They have the instance names `poser1` and `poser2`, and each is on a layer of the same name.

In the code that follows, I scan for the poser movie clips and add them to the `posers` array:

```
for (var i=1; i <= this.maxBranches; i++) {
    this.posers[i] = this["poser"+i];
    this.posers[i]._visible = false;
}
```

The `for` loop uses the `maxBranches` component parameter to know how many posers to find. With the default `maxBranches` setting of 2, the `poser1` clip reference will be stored in `this.posers[1]`, and `poser2`'s reference will go in `this.posers[2]`. This is why the counter variable `i` starts at 1 instead of 0. At the same time, each poser is made invisible.

In the next section, I create two objects that will "film" the *x* and *y* mouse coordinates, and broadcast them to the branches of the tree. These are instances of the *MotionCam* class, which we'll explore in detail later in the chapter. The following code creates the first *MotionCam*:

```
this.xCam = new MotionCam (this.x_txt, "text", this.filmFrames);
```

This sets up an `xCam` object that will control the `text` property of the *TextField* `x_txt`, which is on the current timeline (on the *textfields* layer). The duration of the film is set by the `filmFrames` component parameter.

However, the *TextField* will merely *display* the data running through `xCam`. Therefore, we need to set a target, or an "actor," to *supply* data for the camera. The next line of code aims the *MotionCam* at the mouse's *x* coordinate:

```
this.xCam.setActor (_level0, "_xmouse");
```

The `xCam` is lastly set to loop when it reaches the end of the film, with this code:

```
this.xCam.setLooping (true);
```

Another *MotionCam* object is set up for the `_ymouse` input. The code is almost exactly the same as before:

```
this.yCam = new MotionCam (this.y_txt, "text", this.filmFrames);
this.yCam.setActor (_level0, "_ymouse");
this.yCam.setLooping (true);
```

The difference is that `y` replaces `x` in several places. The mouse's *y* coordinate is recorded from `_level0._ymouse` and displayed in the `this.y_txt` textfield. This concludes the component initialization.

The onMouseDown( ) Handler

The code for the *onMouseDown( )* event handler is quite simple:

```
this.onMouseDown = function () {
    this.xCam.startRecord();
    this.yCam.startRecord();
};
```

When the mouse button is pressed, the cameras start recording. We'll look at the *MotionCam.startRecord( )* method later in the chapter.

The onMouseUp( ) Handler

Likewise, the *onMouseUp( )* event handler is straightforward:

```
this.onMouseUp = function () {
    this.xCam.stopRecord();
    this.yCam.stopRecord();
};
```

When the mouse button is released, the camera objects stop recording. That's it for the component code. Next, we'll look at the class designed to represent each branch of the fractal.

The FractalBranch Class

The branches of the fractal tree are copies of one particular movie clip arranged in a precise structure. Instances of the *FractalBranchSymbol* movie clip are created and attached to other instances of the same symbol. The clips are colored and animated individually as well.

In the Flash 5 version of Fractal Dancer, I put functions inside *FractalBranchSymbol* (named differently back then) to govern the tasks of duplication, coloration, and animation. When I reworked the project in Flash MX, I realized that these functions would work well as methods of a class, which I called *FractalBranch*.

The new *Object.registerClass( )* function also allowed me to easily make *FractalBranch* a *MovieClip* subclass. With this new setup, the functions inside *FractalBranchSymbol* are only declared once—as methods in the class prototype—whereas before, each branch movie clip created separate copies of the functions. At the default settings, the tree has 63 branches. With five functions in each branch, the old setup created over 300 functions in memory. With the new approach, however, only five functions are created. As you can see, *MovieClip* subclassing and *Object.registerClass( )* can really improve a Flash movie's resource management in terms of memory requirements.

NOTE: The *Object.registerClass( )* function is usually linked closely with components, possibly giving the impression that it is used *only* for components. The *FractalBranch* class is an example of *Object.registerClass( )* used for a non-component. Conversely, my *FractalTree* component doesn't use *Object.registerClass( )*.

The FractalBranch Constructor

The code for *FractalBranch* is contained in the file *fractal_branch_class.as*. As usual, we begin by looking at the constructor, which is quite simple for this class:

```
_global.FractalBranch = function () {
    this.init();
};
```

The constructor function merely calls the *FractalBranch.init( )* method to set up the instance. Branden Hall and others have recommended that when coding subclasses of *MovieClip*, such as components, we put all initialization code in an *init( )* method; it makes certain tasks easier later on.

In the next line of code, *Object.registerClass( )* is called to associate the movie clip symbol *FractalBranchSymbol* in the library with the *FractalBranch* class:

```
Object.registerClass ("FractalBranchSymbol",
                       FractalBranch);
```

From now on, the *FractalBranch( )* constructor will be called whenever an instance of *FractalBranchSymbol* is created. In addition, the movie clip instance will inherit the methods of the class. Let's look at the *FractalBranch* methods now.

Methods

First of all, I set up the prototype chain so that FractalBranch inherits from the *MovieClip* class, with the following code:

```
FractalBranch.prototype.__proto__ = MovieClip.prototype;
```

I discuss __proto__ inheritance in Chapter 2.

Next is my usual practice of declaring a shortcut variable to the prototype of the class:

```
var FBP = FractalBranch.prototype;
```

Now we can create methods and attach them to FBP, starting with the *init( )* method.

FractalBranch.init( )

The *init( )* method prepares the *FractalBranch* instance, which is a movie clip subclass, for its life as part of a fractal tree. Here is the method's code:

```
FBP.init = function () {
    this.numBranches = 0;
    if (this.myLevel == undefined) {
        this.myLevel = 0;
        this.fRoot = this._parent;
    } else {
        this.doColor();
        if (this.myBranch == 1)
            this.fRoot.xCam.addListener (this);
        else if (this.myBranch == 2)
            this.fRoot.yCam.addListener (this);
    }
};
```

First, the numBranches property is set to zero, to reflect the fact that no sub-branches have been attached to this branch yet:

```
this.numBranches = 0;
```

Next, an if statement checks whether this branch is the "trunk" of the tree:

```
if (this.myLevel == undefined) {
    this.myLevel = 0;
    this.fRoot = this._parent;
}
```

With the way the tree is set up, each sub-branch will be assigned a level in the myLevel property. Therefore, if myLevel hasn't been defined, the branch is not a sub-branch, and thus, it is the main branch at level zero.

In addition, an fRoot property is defined to store a reference to the *FractalTree* component (found through this._parent). The fRoot reference will be passed later to every branch of the tree, allowing each to access the component easily.

If, one the other hand, the branch is *not* the trunk of the tree, the following `else` clause is executed:

```
} else {
    this.doColor();
    if (this.myBranch == 1)
        this.fRoot.xCam.addListener (this);
    else if (this.myBranch == 2)
        this.fRoot.yCam.addListener (this);
}
```

The first line calls the *doColor( )* method to change the color of the branch. Then an `if` statement checks the number of the branch, which is stored in the `myBranch` property. As it worked out in this movie, the right branch is numbered 1 and the left branch is numbered 2.

Lastly, the current branch is added as a listener to one of the *MotionCam* objects—either `xCam` or `yCam`—with the following code:

```
this.fRoot.xCam.addListener (this);
// or
this.fRoot.yCam.addListener (this);
```

This causes the branch to receive *MotionCam* events, which we'll use to cause the right branches to be controlled by _xmouse and the left branches to be controlled by _ymouse. But we need to define the *onMotionChanged( )* event handler in order to accomplish this.

FractalBranch.onMotionChanged( )

As we just saw in the *init( )* method, the *FractalBranch* instance is a listener for events from a *MotionCam* instance (either `xCam` or `yCam`). A *MotionCam* broadcasts several different events, but we are interested in just one: *onMotionChanged*. As such, we define an *onMotionChanged( )* method to respond to the event, as follows:

```
FBP.onMotionChanged = function (source, position) {
    if (position != undefined)
        this._rotation = position + 175;
};
```

We want the mouse coordinates to determine the rotation of the branch. Thus, when the coordinates change, the `_rotation` property is updated accordingly. If the branch is a left branch, it receives the vertical mouse coordinate; if it is a right branch, it receives the horizontal mouse coordinate.

The value of the new mouse position is broadcast from the *MotionCam* instance through the `position` argument. We do a quick check to ensure that the new position has a defined value. This is necessary because the *MotionCam*'s film is initially filled with `undefined` values before any data is recorded. Thus, we only want move the branch if valid data is received.

Lastly, we set the `_rotation` property to the position plus 175. The number 175 is arbitrary; I inserted it merely to tweak the range of shapes produced by the mouse within the screen area.

FractalBranch.doColor( )

I originally had all the branches of the fractal in the same color. After a while, though, I wanted to make its appearance more interesting. Making the whole tree semi-transparent helped, but I wanted some color variation as well.

I played with various dynamic coloring schemes, and ended up with the following code:

```
FBP.doColor = function () {
    if (this.myBranch == 1)
        var tint = {r:255, g:255, b:255};
    else
        var tint = {r:0, g:0, b:255};

    (new Color (this)).setTint (tint.r,
                                tint.g,
                                tint.b,
                                30);
};
```

The tree is tinted in two different directions. When a branch is a left branch, it is tinted 30 percent white. When it's a right branch, it's tinted 30 percent blue. I'm using my custom method *Color.setTint( )* from Chapter 9 to change the color.

I'm calling the method on an anonymous *Color* object: `(new Color (this))`. Since the color change is a one-time operation, there's no point in keeping a *Color* object around—the anonymous object is discarded automatically after being used.

FractalBranch.newBranch( )

The *newBranch( )* method attaches a new branch to the current one, with the following code:

```
FBP.newBranch = function (bNum) {
    if (this.myLevel >= this.fRoot.maxLevels) return;
```

```
        var p = this.fRoot.posers[bNum];
        var initObj = {
            _x: p._x,
            _y: p._y,
            _xscale: p._xscale,
            _yscale: p._yscale,
            _rotation: p._rotation,
            myLevel: this.myLevel + 1,
            myBranch: bNum,
            fRoot: this.fRoot
        }
        this.attachMovie ("FractalBranchSymbol",
                          "b" + bNum,
                          bNum,
                          initObj);
        this.numBranches++;
};
```

The method has one parameter, bNum. This is a number, either 1 or 2 in this movie, that identifies which sub-branch should be attached (either left or right).

To start things off, an `if` statement determines whether a new branch should be created at all:

```
if (this.myLevel >= this.fRoot.maxLevels) return;
```

The splitting into sub-branches should only happen a specific number of times, as determined by the component parameters in the *FractalTree* component. A reference to the component is stored in `this.fRoot`, and the maximum number of levels is in its property `this.fRoot.maxLevels`, which is 6 by default.

Next, a reference to the correct "poser" is stored in the local variable p:

```
var p = this.fRoot.posers[bNum];
```

A poser is one of the movie clips that can be positioned at author-time, inside the component, to determine the shape of the tree. References to the posers are stored in the array `this.fRoot.posers`, and they are retrieved using the bNum argument as an index. If the new sub-branch is a right branch, bNum will be 1, and the appropriate poser is in `this.fRoot.posers[1]`.

The next section of code creates an initialization object initObj, and then attaches a new movie clip from the library:

```
var initObj = {
    _x: p._x,
    _y: p._y,
    _xscale: p._xscale,
    _yscale: p._yscale,
    _rotation: p._rotation,
    myLevel: this.myLevel + 1,
    myBranch: bNum,
    fRoot: this.fRoot
}
this.attachMovie ("FractalBranchSymbol",
                "b" + bNum,
                bNum,
                initObj);
```

The *MovieClip.attachMovie( )* was given a new fourth argument in Flash MX: initObj. If you supply an object for that argument, all of the properties in that object will be copied to the new movie clip instance created by *attachMovie( )*.

In this situation, I used initObj to store values of _x, _y, _xscale, _yscale, and _rotation for the new branch, along with a few other properties. The visual properties are copied from the poser movie clip. If the poser for the right branch is rotated by 35 degrees, each right sub-branch will be rotated 35 degrees relative to its parent branch. Likewise, if the left poser is 75 percent of the original size, then its _xscale and _yscale will be 75, and each left sub-branch will have these relative proportions as well.

The method finishes by incrementing the numBranches property:

```
this.numBranches++;
```

The numBranches property is important in the *nextBranch( )* method, which we'll look at now.

FractalBranch.nextBranch( )

When the fractal tree first appears, there is just one branch—the trunk. Then, one by one, the branches appear in sequence until the whole tree has formed.

The *nextBranch( )* method moves to the "next branch" in the sequence. The proper next branch is determined in a recursive fashion, with the following code:

```
FBP.nextBranch = function () {
    if (this.numBranches < this.fRoot.maxBranches
```

```
        && this.myLevel < this.fRoot.maxLevels) {
        this.newBranch (this.numBranches + 1);
    } else {
        this._parent.nextBranch();
    }
};
```

In simple terms, the logic is this: If there aren't too many branches, and there aren't too many levels, attach a new sub-branch to this branch. Otherwise, tell the parent branch to do its next branch.

The MotionCam Class

Earlier in the chapter, looking at the *FractalTree* component, we saw how two *MotionCam* objects are used to record and play back the mouse coordinates. The xCam and yCam objects are instances of the *MotionCam* class, which is designed to easily "point and shoot" changing data. A *MotionCam* targets an actor object, records the values of one of its properties onto its film, and plays the data back on demand.

The code for *MotionCam* is contained in the file *motioncam_class.as*. Let's begin by looking at the constructor function.

The MotionCam Constructor

There are only three arguments for the *MotionCam* constructor: obj, prop, and duration. *MotionCam* is a subclass of the *Motion* class we explored in Chapter 7. Like the *Motion* class, *MotionCam* is designed to control a specific property of a particular object, which is accessed by obj[prop]. The duration argument specifies the maximum length of the captured movement. In the *Motion* class, you could specify duration in either frames or seconds. With the *MotionCam* class, however, duration must be given in frames. This is necessary in order for the film to record and play back properly.

Here is the constructor code:

```
_global.MotionCam = function (obj, prop, duration) {
    this.superCon (obj, prop, obj[prop], duration);
    this.setActor (obj, prop);
    this.film = [];
};
```

The first line of code calls the superclass constructor, passing the appropriate parameters:

```
this.superCon (obj, prop, obj[prop], duration);
```

The parameter order for the *Motion( )* constructor is: `obj`, `prop`, `begin`, `duration`. Thus, the `obj`, `prop`, and `duration` parameters are mapped to their counterparts, and `obj[prop]` is sent to the `begin` parameter. This means that the starting value (`begin`) of the controlled property (`prop`) is not determined by the user, but by the current value of the property itself.

Next, an "actor" is defined for the camera to "shoot" with the following code:

```
this.setActor (obj, prop);
```

The *MotionCam* instance will observe the `prop` property of the `obj` object (`obj[prop]`), recording the changing data. As an analogy: in real life, you could set up a camera to record a bird's height. The bird would be the object, and its height would be the property.

Lastly, some blank film is loaded into the camera:

```
this.film = [];
```

The film data is stored in an array property called `this.film`. As it is recorded, the data will be indexed with the time value—for instance, the data for the time 24 is stored at `this.film[24]`.

Public Methods

To make *MotionCam* a subclass of *Motion*, I call the custom *Function.extend( )* method to set up the inheritance chain:

```
MotionCam.extend (Motion);
```

This causes *MotionCam* to inherit all the methods of *Motion*.

Now we'll define additional methods in the *MotionCam* class. A shortcut variable, `MCP`, is created to point to `MotionCam.prototype`:

```
var MCP = MotionCam.prototype;
```

The *MotionCam* methods will be attached to `MCP`.

MotionCam.startRecord( ) and stopRecord( )

The *startRecord( )* and *stopRecord( )* methods switch the *MotionCam* object in and out of recording mode. The code is straightforward, merely toggling the isRecording property between true and false:

```
MCP.startRecord = function () {
    this.isRecording = true;
};

MCP.stopRecord = function () {
    this.isRecording = false;
};
```

MotionCam.cutFilm( )

When you're filming something with a *MotionCam* instance, it often isn't possible to know in advance how many frames of film will be needed. As a result, you start out with an unspecified duration, record as long as you need, and end up with a specific amount of used frames in the film array. At this point, you may want to "cut" the film to a certain length. This way, when you play back the film, it will stop automatically when it reaches the end (or will loop to the beginning, depending on the isLooping property).

Here's the code for the *cutFilm( )* method:

```
MCP.cutFilm = function (t) {
    if (t == undefined) var t = this.$time;
    this.film.length = t + 1;
    this.setDuration (t);
};
```

Notice that the method allows you to designate a specific point in time to cut the film, or it will automatically cut at the current time if the t parameter is undefined.

MotionCam.eraseFilm( )

The *eraseFilm( )* method blanks out the film in the *MotionCam* instance:

```
MCP.eraseFilm = function () {
    this.film = [];
    this.setDuration (0);
};
```

When the `film` property is set to a new array, and the duration to zero, the data is effectively cleared.

MotionCam.toString( )

The *toString( )* method sends a quick printout to the Output window that summarizes the object:

```
MCP.toString = function () {
    return "[MotionCam prop=" + this.$prop + " t=" + this.$time +
        " pos=" + this.$position + " mode: " + this.mode + "]";
};
```

MotionCam.toString( ) overrides the superclass method *Motion.toString( )*.

MotionCam.print( )

The *print( )* method is a quick way to send just the film of the *MotionCam* to the Output window, as a comma-delimited string—for example, "83,9, 41,22,53,10." Here is the code:

```
MCP.print = function () {
    trace (this.getFilmString());
};
```

We'll look at the *MotionCam.getFilmString( )* method shortly; this method turns the film array into a comma-delimited string.

Getter/Setter Methods

In addition to the public methods, several getter/setter methods are defined for the *MotionCam* class, to allow access to characteristics such as position, actor, and film.

MotionCam.getPosition( )

The *getPosition( )* method returns the position for a specific time. Here is the code:

```
MCP.getPosition = function (t) {
    if (t == undefined) t = this.$time;
    return this.film[t];
};
```

The position is retrieved from the `film` array, using the time value as the index. If the `t` parameter is missing, the current time is used.

NOTE: *MotionCam.getPosition( )* overrides the superclass method *Motion.getPosition( )* (which is an abstract method—see Chapter 7 for more details).

MotionCam.setActorObj( ) and getActorObj( )

As mentioned earlier, a *MotionCam* object looks at an "actor" object and records information about the actor onto its film. The *setActorObj( )* and *getActorObj( )* methods allow us to specify and access this object, with the following simple code:

```
MCP.setActorObj = function (ao) {
    this.actorObj = ao;
};

MCP.getActorObj = function () {
    return this.actorObj;
};
```

MotionCam.setActorProp( ) and getActorProp( )

In addition to pointing a *MotionCam* instance toward an actor object, we need to specify which *property* of that object should be recorded. A *MotionCam* can only record the values of one property at any given time, since the film is one-dimensional. The name of the actor's property is stored as a string. The *setActorProp( )* and *getActorProp( )* methods that give us access to that string are shown in the following code:

```
MCP.setActorProp = function (ap) {
    this.$actorProp = ap;
};

MCP.getActorProp = function () {
    return this.$actorProp;
};
```

MotionCam.setActor( )

The *setActor( )* method is simply a convenient amalgamation of the *setActorObj( )* and *setActorProp( )* methods:

```
MCP.setActor = function (ao, ap) {
    this.setActorObj (ao);
    this.setActorProp (ap);
};
```

If you remember, when we looked at the *init( )* method of the *FractalTree* component, we saw how the *setActor( )* method is used to point the xCam and yCam objects toward the mouse coordinates, with these lines of code:

```
this.xCam.setActor (_level0, "_xmouse");
// ...
this.yCam.setActor (_level0, "_ymouse");
```

MotionCam.setFilm( ) and getFilm( )

The *setFilm( )* method lets you load a new "reel" of film—actually an array— into the camera. Conversely, the *getFilm( )* method retrieves the film array. Here is the code for these two methods:

```
MCP.setFilm = function (film_arr) {
    this.film = film_arr;
};
```

```
MCP.getFilm = function () {
    return this.film;
};
```

MotionCam.setFilmString( ) and getFilmString( )

The preceding methods, *setFilm( )* and *getFilm( ),* deal with the film as an array object. Alternatively, it's possible to load or save the film as a string, a series of numbers separated by commas. For example, the string of the recorded positions could be "24,53,62,59,86,23,123." If you have such a string, you can load it into the *MotionCam* with the *setFilmString( )* method:

```
MCP.setFilmString = function (str) {
    this.film = str.split (",");
};
```

The *String.split( )* method is called on the incoming string. This chops the numbers between the delimiting commas into an array.

On the other hand, if you have a recorded film you want to save as a string, you can call the *getFilmString( )* method. Here is its code:

```
MCP.getFilmString = function () {
    return this.film.toString();
};
```

I'm calling the *Array.toString( )* method on `this.film`, which generates a comma-delimited string automatically.

Private Methods

There is just one private method—*MotionCam.update( )*, which overrides the superclass method *Motion.update( )*. Here is the code for *MotionCam.update( )*:

```
MCP.update = function () {
    if (this.isRecording)
        with (this) film[$time] = $actorObj[$actorProp];
    super.update();
};
```

The method checks to see if the camera is in recording mode, and if so, stores the actor's position on the film. Then it calls the superclass *update( )* method to update the screen to match the film.

The actor data is accessed at `this.actorObj[this.actorProp]`. The current frame of film is located at `this.film[this.$time]`. Storing the position is a matter of copying one location to another:

```
this.film[this.$time] = this.actorObj[this.actorProp];
```

I used a `with (this)` statement to shorten and speed up this code:

```
with (this) film[$time] = actorObj[actorProp];
```

After that, it calls the superclass method *Motion.update( )* (discussed in Chapter 7). For reference, here is the code for *Motion.update( )*:

```
Motion.prototype.update = function () {
    this.setPosition (this.getPosition (this.$time));
};
```

Conclusion

In this chapter, we have explored an approach for building an interactive fractal structure. This involved two key classes: *FractalBranch* and *MotionCam*. The former uses *MovieClip* subclassing, while *MotionCam* extends the *Motion* class we discussed in Chapter 7. I hope you will find the *MotionCam* class useful in other situations where you need to record and play back data. In the next chapter, we'll look at another nature simulation: a tornado.

Chapter 14

Cyclone

There is something beguiling about a vortex. Whether it's the satellite photo of a hurricane, the rare sighting of a dust devil on a lazy summer afternoon, or the tiny whirlpool that sucks the bubbles out of the bathtub—a vortex is never boring. It seems so miraculous, that this elegant, symmetrical, stable yet ephemeral sculpture can slide into existence and magically sustain itself. The vortex is rife with contradictions. It has tremendous speed, but it stays almost in the same place. The shape is consistent, stable, orderly; the content sporadic, volatile, chaotic. How are we to understand this strange beast?

I was first introduced to Chaos theory about ten years ago, and it has proved a personal fascination ever since. I have had the privilege of not only subjecting friends and family to numerous mini-lectures, but also wrote an 18-page essay on chaos and determinism as part of my philosophy degree. From the fledgling science of chaos theory comes the concept of the *strange attractor*: a complex, yet orderly pattern that emerges from chaos ("nonlinear dynamical system" is the technical term). What's most interesting about strange attractors is their ability to self-organize through feedback loops.

Tornadoes are excellent examples of these "emergent phenomena." Under special conditions, random atmospheric disturbances, instead of canceling each other out, will become a self-reinforcing system— a cell of rotating air. The storm begins to feed on its own energy until a funnel suddenly forms—the incarnation of a strange attractor. Like a magnetic field, the attractor itself is an invisible, theoretical construct that can be known only through its influence on nearby particles. If you recall the plot of the movie *Twister*, the scientists' mission was to put sensors into a cyclone to obtain mathematical data on the attractor's structure.

The tornado becomes, in effect, a living entity that can only be understood holistically—or rather, a system that is not merely the sum of its parts. An intriguing progression of order-chaos-order (or simple-complex-simple) has occurred. The physics of gravity and fluid dynamics are relatively simple on a small scale (that is, when it comes to a few particles), but give rise to complex, unpredictable behavior at the macro level (say, a pocket of air). However, if conditions are right, and enough energy is fed into the system to throw it wildly out of equilibrium, a higher level of order may spontaneously emerge. Although we encounter the storm physically (certainly the cow in *Twister* did), its essence is not physical. The vortex is a pattern—information, really—that transfers matter to and from its environment in order to survive.

Beyond just the weather, these principles can give us insight into many aspects of human experience. In her groundbreaking book *Leadership and the New Science*, Margaret J. Wheatley suggests that *information*, not matter, is the basic ingredient of the universe. As a case in point, all the cells in your body are replaced within a six-year period. If so, are you a *physical structure*, or are you an *informational process* that organizes matter as necessary? In a sense, you are a vortex. And if you're a designer, your life is full of twisters. Chaos theory helps us understand everything from the spontaneous nature of the creative process and the projects that "take on a life of their own" to business relationships and online communities. In fact, as I'm about to describe, the very *process* of creating Cyclone was itself a kind of vortex.

Near the end of August 2000, Flash 5 was about to be released, and I was beside myself with anticipation. Tantalizing reports had recently come from the FlashForward conference in New York, and I was poring over the list of Flash 5's new features, particularly its custom functions and the *Math* object. In addition, first-hand accounts of Yugo Nakamura's New York session told of mind-blowing motion graphics saluted by multiple standing ovations. Soon after the conference, Flashmove.com posted Yugo's complete presentation. What I saw was astounding—a series of reactive fields that fed on user input and produced breathtaking, flowing patterns—all in code.

At this point, I had been using Flash for nine months, and was just beginning to learn how to duplicate movie clips and change their properties with ActionScript. In early August, I had come up with the simple particle experiments in *swirl_white.swf* and *swirl_purple.swf*.

They sat on the shelf for a few weeks while I learned other aspects of Flash. When I showed the animations to my friend Joshua Dunford, a designer at burnkit.com, he encouraged me to "keep going with those particles; it could be interesting." That night, I created a new "sparks" animation, which you can see in *sparks.swf*.

The next day, I found myself picturing a tornado and thinking, "maybe I could do that in Flash." My brain conducted some quick feasibility projections, sat me down in front of the computer, and held me there for ten straight hours. I finished around 5 A.M., but sat there for at least another half hour, staring at the stupid thing and pressing F5 countless times to refresh the page. Finally, as the rising sun shone through my bedroom window, I went to sleep with the feeling that I had taken a significant step in a new direction.

Dreaming It Up

Let me take you through an overview of my thinking process as I worked to realize my vision. For me, problemsolving usually begins with identifying the vital functional requirements of the piece. To use a Flash metaphor, I look for the technical *keyframes*, the core challenges to overcome. Essentially a quick feasibility study, this stage can save you from wasting your effort and hitting dead ends. For instance, if I want to implement a 3-D engine in a programming environment, one of my necessities is the cosine function. If there is absolutely no way to find the cosine of an angle, there is no point in coding anything else. Once I am fairly confident of producing the keyframes, I add some *tweens*: ways of moving from one stage to the next, working from the simple to the complex. This process may need to be repeated a few times. The first set of keyframes may be spaced quite far apart, but more will be added as the project takes shape. In technical school, working in Visual Basic and Java application development teams, our mantra became "It's an iterative process; it's an iterative process."

With Cyclone, I started with a simplified goal: to build a top-down view. What does a tornado look like from above? It would be a series of concentric circles, with particles orbiting the center. Since the particles have different radii of rotation, my first task was to make a single particle that was able to orbit at variable radii.

I came up with a basic particle movie clip nested within another movie clip. If the parent was rotating, the child would have an orbit radius equal to its distance from the center. So, to move the particle in a circle of radius 10, I set its _x position within the parent to 10, and rotated the parent. The result can be seen in *cyclone_stage1.swf*.

The next step was to make dozens of these things. I worked out how to use the *duplicateMovieClip( )* action to copy my new object. If I left it at that, they would all be on top of each other, so I had to spread them out spatially. I gave them all different radii, spread out over the group. This produced something like *cyclone_stage2.swf*.

Now I had a collection of particles revolving in concentric circles, all in a line and at the same speed. Time to mix it up a bit. I made each particle start at a random point on the circle; this spread them out to cover the area quite nicely, as shown in *cyclone_stage3.swf*.

Next, the particles needed to have different speeds. The closer a particle was to the center of the tornado, the faster it would spin. So I needed to find an equation that would give me an appropriate speed, given any radius. In mathematical terms, speed was to be a function of radius. The varying spinning speeds produced a more convincing rotation, as shown in *cyclone_stage4.swf*.

So far, so good; I had completed a top-down view of the cyclone. It could actually pass for a satellite view of a hurricane at this stage. However, I wanted a three-dimensional view. I decided to go with isometric 3-D, since it was the easiest to render. Isometric 3-D has no vanishing point, so parallel lines remain parallel. (A trick with transparent isometric graphics is that you can mentally turn them inside out; with Cyclone, you can either see the funnel from above, or from below, spinning the opposite direction.) In my case, a circle viewed at an angle was just an ellipse, an oval shape. I had to wrap the rotating particle inside a new movie clip so that I could do a "global squish." I didn't want to squish the particle dot and then rotate it; I wanted to rotate *then* squish.

Now I had a series of ovals that I wanted to separate vertically, stacking them up like layers of a cake. I needed another equation, this time to displace the ovals based on their radii. The equation would not only define a relationship between radius and *y*, it could also be a curve when graphed— a curve that would be the profile of the cyclone. From the many options available, a linear relationship seemed simplest, producing a line when graphed. I would simply multiply radius by some number, perhaps do a simple addition here or there, and I'd be done. Then when the particles rotated, the line would be swept around the y-axis to produce a 3-D shape. A line straight up and down would produce a cylinder; a slanted line, a cone shape. Was a cone satisfactory? It was close, but tornados are not usually that straight along the surface. Their cross section reminded me of a $1/x$ curve, also called an inverse function. Figure 14-1 shows the $1/x$ curve. It's relatively simple—just divide instead of multiply; no trigonometry necessary.

After some trial and error in finding the right numbers for the cyclone particle movie clips, it worked out well. By now, it was about 2:00 A.M., and I was thoroughly captivated by this speckled jewel turning like a music box dancer on my screen. You might think I would be satisfied and call it quits for the day. But I had another idea: wouldn't it be cool if you could make it move, perhaps by dragging it around? I would just drag it left and right to mimic real-world movement. Time for some more math.

This time, my input was an _x value, ranging from –100 to 100 relative to the center of the animation. The cyclone needed to move toward that point, and somehow end up centered there if the mouse remained stationary. But if the whole thing just slid over without changing shape, what fun would that be? Remembering real-world behavior, the thin, lower funnel tends to move quickly, while the thick, heavy base up top plods along. In my animation, lower/smaller-orbit particles should be fast, higher/larger-orbit particles slow.

After several failed attempts to make the cyclone bend towards the mouse, I imagined having the particles pull each other along. I thought in

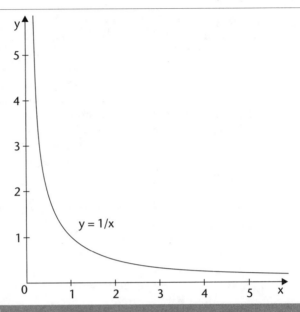

FIGURE 14-1

The 1/x (inverse) curve

terms of the cyclone "wanting" to move to a state of equilibrium. Picture a marble rolling around in a large bowl. You can disturb its equilibrium by injecting energy into the system (by hitting either the bowl or the marble), but it is inevitably drawn toward a single point of rest and stability. I was disturbing my storm system at the bottom, so the changes should ripple from the bottom up. First the lowest particle would arrive at the new center, then the others would follow.

My cursor would pull on the lowest particle, *p1*, which in turn would pull *p2*, which would pull *p3*, and so on. Essentially, a particle would try to stay centered above the particle below it. The farther away the two particles, the faster the "correction" would be. The math involved was quite simple. Find the distance between the two particles and move the top one a fraction of the distance towards the bottom one. Repeat this every frame. This technique is now quite familiar to Flash developers, so I won't belabor the point. This type of "exponential easing" is often used on mouse trailers, menus, and content. In my case, this resulted in a satisfying undulation for my cyclone.

Breaking It Down

Now that we've had an aerial tour of the animation, it's time to land and hack our way through the jungle of code. First off, I have to say that using the proper structure of nested movie clips is an important thing to learn in Flash, even if you don't use much ActionScript. You need to know the different functional levels of an animation, and where the responsibilities lie in the hierarchy. My particle systems have evolved over time to a standard format. I have at least three basic levels in a particle system: the particle, the path of the particle, and a group of paths.

In Cyclone's case, there are four levels of nested movie clips—I had to add a fourth level in order to squish the circular paths into ovals. We will examine Cyclone from the inside out, similar to how someone might build it from scratch. Open *cyclone.fla* and follow along.

Particle

You could open the `Particle` movie clip directly from the library to take a look at it. However, since Cyclone is all about hierarchy, it's best to examine its parts in context to see where movie clips are in relation to each other. The `Particle` movie clip is nested three levels deep inside the `Cyclone` component. Right-click the component instance on the stage and select Edit In Place. Then double-click the symbol three times at the registration point to drill down to the `Particle` symbol. (You could also go directly to `Particle` by double-clicking it in the Library, but I find it useful to go through the layers to get a sense of the movie clip hierarchy.)

This diamond is our basic particle. Particle systems are generally composed of simple shapes duplicated many times and animated in various patterns. I used a diamond shape for Cyclone because it is extremely easy for the Flash plug-in to render, being merely a polygon with four straight sides. Also, the shape itself gives direction and motion to the animation. At small sizes, it resembles a motion-blurred streak. This movie clip doesn't contain any animation, but it could easily be modified to show different stages in the particle's life, or a motion sequence such as a pulsing effect.

Path

With the basic graphic in place, the next level defines the particle's primary motion—the orbit. `Particle` is enclosed in the `Path` movie clip.

Path.onEnterFrame( )

`Particle` orbits, not through a motion of its own, but by being inside `Path`, which rotates. This code, on the `methods` layer, causes `Path` to rotate continuously:

```
this.onEnterFrame = function () {
    this._rotation += this.velRot;
};
```

This rotates `Path` by increasing its `_rotation` property each frame by a certain amount—the velocity of rotation `velRot`. The velocity is set in the *init( )* method.

Path.init( )

The init( ) method sets up the initial conditions for the `Path` movie clip:

```
this.init = function () {
    this.particle._x = this.radius;
    this._rotation = Math.random() * 360;
    this.velRot = _parent._parent.speed / this.radius;
};
```

Looking at the first line in *init( )*:

```
this.particle._x = this.radius;
```

This positions `particle` horizontally within its container movie clip, `Path`. When `Path` rotates, `particle` will orbit around its center, with a radius equal to `_x`.

```
this._rotation = Math.random() * 360;
```

This code picks a random number between 0 and 360 and rotates `Path` to that value. The *Math.random( )* function returns a random decimal number between 0 and 1. When we multiply this by 360, the number now lies between 0 and 360. This starts the particle's orbit at a random angle, to give a nice even distribution over the tornado. A fun exercise for you to try is to disable this line of code by using comment slashes:

```
//this._rotation = Math.random() * 360;
```

The resulting effect looks like either dropping a string into a blender or making spiral metal shavings using a drill press.

The final line of code controls the spinning speed:

```
this.velRot = _parent._parent.speed / radius;
```

The variable `velRot` is the velocity of rotation. A `speed` variable will have been set in a the grandparent movie clip (`_parent._parent`), which is the `Cyclone` component. As we'll see, `speed` is a component parameter that allows you to change the energy of the storm as a whole. As for individual particles, the velocity of rotation is *inversely proportional* to the radius of the particle's orbit. "Inverse" means a $1/x$ relationship, which is why we *divide* by `radius`.

This completes the *init( )* method, which the `Path` movie clip calls to initialize itself in the `actions` layer like so:

```
this.init();
stop();
```

val

We're now going to enclose the `Path` movie clip inside another movie clip. `Oval` squishes `Path` *vertically*, producing a 3-D effect. It also controls the *sidewinding* behavior of the tornado's layers.

Oval.init( )

`Oval's` first function on the methods layer is called "init" (sound familiar?). Movieclips often need to initialize themselves, somewhat like their "morning routine" before they go to work. Our previous movie clip `Path` had a particular morning routine. Our current movie clip, `Oval`, has one that's slightly different:

```
this.init = function () {
    this._yscale = 33;
    var index = this._name.slice(1);
    this.neighborName = "p" + (index-1);
};
```

The first line of code changes the vertical scale of the movie clip:

```
this._yscale = 33;
```

This reduces `Oval` to a third of its original height. Prior to this, the enclosed `Path` was circular; now it's an oval. In the real world, when you tilt a circle away from you, it looks roughly like an oval. It's distorted a bit by perspective—the farthest edge is a bit smaller. But in isometric 3-D rendering, there is no perspective or vanishing point, and a circle appears as an undistorted oval. Thus, Cyclone is rendered in isometric 3-D.

Looking at the next line of code:

```
var index = this._name.slice(1);
```

This command gives `Oval` a sense of self-identity. When we're all finished and the movie is running, there will be 100 (by default) clones of `Oval`. Each cloned movie clip will have a different instance name, ranging from `p1` to `p100`. The preceding line of code takes that name and removes or "slices" the first letter, `p`. The resulting number is stored in the variable `index`.

We use `index` in the next line of code:

```
this.neighborName = "p" + (index-1);
```

This finds the name of the movie clip's *neighbor*. When we're finished, we will have 100 `Oval`s stacked on top of each other. Each `Oval` will need to know who its neighbor is. The neighbor is the `Oval` directly underneath. Thus, if the current `Oval` is named `p50`, its neighbor will be named `p49`. Why does it need to know its neighbor? Because, as we will soon see, each `Oval` will try to move towards its neighbor when the cyclone gets bent out of shape.

Oval.sidewind( )

Besides squishing the circular `Path`, `Oval` takes on the responsibility of controlling the movement of the tornado as it moves back and forth. This undulation is accomplished by having many small pieces each move a little bit closer to each other. The *sidewind( )* method takes care of this:

```
this.sidewind = function () {
    var distance = _parent[this.neighborName]._x - this._x;
```

```
        this._x += distance * _parent.stiffness;
};
```

Looking at the first line of the function:

```
var distance = _parent[this.neighborName]._x - this._x;
```

Imagine you are the tenth `Oval`, named `p10`. Your "neighbor," whom you will follow faithfully, will be named `p9`. You need to find out how far away you are from your neighbor, horizontally, by subtracting its `_x` property from your `_x` property. To look up the neighbor clip using a variable name, I'm using the bracket syntax `_parent[neighborName]`.

Once you know how far away you are from your neighbor, you need to move yourself in that direction, with this code:

```
this._x += distance * _parent.stiffness;
```

We are using a piece of information, `stiffness`, from `Oval`'s parent movie clip. Using a number between 0 and 1, `stiffness` determines how quickly the tornado straightens itself out. If `stiffness` were 0.5, you would move halfway towards your neighbor every frame (`stiffness` is 0.65 by default, but you can experiment with this number in `Cyclone`'s component parameters). The farther you are from your neighbor, the faster you will move towards it.

Stepping back for a moment, what do we have so far? The `Particle` movie clip contains the graphics. The `Path` clip governs the orbit of the particle. The `Oval` clip manipulates the `Path` as a whole, by squishing and sidewinding it. The final step is to make a particle system, duplicating `Oval` and stacking the movie clips in a particular pattern.

The Cyclone Component

We're now going to enclose the `Oval` movie clip inside another movie clip. `Cyclone` is responsible for producing 100 copies of `Oval` and sculpting them into an attractive profile. We currently have one `Oval` on the stage. When we run our finished movie, this single movie clip will be cloned 100 times with ActionScript, forming a tornado.

As with the other movie clips, several functions are defined on `Cyclone`'s first frame, on the `methods` layer.

Cyclone.init( )

Here's the *init( )* method, which initializes a few important conditions:

```
this.init = function () {
    this.p._visible = false;
    this.numParticles = 0;
    this.onEnterFrame = this.grow;
}
```

Going through the function line by line:

```
this.p._visible = false;
```

Oval's instance name within Cyclone is p. It is what you could call a "seed clip"—a movie clip that is duplicated repeatedly at run time. Clones of our seed clip p will form the tornado, but p itself won't be used in the animation. Consequently, we make it invisible by setting the _visible property to false.

Looking at the next line:

```
this.numParticles = 0;
```

We will need a variable to keep track of the number of particles that have been produced. Here we initialize the *numParticles* property to zero. As we add more particles, this will increase.

The final line of *init( )* assigns a function to the *onEnterFrame( )* handler:

```
this.onEnterFrame = this.grow;
```

The *grow( )* method will be executed every frame when the Cyclone starts out, though we will eventually stop this loop. We will look at the *grow( )* method itself shortly.

Cyclone.makeParticle( )

Next is the makeParticle( ) method, which duplicates the seed clip and gives it an appropriate radius and vertical position:

```
this.makeParticle = function (index) {
    var oval = p.duplicateMovieClip ("p" + index, index);
```

```
        var radius = index*index / this.maxParticles + 2
        oval.path.radius = radius;
        with (oval.path.particle) {
            _xscale = _yscale = 60 + radius * .8;
        }
        oval._y = this.funnelHeight / (radius + 10);
    };
```

The *makeParticle( )* function accepts a parameter, *index*, which will range between 1 and the value of maxParticles (100 by default).

Going through the function line by line:

```
var oval = p.duplicateMovieClip ("p" + index, index);
```

This command duplicates the seed clip, p. The clone is given a new instance name and depth, specified by the index parameter. If index is 71, the new name will be p71, and the depth of the movie clip will be 71. Each movie clip needs its own unique depth number. In Flash MX, the *MovieClip.duplicateMovieClip( )* method returns a reference to the newly created instance. We store this reference in a local variable oval so we don't have to worry about its exact name as we manipulate the new clip in the code that follows.

The next line is where the all-important radius is determined:

```
var radius = index*index / maxParticles + 2;
```

I arrived at this equation after quite a bit of experimentation. I discovered that the tornado looks better when there are more particles in the skinny part of the funnel. I chose to square index and divide by maxParticles in order to skew the distribution of particles. With this equation, more particles end up where more detail is necessary.

The next line passes the radius information further down the hierarchy:

```
oval.path.radius = radius;
```

Here we pass the radius property to the *path* movie clip, which is nested two levels deep within *oval*.

```
with (oval.path.particle) {
    _xscale = _yscale = 60 + radius * .8;
}
```

This code does a little touch-up work on the particles. It slightly shrinks the particles with smaller orbits, cleaning up the funnel a bit.

The next line shapes the tornado's funnel with a mathematical relationship:

```
oval._y = this.funnelHeight / (radius + 10);
```

The vertical displacement of each `Oval` is made to be inversely proportional (1/r) to its radius. Through experimentation, I found that a default `funnelHeight` of 1500 and the addition of 10 to `radius` produced a good shape.

Cyclone.grow( )

Next is the process of duplicating the particles gradually over time. We could use a `for` loop, but that would cause the particles to appear simultaneously in a single frame. For dramatic flair, we'll bring in the particles one at a time, one per frame, top to bottom. The twister starts in the sky, gathers strength and extends its funnel to the ground, almost menacingly. The *grow( )* method manages this process:

```
this.grow = function () {
    if (this.numParticles < this.maxParticles) {
        this.makeParticle (this.maxParticles - this.numParticles);
        this.numParticles++;
    } else {
        delete this.onEnterFrame;
        this.p0.appear ();
    }
};
```

Breaking it down line by line:

```
if (this.numParticles < this.maxParticles) {
```

The `if` statement checks the number of particles that have been duplicated to see if any more need to be created. If so, a particle is created in the next line:

```
this.makeParticle (this.maxParticles - this.numParticles);
```

This calls our *makeParticle( )* method and passes it an `index` parameter. The parameter is set to the *difference* between `maxParticles` and numParticles. The subtraction causes the number to go from 100 to 0, rather than 0 to 100. Remember that we want particles at the top of the tornado to appear first. The top particle is named *p100*, so we want to start there and work our way down.

The next line of code increments the numParticles property to keep track of the number of particles that have been spawned:

```
this.numParticles++;
```

If we have created enough particles, we need to stop the loop somehow. When 100 particles have been created, the if statement will skip to the else section, where this code is executed:

```
} else {
    delete this.onEnterFrame;
    this.p0.appear();
}
```

First, the *onEnterFrame( )* handler is deleted. Remember that the *grow( )* method was assigned to it; now it stops being executed every frame. Then we call the *appear( )* method of the p0 movie clip, which is an instance of the Dragger symbol. This is the draggable movie clip that allows the user to control the tornado, which we'll look at later in the chapter.

Cyclone.sidewind( )

Cyclone and Oval each have a *sidewind( )* method, something we already looked at with *Oval.sidewind( )*. The tornado is comprised of 100 instances of Oval. Consequently, the Cyclone sidewinds by telling each Oval to sidewind. Here is the code for *Cyclone.sidewind( )*:

```
this.sidewind = function () {
    for (var i=1; i <= this.maxParticles; i++) {
        this["p"+i].sidewind();
    }
}
```

Cyclone tells 100 Ovals to sidewind in a single frame. The for loop increments the local variable i from 1 to maxParticles, which is 100 by default. This value is used to index the instance name of each Oval and call its *sidewind( )* method. I chose this approach of controlling the particles from the outside (rather than an *onEnterFrame( )* loop inside each Oval) so that I could easily turn the sidewinding on and off. It also guarantees the correct order—it's crucial that the tornado sidewinds from the bottom up, not the other way around.

Cyclone.startSidewind( ) and stopSidewind( )

I gave `Cyclone` simple methods to start and stop the sidewinding behavior:

```
this.startSidewind = function () {
    this.onEnterFrame = this.sidewind;
};

this.stopSidewind = function () {
    delete this.onEnterFrame;
};
```

These methods manipulate the *onEnterFrame( )* handler to either start or stop the execution of *sidewind( )* on each frame.

The Component Parameters

When I brought Cyclone from Flash 4 to Flash 5, I made the main `Cyclone` movie clip into a Smart Clip, with four parameters. When I later brought it into Flash MX, the Smart Clip was automatically converted into a component. Table 14-1 lists the parameters used and their default values.

The `maxParticles` parameter determines how many particles the tornado will have—the number of times the seed clip `p` will be duplicated. The default here is 100, but you can adjust this number to change the amount of detail in the cyclone. The remaining three parameters control the height, rotation speed, and stiffness of the tornado. The stiffness parameter is similar to the elasticity constant in Hooke's Law governing elasticity (see Chapter 8). The value should be between 0 and 1, and governs

Parameter Name	Default Value
maxParticles	100
funnelHeight	1500
speed	300
stiffness	.65

TABLE 14-1

Parameters of the Cyclone Component

how fast each ring of the tornado moves toward the one beneath it. The default value, .65, moves each Oval about two-thirds of the distance towards its neighbor each frame. Feel free to play with the different component parameters to create your own customized storm.

Dragger

Now we look at how to interact with the tornado using the mouse. The Dragger symbol is a movie clip, inside the Cyclone clip, which can be mouse-dragged to direct the storm. The Dragger symbol has an instance name of p0. By naming it thus, we trick the tornado's bottom particle p1 into thinking that our Dragger instance p0 is its neighbor. When we drag p0 with the mouse, p1 will move toward p0, p2 will move toward p1, and so on. Manipulate the leader, and the rest will follow.

Frame Actions

The first frame of the Dragger clip has this simple code in the Actions layer:

```
this._visible = false;
stop();
```

The movie clip hides itself right away, but will appear later.

Dragger.appear( )

Speaking of which, the *Dragger.appear( )* method is defined nearby, on the *methods* layer. It's a nifty little method that automatically positions Dragger at the bottom of the tornado:

```
this.appear = function () {
    this._x = _parent.p1._x;
    this._y = _parent.p1._y + 2;
    this._visible = true;
};
```

When the time is right, the *appear( )* method is called to position the Dragger clip and make it visible. The code finds the *x* and *y* positions of the particle at the bottom tip of the tornado. It then positions the Dragger clip in line with that particle and just slightly below it. This dynamic positioning eliminates guesswork, and works even when you change the maximum number of particles or the height of the funnel.

Dragger.onEnterFrame( )

This last method is purely for aesthetic purposes:

```
this.onEnterFrame = function () {
    this._rotation += 9;
};
```

I like having the little cross hair continuously rotating. The easiest way is to have an *onEnterFrame( )* script that keeps increasing the _rotation property.

Button Actions for dragBtn

The following code is on the button instance dragBtn in Dragger:

```
on (press) {
    this.startDrag (false, -100, _y, 100, _y);
    _parent.startSidewind();
}

on (release, releaseOutside) {
    this.stopDrag();
    _parent.stopSidewind();
}
```

Working through the code:

```
on (press) {
    this.startDrag (false, -100, _y, 100, _y);
```

When the button is pressed, the movie clip containing it will start to be dragged; it will follow the mouse cursor. These particular parameters for the *startDrag( )* method restrict the movement to a horizontal axis, within a range of 100 pixels to the left and right. The *Cyclone.startSidewind( )* method is also called:

```
    _parent.startSidewind();
```

When the button is released inside or outside the movie, its container movie clip will stop being dragged:

```
on (release, releaseOutside) {
    this.stopDrag();
```

As well, a command is sent to the parent clip, `Cyclone`, to ask it to stop sidewinding:

```
_parent.stopSidewind();
```

Conclusion

Thus, we conclude our whirlwind tour of my Cyclone animation (pun intended). I hope you were able to follow along throughout the turbulent math and code. With the right conditions and enough energy, one can ultimately achieve a higher level of order, the simplicity on the other side of complexity, the perfect storm.

Index

Numbers and Symbols

A

B

Q

INTERNATIONAL CONTACT INFORMATION

AUSTRALIA
McGraw-Hill Book Company Australia Pty. Ltd.
TEL +61-2-9900-1800
FAX +61-2-9878-8881
http://www.mcgraw-hill.com.au
books-it_sydney@mcgraw-hill.com

CANADA
McGraw-Hill Ryerson Ltd.
TEL +905-430-5000
FAX +905-430-5020
http://www.mcgraw-hill.ca

**GREECE, MIDDLE EAST, & AFRICA
(Excluding South Africa)**
McGraw-Hill Hellas
TEL +30-1-656-0990-3-4
FAX +30-1-654-5525

MEXICO (Also serving Latin America)
McGraw-Hill Interamericana Editores S.A. de C.V.
TEL +525-117-1583
FAX +525-117-1589
http://www.mcgraw-hill.com.mx
fernando_castellanos@mcgraw-hill.com

SINGAPORE (Serving Asia)
McGraw-Hill Book Company
TEL +65-863-1580
FAX +65-862-3354
http://www.mcgraw-hill.com.sg
mghasia@mcgraw-hill.com

SOUTH AFRICA
McGraw-Hill South Africa
TEL +27-11-622-7512
FAX +27-11-622-9045
robyn_swanepoel@mcgraw-hill.com

SPAIN
McGraw-Hill/Interamericana de España, S.A.U.
TEL +34-91-180-3000
FAX +34-91-372-8513
http://www.mcgraw-hill.es
professional@mcgraw-hill.es

**UNITED KINGDOM, NORTHERN,
EASTERN, & CENTRAL EUROPE**
McGraw-Hill Education Europe
TEL +44-1-628-502500
FAX +44-1-628-770224
http://www.mcgraw-hill.co.uk
computing_neurope@mcgraw-hill.com

ALL OTHER INQUIRIES Contact:
Osborne/McGraw-Hill
TEL +1-510-549-6600
FAX +1-510-883-7600
http://www.osborne.com
omg_international@mcgraw-hill.com

W

X

Y

Z